MAGNETIC NORTH

Recent works by Tomas Venclova

See page 395 for a complete list of works by Tomas Venclova.

MAGNETIC NORTH

CONVERSATIONS WITH TOMAS VENCLOVA

ELLEN HINSEY
AND
TOMAS VENCLOVA

UNIVERSITY OF ROCHESTER PRESS

The publication of this book was supported by the Lithuanian Culture Institute.

First published 2017
Transferred to digital printing and reprinted in paperback 2018

University of Rochester Press
668 Mt. Hope Avenue, Rochester, NY 14620, USA
www.urpress.com
and Boydell & Brewer Limited
PO Box 9, Woodbridge, Suffolk IP12 3DF, UK
www.boydellandbrewer.com

ISSN: 1528-4808
Hardcover ISBN: 978-1-58046-586-1
Paperback ISBN: 978-1-58046-926-5

Library of Congress Cataloging-in-Publication Data

Names: Venclova, Tomas, 1937– interviewee. | Hinsey, Ellen, 1960– interviewer.
Title: Magnetic north : conversations with Tomas Venclova / Ellen Hinsey and Tomas Venclova.
Description: Rochester, NY : University of Rochester Press, 2017. | Series: Rochester studies in East and Central Europe, ISSN 1528-4808 ; v. 17 | Includes bibliographical references and index.
Identifiers: LCCN 2017012502 | ISBN 9781580465861 (hardcover : alk. paper)
Subjects: LCSH: Venclova, Tomas, 1937– —Interviews. | Authors, Lithuanian—20th century—Interviews.
Classification: LCC PG8722.32.E5 Z46 2017 | DDC 891/.928309—dc23 LC record available at https://lccn.loc.gov/2017012502

A catalogue record for this title is available from the British Library.

This publication is printed on acid-free paper.
Printed and bound in Great Britain by TJ International Ltd.

Contents

Contents

Part Three

ACKNOWLEDGMENTS

Earlier versions of some material in this volume have appeared elsewhere, in English and other languages. Chapter 10 appeared in Polish as "Pasternak," translated by Maryna Ochab, in *Zeszyty Literackie* 127, no. 3 (2014): 90–102. An abridged version of chapter 10 appeared in English as "Train to Peredelkino: Remembering the *Doctor Zhivago* Affair," *Berlin Journal* 28 (Spring 2015): 54–58. Chapter 12 appeared in Russian as "Moscow in the Sixties," translated by Tamara Kazavchinskaya, in *Inostrannaia literature* 3 (2015): 250–64. Chapter 13 appeared in English as "Meetings with Anna Akhmatova," *New England Review* 34, nos. 3–4 (2014): 170–82. Chapters 13 and 15 appeared in German, translated by Claudia Sinnig, as "Vom 'Gerben der Seele'—Anna Achmatowa: Erinnerungen im Gespräch mit Ellen Hinsey," *Schreibheft* 81 (2013): 83–94; and "Joseph Brodsky, Zwilling: Erinnerungen im Gespräch mit Ellen Hinsey," *Schreibheft* 81 (2013): 65–82, respectively. We wish to thank the proprietors and publishers of these works for their kind permission to reprint.

Excerpts from Tomas Venclova's "Arrival in Atlantis," "Commentary," and "For R.K.," in *The Junction: Selected Poems of Tomas Venclova*, edited by Ellen Hinsey, translated by Ellen Hinsey, Constantine Rusanov, and Diana Senechal (Tarset, UK: Bloodaxe Books, 2008), are reprinted courtesy of Bloodaxe Books. Excerpts from Venclova's "Instruction," "A projector flickers in the somewhat cramped hall," "Sestina," "Thanksgiving Day," "The twenty-four hours cross the middle," and "Winter Dialogue," in *Winter Dialogue*, translated by Diana Senechal (Evanston, IL: Northwestern University Press, 1997), are reprinted courtesy of Northwestern University Press.

Chronology

1937   Tomas Venclova is born on September 11 in Klaipėda, Lithuania, to Eliza Vencloviene (née Račkauskaitė) and Antanas Venclova.

1939   Following Hitler's annexation of Klaipėda on March 22, the family moves to Kaunas, Lithuania's interwar capital.

              After the signing of the secret protocol of the Molotov-Ribbentrop Pact in August, Lithuania falls within the German, then the Soviet, sphere of influence.

              September 1: Germany invades Poland.

              September 17: USSR invades Poland.

1940   June 14: Stalin demands acceptance of Soviet troops into Lithuania and a change of government. Antanas Venclova is appointed minister of education of the new Soviet-installed People's Government. On August 3, Lithuania is annexed by the USSR. The Venclova family relocates to Vilnius.

1941   June 14: the Soviets begin deportations of Lithuanians to Siberia. Between June 14 and 18, approximately eighteen thousand people are deported.

              June 22: Germany attacks the USSR. The Soviet Lithuanian government, including Venclova's father, is ordered to evacuate. Antanas Venclova survives a ten-hour bombing in Minsk. Separated from his wife and son, who remain in Vilnius, he joins the Soviet Lithuanian government-in-exile in Moscow. A self-appointed provisional government collaborating with German troops proclaims Lithuania's independence, but it is ordered to disperse by the Nazis on August 5.

In early July, Venclova's mother is arrested and held in Lukiškės Prison. Venclova is taken in by relatives. Eliza Venclovienė is released in September 1941.

Establishment of the Kaunas and Vilnius ghettos. Under the German occupation, 94 percent of Lithuania's Jews (nearly 200,000) are killed by Nazi death squads, with the participation of Lithuanian collaborators.

1941–44	Venclova spends the war years at his maternal grandfather Merkelis Račkauskas's house in Freda, a suburb of Kaunas, and with other relatives in Lithuanian villages.
1944	In July and August, the Soviets retake Lithuania and impose Soviet rule. Some sixty thousand Lithuanians, including a large part of the country's intellectuals, flee the Soviet Army and find themselves in displaced persons camps in West Germany. Antanas Venclova returns from Moscow. In September, Tomas Venclova begins elementary school in Freda.
1946	The family resettles in Vilnius.
1947	Venclova enters high school in Vilnius.
1950	Venclova meets Ramūnas (Romas) Katilius, a future physicist.
1954	Venclova enrolls in Vilnius University.
1956	Khrushchev's "Secret Speech" to the Twentieth Party Congress of the Communist Party. Uprising in Poznań, Poland. Suppression of the Hungarian Revolution.
1956–60	A group of like-minded young people forms in Vilnius, including Venclova, Ramūnas Katilius, Pranas Morkus, Juozas Tumelis, Aleksandras Štromas, and Natasha Trauberg.
September 1957–August 1958	Venclova takes academic leave, attends a vocational school for truck drivers.

1958	Venclova participates in the samizdat publishing venture Eglutė. His first samizdat poetry collection, *Pontos Axenos*, appears. The student almanac *Kūryba* (Creation), in which Venclova is involved, is banned by the authorities. On October 23, Boris Pasternak is awarded the Nobel Prize.
1959	At a meeting of the Lithuanian Writers' Union, Venclova is accused of being a follower of Pasternak, which he does not deny (January). Venclova begins his "private war" against the Soviet regime. A purge of the Department of Lithuanian Philology at Vilnius University in connection with the *Kūryba* affair. Venclova visits Pasternak in Peredelkino (December 14).
1960	Alexander Ginzburg visits Vilnius. Venclova gives Ginzburg several poems for his samizdat magazine *Sintaksis*. Graduation from Vilnius University. Pasternak's death (May 30); Venclova is present at Pasternak's funeral. With others, Venclova initiates a self-study group in Vilnius.
1961	Interrogation by the KGB in connection with the self-study group and the Ginzburg affair. In early spring, Venclova moves to Moscow. Construction of the Berlin Wall (August 13).
1961–65	Life in Moscow. Partnership with Marina Kedrova, friendship with Andrei Volkonsky, Gennady Aygi, Natasha Gorbanevskaya, Andrei Sergeev, Leonid Chertkov, and others. Meetings with Anna Akhmatova. Venclova makes his living as a translator and writes two popular science books on astronomy and cybernetics. *Moscow Poems* appears (samizdat, 1962). A collection of translations of Akhmatova's poems, some of them by Venclova, is published in Lithuania (1964). Khrushchev is removed from power (October 14, 1964).
1965	Venclova returns to Vilnius.
1965–76	Venclova's Lithuanian translations of Pasternak, Mandelstam, Eliot, Frost, Auden, Baudelaire, Saint-John Perse, Rilke, Cavafy, and others are published. Concurrently, Venclova establishes contact with Yuri Lotman in Tartu and studies structural poetics and semiotics.

1966	Joseph Brodsky visits Vilnius, where Venclova meets him for the first time.
1967	Venclova meets Nadezhda Mandelstam.
1968	The Prague Spring. A demonstration in Red Square against the Soviet invasion of Czechoslovakia is repressed; the demonstrators, including Natalya Gorbanevskaya, are arrested. Cultural life restricted in the entire Eastern Bloc, including Lithuania.
1969–72	Venclova lives mainly in Leningrad (St. Petersburg). Close friendship with Brodsky and his milieu.
1970	First trip to Poland.
1971	Lithuanian Writers' Union refuses Venclova membership (March 23). Death of Antanas Venclova (June 28). Second trip to Poland, makes the acquaintance of Adam Michnik and Barbara Toruńczyk.
1972	Publication of *Kalbos ženklas: eilėraščiai* (Sign of Speech). Self-immolation of Romas Kalanta in Kaunas (May 15). Brodsky forced to emigrate (June 4).
1972–76	Employment as a literary director for Šiauliai Drama Theater.
1973	Venclova's poem "Dialogue in Winter" is translated by Czesław Miłosz and published in the Polish émigré magazine *Kultura*.
1975	Venclova sends an open letter to the Central Committee of the Lithuanian Communist Party, opposing the system and requesting the right to emigrate (sent on May 9). The text of the letter is leaked to the West, attracting the attention of Czesław Miłosz, Arthur Miller, and others.
1976	Establishment of the Lithuanian Helsinki Group (Venclova is one of the five founding members, together with Ona Lukauskaitė, Karolis Garuckas, and the group's leaders Viktoras Petkus and Eitan Finkelstein). A press conference for foreign journalists presenting the group's manifesto (dated November 25) is held in Moscow on December 1. Meets Lyudmila Alexeyeva for the first

time. Venclova's poem "In Memory of the Poet. Variant," translated by Joseph Brodsky, is published in the Russian émigré magazine *Kontinent*.

1977   Venclova allowed to leave the USSR at the invitation of the University of California at Berkeley, arranged by Czesław Miłosz. Departure on January 25. Secret memo by Yuri Andropov stating that Venclova's fate "in the long-term will be determined by his behavior while abroad." After three weeks in Paris, Venclova arrives in the United States. Authorization by the Lithuanian Helsinki Group to act as the group's representative in the West. Testifies in Washington before the Congressional Commission on Security and Cooperation in Europe (February 24). Teaches at University of California Berkeley as regents' professor (March–May). Stripped of his Soviet citizenship by special decree of the Supreme Soviet of the USSR (June 14). Granted political asylum in the United States. Arrest of Viktoras Petkus (August 23). In September, Venclova moves to Los Angeles, where he teaches at UCLA. His *98 eilėraščiai* (98 Poems) is published in Chicago (in Lithuanian).

1979   "Dialogue on Vilnius" (with Czesław Miłosz) published in *Kultura. Balsai: Iš pasaulinės poezijos* (Selected Translations), published in Michigan (in Lithuanian).

1980   Venclova moves to New Haven, Connecticut; receives invitation to lecture at Yale University, where he teaches Russian poetry.

1981   "Dialogue on Vilnius" published by the underground Polish press. A book of essays, *Lietuva pasaulyje* (Lithuania in the World) published in Chicago (in Lithuanian). Martial law is declared in Poland (December 13).

1985   Naturalized as a US citizen (April 12). Venclova's literary essays, *Tekstai apie tekstus* (Texts on Texts), published in Chicago (in Lithuanian). Venclova is awarded a PhD (Yale University).

1985–90   Assistant professor in the Slavic Languages and Literatures
                 Department at Yale (associate professor 1990, appointed
                 full professor 1993–2012).

1985–91   Perestroika. Venclova visits Hungary (November 1986).

1988   Enters the USSR and travels to Moscow and Leningrad
                 (St. Petersburg) with a tourist group; meets his mother
                 and friends. Following Venclova's interview with the BBC
                 in London about perestroika, he is barred entry to the
                 USSR for five years (June 1988).

1990   Signing of the Act of the Re-Establishment of the State of
                 Lithuania (March 11).

                 Venclova marries Tatiana (Tanya) Milovidova. Vilenica
                 International Literary Prize (Slovenia). *Tankėjanti šviesa*
                 (The Condensing Light, poetry) published in Chicago (in
                 Lithuanian).

1991   Venclova attempts to reach Vilnius as a journalist;
                 permission denied. Face-off between Lithuanian pro-
                 independence supporters and Soviet troops in Vilnius
                 (January 11–13). Thirteen unarmed protesters killed and
                 over a thousand injured.

                 Premio Capri (Italy). In his capacity as president of
                 the Association for the Advancement of Baltic Studies,
                 Venclova returns to Lithuania; sees Yuri Lotman for the
                 last time.

                 Collapse of the USSR, international recognition of
                 independent Lithuania (August–September). *Doctor
                 honoris causa*, University of Lublin (October), followed by
                 other honorary doctorates in subsequent years.

                 Pašnekesys žiemą (Winter Dialogue, poetry); *Vilties
                 formos* (Forms of Hope, essays) published in Vilnius (in
                 Lithuanian).

1995   Commander's Cross of the Order of the Lithuanian
                 Grand Duke Gediminas, awarded by the president of the
                 Republic of Lithuania.

1996	Death of Joseph Brodsky (January 28). Venclova's *Aleksander Wat: Life and Art of an Iconoclast*, published in English.
1997	*Winter Dialogue* (poetry) published in English. Translated by Diana Senechal.
1998	*Reginys iš alėjos* (A View from an Alley, poetry), Vilnius.
1999	*Rinktinė* (Selected Poems), Vilnius. *Forms of Hope* (essays) published by Sheep Meadow Press, Riverdale on Hudson, in English translation. Officer of the Order of the Cross of Vytis, awarded by the president of the Republic of Lithuania.
2000	*Manau, kad . . . Pokalbiai su Tomu Venclova* (I Think That . . . Interviews with Tomas Venclova) Vilnius. Lithuanian National Prize.
2001	*Vilnius: Vadovas po miestą* (Vilnius City Guide) published in Lithuania. Borderland Award (Poland).
2002	Prize of Two Nations (received jointly with Czesław Miłosz), awarded by the Parliaments of Poland and Lithuania.
2003	*Ligi Lietuvos 10 000 kilometrų* (10,000 Kilometers to Lithuania), Vilnius.
2004	Death of Czesław Miłosz (August 14).
2005	*Sankirta* (The Junction, poetry), Vilnius. New Culture of New Europe Prize (Poland). Jotvingiai Prize.
2006	*Kitaip* (Otherwise, selected translations), Vilnius; *Vilniaus vardai* (People from Vilnius, biographies), Vilnius.
2007	Death of Venclova's mother (April 5).
2008	*The Junction* (poetry) in English translation. Translated and edited by Ellen Hinsey, with Constantine Rusanov and Diana Senechal. International Baltic Star Award, St. Petersburg, Russia.
2009	*Vilnius: A Personal History* (prose), in English translation.

2010   *Visi eilėraščiai: 1956–2010* (Collected Poems,
            1956–2010), in Lithuanian. Samuel Fischer Guest
            Professorship, Freie Universität Berlin.

2011   *Vilnius: asmeninė istorija* (Vilnius: A Personal History)
            Vilnius. Qinhai International Poetry Prize (China).

2012   Professor emeritus of Slavic Languages and Literatures,
            Yale. Person of Tolerance of the Year Award (Sugihara
            Foundation).

2013   Honorary Citizen of Vilnius. *Pertrūkis tikrovėje* (A Break
            in Reality, essays), Vilnius. Grand Cross of the Order of
            Merit of the Republic of Poland.

2014   Petrarca Prize (Germany).

2015   Berlin Prize Fellow, American Academy in Berlin. Jan
            Nowak-Jeziorański Award, Wrocław.

Map of Lithuania

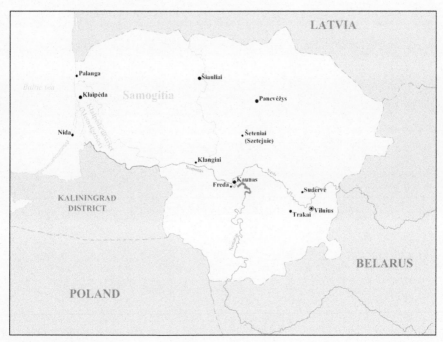

Map by Inga Genytė.

INTRODUCTION

Magnetic North: Iron and Grace

Ellen Hinsey

In the prelude to his Charles Eliot Norton Lectures at Harvard, the Nobel Prize Laureate Czesław Miłosz underscored the fact that the twentieth century—"perhaps more protean and multifaceted than any other"—changed not only according to one's viewpoint, but also according to the volatile coordinates of latitude and longitude, a "point in the geographic sense as well." Miłosz continues: "My corner of Europe, owing to the extraordinary and lethal events that have been occurring there, comparable only to violent earthquakes, affords a peculiar perspective. As a result, all of us who come from those parts appraise poetry slightly differently from the majority of my audience, for we tend to view it as a witness and participant in one of mankind's major transformations."[1]

Tomas Venclova, who came of age under the same sky as Miłosz and attended the same university, albeit in the rebaptized Lithuanian capital of Vilnius, could easily have written these lines. The "peculiar perspective" that Miłosz somewhat obliquely refers to is, of course, a nearly eight-hundred-year-old intellectual tradition, with its distinct, rich, and complex identity and history. And while, as John Donne reminds us, the globe—like a tear—is a perfect sphere, it remains a human curiosity that certain loci on the earth are perceived as being further from "the center," even if, paradoxically, their magnetic ore has endured some of history's most violent earthquakes. Such a state of affairs—compounded by the systematic silences of totalitarianism—has resulted in the necessity of writers from the "borderlands" of Eastern Europe to elucidate its topography and attempt to shed light on the contours of this critical cultural and geopolitical point in space. In this, poetry has indeed been an essential witness and participant.

Such a task was given to Venclova precisely because his life has passed through some of the twentieth century's darkest seismic movements. Born in 1937 in Klaipėda, Lithuania, at the height of Stalin's Great Purge, Venclova's early childhood was first spent in Kaunas at the beginning of World War II, and later in Freda, a nearby suburb, in the home of his maternal grandfather Merkelis Račkauskas. At the start of the 1941 Soviet-German war, Venclova's mother, Eliza Venclovienė, was imprisoned by the Nazis and his father, Antanas Venclova, a writer, fellow traveler, and minister of education, was evacuated to Moscow, where the first Soviet Lithuanian government reassembled.

These first experiences of upheaval remained significant to Venclova, as well as when, following his first day at school, he became lost in Vilnius's early postwar ruins. Already apparent to Venclova in those moments was the chaotic potential of history—what the Czech philosopher Jan Patočka called the experience of "the shaken." At the same time, however, this terrain continued to harbor vestiges of a once-coherent world. As Venclova entered young adulthood during the Stalinist period, such extant fragments began to appear to him as a sign that "made a statement and exacted a demand." Out of this exigency would arise a lifework of intellectual salvage and restoration.

Despite Venclova's father's position as part of the Soviet *nomenklatura*, following the suppression of the 1956 Hungarian Revolution, Venclova broke with the dominant ideology around him. It was during this period that he began to give poetic voice to his feeling that the postwar Soviet world was "out of joint." His poetry began to circulate, and in his third year of university he was accused by the Lithuanian Writers' Union of fostering anti-Soviet tendencies in his work, a fact he did not deny. During his travels to Moscow and Leningrad in the sixties, he sought out the company of like-minded writers and those associated with the so-called Russian Silver Age, including Boris Pasternak, Anna Akhmatova, and Nadezhda Mandelstam, as well as poets of the younger generation, such as Joseph Brodsky and Natalya Gorbanevskaya. Of equal importance was his encounter in high school with Ramūnas Katilius, who became a central figure in his Vilnius circle. Venclova also traveled to Tartu to establish contact with Yuri Lotman, whose studies in structural poetics and semiotics would have an important impact on his work. In 1972, Venclova was allowed to publish *Sign of Speech*, the only volume of his poetry to appear in Soviet Lithuania.

During the stagnation of the Brezhnev years, Venclova became increasingly involved in the Lithuanian and Soviet dissident movements. In

1975, he wrote an open letter to the Central Committee of the Lithuanian Communist Party, publicly stating his views on the Communist system and demanding the right to emigrate. This risky act resulted in both political ostracism and a compromised livelihood, and carried with it the danger of being accused of the crime of "social parasitism," which had been the basis of Brodsky's 1964 trial and subsequent sentencing. In 1976, following the signing of the 1975 Helsinki Accords, Venclova joined Viktoras Petkus, Eitan Finkelstein, Ona Lukauskaitė, and Karolis Garuckas in establishing the Lithuanian Helsinki Group. It was at this moment that Venclova's public opposition to the system and his commitment to dissident and "a-Soviet" cultural activities brought his already contentious relationship with the authorities to a crisis point.

In the wake of the March 1971 decision, prior to the Communist Party of the Soviet Union's (CPSU) Twenty-Fourth Party Congress, to allow for greater emigration of Soviet Jews, an unspoken policy to eliminate political opponents through expulsion or "suggested" emigration also became a common practice. In the mid-seventies, this tactic would be extensively used to dismantle the Soviet dissident movement. Upon his return from the December 1, 1976, press conference in Moscow to announce the establishment of the Lithuanian Helsinki Group, Venclova was summoned by the Lithuanian authorities and "invited" to emigrate—a fate he shared with other key activists, including Yuri Orlov, Lyudmila Alexeyeva, Pavel Litvinov, and Andrei Amalrik. Though Venclova had no knowledge of it at the time, the official decision on his expulsion had been formulated in Moscow at the highest levels and signed by Yuri Andropov, then chairman of the Committee for State Security. In a document dated January 20, 1977, outlining measures to be taken against four dissidents, Yuri Orlov, Alexander Ginzburg, Mykola Rudenko, and Venclova, it was declared that Venclova should be allowed to emigrate but his fate would be "determined on the basis of his behavior while abroad."[2]

After arriving in the United States on January 25, 1977, Venclova continued his political activities, testifying before the House Committee on Security and Cooperation in Europe on religious and political repression in Soviet Lithuania. Following an invitation from Czesław Miłosz to teach at the University of California for a semester, Venclova temporarily relocated to Berkeley. Five months later he was stripped of his Soviet citizenship "for activities that defile the title of a Soviet citizen," and began his period of exile in the United States. In Lithuania, immediately following his emigration, Venclova became an "unperson": his books (already unavailable in bookshops) were subsequently removed from libraries. And yet, as had been the case with Miłosz before him, Venclova's term of exile, though fraught with challenges, became a fortuitous gift for world literature. A number of Venclova's most important books of poetry, essays, and journalistic writings—many of which address persecuted authors—were produced during this period. As was the case with other Lithuanian, Polish, and Russian émigrés, he found shelter within an American intellectual community and, starting in 1980, he began a distinguished career as a professor at Yale University.

Throughout the present dialogue one finds a constant interweaving of this personal, political, and literary history. This approach is intentional because Venclova's life and art are intricately bound up with the time in which he has lived and fate's demands on him. For the same reason, alongside the book's investigation of events and experiences, one encounters a parallel ethical exploration, which becomes its basso continuo. For essential to *Magnetic North* is an examination of how, under the real existing conditions of Soviet totalitarianism and autocracy, it was possible to live a life that can be understood as dignified. Venclova describes his and his friends' attempts to discover ways to resist Soviet reality: a conformist, absurdist but also dangerous universe that had the power, as the poet writes, "to mutilate human souls." What follows in this book is thus an account of daily ethical praxis, which encompasses not only questions of courage and endurance, but also human frailty. For to endure such complexity Venclova argues on the side of compassion, rather than ethical absolutism, which leads to "unconditional condemnation." Reflecting on Thomas Mann's essay "Lübeck as a Way of Life and Thought," Venclova describes this difficult, but essential, challenge:

> Important in [Mann's] world are such categories as reason, responsibility, and home. Certainly this has changed. These categories are no longer handed down to us "from the beginning" by tradition; they can, and can only, be a mission. This means, we must grow up to a sense of responsibility, to a reasonable and dignified life, to some unmechanized place of our own, if not in space then in time. It is a maturity achieved with difficulty, with constant apprehension of losing. This is the result, above all, of the totalitarianisms of the twentieth century.[3]

The acute contemporary relevance and urgency of Venclova's example and ethical struggles, and those of his generation, could hardly have been anticipated in the first years following the collapse of Communism, heralded as "the end of history." Yet Venclova presciently understood that, even if we might be living after the end of the world, such a condition did not "incidentally absolve us from any responsibility."[4]

But, then, from the beginning of his writing career, Venclova has never shied away from difficult topics, and his interventions continue to be essential contributions to contemporary European dialogue. In his essay "Jews and Lithuanians," Venclova was the first writer in Lithuania to address the painful reality of local collaboration in atrocities against Jews during World War II, a topic that remains highly divisive to the present day. In his famous exchange with Czesław Miłosz, the two poets explored the historic conflict over Vilnius/Wilno—their shared "city without a name"—in an attempt to promote Polish-Lithuanian understanding. As with his human rights work in the seventies, since 1989 Venclova has continued to advocate tolerance and reconciliation at a time when issues of territorial sovereignty and the specter of nationalism—so aptly addressed in his recent essays—have reappeared, posing critical questions for the future of Europe.

It is Venclova's work as a poet, however, that stands at the center of his oeuvre. The author of eight volumes of verse translated into more than twenty languages, Venclova has indeed continued the tradition of being a "witness and participant" in history's transformations. While much of Lithuania's native literature and history were banned during Venclova's upbringing (though at times found available in his father's extensive library), Venclova memorized "hundreds of poetic lines" in his native Lithuanian and came to believe that, in the absence of a coherent world, it was within those lines that he felt most at home. For Venclova, poetry was, and remains, one of the most unfettered sites for consciousness; an entirely free contemplative space. Poetry is also a vehicle where recollection can serve as the basis for resistance—something that, early in his career, did not go unnoticed by the Soviet authorities. As Venclova wrote in his essay "Poetry as Atonement": "The forces shattering the spirit of mankind may yet recoil before our consciousness and memory."[5] One might even go as far as to say that Venclova's generation, which took up with passion the ancient practice of *ars memoriae*, memorizing not only poetry but forbidden history, science, and literature, were rivaled only by their Renaissance fore-practitioners. Venclova's lineage might even be traced further back to the tutelary figure of Simonides of Ceos, the ancient Greek poet attributed with inventing the art. For it was Simonides who, after reciting and feasting with others—and being unexpectedly called away from the table—was tasked with recalling from memory the identities of the dead beneath the roof's sudden collapse.

In the pages of *Magnetic North*, Venclova is often left to evoke the memory of those lost under the rubble of the twentieth century, as well as the countless buildings, streets, and monuments that no longer exist and sometimes vanished overnight, their names changed, their foundations dynamited. The structural choice of a dialogical form for *Magnetic North*—in Polish *wywiad-rzeka*, or "an interview like a river"—is therefore not arbitrary. While referential to a number of illustrious examples of the genre, including *My Century* by Aleksander Wat, *Conversations with Czesław Miłosz*, and *Conversations with Joseph Brodsky*, *Magnetic North* employs not only the I-Thou of question and answer, but preserves the identities of a whole generation, whose voices rise from these pages. Thus Venclova reconstructs, with the care of an expert genealogist, the stories of the deported and those whose lives were irrevocably broken by the Stalinist period. We learn of the secret police's "prophylactic talks," shadowy rituals during which the authorities alternated their interrogatory roles like a hydra with multiple heads. Present also are family tragedies such as Venclova's father's failure, despite his position, to save his own brother from deportation, forced labor, and death. And yet, one is also witness to subtle victories, as when one of Venclova's teachers, another master of *ars memoriae*, defied the authorities and recited to her students the whole of a banned pre-war history of Lithuania by heart. Like roundels on a Renaissance *arbor con-sanguinatis*, there are an extensive number of portraits of Lithuanian (as well as Russian, Polish, and Ukrainian) intellectuals, painters, and writers. This dedication to memory also underpins a number of Venclova's other works, such as *Vilniaus vardai* (People from Vilnius) and *Vilnius: A Personal History*, which reflect his long-standing commitment to rescue archaeology regarding the city of Vilnius and its cultural figures.

In Giorgio Agamben's study *The Signature of All Things*, the philosopher states that archaeology is a science of ruins, a "ruinology."[6] *Magnetic North* can be understood as a dialogue-river bordering the archaeological site of the twentieth century, flowing in and among its ruins. And while no single text can ever recover the "empirical whole" of the past, there are moments when it can almost seem—as can happen on a vivid day when one is seated on a bench by a river—that the lost past stands again, reflected in Venclova's wavering lines of prose. There is an implicit victory in this reconstruction of the story of a generation, whose existence was the target of spiritual, and oftentimes, physical extermination. For whereas in the West a reader might be able to recount the interrelationship of Western postwar painters, intellectuals, and writers, a knowledge of Lithuania's cultural and intellectual milieu remains a deleted "white space" in European history, which must be salvaged while still bright in the living waters of human memory. For, as Venclova's mentor Anna Akhmatova believed, it is memory that gathers up the totality of human history, good and evil. And like God, memory ultimately has the power to endure, and in that way triumphs over history's events and its tyrants.

* * *

The genesis of *Magnetic North* is in many ways as surprising as the stories contained within it. Tomas Venclova and I met in the summer of 2003 in Switzerland, at the Château de Lavigny, only five miles from where Miłosz began his classic 1954 memoir *Native Realm*. Due to a mysterious chemistry that can only be explained by the fact that poets are members of an extended family, Venclova and I were immediately at ease and exchanged thoughts on poetry. On that first afternoon, under the shade of a tree, Venclova recounted stories about his childhood, his parents, and his relationships with Akhmatova, Pasternak, and Brodsky, among many other things. Before we had finished our conversation, the seeds for this book had been planted, though we would have to wait until 2009 to begin, and it was a project that would take six years to complete.

Due to the density of the material and our geographic separation—Venclova was in New Haven at Yale, and I was teaching at Skidmore College's program in Paris—it was decided that a written account would best do justice to the project. After research and preparation, I would send Venclova questions; he would then generously respond a few weeks later, sometimes with over twenty-five pages of text. This process survived mutual teaching loads, extensive travels, the deaths of parents, and life's other passages. While research for this volume involved an extensive number of books and articles, I would like to cite a few works that were particularly important to me: Lyudmila Alexeyeva's *Soviet Dissidence* and *The Thaw Generation*, Natalia Gorbanevskaya's *Red Square at Noon*, and Donata Mitaitė's *Tomas Venclova, Speaking through Signs*. I am also grateful for interviews with Lyudmila Alexeyeva in Moscow, Romas (Ramūnas) Katilius in Vilnius, and Eitan Finkelstein in Munich. Romas Katilius and Eitan Finkelstein kindly read specific chapters for us, and provided verification and helpful comments. Respective overlapping fellowships in 2015 at the American Academy in Berlin, and the Berliner Künstlerprogramm des DAAD, provided Tomas Venclova and me with invaluable time for the final editing of the manuscript. We are immensely thankful to Katherina Narbutovic and our editor Katharina Raabe at Suhrkamp Verlag for their ongoing support of the project. At the University of Rochester Press, we extend our deep gratitude to Timothy Snyder and Sonia Kane, as well as to Tracey Engel, Ryan Peterson, and Therese Malhame. Finally, we would like to thank Tatiana Milovidova-Venclova and Mark Carlson for their patience and immense support.

Lastly, despite our attempt at comprehensiveness regarding the book's scope, neither Tomas Venclova nor I believe that an individual is merely the sum of his or her life experiences, or that the latter can explain "the creation of a poet." In contrast to the deterministic Marxist worldview that Venclova escaped early on, it is our understanding that an individual is a free agent, whose life, creations, and passions transcend the purely biographical, as well as the linear boundaries of prose. Like Akhmatova's conviction that all great poetry must "have some mystery in it," we hope that *Magnetic North*, like a work by Rembrandt van Rijn—whom Osip Mandelstam once called the "father of green-black darkness"—nevertheless preserves in its depths certain mysteries that can only be discovered, and if then, in Venclova's verse. For life is also composed of things that can only be understood obliquely, that remain beyond the reach of a lighthouse's beacon at night, yet are a palpable part of experience; whether tragic or joyful, they also constitute life's magnetic iron and grace.

PART ONE

CHILDHOOD AND FAMILY

HINSEY: Why don't we start by speaking about your earliest memories, for example, the house where you were born?

VENCLOVA: The house was in Klaipėda (also called Memel), a harbor town on the Baltic Sea. But I don't have any memory of it since our family moved when I was less than two years old. The history of Memel is as complicated as any history in that part of Europe. The town started as a fortress established in 1252 by German knights on terrain inhabited by pagan Lithuanians (they also founded the much bigger and better-known Baltic cities, including Riga and Königsberg, at approximately the same time). The knights attempted to subdue and baptize the Lithuanians, but without much success; they only managed to impose their rule on a narrow strip of land around the town, a region that later acquired some fame as Memel Territory, or Memelgebiet. In any case, the land was considered to be part of Germany for seven hundred years. After World War I, it was separated from the German Reich by the Treaty of Versailles, and ended up as an autonomous region of Lithuania.

HINSEY: Could you describe what Klaipėda was like at that time?

VENCLOVA: In 1937, the town was small, provincial, and German-speaking. The architecture was typically Prussian: timber-framed houses and Lutheran churches with pointed steeples. Incidentally, Thomas Mann used to spend his summers in Nida, a village not far away (he started writing *Joseph and His Brothers* there), but he did not return after leaving for Switzerland in 1933. In the countryside around Klaipėda, as the town was now officially called, the people mainly spoke Lithuanian, but the Memellanders were Lutheran and looked down on the Catholic and definitely less civilized inhabitants of "Lithuania proper." Most of them succumbed easily to Nazi sloganeering. In March 1939, Hitler took Memel and Memel Territory back: it is still remembered that he arrived on a warship and delivered a speech from the balcony of the old theater, heartily applauded by the majority of Memellanders (even if the speech was on the short side, due to his seasickness).

HINSEY: Your father had moved to Klaipėda a few years before you were born. What was his occupation at the time?

VENCLOVA: My father was a leftist writer from Lithuania proper, who moved to Klaipėda in 1934 after finding a job as a teacher in the only Lithuanian high school in the town (there were several other schools, but they used German as the language of instruction). He also became associated with a company of Lithuanian actors who performed in the old theater building prior to the führer's arrival. Like other teachers and actors, he was expected to take part in the Lithuanization of Memel Territory—a rather hopeless enterprise, to tell the truth. Many years later, reading Günter Grass's *The Tin Drum*, I was struck by the similarities between Klaipėda and prewar Gdansk. Of course, our town was of negligible size and importance in comparison to the Free City of Danzig, but the same type of ethnic composition and tensions prevailed in it. Independent Lithuania tried to do its best in the region. The high school that employed my father was quite modern by the standards of the time—even today, it is one of the architectural highlights of the city. The hospital, also built under Lithuanian rule, was equally spacious and well-equipped. Part of it was dedicated to the maternity ward—to which my father accompanied his young wife when she was ready to deliver. For lodgings, they rented an attic apartment just around the corner that belonged to a German family.

HINSEY: Are there any significant family stories you were told about this period?

VENCLOVA: The only story my mother told me about those years does not sound very agreeable. She took me to a park along with another baby and his mother, an actress from the theater company. Several members of the Hitler Youth, who overheard them speaking in Lithuanian, threw sand into our prams. (The other baby, Pranas Morkus, later became a close friend—I'll talk more about him when discussing my university years). In 1939, when Hitler took Klaipėda, we had no other choice but to leave. Most of the town's not-too-numerous ethnic Lithuanians and its small Jewish population made the same decision. We moved to a suburb of Kaunas, then the capital of still-independent Lithuania, and found temporary housing next to my maternal grandfather's house.

Incidentally, at the end of the war, Memel surrendered to Soviet troops, who found only seven people in the destroyed town (around forty thousand had fled to Königsberg, and then across Poland to Germany. Stalin decided to give Memel back to Lithuania—which was by then a Soviet republic—and to restore its Lithuanian name. I got to know my birthplace only in my adolescence and fell in love with it. It was a romantic place, ruined, almost deserted, very grim, with a black and white lighthouse at the end a stone pier that jutted into a usually turbulent Baltic Sea. The lighthouse and many other parts of the town were actually off-limits since the Soviets used them for military purposes, but I still managed to get a glimpse of them. Some of my earliest poems are about Klaipėda.

HINSEY: Since then Klaipėda has changed considerably: is it possible to see any traces of this earlier period?

VENCLOVA: Klaipėda no longer has much in common with its prewar or early postwar years. It is definitely larger, not a town anymore, rather a veritable city: industrial, with a busy harbor—also visited by cruise ships—and ringed by horrible Soviet-era suburbs consisting of nearly identical five- and six-story apartment blocks, punctuated here and there by taller Western-style buildings. The Germans have long since departed and everyone speaks Lithuanian, including those of Russian origin who make up about a quarter of the population. The old downtown has survived only in part, but is recognizable (the churches have disappeared). The theater is still standing, as well as the high school where my father taught and the hospital where I was born. Even the attic apartment our family once rented is there. You can see its windows from the house's small, neglected garden. I returned there two or three times. Once, while my father was still alive, we knocked on the door and asked permission to visit. The Russian family who lived there was a bit upset—they probably thought we were the house's former owners, come to request our property back (such demands were usually pointless under Soviet rule, but one never knew . . .). Still, we were allowed to look inside. It was cramped and shabby, undoubtedly shabbier than before the war. In 1939, a small secretary desk with two rusty iron hinges on which my father wrote his first novel in Klaipėda escaped the vagaries of history, and made it to our Vilnius flat. It is still there.

HINSEY: Before we return to your childhood, let's speak about your grandparents—

VENCLOVA: On my father's side, my grandparents were peasants. They lived in southern Lithuania, two or three miles from the present-day Polish border. My grandfather Tomas Venclova (I was named after him) was relatively well-to-do and literate: his less literate neighbors would visit his house, where he read Lithuanian newspapers aloud to them—hence, his home functioned as a sort of library or village club. He died of typhus in 1919, while still a young man. During the Soviet period, our family tended his grave. By a strange coincidence, Krasnogruda manor, where Czesław Miłosz spent part of his youth in the 1920s and 1930s, is very close by, just on the other side of the border. My peasant grandmother Elzbieta Vėlyviūtė survived her husband by thirty-eight years. I met her in my early childhood when she sheltered my mother and me during the Nazi occupation, but I never developed a significant attachment to her. In 1957, I attended her Catholic funeral. On this occasion, my father and I participated in the Mass; for my father this was a political transgression, as high-standing Communists were not supposed to encourage "superstitions." As often happens with peasant families, it is difficult to trace one's genealogy: my great-grandfather was named Martynas Venclova, but that's all I know about him.

HINSEY: Venclova is not necessarily a typical Lithuanian name. Did your father have any ideas about its origins?

VENCLOVA: Our family name sounds Czech—or German—rather than Lithuanian. My father toyed with the idea that we were descended from Hussite immigrants (in the fifteenth century, several of these families were granted asylum in Lithuania). More than once, he joked, "You know, Václavské Náměstí (Wenceslas Square) in Prague belongs to us." Of course it's absurd.

HINSEY: What about your mother's side of the family, in particular your maternal grandfather Merkelis Račkauskas?

VENCLOVA: On my mother's side, things look different. Merkelis Račkauskas (Melchior Raczkowski in Polish) was born in the northwestern part of Lithuania, near Klaipėda—though not in Memel Territory—in Catholic Lithuania, Samogitia to be exact. People there speak a specific dialect, practically a separate language. It differs from standard Lithuanian in the way that Portuguese differs from Spanish. Socially, Samogitia is, or was, unique; it had a very large gentry population, who were generally poor and indistinguishable from the peasants in their standards of living (and frequently intermarried with them). Yet they were proud, and stubbornly preserved old traditions. The everyday language of these hidalgos was Samogitian, but they considered Polish their language of culture—everyone was bilingual, and strongly preferred Polish name forms (Raczkowski instead of Račkauskas). They were very active in the 1831 and 1863 uprisings against tsarist rule. At the end of the nineteenth century, when national independence movements separated Lithuanians from Poles, most, but not all, of the Samogitians took the Lithuanian side. However, Józef Piłsudski, the interwar Polish dictator, and Gabriel Narutowicz, the first president of independent Poland, both of Samogitian descent, played significant roles for Poland.

HINSEY: The Lithuanian national movement plays an important role in your grandfather's story. It is difficult to understand his life without touching on historical events. Perhaps you could recount a bit about the revival of the Lithuanian language in the nineteenth century.

VENCLOVA: This is a rather long and involved story. Czesław Miłosz and others have frequently compared Poland to England, and Lithuania to Ireland (Scotland might be an even better example). One has to start with the fact that medieval Lithuania was pagan—the very last non-Christianized area of Europe. In the thirteenth and early fourteenth centuries, these bellicose pagans managed to establish a strong state with Vilnius as its capital—the so-called Grand Duchy of Lithuania. This territory included contemporary Belarus, a large part of Ukraine, and also Western Russia, almost to the suburbs of Moscow. The Slavic regions embraced the Orthodox faith, which came from Byzantium. In general, these populations were more civilized than the pagan "core" around Vilnius.

The Slavic languages—Russian, Belarusian, Ukrainian, and Polish—are closely related, but Lithuanian is as different from them as Gaelic is from English. It is totally incomprehensible to any nonnative speaker without prolonged study. It is Indo-European, that is, it has something in common with Slavic and most other European languages, but it has retained a very archaic vocabulary and grammar structure. If I am not mistaken, the French linguist Antoine Meillet observed that Lithuanian best corresponds to the preclassical Latin of the third century BCE. In the medieval period, it still did not have a written form. The official language of the Grand Duchy was East Slavic: the pagan core still spoke Lithuanian, but the ruling class used it as a sort of secret code, on occasions when Lithuanians preferred not to be understood by outsiders.

HINSEY: However, at the end of the fourteenth century this was to change—

VENCLOVA: Yes, that is when Lithuania entered into a dynastic union with Poland. From that time on, Lithuania, just like Scotland, was considered the "wilder," more romantic part of this kingdom, a land of primeval forests and a valiant but not-too-civilized people. Poland succeeded in converting the Lithuanian pagans (something the German knights had failed to do), and Polish supplanted East Slavic as the official language. The nobility—which, as a rule, knew East Slavic well—easily made the transition to Polish. Incidentally, this was true of Miłosz's ancestors: they became "Polish-speaking Lithuanians," like thousands of other gentry families. Even though books printed in Lithuanian began to appear in the sixteenth century, the language remained that of village folk (and sometimes the poorer gentry). In the nineteenth century, it was well on its way to dying out, like Gaelic or Welsh. Vilnius, now called Wilno in the Polish fashion, was like Edinburgh—an old capital with its own history and traditions, but part of a united commonwealth.

HINSEY: But the Lithuanian language survived, though it had to weather uprisings and partitions—

VENCLOVA: Yes, and very much so. But first let's go back a bit: in 1795, the Polish-Lithuanian Commonwealth, which was in decline, was partitioned by three continental powers (Prussia, Austria, and Russia). Lithuania found itself under Russian rule, which was harsher than that of Prussia or Austria. In the nineteenth century, as I mentioned earlier, there were two uprisings against the Russian tsar, in 1831 and 1863, which had as their goal the restoration of the Commonwealth. Lithuanians participated gallantly in both, making no distinction between themselves and Poles. The second uprising literally ended in a bloodbath, and to keep this from happening again, the tsarist authorities decided to Russianize the Lithuanian peasants (the official line was that these loyal but naive village people had been led into temptation by the treacherous Polish nobility, but deserved a better fate). By then, the old Lithuanian language had already found a literary niche—there were people who wrote poems, stories, and even treatises in it—though it was still something of a local curiosity and these works were published rather infrequently.

HINSEY: Was this connected to the so-called press ban?

VENCLOVA: When we speak of the "press ban" it is a bit of a misnomer. The Russian authorities did not expressly forbid the publishing of Lithuanian books, but instead imposed the use of Cyrillic characters rather than the Latin alphabet. This was perhaps one of the most counterproductive decisions in history. The peasants, not without reason, perceived this as a thinly disguised attack on their Catholic faith and their very identity. Lithuanian books in Cyrillic were boycotted (and soon became rarities). Some priests and intellectuals managed to establish publishing ventures in Germany (not in Memel Territory but in the nearby city of Tilsit). From there, books and newspapers in banned Latin script were smuggled into Lithuania proper—and avidly read, even if this was a punishable offense. The press ban lasted forty years, from 1865 to 1904. By the end of it, there was a steadily growing body of literature in Lithuanian, to say nothing of intellectual ferment and nascent political life.

HINSEY: These national aspirations were part of a much larger picture of course—

VENCLOVA: Yes, all of this was part and parcel of the nineteenth-century national movements in Eastern Europe—which were accompanied by the revival of ethnic languages such as Czech, Finnish, Latvian, and so on. Still, Lithuanian developed under much harsher conditions. Once again, one may easily draw a parallel with the revival of Gaelic in Ireland. While reading Yeats and Joyce, I was struck by the obvious similarities: the same love of archaic and unusual language, mainly preserved in remote villages, the same interest in local mythology—the distant past and its semidivine heroes—in a word, Romanticism. There are other analogies, as well: Lithuania was as Catholic as Ireland, rather poor and, beginning in the late nineteenth century, had a very large and influential diaspora in the United States. However, one can probably say that the Lithuanian revival was more successful than its Gaelic counterpart. It resulted not only in the establishment of an independent republic (in 1918) but also in the complete rebirth of the Lithuanian language, now the native language of three million people, myself included.

HINSEY: But all of this was not achieved without considerable resistance—

VENCLOVA: That's true, it had powerful opponents. Not just the tsarist authorities but also a significant portion of public opinion, which was opposed to the "Litwomaniacs," that is, Lithuanophiles. Inhabitants of Vilnius and its environs may have spoken only Polish but they called themselves Lithuanians, and may even have regarded Poles in Warsaw and Kraków rather cockily, since the best Polish patriots and poets, including the greatest one, Adam Mickiewicz, came from Lithuanian territory. But for them, their identity was just a local variant of Polish identity, and they had no intention of learning an ancient and "barbarian" tongue (and a very difficult one at that), or striving to create a separate state from Poland. Miłosz always insisted that he was one of such Polish-speaking Lithuanians, "the last citizen of the Grand Duchy." He was sympathetic to the Lithuanian movement, and possessed some knowledge of the Lithuanian language, but he was an exception (because of this, certain Poles treated him as a traitor, even expressing their anger at his funeral).

HINSEY: With the rise of the Polish and Lithuanian independence movements, the fate of Vilnius became uncertain—

VENCLOVA: In the nineteenth century, the division of the Polish and Lithuanian national movements led to sharp political conflict. When the two countries succeeded in resurrecting their respective independent states in the wake of World War I, they had in fact virtually returned to their predynastic configuration. This said, Vilnius, the capital of old Lithuania, fell to the more powerful and aristocratic Poland, since most of the city's inhabitants identified themselves as Poles. The Lithuanian-speaking city of Kaunas became the new capital of the Republic of Lithuania. According to the Lithuanian constitution, this was, however, only a temporary measure: Vilnius had to be won back. To better understand this, imagine independent (and Gaelic-speaking) Ireland with a provisional capital in Galway, while English-speaking Dublin remains in English hands. Given Poland's superior size and strength, any struggle for Vilnius seemed hopeless. Yet in 1939, Lithuanians got their capital back, which is perhaps one of the most unexpected developments of the period.

HINSEY: Now, returning to your grandfather's time—and his relationship to the Lithuanian Independence movement—in these matters of allegiance, which side did Merkelis Račkauskas take?

VENCLOVA: My grandfather sided with the Lithuanians, but not immediately. As I mentioned earlier, he was born into one of those Lithuanian families that preferred to speak Polish. His father was a village organist from the gentry, and his mother a veritable noblewoman. My grandfather had some musical talent. In my childhood, he took me to Kaunas cathedral, where he loved to play the organ—with the permission of the organist, who was a friend. By World War I, however, Melchior Raczkowski had sided with the Lithuanian movement (and consequently with the Lithuanian language). He contributed a patriotic poem (a very weak one, to tell the truth) to an illegal magazine during the "press ban," and was active in Lithuanian intellectual circles after that.

As befits a member of the gentry, Merkelis knew quite a bit about his ancestors. They were renowned for their longevity. His great-grandfather Martynas Račkauskas died at the age of 105 (he was born in 1770 in the then-independent Polish-Lithuanian Commonwealth before the tsarist occupation). Juozapas, a son of Martynas, lived to be 102 (he took part in the 1831 uprising). And so on. By the way, my mother inherited their genes. She died in 2007, after her ninety-fifth birthday. Right before her death, she gave a perfectly lucid interview to a Vilnius magazine.

HINSEY: Merkelis's education began prior to World War I, and intersected, at least as he liked to tell it, with some illustrious scholars—

VENCLOVA: Yes. Merkelis was largely a self-made man. Adverse conditions notwithstanding, he managed to graduate from high school (Russian was the language of instruction in Lithuanian high schools at the time), and enroll in the prestigious St. Petersburg University. During the Soviet period, he wrote an extensive memoir about his childhood and early youth, which he attempted to publish. However, the censors saw no point in printing a book about the adventures of a poor youth growing up amid Gogolian landowners and village priests (worst of all, the description of his sexual initiation was a bit too frank for their tastes). His memoirs were only published after 1990, several decades after his death; they were quite successful. I remember a story—not included in the memoirs and probably a bit embellished—that he liked to recount during my childhood. In St, Petersburg, he tried to enroll in a chemistry class taught by Mendeleev, one of the most renowned chemists of all time, but he dropped out because the hall was overcrowded and he could not find a seat. Then he went to the physiology class taught by Pavlov—as illustrious a figure as Mendeleev—yet the throng there was even more discouraging. Finally, he entered a classroom where the professor was reading the superbly difficult Latin satirist Persius with just two students, and there he stayed. Later, he moved to Odessa University, and graduated with a degree in classical languages.

HINSEY: At the time, there were restrictions on Lithuanians practicing their professions. Is this why, after receiving his degree, your grandfather didn't teach in Lithuania?

VENCLOVA: Under the laws of prerevolutionary Russia, educated Lithuanians could not be employed in their native land (the only exception being Catholic priests, which partly explains their important role in the Lithuanian national movement). Therefore, Merkelis Račkauskas (or Melchior Raczkowski, as he spelled his name at that time) became a high school teacher in the town of Bolgrad, near Odessa. By that time, he had already married my future grandmother Helena Łatyńska, a Polish-Ukrainian gentry woman (also from an impoverished family), born in the village of Krivin near Kyiv. They had three children: Witold (Vytautas in Lithuanian), Eliza, and Maria. Maria became an Impressionist painter, one of the better-known Lithuanian artists of the twentieth century. And Eliza became my mother.

I must confess that it is only recently that I have started to take an interest in genealogy, to which I was rather indifferent when I was younger. For example, I visited Bolgrad and even Krivin (today, both are in Ukraine). The Bolgrad high school is still there: built in the tsarist era, it is quite impressive and even contains a small museum about its history. I did not find any traces of my grandfather there, unless you include an old bust of Herodotus that he might have pointed out to his students during his classes. I was unable to find the house where my mother was born, although it may still exist. Krivin is a big village, disfigured by Stalinist collectivization—I doubt my grandmother Helena would recognize it now.

HINSEY: There was great instability in Russia after 1917—how did this affect your grandparents?

VENCLOVA: Immediately after the October Revolution, this part of the family moved from southern Ukraine to Lithuania. This was a wise decision, since life in Lithuania was relatively normal (if not overly prosperous) by European standards, while life in the future USSR was rather precarious, to put it mildly. The journey from Bolgrad lasted several weeks. To travel with three small children by very slow trains through the revolutionary countryside was an adventurous enterprise—one can get a sense of it by reading Babel, Pilnyak, and other early Soviet writers. My grandmother used to tell various stories about it, some funny, others chilling. Finally, they crossed the Lithuanian border and after some additional complications settled in Kaunas.

HINSEY: This was when your grandfather began teaching at Kaunas University—

VENCLOVA: Yes, as Merkelis Račkauskas, my grandfather became professor of classical languages in the newly established Kaunas University. After obtaining Lithuanian citizenship (following the revolution, one could choose between Soviet and Lithuanian citizenship), the entire family began to speak Lithuanian instead of Polish. Grandmother Helena spoke it with a heavy accent all her life, and only read Polish classics, primarily Sienkiewicz (a sort of Polish Walter Scott), but my uncle Vytautas and the girls became Lithuanians *sensu stricto*. They built a house with a large garden in a Kaunas suburb. One might compare it to a professor's house in the United States, but without running water (one used pails, washbasins, and an outhouse in the yard). Still, there was a telephone, a rarity at the time—the family provided poles and cabling at its own expense.

HINSEY: In fact, Kaunas University would also play an important role in your parents' lives—

VENCLOVA: In the thirties, while a student at Kaunas University, my mother Eliza fell in love with a leftist writer, my future father. They married, and Maria, my mother's younger sister—who studied at the Kaunas Art School—married another writer whose name was Petras Cvirka. He was my father's close friend. Several years before their marriages, they coedited the literary magazine *Trečias Frontas* (Third Front). A definitely "reddish" venture, it was closed by the censors after the fifth issue: something that only added to their fame. Thus, Merkelis—who was a liberal but not a pro-Communist—became the "father-in-law of two Bolsheviks." That put him in a dangerous position during the 1941–44 Nazi occupation of Lithuania. He lost his job at the university and returned to teaching high school. Although he was never a teetotaler, he now started drinking rather heavily. Still, he was able to keep his house, and his problems subsided when the Soviets returned in 1944. He was reinstated as a professor, but then the new authorities closed Kaunas University: there was a rule that each Soviet republic, with the exception of the fairly large Ukraine, should have only one university, and that it had to be in the capital, that is, in Vilnius. Well, Vilnius was only sixty miles from Kaunas, and one could commute by train or car (though the latter was an impossible luxury in the early Soviet era).

HINSEY: What was your grandfather's response to these developments?

VENCLOVA: Merkelis, or "Telė," as I used to call him, was a man of independent spirit, and adopted a rather ironic stance toward the powers that be. His anachronistic occupation as a classics professor allowed him to maintain a distance from Marxism and everything that went with it. However hard the authorities might try, they could not enforce Stalinist formulae on *ut consecutivum* or on *passer mortuus est meae puellae* without looking ridiculous. Under the Soviets, Latin was eliminated from the high school curriculum, but a small niche for classical languages remained in the university. Telė taught me some Latin and even Greek. I remember his words: "Generally, Greek is easier than Latin—it is possible to master it in two years, but then you have to learn the verbs ending in -*mi*, which takes three more years at the very least." Even today, I can read Catullus and Ovid (Horace is much more complicated), and I can decipher an excerpt from Homer, though not without effort.

In my early youth, Grandfather provided me with a copy of *The Odyssey* that had been used in tsarist high schools and that contained extensive commentary. Latin sayings peppered our everyday speech: some of them, not necessarily decorous, were invented I believe by Grandfather himself. He could also easily write a burlesque poem in Lithuanian or, for that matter, in Polish. Finally, he was a good chess player—he learned the art in Odessa, a city that produced some of the very best Russian chess masters. My cousin Andrius still has in his possession the small chessboard with miniature ivory and mahogany pieces, a memento from that period. The grim system that surrounded us during my early school and university years was bearable as long as Grandfather was around. He was a living link to better times, not just prewar Lithuania or prerevolutionary Russia, but the Enlightenment, the Renaissance, and Antiquity.

HINSEY: Your grandfather was also an accomplished translator. How was this connected to the development of Lithuanian culture during the interwar period?

VENCLOVA: Between the two wars, the Lithuanian Republic did its best to develop a culture in its own language. Lithuanian was simultaneously ancient and very young: it virtually had to be created from a mixture of dialects (Samogitian was only one of them) and standardized. The literary tradition in Lithuanian was rather sparse (even if there were several fairly good eighteenth- and nineteenth-century poets and prose writers). The market for books was still small as there were only three million Lithuanian speakers, and many of them were still illiterate. All of world literature had to be made available to them and their children in Lithuanian: from Homer to Dante, Shakespeare, Goethe, and Tolstoy, as well as, of course, native authors who wrote in Polish, like Mickiewicz. It was a patriotic duty, a creative exercise, and undoubtedly a great deal of fun—comparable perhaps to the revival of Hebrew in Israel.

Grandfather translated, among other authors, Erasmus, Lucretius, and Plato. As regards Plato, he had a formidable rival, namely, Antanas Smetona, the president of Lithuania, who knew Greek and dreamed of establishing a Lithuanian philosophical republic. To my taste, however, Telė's translations were better. I remember how I roared with laughter in my grandfather's garden reading the *Menaechmi*, the funniest of Plautus's plays, which served as a source for *The Comedy of Errors*. Many years later, in the Albanian city of Durres, I found an ancient amphitheater lost in a maze of dirty, half-Oriental, half-Socialist streets. It stirred elusive memories in me. Suddenly, I remembered that the action of the *Menaechmi* took place in Durres (then Epidamnus), and that the play might have been performed on its stage. My poem "Homage to Shqiperia" addresses that experience: I owe its inspiration to the preclassical Latin lines translated by my grandfather together with a minor Lithuanian poet.

HINSEY: What happened to your grandfather later in life?

VENCLOVA: One of Telė's eccentricities was positively dangerous. We knew that he kept a handgun in a locked drawer. This was a big family secret, since the unauthorized possession of a weapon could result in a long prison sentence or even execution—at least during Stalinist times. How did he get it? It appears he traded it for a lump of lard with a Russian (or German?) officer at the end of World War II. After Stalin's death, he used it once or twice on very special occasions, such as on New Year's Eve. He fired it from our porch, but the lone shot was imperceptible among identical shots; Soviet military personnel, who were numerous in Kaunas, did the same from other porches. In January 1968, on his eighty-third birthday, he drank a bottle of cognac in his study and shot himself. By a strange coincidence, I was in Kaunas at that moment (though not at his house), en route to Palanga, a Baltic Sea resort, where Joseph Brodsky was staying, after his girlfriend Marina had left him. The next day, I returned from Palanga to comfort my mother and other family members. My mother told me that Merkelis had been worried about what he thought to be symptoms of prostate cancer, and presumably had not wanted to become a burden on his family. An autopsy, however, did not show any cancer whatsoever. He could had lived at least another twenty years, as his ancestors had.

2

THE SOVIETS

1939–1941

HINSEY: Could you begin by discussing your family's situation right before the first Soviet occupation of Lithuania?

VENCLOVA: I mentioned that we had moved from Klaipėda to Kaunas. Petras Cvirka and my aunt Maria were living in my grandfather's house, so we rented a small annex building from another professor's family, almost next door. My father again found employment as a high school teacher, but would lose his job at the beginning of 1940. This was due to a pacifist and mildly pro-Soviet poem he published in the literary press; it attracted the attention of President Smetona himself, who telephoned the minister of education and proposed that measures be taken against a politically suspect author. (It was a common practice in authoritarian Lithuania, though the country was far from fascist, even if it was considered as such by Stalinists.) Later, Father found a new job in a leftist newspaper, but our family was in dire straits.

HINSEY: As the war neared, independent Lithuania found itself in an unenviable position—

VENCLOVA: Lithuania had no diplomatic relations with Poland because of the Vilnius question. Nazi Germany, its neighbor to the west, was a genuine threat. In 1938, the Polish government had demanded the immediate establishment of diplomatic relations, which was viewed in Lithuania as a demand to abandon all claims to the capital. After some hesitation, the Lithuanian government conceded—it had virtually no alternative, since a Polish-Lithuanian war would have ended in Lithuania's defeat. Subsequently, Hitler demanded Klaipėda and Memel Territory. Since he could easily have crushed the country in two or three days, the government understood that it would have been pointless to resist. These two calamities had an immense psychological impact on the population. It must be remembered that President Smetona was a leader who had come to power in a coup d'état, established an authoritarian regime, ruled without a parliament, and was strongly disliked by a considerable portion of the country. Now he looked helpless, at the mercy of the surrounding powers. In the national imagination, Vilnius was seen as the heart of Lithuania, and Klaipėda—the country's only harbor—as its lungs. It was unlikely that the country could survive without either.

HINSEY: This touches on the complexity of prewar geopolitical relationships, including with the Soviet Union—

VENCLOVA: Yes, in light of the situation, for some at least, the Soviet Union didn't look so bad. It didn't have a common border with Lithuania (that was established later, after Poland was carved up between Nazi Germany and the USSR under the terms of the Molotov-Ribbentrop Pact). It supported Lithuania's position with regard to Vilnius, if only because Russia was Poland's sworn enemy. Of course, the Soviets were brutal, but the full extent of their crimes was not yet known in Lithuania, or in other European countries, for that matter. Those who tried to alert the public were easily dismissed as "partisans of a lost cause" or "incorrigible right-wingers." People concerned with political and social conditions in Eastern Europe (which were quite serious) tended to consider Communism a panacea—neither my father nor Cvirka were immune to this temptation. In Poland, Miłosz was drawn to it, at least for a time. Both Father and Cvirka were part of a group of Lithuanian cultural figures that visited the Soviet Union in the thirties. They were shown the usual Potemkin villages and left the country with the impression that life there was a viable alternative to capitalism.

Or at least, these are the reasons cited in defense of the interwar leftists who succumbed to Communism in its Stalinist variety. This line of argument may also have seemed persuasive at the time to Western Europeans and Americans, but they never experienced the realities of Soviet rule, which befell Lithuania and the other two Baltic states. (Latvia and Estonia were smaller, a bit more prosperous and democratic, but their experience did not differ much from Lithuania.)

HINSEY: You have just mentioned the Molotov-Ribbentrop Pact. Since this treaty had far-reaching implications for Lithuania and your father's life, perhaps we should speak about it here—

VENCLOVA: The pact was signed between Germany and the Soviet Union at the end of August 1939. As is well-known, it also included a secret protocol.

(Although the Soviets continued to vehemently deny its existence up until the Gorbachev era.) The protocol divided Poland into Nazi and Soviet "spheres of influence" (the territorial division was similar to the 1795 partition, though more brutal, befitting a more brutal age). Latvia and Estonia were to be assigned to Stalin, and Lithuania, which had a common border with Germany, was to be given to Hitler. The German ambassador in Kaunas then proposed a scenario under which, in exchange for a military alliance with Germany, the Lithuanians would take back Vilnius, aided by the advancing victorious German army. They would march on their capital and take it back from Polish hands, already weakened by Germany's overwhelming military superiority.

HINSEY: What was independent Lithuania's response to this?

VENCLOVA: Wisely, President Smetona refused (although some Lithuanian Nazi sympathizers from political circles saw the proposal as a godsend). After this affront, Hitler dismissed the idea of Lithuania as a possible ally and gave the country to Stalin in exchange for a province and a half in Poland (Lublin Voivodeship and eastern Warsaw Voivodeship). After the division of Poland between Germany and the USSR was carried out in September 1939, Stalin took Vilnius and generously presented it to the still independent and neutral Lithuania. It was a fateful decision that survived Stalin and even the Soviet Union. Vilnius remains part of Lithuania to this day, as its capital.

HINSEY: We have a tendency to think that Lithuania had already lost its independence following the 1939 September Campaign—

VENCLOVA: Yes—however, this is, of course, not correct. Even though the war had begun in Poland, along with Latvia and Estonia, Lithuania experienced a modicum of independence for nine more months. In October 1939, Stalin requested permission to establish military bases in all three countries, purportedly to defend them and the USSR from Western aggressors and, more generally, from the vagaries of war. Needless to say, his request was granted. The pressure of the new Soviet ally was such that concession to its demands was inevitable. Some hoped—and prayed—that the present and still bearable conditions might continue. Others secretly prepared to flee, while the Lithuanian Communists, who were a negligible minority, eagerly awaited a full and definitive Soviet occupation.

HINSEY: However, this was to change radically in June 1940—

VENCLOVA: Yes, that was when Stalin sent an ultimatum to Lithuania, demanding entry for an unlimited number of Soviet troops and a change of government. Identical demands were presented to Latvia and Estonia. The Lithuanian government saw that it would be useless to resist, and therefore surrendered. Smetona opposed this, but was outvoted for the first and last time in his rule. He fled, first to Germany, then to the United States—a fortuitous decision, since the presidents of Latvia and Estonia, who remained in their respective countries, ended up in prison camps. The takeover was strongly reminiscent of Hitler's invasion of Czechoslovakia in March 1939, and was clearly patterned after it. Although technically considered an annexation rather than a state of war, this would fundamentally affect our family's situation.

HINSEY: Your father was intimately caught up in these events. Could you explain about that?

VENCLOVA: The new Lithuanian government, installed by the Soviets, was composed of people who had been opposed to Smetona's rule, some of them respectable liberals who did not necessarily understand the events in full, some of them Communists who understood everything very well. My father, who was thirty-four at the time, was in Estonia as a representative of the Lithuanian Writers' Union. On June 17, 1940, on the train from Tallinn to Kaunas, he read in a newspaper that he had been appointed Lithuanian minister of education (no doubt due in part to the reputation he had acquired in leftist circles after being fired from his teaching job). After some hesitation, he accepted the post: other members of the government impressed upon him the fact that any equivocation was unthinkable. All schools in Lithuania, the university, the theaters, and so on, were now under his authority—nominally, of course. (His friend and brother-in-law Petras Cvirka was not appointed to a government post, but welcomed the new regime nonetheless.) Within a month and a half, Lithuania became a standard Soviet republic and was absorbed into the USSR. Father went to Moscow with other members of the government for the official signing of the necessary documents. He and a small group of Lithuanian public figures were invited to meet with Stalin. This encounter with Stalin lasted a couple of hours.

I believe we'll continue talking about all that later. The story is sad and more complicated than it seems. In any case, my earliest memories come from that year (my third birthday fell on September 11, 1940, one month after the Soviet annexation).

HINSEY: Let's take a moment to talk about your first memories from this period—

VENCLOVA: Like most people, I cannot determine my very first recollection. Was it the funeral of Pranas Mašiotas, an old children's writer loved by several generations? He lay in state in the building of the Ministry of Education, and I was brought to say good-bye to him. Or was it a big rally my father addressed, among others? I remember the crowd, red banners, and portraits of the Soviet leaders quite palpably. There is one moment, however, that particularly stuck in my memory: my parents had to leave the house for an evening, and I threw a tantrum, since I didn't want my mother to go. I was told that the maid (we already had a maid) would show me pigeons in the attic. I went there with some interest, the pigeons did not materialize, and when I came back, my parents were gone. For the first time in my life, I understood that one can be lied to, and from that moment on, I hated deception with all my heart.

But my first really significant memory comes from when we moved to Vilnius. After the Soviet occupation, the various Lithuanian ministries were supposed to relocate from Kaunas to Vilnius, but in 1940 only the Ministry of Education did so (the city was almost exclusively Polish-speaking at that time, and none too enthusiastic about Lithuanians, to say nothing of the Soviets). Father got a flat in a comfortable neighborhood where other Lithuanian newcomers, more often than not his subordinates or friends, settled as well.

One such friend was Kazys Boruta, who merits more than a passing mention. He had been Father's classmate, and he was also a leftist writer; in the 1920s he joined the illegal Socialist-Revolutionary party, which fought Smetona's rule by all imaginable means, including terrorism. The Communists hated them heartily, and the Socialist-Revolutionaries repaid them in kind. Boruta had to leave for Vienna (recently, the house where he lived was located, and it supposedly will be marked by a memorial plaque). After returning to Lithuania, he was imprisoned by Smetona, then released, survived the Soviet and Nazi occupations, landed in a Stalinist prison in 1946, and was released again, not without my father's help. I knew him well, and admired him in my youth. He was a fairly good poet (translated, incidentally, into Polish by Miłosz), and a fine fiction writer, but above all a very honest if somewhat naive man.

Well, Boruta had a daughter Eglė (her name means "fir tree" in Lithuanian—Eglė was a mythological figure transformed into a tree, like Daphne), who frequented our flat and played with me every other day. She was already seven, therefore a protective and somewhat condescending girl. (Later, she became a well-known physicist.) Once, Eglė decided to teach me how to read. I believe she was a born pedagogue. To begin, she showed me the letters "m" and "a," and then wrote the word "mama." Then she said, "Now, I'm going to write a different word—"America." But instead of "America" she scribbled "mama" once again. As I have mentioned, I was very sensitive to all forms of deception. So I screamed, "No, it is the same 'mama'!" Eglė laughed approvingly. In a flash, I understood the central idea: one should not focus on individual letters, but grasp entire words. From that moment on, I learned very quickly, and soon astonished my parents during a walk through Vilnius. With a modicum of anxiety, they found that I could read and understand shop signs—"kepykla" (bakery), "kirpykla" (barbershop), and so on. (Some were in Polish or in Hebrew; which was totally incomprehensible to me—these I skipped.)

In any case, I started to read almost everything I could lay my hands on, including Boruta's poems, as well as *Antigone* and *Decameron* (which, needless to say, I understood only in part). That came a bit later, when I was five or six years old. At three, there were mainly children's books by Mašiotas and others. To this day, I remember a gift from my father—the book I read on the first day of the war. It was a Lithuanian translation of *Uncle Remus* stories, which remained in my possession for a long time, although in an extremely shabby state.

HINSEY: What did you know about your father's position and your parents' life at that time?

VENCLOVA: Naturally, I knew next to nothing about my father's work, but I remember that I saw his portrait in a children's magazine next to portraits of the Soviet leaders, and as a three-year-old was rather proud. He did not join the Communist Party (that happened after the war), and remained a typical leftist fellow traveler, not immune to liberal and "bourgeois" illusions. Of course, he was powerless to affect the course of events. Slowly but inexorably, the strict Stalinist order, Stalinist ideology, rhetoric, and censorship were introduced, resulting in abject shabbiness, boredom, and uniformity (*Gleichschaltung*, as they call it in German). Fear started to set in, though the first months of the Soviet regime did not yet reveal the catastrophes that were to follow. That said, some—though not all—members of Smetona's government and the old ruling caste were arrested, exiled to Siberia, and some of them shot without any semblance of due process (their arrests and deaths were never reported). While no killing or arbitrary imprisonment is defensible, at the time such violence was understood by certain leftists in the context of retribution, as Smetona also used to arrest and, from time to time, execute his enemies.

HINSEY: How did your father view the evolving situation?

VENCLOVA: I think my father, like many people around him, and not necessarily just leftists, viewed it as the result of force majeure. He tried to convince himself that things were not so bad (some changes might perhaps even be positive) and that a modicum of normalcy could be preserved. I also tend to believe that he managed to be of some use in those early months, even if his scope of influence was limited. New schools were opened: even if they mainly taught Stalinist material, they helped to reduce illiteracy (and once literate, people have the ability, in principle, to read what they wish). One could also see the secularization of the school system as befitting the spirit of democracy. On the other hand, minority-language schools (Polish, Yiddish, etc.) were shut down.

Although an atheist, Father tried to help a number of Catholic priests; he let them teach Latin in the schools, which was the best method of survival. There was also the case of Juozas Miltinis, an actor and stage director who had spent his formative years in Paris, studying under Charles Dullin (and also making friends—or even more than friends—with Artaud). He returned to Lithuania right before the Soviet takeover. This could be considered exceptionally bad luck, but my father, who knew Miltinis well, helped him to establish a theater in the provincial town of Panevėžys, where ideological conformity was less strict. Miltinis managed to assemble a troupe of young, gifted actors. His theater survived the Nazi occupation and the subsequent Soviet years, even if there was moral compromise involved. In the sixties and seventies, it was probably the only Western-oriented theater in the entire Soviet Union. Miltinis staged half-banned playwrights such as Strindberg and Dürrenmatt, and his actors, known for their European-style training, became film stars throughout the Soviet Union. I had the privilege of meeting the grand old man and members of his troupe more than once.

HINSEY: The events of this period had an important impact on your parents—do you remember anything about your family's routine at this time?

VENCLOVA: I don't remember much about our family life during the first Soviet occupation, in 1940–41. Like most children, my early memories are somewhat idyllic. In my case, however, they contrasted sharply with the war traumas that were to follow. During this period, our daily routine in Vilnius was frequently punctuated by visits to my grandfather's house in Kaunas. We were on very friendly terms with Petras Cvirka, who was high-spirited and witty, quite unlike my calm father. At that time, Cvirka wrote numerous articles praising the new system, but the only book he published—and presented to me—was a fine collection of tales for children (it is still in print).

Aunt Maria gave birth to my cousin Andrius, who was still a toddler when the war began.

HINSEY: However, the "modicum of normalcy" you spoke of would abruptly end two weeks before Germany's attack on the USSR in June 1941—

VENCLOVA: Yes, what happened changed the attitude of the Lithuanians for years to come. I was less than four years old at the time—my earliest awareness of it came later, during the Nazi occupation—but it was a veritable shock for my entire family, as for everyone. For the first time since annexing Lithuania, the Stalinist regime revealed its true colors. In the early morning hours of June 14, 1941, the secret police, assisted by local Communist activists, went to thousands of homes. The families they targeted were given an hour or so to pack some basic belongings, then they were herded onto trucks, taken to railway stations, and loaded into cattle cars—the men separated from the women and children. The deportations were totally unexpected. It took two or three days. Those in the cattle cars belonged mainly, but not exclusively, to the nation's elite—teachers, army officers, civil servants, priests, well-to-do (and not so well-to-do) peasants, even workers, if they happened to be members of non-Communist parties. In fact, all such parties had been banned from the very beginning of Soviet rule (Trotskyites, Socialist-Revolutionaries, and other leftists were considered the most suspect, followed by those on the right), but their rank and file had escaped relatively unscathed. Now all that changed entirely. Moreover, anyone who had had any contact with foreign countries, including Esperantists and postage-stamp dealers, were to be rounded up by the police en masse. Those arrested were transported to Siberia, some to labor camps, but the majority to godforsaken Russian villages where they had to start their life from scratch. Many died en route; even more perished within a year. A small number survived, adapted to their grim surroundings, and returned after Stalin's death, but these were the exceptions. They never received any compensation from the Soviets.

The June 1941 events were similar in brutality to Nazi deportations. Incidentally, the Gestapo used to publish announcements regarding deportations, and executions. In this case, everything took place in silence—no orders pasted on walls, no notices in the newspaper, nothing at all. People simply vanished without a trace. The Nazis primarily targeted Jews; the Soviets targeted "class enemies" (including, of course, the Jews, especially members of the bourgeoisie), but they did not pay much attention to ethnic background, religion, or race. In today's Lithuania, the deportations are often labeled "genocide." I don't believe this is an accurate term. "Stratocide" would be more appropriate, for Stalin was actually uprooting those strata of society he considered a potential threat to his power. But terror remains terror, no matter what you call it.

HINSEY: Was your own family in danger?

VENCLOVA: Our family was spared (at that time, Stalin was not carrying out purges within the Soviet government, although that changed during the postwar years). One should also note that many people who might have been targeted for deportation were temporarily left at large. But the experience was undoubtedly stressful for my father, mother, and grandparents. It was perhaps at that point that my father understood, for the first time, what kind of horrendous mess he was involved in. Teachers, who were under his nominal control, perhaps suffered the most. I know for certain that he attempted to save several of them. When I was growing up, we rarely discussed these events, but when we did, he always talked about them with visible distress.

HINSEY: Then on June 22, 1941, Germany officially declared war on the Soviet Union, breaking the nonaggression pact—

VENCLOVA: This happened at the height of the Soviet deportations. For this reason, some people viewed the start of the war, and the subsequent Nazi occupation, as an escape from Soviet rule—at least initially. True, the war immediately put an end to the deportations. Today historians estimate that some seventeen thousand people were exiled, and many more might have shared their fate had the Soviets remained in power. In the two smaller Baltic countries, Latvia and Estonia, the numbers were not quite as high, but still considerable. The same thing happened in Western Ukraine and Western Belarus, which had been part of interwar Poland.

HINSEY: What was the immediate Soviet military response to the German invasion of Lithuania?

VENCLOVA: The Soviets were totally unprepared to fight and hastily fled, leaving Lithuania to the mercy of the Germans (in Latvia and Estonia, they at least managed to put up some resistance). The Soviet Lithuanian government retreated together with the troops, in disarray. Armed groups of anti-Soviet activists (or insurrectionists, as they are increasingly called in present-day Lithuania) appeared on the streets on the very first day of the invasion. They prepared the ground for the Germans' advance, but also had their own agenda, which differed from the Nazis. These groups, commonly known as Baltaraiščiai, "White Armbands," were mainly active in Kaunas and smaller towns, but much less so in Vilnius, where the population was rather indifferent to their cause. They attacked the retreating Soviet troops, took the Kaunas radio station by force and used it to broadcast the restoration of Lithuania's independence—in Lithuanian, German, and French, as I was told many years after the fact. Power was in their hands for at least several days, and they maintained control in the Lithuanian periphery for months.

HINSEY: How did your parents learn of the German invasion?

VENCLOVA: Unaware that the Germans had invaded that day, my parents had gone to Trakai, a popular spot on a lake with a medieval castle, some thirty kilometers from Vilnius. I had been left at home with the maid. In Trakai, several students greeted my father (whom they recognized as the minister of education), and proposed a boat ride, which my parents readily accepted. Out on the water, they all noticed several non-Soviet planes overhead, but they didn't pay much attention. When my parents returned to the city, they learned that Germany had attacked the USSR. Molotov gave a speech on the radio promising a swift victory (Stalin was scared to death and did not appear in public until early July). The radio broadcast that the Red Army was already fighting the Germans on their own territory, bombing Königsberg and Berlin, and so on. In reality, the Germans bombed Vilnius that first night, and ferociously. One bomb exploded next to our house, and a fragment broke the window of the flat below us, where my father's deputy, a former Social Democrat, lived. It crushed and virtually cut off his young wife's legs. My mother, who was also young at the time (she was twenty-nine), rushed to help and did her best to bandage the woman's legs. It was in vain; the woman died two hours later.

HINSEY: How long did you remain in the center of Vilnius?

VENCLOVA: After that night, my father decided to move our family away from downtown Vilnius to a neighborhood called Jeruzalė. It was essentially a village, and he did this in the hope that there would be nothing to bomb there. (The name Jeruzalė, that is Jerusalem, was given to the neighborhood because there was a Catholic church and monastery in the vicinity, with a Via Dolorosa.) In Jeruzalė, my father placed my mother and me in the home of Vilnius's mayor, also a leftist and fellow traveler, who provided shelter not just for us, but for an entire group of intellectuals. He then went back to his office in downtown Vilnius (as a minister, he had a car and driver), and attempted to do his job as usual. But the Ministry building was almost empty. Only a few Baltaraiščiai could be seen on the streets. With great difficulty, my father contacted Kaunas (as I mentioned, all government offices except the Ministry of Education were still located there) and learned that he had been ordered to move—temporarily—to Minsk, two hundred kilometers east. He did this, and in Minsk he survived a ten-hour bombardment that flattened the city. At that time the Nazis were already approaching Vilnius, and in a couple of days he was cut off from his family by the front line. In several more days, he reached Moscow, where the Soviet Lithuanian government was gradually gathering, as a sort of government-in-exile.

HINSEY: What did you and your mother do?

VENCLOVA: My mother and I remained in Jeruzalė, having no idea of Father's whereabouts, and almost no idea of what was happening. One of my most vivid childhood memories comes from that time. We were standing on a wooden veranda and saw air combat in the skies above Vilnius. The Germans had shot down a Soviet plane, and the pilot and the navigator bailed out. The sight of their parachutes opening was unforgettable—they looked so small, almost toylike. The German plane then turned around and followed up with a machine-gun salvo in their direction. These were the new rules for new times.

HINSEY: How swift was the German advance?

VENCLOVA: In two or three days, Kaunas was taken by the Germans (who were welcomed by the Baltaraiščiai and by a considerable part of the population), and Vilnius fell a day or two later. After the initial fighting, my mother walked from Jeruzalė to central Vilnius—a distance of around ten kilometers (there were no buses or cars)—to go to the food market and our flat, for which she still had the keys. The city was more or less intact and under the control of the Baltaraiščiai. The German army was not particularly visible—it was fighting farther east around Minsk. A couple of times she came back to Jeruzalė, but once she did not: several Baltaraiščiai were waiting for her in our flat, and she was arrested. She recognized one of them: he was a student from the group who had given her and her husband the boat ride in Trakai only a week or so earlier.

She was taken to Lukiškės prison—in Polish, Łukiszki—and put in a cell with several prostitutes and women arrested on the street by accident. All the guards were local people who had served there through Polish, Lithuanian, and Soviet times. She was then questioned by the interrogator (who was Lithuanian). He wrote down her personal data and asked, "Are you Jewish?" "No," my mother answered, which was the truth: she was an ethnic Lithuanian, and had been baptized in a Catholic church. "But your father's name is Merkelis, which is Melchior." "It is a Catholic name—one of the three Magi." "Well, your husband is a Communist, and all Communists marry Jewish women." To that, my mother did not know what to say. "Go back to your cell," the interrogator said, "we'll deal with you later."

HINSEY: How long was your mother in prison?

VENCLOVA: She spent a month and a half in Lukiškės, under rather harsh conditions, but she survived. Her primary worry was about me, her four-year-old son about whom she had no news. Nor did she have any information about her husband, although her interrogators believed he was hiding somewhere in Lithuania and expected her to divulge his whereabouts. She heard that many of her fellow inmates, primarily, but not exclusively Jews, had been executed. Once or twice she was assembled with a group of Jewish women waiting for a truck that was to drive them to an unknown destination. But then she was called out of line and brought back for further questioning. In August, the Germans disbanded the Baltaraiščiai and took over the administration of the country, including the prisons. After looking into her file, they decided that there was no sense in keeping her in Lukiškės. Given the fact that she was Aryan, she could remain at large but under police surveillance. Outside the prison gates, her mother was waiting for her, accompanied by Merkelis's brother. They noticed (and only then did she notice it herself), that a front lock of her hair had gone completely gray. She left it as it was. After the war, people used to say that it gave her an elegant touch (she was a very beautiful woman even into old age).

HINSEY: What happened to you after your mother was imprisoned?

VENCLOVA: After my mother disappeared, I was taken care of by people in the Jeruzalė house, primarily our maid. After some time, we were allowed into our Vilnius flat to recuperate some of my toys (a German officer was billeted there, and I remember the toys were strewn about). I was then brought to Kaunas where my grandfather Merkelis lived, but for some reason not directly to his house. Instead, I was taken to a flat downtown next to the railway station, which belonged to a very close friend of my grandmother's. I believe there were two reasons for this. First, Petras Cvirka and Aunt Maria had fled Kaunas and reached Moscow, just as my father had. Their son, Andrius, who was then only a year and a half old, remained with Grandmother—temporarily, of course. This "temporary" separation lasted for three years, as was our case. Since Grandmother was already very busy with a toddler, she could not take me on as well. Second, she was very occupied with trying to find out what had happened to my mother, and then attempting to secure her release. The maid disappeared for good (later, I learned that she fell ill and died before the Soviets returned), but the elderly woman who took care of me was very kind. This said, losing both parents in the space of several days is not the best imaginable experience for a four-year-old. I was rather precocious and could read, but I understood very little of what was going on around me. However, I remember a moment when I was playing in a garden near the railway tracks and suddenly felt entirely abandoned. But that did not last long.

HINSEY: After staying with your mother's friend, where did you go?

VENCLOVA: Soon, I was taken to the flat of Grandfather's brother. I should probably say a word or two about him. He was a year older than Grandfather, and his first name was Karolis. Around 1905, he had left his native country for America, specifically for Pennsylvania, where there was a large Lithuanian diaspora. They were mainly miners. Karolis edited a Lithuanian newspaper for them, in one of the smaller Pennsylvanian towns—was it Scranton or Shenandoah? He wrote under the pen name Karolis Vairas. Since he had mastered English, he began to make his living as a translator, and translated dozens of volumes throughout his life, from James Fenimore Cooper and Longfellow to H. G. Wells and Steinbeck. He collected rare Lithuanian books, and before leaving the United States donated his collection to the New York Public Library, where it remains to this day. After returning to interwar independent Lithuania, he joined the diplomatic service, and was posted to London, and for several years served as Consul in Cape Town. (I visited South Africa some time ago, and with the help of an old phonebook found the house where he had lived.) At the risk of name-dropping, he met Bernard Shaw and Winston Churchill; Nadine Gordimer's parents, who were Lithuanian Jews, were under his aegis during his Cape Town years. A rather well-connected man, he was instrumental in securing my mother's release from prison. He was a leftist and a freethinker. His links with America and England put him in a precarious position both during and after the war, but he managed to survive. During the German occupation, he was head of the city's public library, and in the Soviet years, the director of a literary museum. For this latter position, his friendship with my father most likely helped.

HINSEY: Would you say a bit more about staying with Karolis?

VENCLOVA: Karolis and his wife Nina, who was at least thirty years younger than he, maintained a European middle-class—even upper-middle-class—lifestyle, but they didn't have a child's cot. I had to sleep on two armchairs placed together (which amused me quite a bit). They had two dogs, however—Billy the German Shepherd and Cheebie the Pekingese—with whom I made friends immediately. Uncle Karolis taught me to sing "*a, b, c* . . ." in English, and showed me photos of elephants and a puzzle map of Africa that I gradually learned to assemble. Life improved considerably when my mother was released from prison. True, at first I feared she might disappear again at any moment, and I tried to follow her everywhere, including to the bathroom. After a couple of days, we left for Grandfather Merkelis's house on the other side of the Nemunas River. My mother also looked after Andrius, thus relieving Grandmother of her duties. We grew up as brothers (and considered ourselves brothers, not cousins) until the Soviets returned. Andrius called my mother "mama," and continued to do so even after his real mother, my Aunt Maria, returned from Russia. (He inherited Maria's artistic talent, and in the sixties and seventies became a well-known cartoonist whose work was also published outside of Lithuania.) Our life took on a semblance of normality, even if Mother was under police surveillance.

HINSEY: This might be a moment to speak about the tragedy that befell the Jews in Kaunas and Vilnius.

VENCLOVA: The Jewish community represented roughly 8 percent of Lithuania's prewar population. This included prosperous businessmen and intellectuals, but also many poor people who were usually Orthodox. My parents were on friendly terms with a number of Jewish families (Father taught Lithuanian literature and language in a Jewish school for some time—there were both religious and secular schools, whose languages of instruction were Yiddish, Hebrew, or Lithuanian). Vilnius was nearly 50 percent Jewish (the other half was mostly Polish), and in Kaunas the Jewish population made up probably 20 percent. There was also a high concentration of Jewish families in the small towns (Catholic Lithuanians lived in villages). Lithuanian-Jewish relations were neighborly, and pogroms were practically unheard of—in this, Lithuania was quite different from Ukraine, Moldova, and Poland. Generally speaking, Jews felt more comfortable here than in many other places. Bernard Berenson, Jacques Lipchitz, and Emmanuel Levinas all came from Lithuania, and have contributed to its renown.

Yet during the Nazi occupation more Jews perished in Lithuania than anywhere else in Europe: around 94 percent. An entire world was lost. The Poles in Vilnius also disappeared to a large degree, and the Germans in Klaipėda disappeared entirely, but they were not, for the most part, persecuted or killed. A large number of Jews were summarily executed in the first days of the German occupation by the Baltaraiščiai and other Lithuanian collaborationists, particularly in the small towns, but also in the two capital cities. After the Germans assumed administrative authority, the remaining Jews were driven into ghettos, subjected to hard labor and gradually exterminated by Nazis and helpers of Lithuanian origin.

These are well-known facts, but during the Soviet era, my generation was largely unaware of them. The Stalinist purges and deportations, as well as the Holocaust were forbidden or half-forbidden topics, and went virtually unmentioned in both the press and the schools. But it was impossible to suppress them completely: everyone, myself included, had heard something from relatives and friends, yet as a rule we never understood the extent of the tragedy.

HINSEY: Do you remember any specific events connected with this?

VENCLOVA: Once in Kaunas, perhaps during the second year of the German occupation, my mother and I met a man wearing a yellow star on his clothes. Instead of using the sidewalk, he was walking along the road. Mother greeted him—perhaps they knew each other—and when I asked what the star meant, she replied: "He is a Jew. Jews have been ordered to wear them." I also came upon the word "Jew" in a children's magazine published during the German occupation. The author of the story claimed that the Jews and the Soviet secret police were basically one and the same—criminals who had slaughtered and deported the Lithuanians (I even remember the name of this children's writer: after I emigrated, I used to come upon it in the Lithuanian diaspora press—he is now dead). It was only after the war that my mother told me about her own prison experience, and how perilous being Jewish could be.

HINSEY: Now, in retrospect, what do you think gave rise to this virulent anti-Semitism?

VENCLOVA: Antanas Smetona and his generation were largely immune to anti-Semitic sentiment. But in the second half of the thirties, a new generation of right-wing politicians appeared, who very much resembled the generation of Romanians depicted by Ionesco in his play *Rhinoceros*. They all considered Smetona to be excessively soft, and took great interest in what was happening in and around Berlin. They were not necessarily pro-German (due to the fact that Lithuania had the territorial dispute with Germany regarding the status of Memel Territory), but Hitler's discrimination against "foreigners" seemed worthy of emulation. The Poles, and, in an ironic twist, the Klaipėda Germans were looked upon as "foreigners," but above all the Jews, which was also due to the fact that there wasn't a state that stood behind them, and therefore they were defenseless. The Lithuanian "rhinoceri" did their best to exploit all the old anti-Semitic stereotypes as well as a primitive distrust of intellectuals and educated people, which is not uncommon in peasant societies. There was another important factor. As in many countries at that time, the Jews were identified with Communists. The underground Communist Party in

Lithuania was minuscule, but there were some Jewish members (even if Stalin preferred appointing ethnic Lithuanians to the key positions).

HINSEY: What is the mythology about how this is connected to the June deportations?

VENCLOVA: The Soviet deportations of June 1941 were a collective trauma, and remain unhealed to this day. It is crucial to understand that there is a persistent delusion, on the part of many Lithuanians, that only ethnic Lithuanians were targeted. It is also believed that the Soviets intended to annihilate the Lithuanians as an ethnic group, which was thus fortunately prevented by the German invasion. Many historians and journalists still cultivate this myth through omission and misplaced emphasis. In fact, as I mentioned earlier, Stalin practiced *stratocide* instead of *genocide* in the Baltic states. All ethnic, religious, and racial groups, including the Jews (as well as Poles and even Russians), suffered from it to a more or less equal degree. Yet the "rhinoceri" managed to present the deportations as the result of a sinister Jewish plot against the Lithuanian nation, exploiting the presence of Jews in the ranks of the secret police. Of course, Lithuanians, Russians, and Poles were also present in this organization (if Martians could be found in Lithuania, Stalin would have employed at least some of them without hesitation). But that was conveniently overlooked.

HINSEY: The actions of the Baltaraiščiai continue to be a complex subject in Lithuanian history—

VENCLOVA: The events of the beginning of the 1941 German occupation—when the Baltaraiščiai took power and proclaimed the restoration of Lithuanian independence—came to be known as the June uprising. I believe that taking up arms against Stalinist oppression was a legitimate act, and that restoration of independence was necessary for Lithuania. But from the beginning it took a terribly wrong turn. The uprising was, to a large degree, prepared and controlled by the young "rhinoceri" who made their headquarters in Berlin and collaborated with the Nazi authorities. True, their objectives were not quite the same as Hitler's. They were going to found a new Lithuania that would fight alongside the Nazis, like Slovakia and Croatia (or, better still, Finland). However, Hitler had no intention of creating any such state and treated Lithuania as just one more *Raum* for German colonization. In August 1941, when the Germans disbanded the self-appointed Lithuanian government and its Baltaraiščiai units, some of the Baltaraiščiai enlisted in Einsatzgruppe A—a Nazi mobile killing squad—but others did not, and several members of the government were even arrested by the Nazis.

HINSEY: This is a painful episode—

VENCLOVA: I do not condemn people who fought for their country and did not take part in pogroms (there were such people, though it is very difficult to draw a line between them and the collaborators after all these years—and the line was somewhat blurred even at the moment of the uprising). But a government that promulgates anti-Semitic laws and is willing to sacrifice a large part of its citizenry in the name of an illusory independence does not deserve more respect than, say, Pétain's followers in France. If a nation is to be saved by such means, it would, as a consequence, lose the right to be called a nation.

A Lithuanian must be able to talk about all this with complete frankness. It is not easy for me. I love my people and my country; I know that its history is complicated and rife with contradictions, like any history, and many of its traditions are honorable. In the context of its times, the Grand Duchy of Lithuania was a tolerant and relatively democratic state. Vilnius was and is on a par with the great European cities with respect to architecture, poetry, and science. The story of Lithuania's struggle with the German knights, and Lithuania's revival following the years under the "press ban," are noble and often moving stories. The same can be said about the independence movement in the 1980s and 1990s. Even under the German occupation, many Lithuanians—priests, physicians, intellectuals, and ordinary people—risked their lives to help and hide Jews. Another source of my love for my country is the fact that the Lithuanian language is not only archaic, but rich and sonorous, virtually on par with the Greek of Homer and Aeschylus. To me, as a poet, this has been rewarding. But the story of the pro-Nazi government and its armed units must be told in full, without evasions and attempts at justification. Otherwise this dark chapter of our past will never be overcome.

HINSEY: In fact, you wrote about this before 1989—

VENCLOVA: In my years as a Soviet dissident, in 1975 or 1976, I wrote an essay about it, although it was still difficult to have access to information about wartime events in Lithuania. It was published in samizdat and triggered quite a heated debate. After I emigrated, I found out that right-wing members of the diaspora were not too happy about it—to tell the truth, a few of them had been personally involved in some of these anti-Semitic actions and propaganda, like the children's writer I mentioned. But there were other liberal émigrés who shared my point of view. When Lithuania once again became an independent nation in 1990, I was deeply disturbed by the fact that the right-wing version of these events prevailed almost universally—in the press, in school textbooks, and in public opinion in general. The Baltaraiščiai were hailed as national heroes, and there were official attempts to portray the pro-Nazi government as legitimate and glorious. Lithuania was no exception: very similar attempts were made in Croatia and Slovakia, to say nothing of Latvia, Estonia, and Ukraine. The Communist regime was so thoroughly hated that any anti-Bolshevism was immediately embraced, despite the fact that Hitler had been the most ardent anti-Bolshevik of all time. Perhaps this trend has subsided a bit. But I still consider it a public duty to speak out against it wherever possible.

When Lithuanian president Algirdas Brazauskas addressed the Israeli Knesset and apologized for what had happened half a century before, his words were interpreted by far too many in Lithuania as a national humiliation. Well, repentance does not humiliate. The truth does not humiliate. Telling the truth is the only proper way of restoring dignity.

3

WAR YEARS

1941–1944

HINSEY: After Germany's invasion of Lithuania and your mother's return from prison, you were living in Freda near Kaunas. What was the state of Kaunas?

VENCLOVA: Kaunas had escaped destruction and appeared peaceful on the surface, except that certain buildings were guarded by soldiers. Kaunas was a fairly modern city at that time, full of Art Deco buildings, and its cinemas, cafés, and dancehalls were all still open. As far as I remember, the buses were also running, and the numerous city gardens were full of people. Even the bridges, if I am not mistaken, were intact and had not been blown up by the retreating Soviet Army.

HINSEY: Do you have any other precise visual memories of the German occupation?

VENCLOVA: Once or twice my mother took me to Laisvės Alėja, the main boulevard, where she used to stroll during her student years. A German sentinel at one building offered me a candy, but my mother ignored this proposal, to my great dissatisfaction. A black flag with two lightning bolts flapped in the wind atop of one of the buildings some distance from Laisvės Alėja—my mother explained that these were, in fact, the letters "SS." "What is the SS?" I asked. "Well, it's a sort of military office, but it's best not to speak about it." In Freda, we almost never saw Germans, but there was at least one outright collaborator who sometimes visited us uninvited; once, in a tipsy state, he took a handgun from a satchel and demonstrated his prowess by shooting a bird in the garden. He made his living by black-market profiteering, and disappeared without a trace just before the Soviets returned.

HINSEY: Did your mother experience further problems with the Germans?

VENCLOVA: Technically, my mother was under police surveillance, at least for a time. Once policemen came to Grandfather's house and searched the barn, as somebody had informed them that a Russian soldier, who had escaped from a POW camp, might be hiding there. They ordered Mother to enter the barn before them, threatening her with a gun—apparently they were afraid that a gunfight might break out. The barn was empty. (The POW camp was on the banks of the Nemunas, not far from the railway bridge, and we knew that the fate of the POWs was unenviable. A young Lithuanian, the son of our neighbors, threw a cabbage to the hungry Russians through the barbed wire. This was strictly forbidden and he was shot on the spot.) On the other hand, an old policeman who lived nearby, as well a former classmate of my mother from a professor's family, who had some "connections," would warn us now and then that an action was being prepared, and that Mother could be arrested if she were found at home. In such cases, she went downtown and spent a night or two in Karolis's flat. If this occurred in winter, she had to cross the frozen Nemunas River, since the bridges were off-limits (in summer, one could count on the help of a boatman).

Of course, our fate cannot be compared with that of Kaunas's Jews, who were driven into the ghetto in the suburb of Vilijampolė and subjected to gradual extermination. Vilijampolė was quite far from Freda, and one rarely saw Jewish people outside of it—I remember only one such occasion, which I mentioned earlier. Two Jewish children who were saved by Lithuanians who hid them on the Aryan side became my close friends after the war: Aleksandras Štromas, a political scientist who emigrated from the USSR almost at the same time as I did and ended up as a professor at Hillsdale College (in Michigan), and Kama Ginkas, one of the best stage directors in contemporary Russia (I met him not only in Vilnius and Moscow but also in New Haven, since he was invited to work at the Yale Repertory Theater on more than one occasion). It was from them that, much later, I learned in greater detail about the Kaunas ghetto and the rescue network. Our family was not a part of the network, but knew about it, since many of our friends were involved. A young Lithuanian doctor sometimes visited our house with his wife Johanna, who was purportedly German: in reality, she was Jewish, and the marriage (with fake papers) had been arranged to rescue her. But that was a big secret, which of course my mother didn't share with me until after the war. Kazys Boruta, whose daughter Eglė had taught me to read, also belonged to this network.

HINSEY: What were the repercussions of your father's being in Moscow?

VENCLOVA: Most of our family's former friends refused to have any contact with us, and some cursed my mother on the phone for being "the wife of a Bolshevik." Boruta was one of the few who didn't break off his friendship. He continued to live in Vilnius, but came to Freda rather frequently. I learned his long poem about the polar explorer Amundsen by heart and used to recite it in his presence—he accepted this as God's just punishment. He also took care of Father's library (only part of it survived since German officers billeted in our former flat had thrown out a number of books), and brought it to the Freda house, thus providing me with additional reading material. Another writer who did not shun us was Henrikas Radauskas, a very fine poet who came of age in the interwar period and who was a close friend of Father's during the Klaipéda years. I remember how he pushed me on a swing. Though he held leftist views, he fled the Soviets in 1944 and ended up in Washington, DC. As a young man, I avidly read his poems, which found their way to Soviet Vilnius via the émigré press. Radauskas became the best Lithuanian poet of the twentieth century, a sort of Lithuanian Mandelstam. Unfortunately, I never met him again: he died seven years before my own emigration.

HINSEY: How long did you stay in Freda?

VENCLOVA: We lived in my grandfather's house for three years. Of course, my mother and grandparents tried their best to give us a reasonably happy childhood despite adverse circumstances. They invented various distractions, and even staged plays in which we, the children, were expected to perform. Moreover, the war, the postwar, and even the prewar years in Freda are somewhat intermingled in my memory, which may make wartime seem a bit more bearable. Freda was a tolerable refuge, at least in our eyes. But the Nazi occupation was there and all around, and nothing could be done about it.

HINSEY: Before we return to the war, would you describe your grandfather Merkelis's house?

VENCLOVA: After the war, we frequently visited my grandparents and stayed with them for months at a time, especially in the summer, and therefore the house is very much alive in my memory. (It's still there, but after my grandfather's suicide it was sold to a different family and has deteriorated woefully.) It was a two-story wooden lodge with a large garden full of apple trees and a pond where one could hear frogs and observe newts. Once, my small cousin Andrius fell into the pond and nearly drowned but was saved by Grandfather who dashed out of the house at the last moment. On the ground floor, there was a drawing room with stuffed armchairs, Grandmother's bedroom with an Orthodox icon over the headboard (she was a Catholic but had no qualms about praying to it), and two spacious rooms that belonged to Grandfather. These were virtually off-limits to children. We knew that he kept his library there, and sometimes I caught a glimpse of an immense map of Lithuania that hung suspended next to his work desk.

No doubt, the words "spacious" and "immense" are overstatements since they are colored by my perceptions as a child: I'm sure everything in the house was of rather modest size, but in my eyes it seemed like a labyrinth full of secluded nooks and strange objects—an old clock that chimed throughout the night and a mirror that reflected a plethora of small perfume bottles. There were photographs on the walls, including a large portrait of Grandmother taken just before her wedding, and a picture of an unknown young lady repos-ing in a meadow with a castle in the background (I was told that the lady was my absent Aunt Maria, and the meadow was in Corsica, which she had visited before the war). Many years later, I attempted to describe that house from childhood in the poem "A View from an Alley."

HINSEY: And the other parts of the house?

VENCLOVA: From the drawing room, one could proceed either to the veranda, which had glass doors that opened onto the garden, or to the bathroom and kitchen. I mentioned that the house had no running water, so we used wash-basins. Nor was there any central heating: Grandfather kept piles of firewood under a lean-to in the yard and used it for the tile stove in the drawing room and a very ancient-looking kitchen stove where Grandmother prepared meals. She was sometimes helped by my mother, and sometimes by a local girl who was not exactly a maid, just someone who was trying to earn some money in her spare time. On the back wall of the veranda there was a large mural-like painting; the work depicted peasants picking apples and had been done by Aunt Maria in her student days. In the hallway there was a telephone and a thick prewar phone book, where one could find instructions on how to make calls to Stockholm and Liverpool, and a spiral staircase that led to the first floor. The upper floor consisted of two rooms: before the somber years, my parents used to stay in one of these, and Petras Cvirka and Aunt Maria in the other. The rooms were separated by an attic that was larger than both of them put together. Grandfather kept hundreds of old books there, and I used to avidly leaf through them, gleaning bits of totally superfluous information from their pages.

In the rooms there were iron-frame beds with brass bedknobs, and a wooden cradle with dowels for sides in which I slept as an infant (later, my daughter slept there as a baby). From the kitchen, one could enter the yard, where there was a cement well and a barn. There was a chained German Shepherd named Jim. If you managed to pass him unharmed—which was not necessarily guaranteed—you reached a vegetable garden, where some tobacco plants grew as well. This was under the shade of an oak tree, the tallest one on the property. In the second and larger garden—consisting mainly of apple trees—there were thujas, larches, a fir tree, and an aspen just beyond the fence. There was also a small dog of unknown pedigree called Rudis, that is, Brownie. We liked him enormously. Rudis died of old age, many years after the war, and was buried by the fence of the vegetable garden, a fact I mention in "A View from an Alley."

HINSEY: What was Freda like at this time—was it still agricultural?

VENCLOVA: Though Freda was a suburb, it was still somewhat rural as well. There were no livestock, though there were hens and a duck or two in the yard. At the end of the German occupation, Grandfather rented out part of the house to tenants—an enterprising family who immediately started to keep cows and sheep on the premises, though that did not last long. The entire suburb consisted of similar houses with gardens, vegetable gardens, and flowerbeds. These homes, which were mainly inhabited by university professors, flanked narrow leafy lanes where one never saw any vehicles (a bus stopped two or three times a day on the main street that was, as far as I remember, the only one that was properly paved). Generally, one just walked or used a bike. The streets dead-ended in a steep slope lined with ravines, where we tobogganed in the winter and played Tarzan in the summer. At the base of the slope there was a railway line, and then beaches along the Nemunas River. Across the river was downtown Kaunas (actually, the downtown was a bit to the left; from the crest of Freda's hill, you could see the poorer part of the city, a sort of Kaunas East End). Nearby, there was a botanical garden with greenhouses, where some of the professors were employed: my mother often took us there for walks. In a different direction was Napoleon Hill on the banks of the Nemunas, from which the emperor supposedly watched as his troops forded the river, invading the Russian empire. Finally, there was an airfield a mile or two away. One of the proudest projects of interwar Lithuania was an attempt to create an air force on a par with its mightier neighbors, not without some success. I believe the airfield was used by the Nazis during the war, and it then became a landing field for Soviet planes.

HINSEY: You mentioned that your grandmother was religious. Lithuania is a country with a strong Catholic tradition. Do you have any other memories related to religion?

VENCLOVA: Grandmother was a believer, and Grandfather (like his brother Karolis) was a freethinker, though he was discrete about it: incidentally, he used to teach New Testament Greek to theology students. Father was an atheist, and he persuaded my mother to accept a civilian marriage, which was a difficult choice at the time. The main cultural tension in independent Lithuania, however, was between Catholics and liberals, just as in Spanish-speaking countries. The Catholic Church prevailed, and Lithuania was, as far as I know, the sole European country that only recognized marriages blessed by the church. Yet Memel Territory, that is, the Klaipėda region, had an autonomous (pre–World War I German) set of laws, and civilian marriages were recognized there. Thus, my future parents went to the first village on the Memel Territory side, registered their marriage at the local office, and came back to Kaunas (this was before my father accepted a teaching position in Klaipėda). Predictably, this resulted in a scandal that was taxing for my grandparents and my mother as well. My mother endured it with her typical tenacity, but her sister Maria, when it was her turn to marry Petras Cvirka (another notorious atheist), insisted on a church wedding and succeeded.

HINSEY: What about baptism?

VENCLOVA: My parents didn't baptize me—in Klaipėda, this was acceptable. But during the war, my grandmother started to talk about correcting this omission. As a believer, she naturally wanted to have a Catholic grandson (Andrius was baptized); but she most likely also knew that an unbaptized child could easily be denounced to the Nazi authorities as a Jew, with obvious consequences. After some effort, she convinced my mother, and I was taken to the small Freda church where the priest (who was a family acquaintance) performed the rite. I was five at the time, and therefore I remember the event very well. Some salt was put into my mouth: I asked if I might spit it out, but was told to swallow it. My godfather was Antanas Bendorius, a geography teacher and a former colleague of my father's in Klaipėda. After the ceremony, we visited his flat in downtown Kaunas, where I was positively thunderstruck by an immense globe: I climbed a stepladder and investigated the continents for an hour or two.

After being baptized, I sometimes attended Mass with Grandmother. The Freda church stood next to the botanical garden: actually, it was an old Russian Orthodox chapel from tsarist times, which now served the small Catholic parish. Around the cupola, a tricolor band had been painted. These were the colors of the Lithuanian national flag, which underscored the fact that the church had been claimed by patriots. I must confess this was the thing I remembered most about it. We observed the traditional Catholic feast days, but more as folk customs than religious events. On Christmas Eve, Grandmother prepared twelve traditional dishes; there was a fir tree decorated with simple toys and bric-a-brac, and Grandfather played Santa Claus. On Easter, Mother taught us how to paint eggs. All that continued in our family into Soviet times, but it was gradually abandoned. I don't think this was a sign of obedience to the atheist regime. The main reason was the end of childhood.

At the end of the German occupation, when I was six or seven, Grandmother presented me with three books that summed up the main stories of the Old and New Testaments. The Old Testament made the biggest impression on me: it was the story of the Israelites and full of fascinating events; and Israelites, as I was told, were Jews (ancient ones), thus belying in my young mind the notion that Jews were necessarily Communists. I learned prayers, including the Our Father, Hail Mary, and the Nicene Creed (I particularly enjoyed long litanies), and for a time, became quite an ardent believer, though I was less than eager to share my new faith with my family—it was too intimate. As befits a person familiar with the Old Testament narrative, God inspired mainly fear in me. But that bout of youthful religious enthusiasm soon passed.

HINSEY: Returning to the war, what were you told about your father in Moscow?

VENCLOVA: At the beginning, I was told that Father was busy with his work in Vilnius and could not see us for a time. But once, as I stood by the fence in our garden, two neighborhood boys on the other side started to tease me. Among other things, they yelled: "Do you know who your father is? He's a Bolshevik!" I was shocked, since I had learned from children's magazines published under the Nazi occupation that the Bolsheviks were definitely the bad guys. Mother then explained our situation to me, gradually and in rather vague terms. By the end of the German occupation, I knew that my father was in Moscow, but that one should not mention this fact in public.

I have said that the Lithuanian Communists who fled the German army established a rudimentary government-in-exile in Moscow (which, of course, did not have the slightest semblance of authority and was totally dependent on Stalin). In time, it started to organize guerrilla units in Lithuania, which consisted mainly, though not exclusively, of servicemen who were trained by the Soviet secret police and parachuted into Lithuanian forests. These units were not particularly successful. The Sixteenth Lithuanian Division of the Soviet Army was also organized, consisting of men who had left Lithuania in the early days of the war (many of them Jewish) and of Lithuanians living in the USSR.

Its command included several officers who had served in the former independent Lithuanian army. Just before the German invasion, the bulk of the officer corps had been deported, but a few were employed as teachers in the Moscow Military Academy. Most likely this was conceived as a prelude to their arrest and execution, but Germany's invasion of the USSR changed all that, and Stalin decided to draw on their experience. The Sixteenth Division lost half of its men in its very first engagement, but it was able to recover thanks to these officers, and it fought quite well, entering Lithuania in 1944 (it participated in the retaking of Klaipėda). For some time, my father continued to nominally serve as minister of education, but only one school remained under his control: its pupils were mainly Jewish Lithuanian children evacuated at the beginning of the war. One of these children, my colleague at Yale, Benjamin Harshav, once told me that my father managed to provide blankets for them and thus probably saved their lives during the Russian winter of 1941. (The Lithuanian children who managed to survive the deportations of early June 1941 attended Russian schools in Siberia. These were beyond his aegis.) Later, Father resigned and became a war correspondent, covering the battles and the everyday life of the Sixteenth Lithuanian Division. He also wrote nostalgic poems, sometimes dedicated to his lost wife and son (he was almost certain we had perished). Our family didn't have a radio, but a neighbor lady in Freda listened clandestinely to broadcasts from Moscow. She described these poems to Mother whenever they met.

HINSEY: And survival under the Nazi occupation?

VENCLOVA: It was bearable. My grandfather was the only employed person: he taught Latin in a high school and his salary enabled us to survive, albeit modestly. True, his position was precarious. The garden provided us with apples, currants, and gooseberries, we bred hens and had vegetables, and a friendly musician's family gave us milk free of charge. Except in the ghettoes, there was no famine or widespread hunger in Lithuania at that time. But we children came down with typical childhood diseases, and there was a marked lack of medical supplies (antibiotics were as yet unknown). Andrius almost succumbed to diphtheria, which killed a great many children his age. In 1944, or perhaps already in 1943, the Russian bombings began. Together with the other inhabitants of Freda, we took shelter in a rather strange place: not far from our house, there was a stone tunnel under a road, with a small brook running through it and wooden benches. However, Grandmother never joined us there during the bombardments. She was a fatalist and, moreover, supposed that an empty house provided a marvelous opportunity for thieves. Her instincts were right: the Russian planes never harmed the city or its environs. Not a single bomb fell in Freda; two or three fell in downtown Kaunas, but these landed in vacant lots (I saw one of the craters—which was impressive—but the surrounding houses remained untouched).

My mother did her best to protect us. The simplest way was to explore the countryside; in Lithuanian villages, food was abundant, there was nothing to bomb, and contagious illnesses were supposedly less prevalent. The fact that there were fewer informers outside of the cities also played a role. Luckily, we had many peasant relatives in various parts of the country. We spent a month or two in southern Lithuania, at my paternal grandmother's home, and stayed in the houses of my father's siblings, including his brother Juozas (it was a big family, scattered throughout a region of hills and lakes near the Polish border). A couple of times we were put up by Petras Cvirka's relatives in a village called Klangiai, which was somewhat closer to Kaunas, on the high bank of the Nemunas River. Cvirka had chosen it as the location for his fictional stories, which are still popular in Lithuania. Even the names of Klangiai's inhabitants are known to anyone who has read them. His family was poorer than my father's relatives and a bit less disciplined, but also jollier, especially Petras's mother, a woman as high-spirited as her son. But I did not feel very comfortable in the countryside: in comparison with the civilized life in Freda, the peasant hut where we stayed was rather primitive—in Klangiai there was an earthen floor, across which small toads hopped from time to time. In the summer of 1944, one of Petras's relatives once took me with him on horseback, and we rode to a windmill he owned—it was no doubt the high point of my day. That summer, the Soviets returned.

4

RETURN OF THE SOVIETS

HINSEY: What was the reaction of the population to the return of the Soviets?

VENCLOVA: Up until the spring of 1944, the Soviets' return did not seem imminent. The intelligentsia, as well as the general population, felt that Germany was losing the war, but hoped that the Allies would convince the Soviets to stop at the borders of the former Baltic states. This time, the Soviets were much more feared than in 1940. The deportations and general tenor of life under the Bolshevik regime had been more than enough to disillusion even those who had once held pro-Soviet views during the interwar period. But the population had also suffered under the Nazis. Even many of the former Baltaraiščiai had been profoundly disillusioned by the fact that their German allies had not had the slightest intention of restoring Lithuania's independence and did not treat them as full-fledged Aryans.

HINSEY: How did the Soviet advance affect the German command?

VENCLOVA: When it became clear that Hitler might be defeated, the attitude of the German command toward the Lithuanians changed. Germany needed as large a fighting force as possible, thus it attempted to form a Lithuanian Waffen SS legion. Even if there were young people who were eager to defend the country against the Soviets, the attempt failed miserably (it succeeded in Latvia and Estonia). In retribution, the Germans closed Vilnius University and sent dozens of intellectuals to the Stutthof concentration camp. They were suspected—not without cause—of anti-Nazi propaganda. Among them was Balys Sruoga, the famous poet and playwright whom my parents knew well. There was then a second attempt; the Germans proposed the creation of Lithuanian units that would defend the country's borders (and that might be construed, with a stretch of the imagination, as the nucleus of a future army—in a sense, a counterpart to the Soviet Lithuanian division). This proposal was accepted, but when the Nazis decided to use Lithuanian units against the Allies (D-Day was imminent), most of the enlisted men deserted, and, fearing unrest, the Nazis forcibly dispersed some units.

HINSEY: How much of this were you able to perceive as a child?

VENCLOVA: Of course, I was only vaguely aware of these developments, although our family followed them closely, and some people from the surrounding countryside enlisted in the ill-fated units. However, I do remember hearing a lot about the approaching Bolsheviks. The prospect of Soviet rule profoundly frightened most of the intelligentsia. (The peasants showed more sangfroid and were sometimes indifferent; if there were Bolshevik sympathizers among them, they were virtually invisible.) I recall scraps of information and pro-Nazi propaganda: the newspapers claimed that the villains Churchill and Roosevelt had sacrificed Lithuania to Stalin, whose army, consisting mainly of Mongolians, tortured and killed everyone in their path, especially children. No wonder I was scared as well, though Mother attempted to reassure me. When the Soviets approached and took Vilnius in early July 1944, thousands of people, including many of our acquaintances, fled toward Germany. Kaunas fell to the Soviet Army on August 1, 1944 (the Normandy invasion was by then in full swing). All this contributed mightily to the exodus. Throngs of Lithuanians, usually on carts but sometimes on foot, flooded into the border towns. At first the German guards did not let them in, but soon yielded. The refugees dispersed throughout Germany and Austria, some reached Denmark and other countries. After a long stint in displaced persons' (DP) camps, most of them found their way to the United States, swelling the ranks of the old diaspora from tsarist times.

HINSEY: What was the exact percentage of the population that fled Lithuania at this time?

VENCLOVA: We have only an approximate number—but probably around sixty thousand people. For a country like Lithuania, with three million inhabitants, this may not seem like an exceedingly large number, yet it was significant because it included more than half of the intellectual class. The working classes usually remained where they were, with some exceptions, particularly well-to-do peasants who knew that they might be targeted for deportation. Scores of writers, artists, and scholars chose exile over life under the Soviets. Their political views spanned the spectrum: there were Nazi sympathizers, including those who had committed war crimes, but the majority were decent people, from the left as well as the right. As I mentioned, my father's friend Henrikas Radauskas and my godfather Antanas Bendorius ended up in the United States, as well as the famous writer Vincas Krėvė, the head of the first 1940 pro-Soviet government in which my father was minister of education. Some of our close relatives also fled, including Vytautas Račkauskas, my mother's brother, and Pijus Venclova, an uncle on my father's side. The refugees also included many young students and children. A number of them later became well-known in their fields, for instance, the archaeologist Marija Gimbutas and the New York film-maker Jonas Mekas, to mention only two. Valdas Adamkus, who fought for a time in one of the Lithuanian units that attempted to stop the Soviets, ended up in Chicago as a displaced person. He later became a liberal politician and the second president of newly independent Lithuania.

HINSEY: There were also the members of the interwar government—

VENCLOVA: Of course, nearly all the political figures who succeeded in escaping the 1941 deportations found themselves in DP camps and then in the United States. They did not manage to form a government-in-exile; that role was played, to a degree, by the Lithuanian diplomatic service, which still existed in many countries. Its members, headed by minister of foreign affairs Stasys Lozoraitis, refused to obey the Soviets and became a splinter of the pre-war republic, whose territory shrank to the size of several embassies. It continued to shrink during the entire postwar period, as one country after another recognized the Soviet annexation, but it never disappeared entirely because the embassies in Washington, DC, and Rome stood firm. (Latvia's and Estonia's cases were almost identical.) This was one of the most bizarre situations in diplomatic history. I believe we'll talk more about that later, since the Lithuanian postwar diaspora was to play a role of some significance later in my life, and in the end I became a part of it.

HINSEY: What were some of your personal experiences of the Soviet return?

VENCLOVA: Well, at first everything looked much milder than the propaganda had predicted. We were in Klangiai (I believe that was our second stay there). The Soviets shelled the nearby German positions for several days: once or twice, shells flew over our heads, but they were high in the air and generated more interest than fear. One evening, we saw a small German cavalry regiment in the field near the Cvirkas' house; the next morning, a group of Russian sappers crossed the same field. After some hesitation, they entered our house. At first, the atmosphere was quite strained, but it soon relaxed, as the sappers did not in fact look threatening and obviously did not intend to do us any harm. My mother and grandmother knew Russian well, and some Klangiai people also knew it, therefore a rather lively exchange followed. It turned out that the commander of the group was Ukrainian, so Grandmother switched to

Ukrainian, which she also knew. Believe it or not, it turned out that he came from a village close to Krivin, where she was born. The soldiers left after having drunk some homemade vodka. Nothing else happened.

HINSEY: On the other hand, there are many accounts of violence—

VENCLOVA: In memoirs published in today's Lithuania, I frequently read about the destruction caused by the Soviets, about petty thefts and ruthless looting, brutish behavior, killings, desecration of holy places, and so on. This may have been true in other areas, but it did not happen in Klangiai. In 1944, Stalin was not necessarily looking to immediately increase the level of antipathy that already existed toward Soviet troops in non-German areas. Therefore, the soldiers were instructed to more or less behave themselves. Only after crossing the German border, "in the nest of the Fascist enemy," robberies, atrocities, rapes, and so on were allowed and even encouraged. The real destructive force in Lithuania, and in the countries that suffered similar fates, was not the Soviet army but the security forces—the SMERSH ("Death to spies") units—that followed in their wake. Further atrocities were carried out by the newly established administration, mainly by the secret police, at that time known as the NKVD.

   Thus in Klangiai, our first encounter with the victorious Soviets was bearable. They may have been shabbier and hungrier than the Germans (although not by much, since at the time the Allies were providing them with various supplies), and frequently primitive, but certainly not inhuman. True, later there was a case of rape in Klangiai when more soldiers arrived, but people considered such things to be inevitable in wartime. (Of course everyone spoke about it in hushed tones, especially in my presence. Yet I understood for the first time that something really dreadful could happen between a man and a woman.)

HINSEY: At this point, your father returned to Lithuania. How were you reunited?

VENCLOVA: On the third or fourth day after the Soviets' return, one of my father's friends appeared in Klangiai. He was the leftist writer Jonas Marcinkevičius, better known for his drunken escapades and jokes than for his novels, which were definitely second-rate. Now he was serving in the Soviet Lithuanian division and was in uniform (he had fled Lithuania in June 1941). From him, we received the news that Father was already in Kaunas. The Lithuanian Communist government had arrived on the heels of the Soviet army and was reestablishing itself in its former capacity. As I mentioned, Father was no longer a member of the government, but had returned to

Lithuania as a war correspondent. Mother, Andrius, and I went immediately to the Kaunas highway, a couple of kilometers from Klangiai, and stopped a military truck full of Soviet soldiers heading in the direction of Kaunas. This is how we reached the city. (Klangiai is approximately fifty kilometers west of Kaunas, and so the Soviets took it at almost the same time as the city, or at most a day or two later.) At six years old, I remember the trip with the soldiers as safe and amusing, and did not at all understand that my mother had exposed herself to considerable risk. Perhaps her fluent Russian and independent character protected her a bit.

HINSEY: How had Kaunas fared?

VENCLOVA: Kaunas had again remained intact but it was totally deserted: the inhabitants had either fled or didn't dare show themselves on the streets. Our truck stopped next to the railway station—I recognized the neighborhood since I'd spent the first days of the war there. Suddenly, a solitary motorcycle with a sidecar went by at full speed. "Petras!" my mother shouted at the top of her voice. In the sidecar was Petras Cvirka, whom she had not seen in over three years. He didn't hear her and sped away: he was going to Klangiai in search of our family (my father did the same, though by other means of transportation).

HINSEY: What happened next?

VENCLOVA: We crossed the Nemunas River by boat (this time, the bridges had been blown up—it was the only trace of the war in the city) and reached Freda. Father arrived the next day. Petras Cvirka also turned up, but Aunt Maria only returned a month or two later—she had to wait in Moscow until the military situation stabilized a bit (the German army, aided by some Lithuanian units, continued to fight in Western Lithuania until late fall 1944, and in Klaipėda until January 1945).

HINSEY: But your family was intact—

VENCLOVA: Yes, that was a family reunion. Only my grandmother Račkauskas was aggrieved, since her son Vytautas had left for the West. "One of my children is always missing," she used to say.

We were an exception among the Lithuanians, since we actually felt liberated. Another exception were the few Jewish survivors of the Vilijampolė ghetto. Of course, one cannot compare our two fates. Most of the remaining population was frightened and guarded, though a business-as-usual attitude gradually returned. For approximately a year, there were no large-scale atrocities. Schools reopened, newspapers and publishing houses were reestablished—though of course, under quite different management. Public services began working again, albeit intermittently, and small private businesses were temporarily allowed. I remember visiting a pastry shop in downtown Kaunas run by a female friend of my mother's.

HINSEY: You have said that you continued to stay in Freda for some time—

VENCLOVA: Yes, for a year or so. I have also mentioned that we used to spend summers in Freda throughout the postwar period. I remember the early postwar years as a happy time. In reality, however, the mood was strained, and not just because of the political situation. In Moscow, my father had had a serious love affair with a Lithuanian girl, who had returned to Kaunas with him. Eventually, he decided to rejoin his former family, but it took time and effort. As a seven-year-old I didn't completely understand this, but it was quite taxing for everyone involved. I never met my father's love, who later married another man and lived in Vilnius for many years after she and my father parted; she had a daughter, whom I also never met.

HINSEY: What did your father do for work right after the war?

VENCLOVA: Father stayed with us in Freda, though not always. He began teaching a survey course in European literature at Kaunas University, the aim of which was to give students an introduction to Shakespeare, Goethe, and Byron. Grandfather also returned to the university. As for us, the children, we continued to spend our time playing—in the leafy streets and on the hills and beaches of Freda. We also learned to play chess, and later, Grandfather taught us to play Preference, a complicated card game similar to whist (Andrius was much more successful in this than I). In the evenings, there was harmonium music and socializing. In Freda, Father wrote a dozen or so of his best poems, which are still in print: they were hardly Socialist Realist—just lyrical pieces somewhat in the style of Pasternak (whom he had met in Moscow once or twice). He also translated *Eugene Onegin* into Lithuanian; he used to read parts of his translation aloud, soliciting our responses. Later the translation was published, accompanied by prewar illustrations by Mstislav Dobuzhinski, a renowned Russian artist who, incidentally, emigrated to the United States— this perhaps serves as an example of the relative cultural freedom of the early postwar period. Imitating Father's poetry, and doggerel I'd read in children magazines, I also tried to write verse.

HINSEY: This period also marked the beginning of your schooling—

VENCLOVA: In the fall of 1944, I began to attend a primary school housed in a modest farm-style building just around the corner. Since I could already read and write, I skipped a year and was put in second grade. I remember my first wooden briefcase well: Mother painted it with flowers, which made me proud. Then we moved to a flat in downtown Kaunas, not far from Uncle Karolis, and I did not attend school for two years—I enjoyed this period of idleness immensely. To tell the truth, I was not totally idle, since I was an avid reader. Mother also taught me at home, with the help of an elderly lady who lived nearby; this same woman also gave me my first English and French lessons.

HINSEY: Your family's situation directly following the war sounds as if it were relatively comfortable—how was it affected by the Soviet occupation?

VENCLOVA: Our family was an exception because of Father's official standing, but there were other such cases. Despite the surrounding poverty and chaos, certain intellectuals—including those hostile to the regime—managed to maintain their prewar lifestyles and mores somewhat, at least for a time. True, they were tormented by fear, which soon proved well-founded. The greater part of these intellectuals who did not emigrate were leftists (which did not necessarily spare them in the end), but there were also Catholics and Western-style liberals. Lithuania clearly differed from Stalinist Russia in many respects, and reminded one of other not yet totally subdued Eastern European countries like Poland. But this did not last long.

HINSEY: What were the first signs of Stalinization?

VENCLOVA: Portraits of Stalin appeared here and there. A farcical election campaign was organized in 1947—which proposed only one candidate for every district—for the Supreme Soviet of the USSR. (Father was among the candidates and was duly elected, like everyone else.) The newspapers were full of propaganda, but in the beginning it could be construed as anti-Fascist. I remember how Father once said, "In Nazi times, you heard a lot about the Red Terror; now you will hear about the Brown Terror"—and he showed us an article describing the fate of Pirčiupis. This was a Lithuanian village that the Nazis had burned down, along with its inhabitants, since a Communist guerrilla unit was active in the vicinity. The story was true, and for decades it was used for Soviet propaganda purposes. There were poems and statues elevating Pirčiupis to the rank of a Lithuanian Oradour or Lidice.

HINSEY: Did Russification with respect to language start right away? How was this carried out?

VENCLOVA: In school, we were taught Russian right from the beginning, though all other classes were conducted in Lithuanian, and old textbooks were used for a time (the new ones, full of Soviet material, were printed a year or two later). Prewar books were removed from the libraries and gradually destroyed (Uncle Karolis, who was the head of the Kaunas public library, was ordered to place prewar and Western literature under lock and key; during the Nazi occupation, he had been requested to eliminate all books written by Communist and Jewish authors. However, instead of throwing them out, he had hidden them). New books, mainly printed in Russia, took their place. In the bookshops, Lithuanian-language literature prevailed, but until the sixties, it consisted primarily of translations of Gorky and Soviet Russian authors, and less frequently Pushkin and Chekhov.

HINSEY: What about the military presence in Freda?

VENCLOVA: Soviet soldiers were highly visible, much more than the German soldiers had been. In May 1945, following the Allied victory, there were lots of fireworks and heavy drinking. After that, the number of Russians continued to increase, since the nearby airfield had been taken over by the Soviet air force. Grandfather was ordered to allocate two rooms in our house to a pair of pilots (one of them perished soon after in a plane crash). Everywhere in Freda, families of Russian servicemen appeared, requisitioning rooms in our neighbors' homes free of charge, and sometimes occupying entire houses if the owners had emigrated. Still, they did not appear arrogant or mean, at least to me. The Lithuanians avoided mixing with them, but I played with Russian children my age and quickly learned the language. One summer, I was quite interested in a Russian girl named Vera, several years older than me. She always walked barefoot and obviously enjoyed it (something uncommon in conservative Freda). She was perhaps the very first person who stirred vague sexual feelings in me. Around 1960, the airfield was reassigned to civil aviation—a much larger military one had been built north of Kaunas—and the Russians left Freda.

HINSEY: What about the Soviet persecution of religious expression?

VENCLOVA: Immediately after the war, most of the churches in Kaunas, as well as in provincial towns and villages, remained open, though many priests, including most of the bishops, had emigrated, and religious observance was officially discouraged, especially for children. My first day of school had begun with a prayer, as was customary in pre-Soviet times; then the teacher abruptly announced that the Bolsheviks had banned praying in schoolrooms. By 1946, Bishop Vincentas Borisevičius had been arrested and executed. Yet it was not until 1948 that an extensive and brutal antireligious campaign began. This was connected with Soviet efforts to eradicate Lithuanian partisan warfare, which was then at its zenith.

HINSEY: Perhaps this is a good place to speak about the partisan warfare—

VENCLOVA: During the first Soviet occupation in 1940–41, there was almost no armed resistance. But after the Germans left, many young men found themselves in the forests (they were usually called *miškiniai*—"forest people" or "forest brothers"). Many parts of Lithuania were actually under their control, especially at night. It was rather easy to obtain weapons, which had either been abandoned by the retreating Germans or stolen from the Soviets (who sometimes even sold them to the *miškiniai* on the sly). These partisans were a mixed bag: some were former Baltaraiščiai, including Nazi sympathizers and men trained by the Nazis to sabotage the retreating Soviet Army. There were also common criminals, whose numbers increased as time passed. The majority, however, were young boys from the countryside who did not want to serve the Soviets, and who hoped that the Allies would soon help reestablish an independent Lithuania. Former students and teachers also withdrew into the forest because they felt it was their duty to resist the occupiers. There were quite a few servicemen from the interwar Lithuanian army who considered themselves bound by their oath. And so on. In the beginning, these groups were not overly active, and the Soviets tried to coax them out of the forests, promising amnesty and legalization. These promises, of course, proved largely false—as a rule, the men who surrendered landed in prison. Gradually, the ranks of the "forest people" increased as the Soviets started to lay the groundwork for collectivization, which the peasants strongly opposed. By 1947–48, the war in the countryside was in full swing.

HINSEY: This led to a sustained and violent conflict—

VENCLOVA: Yes, as is often the case with guerrilla warfare, it was brutal. Thousands of people perished, women and children were sometimes savagely murdered. The Soviets organized so-called destroyer units (*istrebiteli* in Russian, or *stribai* in Lithuanian). These were also made up of village people and were known for their ruthlessness. One of the most traumatic experiences—remembered to this day—was how the corpses of partisans were publicly displayed in town squares. This was allegedly for purposes of identification, but in reality it was to profane the dead. As a rule, a dead man's relatives refrained from recognizing the body, since this usually led to arrest, cruel interrogation, and Siberian camps. The *miškiniai* were often ruthless as well, killing Soviet collaborators or people suspected—sometimes unjustly—of collaborationist sympathies. All that lasted until 1953, the year of Stalin's death, though some partisans hid in their bunkers long afterward. It is interesting to note that in the late forties and early fifties, certain young émigrés attempted to cross the Baltic Sea from Sweden in landing boats to join the partisans. Thanks to the British double agent Kim Philby, the Soviet secret police usually knew about them in advance. NKVD agents met them, disguised as freedom fighters, and then either killed the naive émigrés or recruited them to the Soviet side through torture or other means.

HINSEY: What was the attitude of the general population toward the partisans?

VENCLOVA: It was largely positive, though not without reservations. Many families had a son or brother in the forest. That said, as I mentioned, some young peasants joined the *stribai* units, and more than one was tempted by the fact that the authorities allowed them to plunder the property of "class enemies." The partisans also committed atrocities from time to time (in Klangiai, for instance, an entire family we knew was executed by the *miškiniai*), and these cases tended to diminish one's sympathy for the cause. As a rule, the intelligentsia respected the fighters, though silently, of course. A number of intellectuals had contact with them, contributed to the partisans' underground press, and so on. It was gradually acknowledged, however, that the struggle was hopeless. A sort of consensus emerged: since the Western powers would never come, it did not make any sense to spill blood and risk the very survival of Lithuania. As for Catholic priests, most of them sympathized with the partisans, and sometimes joined them, though such cases were infrequent.

HINSEY: Did you personally have any experiences related to this warfare?

VENCLOVA: I knew that it was going on (by this time I read the newspapers, and these were full of virulent propaganda against the "bandits," who were also labeled "bourgeois nationalists"). In Freda, and later in Vilnius, there was virtually no warfare. That said, quite a few city people had connections with the partisans, or even belonged to their command. In second grade I had a classmate whose family's name was Gečiauskas, and his older brother was killed at home one night. Presumably, it was a *miškiniai* execution. The story was not entirely clear: some said the victim was a Young Communist activist, some insisted that he himself belonged to the "forest brothers" but had denounced them to the NKVD, while others maintained that his death was the result of a settling of accounts.

My father, who was considered to be a collaborator, was in some danger (Soviet officials were assassinated from time to time, though usually only in the provinces). But Father never had any bodyguards—high-ranking government and party members were often provided with them (nor did he own a gun). Many years later, a man, who had been a member of the partisan network and had spent many years in Soviet prisons, told my father in private that there had been a decision by the *miškiniai* to spare both him and Petras Cvirka, since they were significant cultural figures who might prove useful to an independent Lithuania. This may or may not have been true, but Father was rather proud of it.

HINSEY: I believe you moved with your family to Vilnius in 1946—what was the house like?

VENCLOVA: We moved in either 1946 or 1947. My recollection is that we spent two years in downtown Kaunas, but one's sense of time in childhood is not entirely reliable. The government, as well as the entire Soviet (and not only Soviet) elite gradually moved to Vilnius during this period. Not every-body was happy about it, since the city had sustained far more damage during the war than Kaunas. Several decades would be needed for its reconstruction. We were assigned a flat in a house not far from the center, on Uosto (in Polish, Portowa) Street, which, incidentally, Czesław Miłosz mentions in his mem-oirs: he used to walk there on his way to high school some twenty years before. Our family lived there until my father's death in 1971; I had left home by then, but was still a frequent visitor.

The two-story white house stood on a hill, surrounded by a fairly large garden. It was built in the thirties, when Vilnius was under Polish rule. Our flat, quite decent by Soviet standards, occupied the entire ground floor (when Joseph Brodsky visited for the first time, he joked: "Tomas, even if we were in power, we still wouldn't be able to provide you with such a good apartment"). Of course it would have appeared rather modest by Western standards. It con-sisted of two bedrooms, a dining room, and Father's library with his working desk. Cherry trees grew next to the windows. There was a bathroom with a heater and an additional room where the housekeeper slept. We called her *šeimininkė* (mistress). She came with us from Kaunas and was practically a member of the family: an elderly lady who treated my mother as a daughter and me as a grandson. On the upper floor, there was a similarly sized flat belonging to a party official with whom we were not on the best of terms.

HINSEY: Can you speak a bit more about the impact of the war on Vilnius?

VENCLOVA: The center of Vilnius was virtually in ruins. Along Gedimino Prospektas, the city's main street, every other house was burned-out. Strangely however, a large wooden building had survived: the movie house Helios, men-tioned by Czesław Miłosz in one of his poems. The old part of the city was to the south, toward the railway station. It was a labyrinth of crooked lanes, full of Baroque churches and monasteries, almost Venetian (though without canals), very beautiful, but run-down and neglected. Only gradually did I learn to appreciate its magic. Father showed me the Cathedral, Saint Anne's Church, and other buildings, but it took five or ten years for me to become really fond of them. The Christian part of the city hadn't been badly hit, although artillery shells had damaged several churches. The Jewish ghetto on the other hand (which had made up almost half of the old city) was a night-marish wasteland: in the middle of it, the walls of the ancient synagogue still jutted up, but these were soon pulled down by the authorities. The debris of war was everywhere. The suburbs were miserable and chaotic. In comparison with Vilnius, Kaunas looked civilized, with a chessboard grid of streets lined with respectable Art Deco buildings. After my first day at school in Vilnius, I got lost in the ruins and wandered for several hours (passersby were infrequent and mainly spoke Polish). When I managed to find my way back to our flat I felt dreadfully exhausted. I have written about how this hopeless wandering in search of home became a sort of personal symbol for me.

HINSEY: At this point, who were the inhabitants of Vilnius?

VENCLOVA: Well, the city was half-empty. Before the war, it had about a quar-ter of a million inhabitants; now, there were one hundred thousand at most, fewer than in Kaunas. And the population was in permanent flux. Almost all the Jews had perished. Some Jewish families, who had managed to flee Vilnius in the first days of the war, returned and joined several dozen survi-vors, but as a rule they did their best to emigrate to Israel (which was just then being founded). Not everyone succeeded, and subsequently many ended up in prison because of their "intent to betray the fatherland of the proletariat." Poles and Polish-speakers had previously composed more than half of Vilnius's prewar population. Some of them were of Lithuanian heritage—and might even have called themselves Lithuanians, but they were Polish patriots and their knowledge of Lithuanian was at best rudimentary. They were presented with a choice: become Soviet citizens or leave for postwar Poland. Not surpris-ingly, few opted for the USSR. True, Polish-speaking peasants around Vilnius tended to remain where they were, but with few exceptions, almost the entire middle and intellectual classes left. They were sent to the former eastern ter-ritories of Germany acquired by Poland following the Potsdam Conference. Actually, it was a brutal eviction, comparable to a deportation. These Poles cherished their memories of Wilno/Vilnius until the end of their days, and their children and grandchildren remain interested in their roots. There is an entire branch of literature in today's Poland that deals with the so-called *Kresy* (Eastern provinces—that is, the former Polish areas of Lithuania, Belarus, and Ukraine). Miłosz and other fine writers, such as Tadeusz Konwicki, made significant contributions to it, even though Miłosz considered the very term *kresy* to be inappropriate, that is, having imperialist overtones.

HINSEY: Thus, your family intimately witnessed this displacement and change in population—

VENCLOVA: When our family arrived in Vilnius, the Polish population was still in the process of leaving. At the beginning, the vacuum it left was filled by Russians. They were of various sorts: military personnel and their families (as in Freda), Soviet administrators, factory foremen, but also many hungry and dejected Russians who had suffered in villages under Stalin's rule (and, more often than not, under the Nazi rule that followed it). They had heard that new lands had been annexed by the USSR, where abandoned houses stood empty and food was relatively plentiful. Thus, they attempted to move to the Baltic states, regardless of whether this was officially permitted or not. Many of these people went to Klaipėda (now entirely emptied of Germans), and especially to Königsberg—now the Russian city of Kaliningrad—though they were quite visible in Vilnius as well. There were also Belarusians from the surrounding countryside (Lithuania's border with Soviet Belarus was not far, and at that time it was just a line on a map, with neither guards nor fences). For all practical purposes, the Belarusians were indistinguishable from the Russians. Ethnic Lithuanians were unquestionably in the minority. They were either government officials or remnants of the country's prewar intelligentsia, who had rather reluctantly moved to Vilnius from Kaunas. True, some Lithuanian-speaking families remained in the city from prewar times, but there were literally a dozen or so of them.

HINSEY: This made for a complex and volatile population—

VENCLOVA: Yes, the ethnic and linguistic landscape of Vilnius was unusual, to put it mildly. Our neighbors were mainly Russian-speakers (including two or three Jewish families who had spent the war years in the USSR). Polish was prevalent on the streets, but not for long: it was replaced by Russian, which I mastered. This "Russian Vilnius" period lasted at least a decade. However, by the time I graduated from Vilnius University—that is, in the sixties—I could communicate in Lithuanian almost everywhere (even if Russian remained the lingua franca in certain situations). This stemmed mainly from the fact that most courses at the university were taught in Lithuanian, and its graduates, born mainly in Lithuanian-speaking villages, easily found jobs in the capital city. There is a theory—we'll come back to this later—that the Lithuanian Communist Party, which was rather nationalistic under a thin internationalist veneer, took pains to change the city's ethnic composition in order to fulfill the dreams of the old national movement. This is debatable, but I am inclined to believe it.

One must add that there was a great deal of ethnic stereotyping and friction between the various groups. This was aggravated by memories of traumatic wartime events in the Vilnius region. During the war, Polish partisans (the Armia Krajowa, or Home Army) were active in the city and particularly in its environs. They treated Lithuanians as occupiers, less dangerous than the Nazis and the Soviets, but hardly worthy of deferential treatment. Lithuanians paid them in kind. Under Soviet rule, this old enmity was reduced mainly to swearing and scuffles between groups of youths. The Russians, as the occupiers, were scorned by both Lithuanians and Poles—not without racist overtones— and in turn, the Russians considered both of the others to be dyed-in-the-wool fascists. And anti-Semitism did not disappear. Because of all this, the city was rather dangerous, in particular at night (criminal gangs of various ethnic origins were numerous in the first postwar decade, and they fought among themselves). On the other hand, if I learned tolerance, it was in Vilnius. I was probably an exception, yet in time I found a group of like-minded friends about whom I'll speak later.

HINSEY: How long did it take for the Stalinization of Lithuania to be carried out?

VENCLOVA: My first years in Vilnius coincided with the total imposition of the Stalinist order and *Gleichschaltung*. Many Russian memoirists recount, however, that immediately following the end of the war there was a glimmer of hope in the USSR: the system could be, to a certain extent, ignored, and there was a modicum of freedom in both daily life and culture, influenced in part by the Western allies. There were those who expected genuine rapprochement with Great Britain and America, which logically would be followed by democratization. I believe my parents, together with Petras Cvirka, harbored such hopes as well. In Lithuania, the memory of a fairly free and civilized prewar life was far from extinguished. There was also a strong feeling of European cultural identity.

Thus, for a year or so, it was difficult to imagine how horrible things would later turn out. I have already said that directly after the war the old intelligentsia tried to maintain at least some of its traditions. Now when I look through the Soviet Lithuanian press from that period, I am struck by the caesura of 1946. Before that, it was possible to find traces of diversity and civility; afterward, Lithuanian society became entirely totalitarian. Stalin did his utmost to impress upon his subjects that nothing was going to change, and if something did change, it would be for the worse. Very quickly, the Western allies were declared sworn enemies of the USSR, all relative liberties were revoked, and the omnipotence of the secret police was reasserted. In Lithuania, there was the additional task of bringing the formerly independent, bourgeois—and resistant—country into the Soviet fold: thus, the callousness of the regime was even more pronounced there.

HINSEY: This brings us to the question of postwar *règlement de comptes* and deportations. How did these deportations differ from those that took place in early June 1941, just before the Nazi invasion?

VENCLOVA: After the Soviets returned in 1944–45, the SMERSH security forces carried out a series of arrests, which frequently resulted in summary executions. All in all, around fifteen thousand people were killed, including some Nazi collaborators, but also many who fell into the hands of the SMERSH by accident. Then there was a pause. As I have said, the Lithuanian partisans were rather passive at first, and there were attempts to pacify them by promises of legalization. But from 1947 on, as Sovietization started in earnest and the partisan warfare intensified, Stalin decided to annihilate its very basis in the Lithuanian countryside.

The 1941 deportations had been primarily directed at the political and intellectual class, which was destroyed to a large degree. After the war the survivors were often out of reach because they were in DP camps in Germany, under the protection of the Western powers. That meant only one group of relatively independent-minded people remained, namely, the peasants—and the partisans could not fight or even exist without their support. Therefore, the peasants became the next main target. In 1948, some forty thousand of them were sent to Siberia and Kazakhstan, and the following year, an additional thirty thousand followed. Thus, the scope of the postwar deportations was much greater. Further, it generated a veritable panic: most people were convinced that all Lithuanians would be deported sooner or later—and sooner rather than later. This did not happen, but the horror was sufficient to break the back of the peasant class. To make matters worse, in 1948–51 even villagers who had escaped repression lost their property and were herded into kolkhozy, or collective farms, as in Russia. This was hailed as a great victory for the Lithuanian nation and glorified in poems and paintings. Actually, it was a step backward, almost to the era of serfdom.

HINSEY: What was the fate of this group of postwar deportees?

VENCLOVA: Luckily, this time many of the deportees survived. Around 1956, after Khrushchev's Secret Speech, they started to drift back to their homeland. Even some of those deported in 1941 returned after Stalin's death, though these were hardly more numerous than the survivors of the Nazi concentration camps. It may be worth mentioning that the head of the Lithuanian Communist Party, Antanas Sniečkus, addressed the Moscow authorities in the fifties, stating that the returnees were still dangerous class enemies and, in his opinion, should not be allowed to live in Lithuania. After his letter, various bureaucratic hurdles were created for those seeking to return. Many of them had to settle in Latvia or in the Kaliningrad region, next to the Lithuanian border.

HINSEY: How visible were these postwar deportations to the general population?

VENCLOVA: They were never mentioned in the press or in any public documents, but everybody knew about Siberian exile and feared it. Two of my Vilnius High School classmates suddenly disappeared. We learned that they had been deported, along with their father, an officer of the prewar Lithuanian army, but it went without saying that one should remain silent about such matters. Even now, I have no idea what happened to them.

HINSEY: Did the deportations have a direct impact on your family?

VENCLOVA: Despite my father's status, some of our relatives were among the deportees. My father's brother Juozas, who had sheltered my mother and me during the Nazi occupation, was one of them. Father wrote a long letter to the authorities requesting his release, but it did not help: Juozas died working in a Siberian mine. Only his widow and daughter returned several years after his death. Then, Father's sister Izabelė came to Vilnius from her home in southern Lithuania. She had walked a hundred miles, avoiding all public transportation. During roundups, she had managed to hide, but her husband Černikas was loaded into a cattle car and disappeared. This time, my father was more successful: he proved that his brother-in-law was not a class enemy. In a week or two, at a small railway station in the Ural Mountains, Černikas was called out of the car and informed that he was allowed to return to his village. This was in fact not all that easy, since he had no money and did not speak Russian. But he finally succeeded. This kind of release, of course, was a rare exception.

HINSEY: What was your family's reaction to these events?

VENCLOVA: Grandmother never hesitated to curse the Bolsheviks for their atrocities. The men in our family were much more reserved, but it was obvious that they were also quite shaken up by what was going on. Once, I asked my mother: "Do they just leave the deportees in the forest when the trains reach

Siberia?" "No," she answered, "they are given a place to live, but their life is of course difficult." Needless to say, I was frightened by the prospect that our family could one day find itself in the Siberian forests, like everyone else. That was improbable, but not impossible. Toward the end of his rule, Stalin frequently purged members of the privileged Soviet class who were perfectly loyal to him. One may recall here the so-called Leningrad Affair, in which the entire party elite of the second-largest Russian city was unexpectedly imprisoned and executed, or the case of the Jewish Anti-Fascist Committee (Father knew at least one of its members, Emilia Teumin). Several Lithuanian Soviet officials were arrested at that time because of their "leniency toward bourgeois nationalists" (in Latvia and Estonia, such cases were even more numerous).

Many years later, I learned that both my parents had helped some of the deportees, and not just their own relatives. Mother arranged temporary shelter for a female friend, Pazukienė, a painter who had returned from Siberia without permission, and used her contacts to provide documents that allowed her to remain in Lithuania. I remember that Father mailed Lithuanian books to the Siberian address of one of his former students. Of course, these were small gestures—there were people who did much more—yet even these were decidedly risky ones.

5

POSTWAR AND CULTURE

HINSEY: We've just spoken about the political climate directly after the war. Let's now explore what was happening in the intellectual and cultural milieus—

VENCLOVA: In August 1946, when we were still living in Kaunas, a cultural crackdown started in Russia. One of Stalin's henchmen, Andrei Zhdanov, gave a speech in which he castigated two famous Leningrad writers, Mikhail Zoshchenko and Anna Akhmatova, for their work, which was, according to him, antipathetic to the heroic Soviet people. Even by Soviet standards, it was an exceptionally virulent attack. The abuse that Zhdanov poured on both writers' heads was obviously dictated by the Great Leader himself. This marked the end of the relative cultural freedom I previously mentioned, and the onset of the Cold War.

Joseph Brodsky, who later became one of Akhmatova's disciples and heir apparent, says in his memoirs that he was unaware of Zhdanov's speech until his early youth, although he lived in Leningrad, where the event occurred. Yet he was three years younger than I was and had not grown up in a literary family. I knew what was happening, though I could not of course understand its full implications. At nine years old, I was able to read not only in Lithuanian but also in Russian, and I remember the journals and newspapers reviling the "decadent" Akhmatova and "cynical" Zoshchenko. Both names were well-known to my parents. Akhmatova's poetry and Zoshchenko's short stories (incredibly funny, by the way) were almost as popular in prewar Lithuania as in Russia itself. Petras Cvirka had even made friends with Zoshchenko in the Kazakh city of Alma-Ata (present-day Almaty) where he had stayed for a period during the war. Therefore, excerpts from their works were in Father's library, and I managed to get hold of them. They looked, well, quite interesting.

HINSEY: What were the repercussions of the Akhmatova-Zoshchenko affair in Lithuania?

VENCLOVA: As a general rule, every Soviet ideological campaign had to be imitated in each Soviet republic, and not only there, but also in the so-called people's democracies, such as Poland or Czechoslovakia—an old Russian custom, as Brodsky liked to call it. Thus, Lithuanian counterparts to Akhmatova and Zoshchenko had to be identified and discredited.

A month and a half after Zhdanov's speech, a meeting of the Writers' Union took place in Vilnius. Kazys Preikšas, a high party functionary—a sort of Lithuanian Zhdanov—addressed the assembly. He was a Communist of peasant origins, had fought in the Spanish Civil War, and had become a genuine Stalinist there. His knowledge of literature was nonexistent, but he was fully aware of the dangers that awaited anyone who was less than active in fulfilling Stalin's orders: therefore, he did his utmost, even if awkwardly.

HINSEY: Who was present at this meeting?

VENCLOVA: The writers who attended were of different provenance. Some, like my father and Cvirka, who had spent the war years in Russia, were considered loyal to the Soviets and worthy of guiding the Writers' Union. But in the auditorium, one could also see intellectuals who had survived the Nazi occupation of Lithuania, and were therefore, by definition, suspect. Preikšas attacked many people (belonging, incidentally, to both groups) in an unbelievably caddish manner, emulating Zhdanov to the best of his abilities. Balys Sruoga was there—as I mentioned earlier, he was a highly respected writer from the older generation, a former Symbolist who had rubbed shoulders with Gorky and Andrei Bely in his youth. As you may remember, he was arrested by the Nazis and sent to the Stutthof concentration camp. Well, the Soviet army liberated the camp and Sruoga returned to Vilnius, where he wrote a book about his experience, titled *The Forest of the Gods*. It was a work in the vein of Alfred Döblin or Tadeusz Borowski, with poignant images of human degradation and a tinge of black humor. Sruoga presented his manuscript to the State Publishing House (there were no others). It frightened the censors since it was very far from the requirements of Socialist Realism. At the writers' meeting, Preikšas attacked Sruoga ferociously. He said, more or less: "Instead of showing us the heroic deeds of the Soviet people in the Nazi camps, Balys Sruoga cynically portrays petty people and wretches, concerned with physiological functions. Based on such an account, our enemies would be justified in saying that the Nazis were right to keep such pathetic creatures in concentration camps." Sruoga was shocked. He understood, quite correctly, that after the Nazi camp he might land in a Soviet one. That did not happen: he died a year later, in the aftermath of the meeting. His manuscript was published ten years later; it is now considered a significant contribution to prison camp literature.

HINSEY: What was the reaction of your father and the other writers?

VENCLOVA: My father and Cvirka spoke at the meeting in a loyal vein, as was expected of them. Neither they nor anyone else dared to defend Sruoga. Lithuania was already in the grip of the "Great Terror" described by many witnesses of Stalinism. People compromised themselves, sometimes trying to justify their behavior by quasi-rational arguments. Well, this is a sad fact. Incidentally, Cvirka wrote privately to Sruoga, attempting to convince him that Socialist Realism could be reconciled with good writing.

HINSEY: As we will be speaking extensively about Lithuanian literature throughout this book, before we continue with the postwar period, perhaps we could address a bit of Lithuanian literary history, and the aesthetics and trends that were prevalent before the war—

VENCLOVA: In general, our literature followed Eastern European and, to some extent, Scandinavian patterns. It matured later than the literatures of the neighboring states, and of course it was not as rich as Russian, Polish, or Czech writing. Nevertheless, readers are presented with an extensive and interesting body of work. Borges once said that any national literature satisfies the spiritual needs of its people as fully as any other, and I tend to agree with him.

Our first significant poet was Kristijonas Donelaitis, an eighteenth-century Lutheran pastor who lived in East Prussia. He wrote in classical hexameters about everyday peasant life, attracted Goethe's attention, and is still considered a great master of poetic language. Some compare his long poem *The Seasons* to Hesiod and to Virgil's *Georgics* (with which he was familiar). Several writers of the first half of the nineteenth century were connected with the University of Vilnius and were influenced by Polish literature of the time, primarily by Adam Mickiewicz—some of them were his classmates. During the period of the "press ban" and the national movement, many authors left their mark. One of them, Maironis, became a national poet: in Lithuanian letters, he played a role comparable to Pushkin or Schiller in their respective literatures. He also transformed Lithuanian versification, introducing into it patterns similar to Russian ones (before him, Polish syllabic patterns were traditionally used). This was a political choice, at least in part: Lithuanians were striving to affirm their non-Polish identity, something that had to be reflected even in their versification. (In a similar way, around the same time our orthography was switched from Polish to Czech.) Most poets after him employed his iambs, trochees, and anapests—only recently have these been supplanted by vers libre. (I am an exception in Lithuania, since I'm still fond of Maironis's verse, even if I frequently use other patterns. Joseph Brodsky was similarly fond of Pushkin's verse.) There were also several significant fiction writers. Continuing in the tradition of Donelaitis, they usually depicted the life of the peasants (who, in any case, made up the majority of Lithuanian speakers at the time). Their short stories and novels followed the precepts of nineteenth-century Realism, concentrating on social and psychological issues.

HINSEY: And when Lithuanian literature entered the modern era?

VENCLOVA: When our literature entered the era of Modernism, it followed the main European trends. Even prior to World War I, Lithuania produced its own variant of Symbolism, and in the interwar period many Futurist and Expressionist works appeared—as a rule, they were comparable in quality to Russian, Polish, and German writing. Just before the Soviet occupation of 1940, Lithuanian literature included a wide spectrum of groups and styles. Older poets, like Sruoga or Vincas Mykolaitis-Putinas, still wrote Symbolist verse with a metaphysical slant, but they did not shy from producing Realist plays or psychological prose as well. Vincas Krėvė, who was considered a candidate for the Nobel Prize, described village life in a rather traditional way, but also created historical dramas in the vein of early Ibsen. Kazys Binkis was an inventive and sharp-witted Futurist. There were some Catholic writers influenced by French authors such as Bernanos and Mauriac, and young poets interested in Rimbaud and Rilke (also in Pasternak and other Russian poets).

HINSEY: More specifically, what about the poets from this generation?

VENCLOVA: I've mentioned Henrikas Radauskas, who was one of the younger poets; he was rather on the leftist side, even if he expounded an "art for art's sake" philosophy. An important figure for many Lithuanians was Oscar Miłosz—a not very well-known but powerful poet who lived in Paris, was employed by the Lithuanian diplomatic service and wrote in French (he was an elder relative of Czesław Miłosz, who valued him highly). Some had heard of Yeats, Pound, and Eliot, though the influence of these authors was rather negligible—in the interwar years, Lithuanians knew French, German, and Russian but rarely English. Finally, there was *Trečias Frontas*, which I have mentioned before—a radical leftist journal edited by my father, which promoted Mayakovsky, Aragon, and similar authors (also Whitman and Sandburg). Petras Cvirka and Kazys Boruta belonged to this group; but its most celebrated member was Salomėja Nėris, a young and gifted female poet who was considered the Lithuanian counterpart to Akhmatova. In 1931, she astonished the reading public, crossing over from the Catholic group to the radical left and embracing the proletarian cause. That was, I believe, mostly due to personal reasons and a youthful desire to épater le bourgeois, yet it had serious consequences. When Lithuania was occupied by the Soviets, Nėris wrote a paean to Stalin. She read it at the Kremlin, in the presence of the Great Leader himself, during the session of the Supreme Soviet when Lithuania was gracefully accepted into the USSR. From that moment on, she was—and still is—considered by many a traitor of the first order. She spent the war years in Russia, like Cvirka and my father (who were her close friends), then returned to Kaunas with the Red Army and died of cancer in 1945. She wrote beautiful poems up to the end of her life (Akhmatova translated some of them into Russian) and continued to be adored by a large part of the reading public. Notwithstanding her controversial reputation, she remains a classic of Lithuanian letters. I met her once, as a seven-year-old boy and, at the urging of my father, recited one of her popular poems. I remember her as a lady of small physical stature, reserved and shy. After I had finished, she made a critical remark about the poem, saying it used unnecessarily archaic language.

HINSEY: Did any of these prewar trends survive in Soviet times, especially after the Zhdanov speech?

VENCLOVA: All writers who did not emigrate had to conform. Some attempted to take a wait-and-see attitude, but they were officially dubbed *tyleniai* ("the silent ones"), which for all practical purposes meant "enemies of the people." Vincas Mykolaitis-Putinas, perhaps the most respected member of the literary community, wrote several propagandistic verses, which probably saved his life. (He lived next to us, and my father, who was his former student at Kaunas University, visited him frequently, trying to reconcile him with Soviet mores with which Father was more familiar.) Antanas Vienuolis, another classic prewar writer, wrote a novel about village life in his usual vein, but was forced to rework it, stressing the class struggle and the role of the city proletariat. Since he knew next to nothing about such topics, the censor produced several chapters himself and mechanically inserted them into the text. The book was consequently praised by critics as an exemplary work of Socialist Realism (it was also translated into German and printed in East Berlin). The curse of Soviet censorship was not only the fact that unacceptable words and paragraphs had to be expunged, but that you were forced to add requested ones.

HINSEY: Among this group of writers, how many were imprisoned or deported?

VENCLOVA: There were many victims. One of them was our close friend Kazys Boruta, whom I mentioned earlier. He had an affair with a woman writer, Ona Lukauskaitė. Like Boruta himself, she belonged to the Socialist-Revolutionary party, which had fought Smetona's regime. During the first Soviet invasion in 1940 when Smetona fled, she was among the leaders who stormed the Kaunas prison and liberated all the Communists, as well as members of her own party. Very soon the prison filled up again, which made Lukauskaitė indignant. She was completely fearless, and thus began to pester the Communist functionaries (many of whom, including the above-mentioned Preikšas, she knew well), demanding the release of their political opponents. After the war, she joined a clandestine group that planned anti-Communist actions. The group allegedly intended to take over Vilnius's radio station and address world public opinion from there; preparations were also supposedly made to hijack a plane and attempt to reach the West with a sort of freedom manifesto. Perhaps such extensive plans did not exist at all (these kinds of offenses were, more often than not, invented by the Soviet secret police during interrogations). In any case, Lukauskaitė wrote a letter—as far as I know, to none other than Winston Churchill—explaining to him the unenviable fate of Lithuania and requesting help from the Western powers. She showed the letter to Boruta before attempting to have it smuggled to London. Boruta did not support the idea, but did not denounce her or her group. He was imprisoned for this, yet was released after three years; she got a ten-year sentence and spent it in Vorkuta camps north of the Arctic Circle. The leader of the group, a prewar army officer and lawyer, was executed.

HINSEY: Your father was present at Lukauskaitė's trial, and you would work closely with her in the 1970s—

VENCLOVA: Yes, I knew Lukauskaitė and worked with her during my dissident years, thus I'll come back to her amazing life. My father was summoned to testify at her trial, and I was happy to hear from her that he behaved quite decently. He tried to help not only her but also Boruta, and in the latter case he may have been successful—three years was considered a negligible sentence.

Boruta returned from prison unbroken. For many years, he could not publish his work and made his living translating Schiller and Ibsen (which he was only allowed to publish under a pseudonym), but he never repudiated his views. That was far from common. The well-known essayist and editor from the prewar period, Juozas Keliuotis, also ended up in prison but was broken by it. (He had been the first to promote Joyce and Picasso in Lithuania, and when Czesław Miłosz came to Kaunas after Poland's downfall in 1939, Keliuotis did a great deal to support him.) After two stints in the camps, Keliuotis began to glorify the regime (true, at the same time he wrote secret memoirs in which he gave free rein to his hatred). Incidentally, Keliuotis was a homosexual; this was a punishable offense in the USSR and it left him vulnerable to blackmail. Needless to say, he was eager to avoid a third prison term.

HINSEY: It is important to remember the fates of these individuals—

VENCLOVA: Yes, there are many such stories. More than half of the writers who did not emigrate suffered in one way or another. Prison and deportation were not the only possibilities: frequently one was left at large, but lived in constant fear, which often led to minor (and not so minor) compromises. For example, a son or a lover might be arrested, and the implicit price for his or her release would be to pen pro-Soviet pieces (though release did not necessarily follow). That happened to Akhmatova, and to more than one Lithuanian.

HINSEY: Was the situation for writers in Lithuania comparable to that in Russia?

VENCLOVA: Well, perhaps not. Before the war, hundreds of Russian authors, including the very best ones like Isaac Babel, were executed. This also happened after the war, though less frequently. In Lithuania, there were no executions of writers, as far as I know. Those who landed in prisons or in Siberia often survived and returned after Stalin's death. Two or three young writers joined the partisan units and perished in the forests. The biggest threat for those who did not join the partisans' ranks was not death but succumbing to abject conformism.

HINSEY: What about those teaching in the universities?

VENCLOVA: As we discussed earlier, there was only one university left in Lithuania, namely, in Vilnius. Grandfather commuted to Vilnius from Freda, but later had to move to the capital. There was a wave of professors' arrests and imprisonments in the late forties and early fifties. This took place at approximately the same time as similar events among writers, but a handful of professors were spared and did their best to uphold some of the previous teaching standards. Among these was the old historian Augustinas Janulaitis, a Social Democrat (who, by the way, had translated the Communist Manifesto into Lithuanian as early as 1904). He was critical of the regime, to put it mildly. Kazys Preikšas once said: "The only thing I cannot forgive myself for is the fact that Janulaitis died in his own bed." University chairs that fell vacant due to arrests were filled either by young conformists and informers or by hard-line Stalinist professors from Russia. One of them, as Grandfather once told me, taught Greek philosophy insisting that Plato was a materialist.

HINSEY: One can imagine the impact on the university. But what about the visual arts?

VENCLOVA: Of course, the professors were expected to teach in the Marxist vein. The older generation adapted to it with mixed success: usually, it boiled down to reciting some mantras about class struggle. I now understand that this kind of Marxism was especially irritating for old leftist intellectuals like Janulaitis.

Artists, as well as musicians and theater people, are usually of lesser concern to totalitarian governments than writers and professors. Consequently, less open persecution and fewer arrests happened in these professions. Still, the strictly Soviet style (that is, pedestrian Realism with quasi-revolutionary overtones) was promoted everywhere, and all remnants of Modernism were fiercely attacked. Aunt Maria continued to paint as she had been taught in Paris—she admired Gauguin and Bonnard—but produced one or two pieces in the official style, just in case. These canvases depicted large, nebulous blots with smaller red spots that, with a stretch of the imagination, might be taken for crowds with red flags. Petras Cvirka, who loved the Impressionists and post-Impressionists no less than she did, published a review of an exhibition in which he mildly reproached her for lagging behind in Socialist reeducation. The irony of the fact that she was publicly admonished by her own husband did not escape anyone's attention.

6

GYMNASIUM

HINSEY: Let's return to your personal experiences. Could you describe the beginning of your high school education in Vilnius?

VENCLOVA: I previously mentioned that I attended only the second grade of primary school in Freda, and then enjoyed two blessed years of idleness. As often happens under such circumstances, I learned quite a bit, including Russian as well as the rudiments of English and French. My mother tried to teach me piano, but I had no aptitude for it. Neither could I paint or draw. In time, I learned to understand and appreciate painting, but I only started to enjoy serious music later in life. The area that really interested me was literature, especially poetry.

When we moved to Vilnius, it was time for me to undertake a regular high school education. The Soviets prided themselves on mandatory secondary schooling, in contrast to bourgeois Lithuania. Actually, only a seven-year school, the so-called *semiletka*, was mandatory; after this, some continued their education for three more years (this was the ten-year school, or *desiatiletka*), while others went to vocational schools or simply joined the workforce. Since Vilnius was half-empty, secondary schools were not numerous. In the beginning, only two of them were Lithuanian and the rest Russian (later, a small number of Polish schools were also allowed). Moreover, they were not coed. Stalin eliminated coeducational schooling throughout the Soviet Union after the war, having gotten it into his head to restore the old tsarist custom of his youth. Later, this was reversed, but I graduated from a boys' school. I believe this may have resulted in some psychological damage: for a rather long time, I had very little information about girls and was shy with them (which, in turn, led to stupid escapades when I became more self-confident).

I was easily accepted into fifth grade (the first level of gymnasium, in prewar terms); the only requirement was an informal dictation test. However, this was not all that easy. Lithuanian orthography is rather complicated: most of the vowels have three variants that differ only slightly in pronunciation. Second, the dictation's subject was village life: an imaginary conversation about various agricultural tools (it was probably intended for peasant boys, and not for city dwellers like me). Anyway, I passed, and attended the school for seven years, until 1954. (Our *desiatiletka* was actually an eleven-year school since we had an additional workload in comparison to usual Soviet schools—namely, Lithuanian language and literature.)

Hinsey: Could you describe what the Vilnius high school was like at the time?

Venclova: My Freda primary school had been an unpretentious wooden building; Vilnius High School was something quite different—a stone edifice befitting a big city. It stood next to the old town hall and the very large Jesuit Church of Saint Casimir. In fact, the school occupied part of the former premises of the Jesuit monastery. A Catholic martyr and patron saint of Poland, Andrew Bobola, had lived there in the seventeenth century (he was tortured to death by the Cossacks). In the nineteenth century, the Church of Saint Casimir had been transformed into an Orthodox church under Russification: Dostoevsky prayed there when he visited Vilnius in 1867. Later, it reverted to being a Catholic church. Neither my schoolmates nor I knew anything about this. The beautiful Baroque church was closed by the Soviets and neglected; some schoolboys managed to squeeze in through its boarded-up windows in order to steal old paintings and organ pipes. Later, it became a vodka warehouse, and after that it was a Museum of the History of Religion and Atheism designed to demonstrate the pernicious role of Catholicism in Lithuanian history. The authorities didn't mention Dostoevsky or, needless to say, Saint Andrew Bobola. Today it is once again a working church, but it still is not in the best of shape.

Hinsey: And what about the monastery buildings?

Venclova: The former monastery was mainly used to house students who came from the countryside. In the thirties the Jesuits, true to their educational vocation, built a big modern annex for their classrooms. These rooms were light and spacious, with comfortable prewar desks. Very well-equipped physics and chemistry labs had also survived. There, we were shown and could ourselves conduct experiments, which were the most fascinating part of our schoolwork. Of course, the Jesuit teachers were no longer there (they had left for Poland, and some no doubt landed in Siberia). No one ever spoke about them.

I had to walk approximately two kilometers from our house to the school, as there were almost no motor cars in postwar Vilnius and almost no buses. The Church of Saint Casimir stood next to the ruins of the ghetto that I passed every morning.

HINSEY: What was the structure of the school curriculum?

VENCLOVA: The seven years I spent in high school, from 1947 to 1954, were among the worst Stalinist years. Still, I believe the school provided us with a rather adequate education. Our teachers, as a rule, were decent people— mainly middle-aged, which meant that they had been brought up in prewar Lithuania and had at least some pre-Soviet pedagogical experience. Strange as it may seem, none were arrested or deported during my school years; once, an article was published in a Vilnius newspaper denouncing one or two of them as covert bourgeois nationalists, but it didn't come to anything. Our school was one of the best in Lithuania, and maintained, to a degree, the traditions of the prewar gymnasia (a few schools in Kaunas and one or two smaller towns may have had a comparable level).

All classes were mandatory (there were no optional subjects or elective courses) and grading was generally tough. We had to learn most material without much student discussion, and sometimes by rote. Still, we were given a great deal of information—perhaps more than our Western counter- parts—and in many cases it was quite valuable. A certain balance between the hard sciences and humanities was maintained. We were expected to master math up to, but not including, calculus. I was not particularly fond of it, though generally successful. To tell the truth, I frequently neglected my math homework and cribbed it in the early morning before the lessons started from my friend Romas Katilius, a future physics professor (I'll speak much more about him later). Our math teacher was a reserved but very likable man: he encouraged me to take part in an all-Lithuanian "Math Olympics," and was genuinely disappointed when I failed (Romas, predict- ably, was the winner). I was more fascinated by physics, chemistry, and par- ticularly astronomy, which was taught during our final year. As I mentioned, the students all loved conducting experiments; I even tried to set up a chem- istry laboratory at home. There, I produced hydrogen from sulfuric acid and filled small balloons with it, which was a dangerous procedure. Incidentally, the balloons were actually condoms, the main purpose of which was some- what mysterious to me at the time. I also made a primitive telescope and observed a lunar eclipse through its lenses.

HINSEY: And the specifically Marxist subjects?

VENCLOVA: There were two classes of a decidedly Soviet nature. One was entitled "The Constitution of the USSR." It supposedly provided us with some Marxist ideas about society and the state, based on the notion that the Soviet Union was the freest and most humane country in the world (if the facts did not necessarily support this, so much the worse for the facts). Once, I expressed some doubt concerning the inviolability of personal correspondence and the lack of censorship in the USSR, and was ordered to leave the classroom immediately (which was a rather serious and unusual punishment). The teacher was a pitiful little man: much later, I learned he also had a sexual problem—he was an exhibitionist. It appears it wasn't all that easy to find individuals willing to teach that kind of Stalinist stuff. The other class was on Darwinism. This provided us with an introduction to natural selection, the origin of species, and so on, but the bulk of the class was devoted to the denunciation of "bourgeois genetics" and praise for the so-called Michurin-Lysenko doctrine.

HINSEY: This was one of Stalin's typical intrusions into scientific life—

VENCLOVA: Yes, in 1948, the self-taught Soviet agronomist Trofim Lysenko attacked several pillars of world biology, namely, Mendel, Weismann, and Morgan (their names sounded suspiciously Jewish) for their theory of heredity, and proposed his own unorthodox theory based on research that was later exposed as fraudulent. He claimed Ivan Michurin, an amateurish Russian biologist, as his immediate predecessor. Lysenko's theory was positively crazy (he insisted, for example, that it was possible to transform one species of bird into another by feeding it a specific sort of caterpillar), but he managed to persuade Stalin that his ideas were a panacea for the numerous ills of Soviet agriculture. What followed was essentially a repetition of the Akhmatova-Zoshchenko case, but in biology. Lysenko's opponents were purged, and every Soviet schoolboy and schoolgirl was forced to learn his nonsensical fabrications. (After Stalin's death, Lysenkoism was rejected and the science of genetics was reinstated, but not immediately, since Khrushchev was also fascinated by Lysenko's ideas.) My friend Romas, in protest against the insane material he was fed in his school years, later became seriously interested not only in physics but also in genetics.

HINSEY: What about language instruction?

VENCLOVA: Essentially, we studied two languages, Lithuanian and Russian. Every day, we attended a Russian class, though all other subjects were taught in our native tongue. After graduation, we were expected to speak, read, and write Russian as fluently as Lithuanian (there was a term for it—Russian had to become our "second native language"). Most of us achieved that level of fluency, especially since Russian was ubiquitous in the streets of Vilnius, and almost everyone had Russian acquaintances (who rarely, if ever, learned Lithuanian). In Latvia and Estonia, as well as in Poland, Russian was generally boycotted by the local people, who did not bother to learn it. But that was not the case in Lithuania. I don't think this was due to a lack of patriotism—many Lithuanians were passionately nationalistic: the resistance simply took place on a deeper level. That said, there was certainly ambivalence here as well. Russian was disliked, and even despised by some, as the language of the occupying power, but it also opened broader vistas. In any case, that was my point of view.

We did not have much linguistic instruction aside from these two languages. Latin, which had been fairly common in pre-Soviet Lithuanian gymnasia, was eliminated. Essentially the only admissible Western European language was English (French, German, and Spanish were present in some schools instead of English, but this was infrequent). However, it was taught in a very elementary and superficial way. This is hardly surprising, since it was the language of Churchill and Truman, that is, of world imperialism: one had to obtain some knowledge of the enemy's linguistic tools, but without overdoing it. We called our English teacher "Mary." She was a fairly young lady who did her best to look fashionable; most of the boys, therefore, were interested in her more from a sexual, than a pedagogic, point of view. These lessons were responsible for my rather miserable knowledge of English, which improved only after I had emigrated. The crowning achievement of the course was reading an English translation of Comrade Stalin's speech for the thirtieth anniversary of the October Revolution. Mary also taught us to sing English songs: that was a popular pastime, but not for me since I had no musical ability.

HINSEY: You have spoken about Russification and Sovietization in the curriculum. What were the other signs of them?

VENCLOVA: We haven't yet discussed the geography and history classes; these are important subjects, since they provide one with an understanding of the fundamental categories of space and time. I had loved geography from early childhood, when I studied my godfather's globe. For instance, I knew the names of almost all the world capitals by heart. In school, geography was taught by Šimonis, a high-spirited instructor with a good sense of humor. (It was he who was denounced in the newspaper as a member of a prewar paramilitary organization.) He shared with us extensive information about islands, mountains, and waterfalls, but I understood that all of this was off-limits for a person living in the USSR. Later, we studied mainly Soviet, that is, Russian geography.

As for history—we had to learn something about ancient Egypt, Greece, and Rome. The textbook on Roman history made for informative and interesting reading—Julius Caesar, Augustus, and Caligula thereafter became household names for me. (Almost all the textbooks were translated from Russian, which does not mean they were uniformly bad.) Medieval history was rather boring, in part because the authors of the textbook did their best to pass over Christianity in silence or to denigrate it. Modern history consisted mainly of chapters on Marx, Engels, and the Paris Commune (well, the freedom-loving Jacobins with their guillotine were also mentioned). Yet all that was nothing in comparison with the large three-volume *History of the USSR*. For all practical purposes, this meant the history of Russia, even if it began in Urartu—a primordial ancient kingdom situated in today's Armenia that used cuneiform writing. This three-volume set has remained in my memory as one of the nightmares of my early teens. It was cultural imperialism at its worst. Moreover, the image of Russia that emerged from these pages was far from attractive: a despotic, aggressive, stagnant, and isolated country that for some reason insisted on its noble mission. (Geographically, it was also rather inhospitable—flat, cold, and monotonous.) We had to learn by heart the names and deeds of virtually all Russian rulers, military commanders, and leaders of peasant uprisings, who were indistinguishable from one another. Then came the October Revolution, the Civil War, industrialization, and collectivization, again with hundreds of names (except, of course, those of Trotsky and Bukharin), dates, percentage points, and so on. During the final examination, everybody was expected to demonstrate a good knowledge of all three volumes. It was a horror, pure and simple.

Since Lithuania was now only a small part of a larger whole, its geography and history did not merit much detailed treatment. Still, some of our teachers attempted to give us at least an idea of the country in which we lived, with its unique past and complicated identity. We had no knowledge of the prewar textbooks, which were strictly banned, but a female teacher of ancient and medieval history orally dictated an entire course about Lithuania. It took several months, and the very fact of doing it most likely put her in a precarious position (she obviously used a forbidden book by Adolfas Šapoka as her source). Only later, when I was already at university, Lithuanian history was formally reintroduced into the high school curriculum, and short textbooks appeared, written in lame Marxist discourse.

HINSEY: What about the teaching of literature?

VENCLOVA: Homer, Ovid, Shakespeare, and Goethe were omitted (later, elements of world literature in translation were included in the curriculum). I knew something about them thanks to my father and his library, but that was far from the general rule. Instead, we had to study the principal Russian authors, and twice at that: first in Lithuanian translation and then, during our Russian lessons, in the original. To tell the truth, this was not so bad: one cannot be harmed by Pushkin or Leo Tolstoy. Still, names such as Dostoevsky were excluded, to say nothing of Akhmatova or Pasternak (although we were expected to know Comrade Zhdanov's unforgettable speech). On the other hand, we read certain minor writers without whom one could get along perfectly, such as the eighteenth-century classics Radishchev and Karamzin, significant for specialists but rather unreadable nowadays. The Soviet authorities, of course, were not primarily interested in broadening our literary horizons, but in watering down our Lithuanian (and non-Soviet) identity. They were not very successful, due to the efforts of our teachers and the fact that Lithuanian literature was also taught—and not without patriotic fervor—during our Lithuanian lessons.

HINSEY: What about the banned authors we have previously discussed?

VENCLOVA: All the émigré authors, such as Krėvė and Radauskas, became "unpersons" and could not even be mentioned. The same fate befell writers who were imprisoned or deported, like Boruta. The classics of the previous centuries were not necessarily banned: Donelaitis and Maironis, just like Pushkin and Tolstoy, were still in print, although the print runs were limited. Some of them—perhaps even most—could be interpreted as representing progress, in other words, as supporting the Soviet side. Was it not true that Donelaitis praised serfs and exposed the vices of the aristocrats (those very German aristocrats who were the predecessors of Nazism)? Of course, overtly religious or anti-Russian (that is, anti-tsarist) authors and texts were strictly forbidden. Almost all of the Lithuanian classics were published with excisions (inclusions could happen as well, though rarely). Still, they were included in the curriculum, and we could acquaint ourselves with approximately half of our native literature.

We were lucky to have an honest and sensitive Lithuanian teacher, Bronė Katinienė. She was also our preceptor. As a maternal figure who had been educated before the Soviet period, she could be trusted in any complicated situation—and one never lacked for such occasions in Stalinist times. Moreover, she possessed an ear for literature, and especially its moral dimensions. (I had the good fortune to meet her again, when she was quite elderly, on my first return trip to Vilnius after emigrating.) She did her utmost when teaching Lithuanian authors; she explained their historical context as clearly as possible under Soviet circumstances, and above all, she gave us a feeling for their unique literary qualities and talents. To the best of her ability, she also attempted to avoid all propaganda. True, she had to teach, for example, the mediocre pro-Soviet poems of Vytautas Montvila, a minor leftist writer executed by the Nazis, and a long poem about the blessings of collectivization by Teofilis Tilvytis. But she concentrated her efforts on old Lithuanian classics, as well as on Nėris and Cvirka, who were highly talented. During her classes, and also outside of them, I repeated hundreds of poetic lines in my native language. As my school years passed, I became acutely aware that these lines in Lithuanian actually represented the sphere in which I felt most at home. As graduation neared, I already knew that the most natural choice for me at university would be to study Lithuanian literature.

HINSEY: In some of your essays and interviews you also mention the impact of Mikhail Schneider's teaching of Russian literature—

VENCLOVA: Mikhail Schneider was an exception among our teachers since he was young, Jewish, and Russian-speaking. I know nothing about his personal history. Most probably, he was not a survivor of the ghetto, but had come to Lithuania from Moscow or St. Petersburg (Leningrad at the time). Previously, we had had several teachers of Russian literature, but none of them had been particularly successful. But Mikhail Izraelevich (we addressed him by his patronymic, according to the Russian custom) was a born pedagogue: an inspired orator, a sharp connoisseur of letters, and a man of strong and independent opinions. At first, we used to call him "Pushkin" among ourselves (he looked a bit similar to the great poet; moreover, he sported Pushkinian sideburns). But later we began to respect him to such a degree that he became our only teacher who was not given a nickname. His task was rather unrewarding—he had to teach us Soviet literature, which according to the textbook consisted of four authors: Maxim Gorky, Vladimir Mayakovsky, Mikhail Sholokhov, and Aleksandr Fadeyev. As far as I remember, he skipped the notorious Socialist Realist Fadeyev altogether, addressed Gorky and Sholokhov in a cursory fashion, and concentrated on Mayakovsky, who was, say what you will, a powerful and innovative poet. His discussion of Mayakovsky brought into our classroom, although in a roundabout way, the entire range of world and Russian Modernism. Mikhail Izraelevich taught us to enjoy the very texture of Mayakovsky's language, its strangeness, its shocking imagery, and provocative humor. I fell in love with Mayakovsky so deeply that I translated into Lithuanian his long poem "A Cloud in Trousers," arguably the best of his prerevolutionary works. The translation, my first poetic undertaking—if one does not count childish doggerel—was of course horrible, and, thank

God, it did not survive. (A translation by a professional Lithuanian poet was printed shortly thereafter, but it also did not do justice to the original, to put it mildly.) I read Mayakovsky's entire collected works in Russian.

HINSEY: However, you have said that you noticed that something was amiss with the poems—

VENCLOVA: Yes, in the process of reading, I was struck by an unusual fact: although Mayakovsky was rightly famous as the foremost Russian master of rhyme, some of his lines did not rhyme at all and looked somewhat truncated. Much later, I found out that the names of purged Communists, such as Trotsky and Zinovyev, had been expunged from his poems (and Mayakovsky, as a rule, used to place them in a rhyming position in his line for the sake of emphasis). On the other hand, he mentioned many poets about whom I knew next to nothing: Blok, Esenin, Pasternak, Khlebnikov, and others. From his comments in verse, one might deduce that these were definitely poets of interest. I decided to look into their work and was happy to find all of them in Father's library. For a time, I liked Esenin, a peasant poet whose slightly kitsch but moving verses about love and alcohol were virtually banned, yet known by heart by many in Russia. Soviet critics denounced them as the very epitome of decadence, which was obviously an overstatement. (Esenin had a rather strong influence on interwar Lithuanian poetry.) As for Pasternak, I did not grasp him at all on first reading, although I knew that I had encountered something extremely powerful. I only managed to fully understand him at university and, from that time on, could not live without his verse.

Thus Mikhail Izraelevich opened up totally new vistas for me, and for some of my friends—including Romas Katilius—albeit somewhat indirectly. As it turned out, our good teacher was a naive and relatively helpless man in everyday life. Many years after my graduation, he left for Israel, but could not find a teaching position and made his living as a night watchman until his death. He wrote to me once or twice, describing his hopeless battle with the Israeli musical establishment, which refused to play Wagner (whom he loved and did not consider a precursor of Nazism).

HINSEY: What were the personal dynamics of your everyday school life?

VENCLOVA: I was one of the top students, partly because I possessed an innate curiosity for almost everything in the world, and partly because I had grown up in an intellectual household. But I wasn't particularly macho, and failed miserably at sports like soccer, which my schoolmates played, as well as at the gym classes we attended once or twice a week. This was a constant source of despair, since the other boys made fun of me—and I was a proud, even vainglorious person. During my university years, I did my best to improve my physical abilities: I practiced canoeing and mountain climbing, I hitchhiked throughout the Soviet Union, and so on, but I was only partially successful. I was also far from the top of my class when it came to music and drawing, which made my grade average a bit uneven. My schoolmates were from varied backgrounds: some came from the so-called intelligentsia, that is, from the families of teachers, doctors, engineers, or civil servants; others had grown up in a blue-collar milieu. There was one additional difference between them: the Lithuanian-speaking intelligentsia had generally moved to Vilnius from Kaunas after the war, just as our family had, yet working-class boys were usually locals, and their Polish was as good as their Lithuanian, if not better. In short, it was a mixed bag: habits, manners, and previous levels of education diverged greatly, sometimes wildly.

In the beginning, I was generally disliked by the other schoolboys and felt rather unhappy and lonely (even though I managed to make a friend or two—initially, as it turned out, among the working-class boys). The main reason for this was my background. Father was a well-known figure, who belonged to the Soviet establishment, and the Soviets were almost universally hated. Against a backdrop of prevailing poverty, our living conditions were also relatively comfortable (the intelligentsia were, as a rule, impoverished by the new regime). Further, top students are rarely popular. Politically, I was also very naive—but I will explain more about that later. My precociousness (I was the youngest boy in my group), combined with nervousness and stupid bouts of arrogance, did the rest.

HINSEY: But then there was a change in your situation—

VENCLOVA: Yes, in my third year of high school, I underwent an appendectomy that proved rather difficult and I was laid up for a couple of months. Around that time, my relations with my classmates had reached their lowest point. But I had a friend across the street, Virgilijus Noreika, who was more or less my age and attended the same school, but in a parallel group (every grade was divided into several such groups—for example, 7a, 7b, 7c, etc.). He came from a blue-collar family and had great musical and theatrical talent. He later became an opera singer, the best in Lithuania and one of the best in the USSR. He was also quite good-natured and used to accompany me to school, since walking proved rather difficult before I had fully recovered. One day, he suggested that I join his school group where, according to him, there was a much friendlier atmosphere. He succeeded in persuading my parents, and after some bureaucratic paperwork, I found myself among a new group of boys who were generally more mature and sympathetic. My new classmates decided that I could not be held responsible for my father's position, and gradually learned to pardon the less pleasant aspects of my character. To begin with, there was still some friction, but I soon fit into the new milieu perfectly; in my final high school years, I became one of the group's leaders. Another leader was Romas Katilius, who was not just a top student but a born moderator.

Our school, as I have said, was for boys only. The feminine world seemed very enigmatic to me for a rather long time (this was aggravated by the fact that I did not have any sisters). Not very far away, there was a Lithuanian girls school, named after Salomėja Nėris: from time to time, there were common gatherings, festivals, and dancing parties held under strict teacher supervision. Of course, hormones did their work. As in every school, scraps of sexual information circulated, and rough sexual jokes were quite common. In those chaotic postwar years, mores proved fairly loose. More than one among us became initiated early enough, yet this was not my case: I lost my virginity later than I would have liked. We knew about homosexuality, but, as far as I know, no one in our group (and even in the entire school) was gay. It seems everyone dreamed exclusively about girls. Well, no doubt homosexual relationships did exist, but these would have been kept completely secret, not only out of fear of ostracism, but because there was the very real threat of criminal punishment. Two or three well-known Lithuanian intellectuals were gay, but this fact was never made public.

HINSEY: You have said that at this time you were politically naïve—

VENCLOVA: Even though I knew about the deportations and a number of the system's other ugly traits, I tended to believe it was generally good, and promoted equality, the brotherhood of peoples and so on. The deportations stopped or, in any case, abated around 1950. The partisan war was also starting to die out at approximately the same time. I was sure the Red Army was a liberating force, and that the Communist future would be beneficial for all mankind. This kind of thinking was sustained not only by the ever-present propaganda but also by my father (he may have had his doubts, but never shared them with me, since he understood very well that that would have been extremely dangerous).

In all this, I was an exception among my friends and schoolmates. Nearly all of them considered the system to be cruel and hostile, but they very rarely (if ever) discussed this openly. Well, I was not totally alone. I have mentioned Aleksandras Štromas, a survivor of the Kaunas ghetto, who much later became a close friend. He was a believer in Communism until Stalin's death.

There may have been intellectuals who perceived some truth in Marxism, or at least saw some raison d'être in the shakeout that was going on. But most inhabitants of Lithuania did not believe a word of the propaganda, and just tried to conform to save themselves and their families. In private, they may have told jokes about Communism and expressed their hatred of it, but in Stalin's lifetime this was strictly limited to whispers. Most of those on the right—as well as on the left—secretly regretted Lithuania's loss of independence, and many were privately indignant about the coercive atheism. Many also mourned the deportees and the dead partisans. Countless lives were ruined, purely and simply. Lots of Lithuanians also dreamed of liberation by the Western powers (who, for some unknown reason, did not seem to be in a hurry to help). But informers were always nearby, so one had to conceal such resentments and dreams.

Later, things started to change. Jokes became more frequent, and hatred less concealed, yet everyone understood that the regime was there to stay. Therefore, one had to express one's loyalty on all possible occasions if one was to advance (which is to say, attain a slightly more adequate standard of living for oneself and one's children). Fear was replaced by cynicism. Moreover, there was something that could, by many, be construed as positive: namely, social mobility. People who would never have risen from the bottom of prewar Lithuanian (or Polish) society could now obtain an education—albeit a flawed one—and embark on a career. Of course, such a career involved high moral costs and had fairly well-defined limits, but it was a career all the same.

In the middle of all this, there was me: a true believer who considered Comrade Stalin a very great man (perhaps not the greatest man of all times, but a warrior of genius, the victor over Nazism, and a likable "Uncle Joe"), and who sobbed sincerely on the morning when the radio announced the untimely death of the Leader. I was sixteen at the time, and in my penultimate year of high school.

HINSEY: This might be a moment to speak about the mechanisms of political indoctrination—

VENCLOVA: Yes, of course. All the media and most of the books were full of it. You know that I was an avid reader from early childhood; now, much of my reading consisted of Soviet books for young people (usually translated from Russian or in the Russian original), which did their best to instill the correct Weltanschauung. Some were rather primitive, but others were more sophisticated. For instance, Arkady Gaidar, a master stylist, created in his stories a rather fanciful world of brave and honest people who fulfilled their duties toward the motherland and all of mankind with Romantic enthusiasm and a healthy sense of humor. These duties included helping old people, caring for abandoned children, being loyal to one's friends, facing criminals fearlessly, and so on. And even if his stories were clearly didactic and depicted the USSR in an attractive light, Gaidar never stooped to cheap propaganda—one could not even find Stalin's name in his writings, which was a rare exception. (Gaidar's grandson Yegor became prime minister of Russia during perestroika, and left his mark on that period.) Many books depicted resistance to the Nazis and the struggle of Soviet partisans as adventure stories. More frequently than not, they were quite readable and were a substitute for cowboy novels and whodunits from the West (these were generally unavailable, though some prewar editions clandestinely circulated in our school, in very worn-out copies).

In school, propaganda seeped not just into classes such as "The Constitution of the USSR," but into virtually every lesson, be it literature, history, languages, or even physics. We were taught that Soviet science was the best in the world. Further, Stalin fought cosmopolitanism by encouraging Russian patriotic pride, which meant that all significant technical innovations were proclaimed to be the work of Russian scientists (the electric bulb was allegedly invented by Lodygin five years before Edison, the radio by Popov a month or two before Marconi). Here, much depended on our teachers. Bronė Katinienė and Mikhail Schneider knew how to avoid propaganda: from time to time, they paid the necessary tribute to it, but managed to convey to us that they viewed it with more than a grain of salt. As for Lodygin and the other claims, the idiocy was only too obvious. Still, the endless repetition of certain ideas and sentences produces results—one did not necessarily believe them, but mastered the art of repeating them when required.

HINSEY: And there were the youth organizations dedicated to indoctrination—

VENCLOVA: At the age of seven, everyone was expected to join the Young Pioneers (I did so in Vilnius, since it was not yet mandatory in Kaunas immediately after the war). This children's organization was patterned after the Boy Scouts, but came with more than a modicum of Soviet ideology. We had to wear red neckerchiefs (which was rather festive); it was explained to us that the three corners represented the Communist Party, the Young Communist League, and our own Young Pioneer organization, which would prepare us for the next two stages of ideological maturity. With our red bandanas around our necks, we attended meetings, celebrated revolutionary anniversaries, staged anti-imperialist plays, arranged readings of Soviet poetry, and so on (I read Salomėja Nėris's paean to Stalin on one such occasion). There was much drumming and bugle playing in a rather Fascist style. I even made a sort of a career in the organization by becoming a company, and later a brigade, "leader" (all Young Pioneers in a school made up a brigade, which was then divided into companies, and these, in turn, into teams, each with its leader). To tell the truth, my duties as leader were next to nonexistent: on one occasion I was asked to report on any schoolboys who attended church but, thank God, I failed to fulfill this request. There were summer camps where Young Pioneers learned survival skills and prepared for military service more or less in the same spirit as the Boy Scouts. The most famous camp, Artek, was in Crimea, in a very beautiful southern setting. But I was never sent to any such camp, even if I had no objections to visiting Crimea or the like.

The next stage for young people was the Young Communist League, which one joined at fourteen (therefore, I did so in 1951). Whereas membership in the Young Pioneers was, for all intents and purposes, mandatory, here some exceptions—though infrequent—were possible. A person whose relatives were subject to repression might be considered unworthy, and a very stubborn person could avoid enlisting, though this might seriously harm his or her prospects. But I do not remember any such cases: our entire group became *komjaunuoliai* (Young Communists, *komsomoltsy* in Russian), which did not mean, however, that we succumbed to the system in full. Notwithstanding the Orwellian reputation of the organization, membership was rather a formality. Not everyone in it believed in Communist ideology or prepared themselves for a party career. Romas Katilius, Virgilijus Noreika, and other decent fellows were *komjaunuoliai*, like everyone else. At the Young Communist meetings, real problems of the group and school life were sometimes discussed and solved, as might happen in a Western high school or college. After graduating, none of us chose studies or jobs connected to politics. Most decided to study geology—a vocation that was about as far from Communist ideology as possible.

Nevertheless, the purpose of the league was indoctrination. For example, it was responsible for organizing the so-called *politinformacijos*—fifteen minutes of information on current events. As far as I remember, these were usually led by a teacher who was a party member. They were highly reminiscent of Orwell's "Two Minutes Hate" in *1984*. Scorn was heaped on Truman, Churchill, de Gaulle, and especially on Tito who was considered the worst of the enemies of the people. Even before joining the league, we were ordered to study the trials of László Rajk and Trajčo Kostov (one was a Hungarian, the other a Bulgarian Communist; both showed signs of independent thinking and were duly executed). This meant that we were required to read accounts of these trials as published in the newspapers, learn the names of the accused, and summarize their alleged crimes. (It is sad to recall that my father published a poem attacking Rajk, about whom he knew next to nothing.) Our teacher emphasized that Rajk was actually *Reich*, that is, not an authentic Hungarian; I tended to think that he was German (a clandestine Nazi, perhaps?), and only understood much later that my teacher's comment was a veiled reference to Rajk's supposed Jewish background. Later, in 1952, the Slánský trial (in Czechoslovakia) was very similar to these two.

As someone who came from a literary family, I was assigned the editorship of the "wall newspaper." This was a typical Soviet enterprise for which the Young Communist League was responsible: there were short political and not-so-political articles, as well as topical satire, which imitated the official press. These were typewritten and posted on a wall under a red banner heading. I published several very bad poems there, one of them about General Cherniakhovsky, whose troops took Vilnius in 1944 and who was buried in the city's central square. (After Lithuania became independent, his remains were transferred to Russia). I believe the last issue I edited was posted in commemoration of Stalin's death. It consisted of various mournful items, most of which I concocted myself.

HINSEY: More than once you have said that you remained a "true believer" until Khrushchev's report to the Party Congress, more precisely, until the Hungarian Revolution—

VENCLOVA: My naiveté prevailed until 1956, but not without certain reservations. Even if I thought that Communism was basically a good idea, I was influenced by my friends and by the general tenor of life under Stalin. I had a strong, though mostly unarticulated, feeling that the world was out of joint— there was simply too much shabbiness, boredom, and unhappiness around me. People were poor, and most of them were obviously frightened. I tried to ascribe this to the aftermath of the recently ended war, and to consider it a temporary phase that would, in time, give way to a more satisfying life. At the outset, of course, my skepticism regarding official ideology was immature and undeveloped, but in my last years of school it became more coherent.

Nevertheless, for a certain time I was still persuaded that although terrible events had occurred, some of them surely were accidental, or even necessary in extreme situations (however sad that might be), and most, if not all, would be remedied in the near future. The Nazis, in my opinion, were the absolute evil—that was easily confirmed by my mother's experience—and victory over them redeemed virtually everything. In such views, I was heartily supported by Father, who himself no doubt attempted to reason along similar lines.

Incidentally, these justifications of Stalinism were typical not only of a Vilnius schoolboy born into a family of leftists but also of many intellectuals in Russia and the West, including Pasternak and Sartre (in Lithuania, there was a much smaller percentage of such people).

At the same time, I was disturbed by the absolute uniformity of the media, by the insanely redundant propaganda, and by a vague sense of isolation. After learning a bit about Paris, Florence, and Corsica, I dreamed of seeing Europe, but this was obviously impossible (though quite possible before the war—as I've said, my parents, Aunt Maria and Petras Cvirka had all been there more than once, even if they were leftists disliked by the prewar Lithuanian authorities). Now, Europe had become a sort of lost Atlantis or a country imagined by Jules Verne. Perhaps Western imperialism was to blame, but the very thought that I'd never be able to visit such places, no matter how hard I might try, was maddening.

HINSEY: But it wasn't just concrete places that were beyond your reach—

VENCLOVA: Yes, early enough, I understood that there were many names and events that one was expected to pass over in silence. Soon, that began to anger me as well. For instance, I discovered in Father's library a book by a Roman poet (Catullus, I believe) in Russian translation, which I started to leaf through with some interest. However, the name of the translator on the front page had been cut out with scissors, leaving a hole. In answer to my query, Father told me that he had bought the volume in this deplorable state in a Moscow bookshop during the war, and knew nothing of its origin. (Many years later, I found out that the translator, Adrian Piotrovsky, a gifted writer and stage director, had perished during the Stalinist purges, like Isaac Babel and countless others.) This turned out to be hardly an isolated case. I came to realize that I was cut off from a good half of Lithuanian and world history, and that infuriated me as much as spatial isolation. Information about the prewar period was especially scarce. Because of this, I began to suspect that the independence period was perhaps not as bad as the media insisted. Of course, there was Smetona's rightist dictatorship, but could everything be reduced to that?

One summer, we visited our old friends in Klangiai who had helped us during the war—Petras Cvirka's family and their neighbors. During the German occupation, Klangiai had remained fairly prosperous, even if it had been poorer and shabbier than villages in Southern Lithuania. Now, it was extremely run-down, and the war had played no part in that. Although there was not a famine, food was far from abundant. Some families had been deported (one had been assassinated by the partisans), and everyone else worked on a collective farm. Workers were paid according to their number of *darbadieniai*, which were assigned to them by the administration (*darbadieniai* was a bureaucratic invention meaning "workdays" but did not have much relationship to actual work). Payment, in rubles and in food, was negligible, and no one hid the fact that the new system actually amounted to serfdom. We were taught that collectivization was a blessing for the peasants, and I myself praised it in my term papers; but what if it was, after all, a failure?

HINSEY: This is when the influence of your schoolmates became especially significant—

VENCLOVA: As I have said, they rarely, if ever, openly criticized the system: everyone understood the inherent dangers of so doing. You might not necessarily be imprisoned for it, but your family might suffer. There was the very real danger of being thrown out of school, which resulted in conscription into the Soviet army—an ordeal young men did their absolute best to avoid. Also, excessively critical people were often summoned to the offices of the secret police and invited to serve as informers: it was very difficult (though not totally impossible) to reject such an offer. Perhaps my schoolmates were more open between themselves than with me, due to my social origin and generally loyal views. But in any case, they finally managed to instill a dose of skepticism into my head, which proved to be quite healthy. Besides, I learned from them (and from my parents) the essential principles of ethics: one does not denounce one's friends, or enemies, to school authorities or any other authority; one does not toady or demonstrate excessive zeal in anything; one should maintain one's dignity in all situations, however hard that might be. Actually, these were the principles of the "old bourgeois" ethics, which the new system was attempting to eliminate once and for all.

HINSEY: Here we return to a particularly important friendship that you touched on earlier—

VENCLOVA: Yes, here I come back to Romas Katilius, who has been my best friend for many years. On my very first day in the new group, I fell out with him and knocked him down, even though I was not particularly strong or combative. I did not know that he had been sick with polio in early childhood, and had some problems with his equilibrium. Consequently, I went to his flat to apologize. That day, we talked for several hours, and thereafter we began to meet for frequent talks. His parents belonged to the old Lithuanian intelligentsia (his father was a professor of mathematics, and his mother a professor of French); he himself was very gifted, well-read, and interested in everything, like myself. Our talks, which lasted for years, shaped both of our worldviews to a considerable degree. We discussed literature and physics, history and biology, morality and philosophy; if one of us managed to get hold of any new information, not easily available in school or elsewhere, he would immediately share it with the other. At the beginning of our acquaintance, Romas also considered Communism a generally sound idea, but he possessed a more developed sense of skepticism. By the last year of high school, he had definitely become a freethinker regarding political matters, which naturally had an impact on me. Once, he showed me a large volume of documents about the Soviet deportations, printed under the Nazi occupation. He had discovered it in his parents' library; it was of course a dangerous book to have in one's possession. Both of us were disgusted at the prevalence of anti-Semitism in the volume (even at an early age, we were allergic to racism and extreme nationalism), but the facsimiles of the documents themselves, alas, looked convincing.

Romas could also have easily become a philologist, but he chose to study physics as it was much less contaminated by ideology. Following his example, I toyed with the idea of choosing zoology (of all things) after graduation, but he dissuaded me. "You are born for literature, there is nothing to be done about it," he said. At university and afterward, our talks continued, as they do to this day.

HINSEY: What were the other influences that contributed to your changing worldview?

VENCLOVA: All natural life processes work against totalitarian utopias and their Weltanschauungen. For that reason, totalitarianism can never become all-pervasive (as in *1984*), even if it may go a long way toward perfection. First, there is literature. I believe one of Stalin's biggest mistakes was that he never banned non-Soviet literature altogether. Dostoyevsky, Proust, and Modernism as such were banned or at least semibanned, but Cervantes, Schiller, and Dickens were not. One could easily buy their works or read them in the library. The same was true of Pushkin and Donelaitis whom, as I have said, we studied at school. And any literature of quality sustains an antitotalitarian world outlook and antitotalitarian mores by definition.

Second, there were the movies. Joseph Brodsky once said that *Tarzan* did more to liberate the USSR than all the dissidents put together. This is basically true. The movie houses in Vilnius and elsewhere were expected to make a profit; this was next to impossible if they showed only Soviet films. (There were some good or at least popular prewar Soviet productions, but they were not particularly numerous.) This problem was solved by so-called trophy movies, that is, American, English, and other classics brought from Germany after its defeat. These movies were never advertised in the newspapers; thus, official repertories frequently listed only a few Soviet pictures shown in one or two movie houses—as if all the other cinemas had ceased to exist. This is because they were showing *Tarzan* or a film about Caribbean pirates, which created immense lines and provided marvelous opportunities for scalpers. We saw many historical films about Robin Hood, Richard III, and so on, including some that had been produced in Germany under the Nazis (for example, a movie about the Boer War saturated with anti-English propaganda). Strangely, I do not remember any Chaplin or Greta Garbo films. But the ones we saw provided us with a taste of a different life. Of course, jazz was also very significant in this respect, but this happened later: during the Stalinist period, it was practically nonexistent.

And then there was the city of Vilnius. In my last years at school, I began to understand and savor its beauty. It remained partly ruined and quite neglected. Its newer part was made up of nondescript streets, abject buildings, and primitive industrial enterprises, some of which became military factories called "post boxes" (they did not possess a regular address, just a PO number). Soon, three radio towers were also installed in that part of town, which dominated the entire skyline: their primary function was to jam the radio broadcasts of Voice of America, the BBC, and Vatican Radio, not to mention Radio Free Europe. On the main street stood a monument to the aforementioned General Cherniakhovsky, and soon a statue of Lenin was erected as well. Allegedly, there were plans to change the name of Vilnius to Cherniakhovsk, but in the end they were rejected: the name was given to the former German city of Insterburg, which bears it to this day. Yet Vilnius's old downtown retained much of its grace, once praised by Mickiewicz and Miłosz. For me, the city became an enigmatic sign that spoke of another—and better—reality. True, around three-quarters of the churches had been closed, the ghetto had been razed, and the Three Crosses—a large white monument on the hill next to the castle—was blown up one night in 1950. But the downtown cityscape was nearly intact, at least for the time being (luckily, it survived the entire Soviet period). I also traveled with my father to small Lithuanian towns, which had lost a large number of their prewar populations, but which were still a testament to a unique and beautiful world.

7

ANTANAS VENCLOVA

HINSEY: Let's begin by discussing your father's responsibilities from 1945 to 1954—

VENCLOVA: My father had no formal duties except being a member of the Supreme Soviet: this meant he made frequent trips to Moscow, where the MPs unanimously voted for all laws proposed by the Kremlin. However, he was a freelance writer of official stature. His friends Salomėja Nėris and Petras Cvirka had died immediately after the war. Cvirka's death in 1947 was a particular blow to our family—he had been very close to us for many years, and he succumbed to a heart attack at the young age of thirty-eight. (There were attempts to link his death to the notorious "Doctor's Plot," but these were unsuccessful. Today, some say he was murdered by Stalinist Bolsheviks, but I consider this an unfounded rumor.) Cvirka was adored by a large part of the general public, and therefore his death and funeral were memorable events in postwar Lithuania. After Nėris and Cvirka passed away, my father became perhaps the most visible author in Lithuania, although he was never as popular as his friends, and also of lesser talent (a fact of which he was well aware). There were famous living writers from the older generation—Sruoga, Mykolaitis-Putinas, Vienuolis—but they had to be "reeducated," whereas he was a loyal party member.

HINSEY: What was your father's literary production during this period?

VENCLOVA: As I mentioned, a book of his poetry had appeared in the immediate postwar period, written in Russia during the war. The poems were by and large nostalgic, and often did not contain any Soviet ideology. He edited the collected works of Cvirka and Nėris and certain Lithuanian classics; in addition, there was his translation of *Eugene Onegin*. However, in 1947 or 1948, he was publicly accused of following the "single stream theory" (which had qualified all classics as uniformly progressive—whereas, according to the authorities, many were now seen as reactionary and had to be forgotten). In addition, there had been a secret denunciation accusing him of Lithuanian nationalism. He only learned about this much later, but he had undoubtedly begun to feel an impending threat. His next several books of poetry were by and large propagandistic. They included the mandatory paeans to Lenin and Stalin, condemnatory pieces about Churchill, László Rajk, and others, as well as praise for collective farms and attacks on reactionary priests. In 1950 he also won a competition for lyrics to the Soviet Lithuanian anthem (during the war and immediately after, the old independence period anthem was played, but around 1950 this was deemed unacceptable). While my father practiced avant-garde poetics in his youth, he now wrote impeccable classical verse, which was generally preferred by the authorities, but also fit well with his taste: he was, in the deepest strata of his person, a man of order and discipline. Soon, the dark clouds that had begun gathering around him dissipated.

It is difficult and painful for me to speak about this. Father was far from the only Lithuanian writer who ascribed to Communist ideology during this period. Moreover, I think he was more sincere than most. Others mainly (though not exclusively) conformed and toadied out of pure fear, while he had already chosen a leftist worldview during Smetona's times (when it demanded a certain degree of courage). As we spoke about earlier, I frequently had the impression that he was trying to convince himself of the general soundness of the system, in the hope that it would ultimately be beneficial for his country. Of course, this required more and more self-deception with every passing year. At the same time, he never lost his faith in culture and its ability to mitigate excesses of "revolutionary" fanaticism: during our private talks, he often said that Lenin had been correct in demanding a complete knowledge of mankind's significant contributions. Father undoubtedly aided in the preservation of Lithuania's cultural heritage, particularly during the post-Stalin era—I'll talk about that later. One of his traits that appealed to me was his lack of strident nationalism: he genuinely believed in the brotherhood of all nations, no matter how hypocritical the reality of such a brotherhood was in the Stalinist USSR. This was a source of considerable friction between our family and most of the Lithuanian intelligentsia, who considered the Russians to be nothing more than cruel occupiers, and did their best to distance themselves from all non-Lithuanians.

Of course there were other reasons for my father's conformist stance. One of them, shared by almost everyone, was anxiety for the fate of one's family. Other justifications were less excusable—such as a drive for comfort or a concern for social status, even if this meant paying a hefty price and conforming to disagreeable rules (these are typical peasant traits, and Father was very much a peasant in his inner makeup). As regards some of his other choices, there is simply no excuse. But in attempting to judge such cases—which were only too numerous at that time—there are essentially two approaches. One is ethical absolutism, which leads to unconditional condemnation. The other is compassion. I can only choose compassion, and not simply because I am speaking about someone close to me. My own life took a different direction, but I cannot state with any confidence how I would have conducted myself if I were in my father's place.

HINSEY: Your father was also a well-known figure outside of Lithuania—

VENCLOVA: My father met and even made friends with many Russian writers who had chosen similar paths, such as Ilya Ehrenburg, Nikolai Tikhonov, and Konstantin Fedin. Most of these relationships dated back to the war or even before (Tikhonov, a gifted if conformist poet, had visited independent Lithuania in the thirties). Father spoke Russian well and felt rather at home in Moscow and Leningrad where the atmosphere, however stifling, was somewhat less provincial than in Lithuania. Once, during my high school years, my mother and I traveled to Moscow: Father was staying there for several weeks and we simply missed him. That was my first airplane trip, which made a strong impression on me; we flew for four hours at a rather low altitude. I also visited Leningrad and immediately fell in love with it, which was—and is—the common reaction of nearly all newcomers. It was very different from Vilnius—immense, built on an ideally flat surface, cut in two by a mighty river, full of Classical palaces and gold-domed churches. Father showed me places mentioned in his favorite works by Pushkin—*Eugene Onegin* and *The Bronze Horseman*—which we both knew by heart. He also took me to a boulevard described in *Crime and Punishment*, thus providing me with an incentive to read it, which was far from recommended at school.

HINSEY: Your father's position allowed him to travel—

VENCLOVA: Even in Stalinist times, Father was allowed to visit Eastern European countries (though, of course, not Western ones). That was a rare privilege, and was partly due to the fact that he knew German and French (an exception among Soviet writers) and therefore could communicate with European fellow travelers. Neither Mother nor I could ever hope of accompanying him. Just after the war, he visited Berlin, which he remembered from the prewar years, and which now lay in ruins; also Prague and Vienna, which had been taken by Soviet troops but were almost intact. Later, Stalin encouraged the so-called peace movement, which provided ample opportunities for denouncing America and the West while at the same time preparing for the new war that the Politburo considered inevitable. Father became heavily involved in this movement, just like his Muscovite friends Ehrenburg and Tikhonov (this was perhaps due, in part, to some of his pacifist writings from the thirties). He attended Peace Congresses in the Polish cities of Wrocław and Warsaw, and met Pablo Picasso. Among the modest gifts he brought me from abroad was a booklet with the signatures of the famous participants of the Wrocław Congress, Picasso foremost among them.

HINSEY: Wasn't your father responsible for preserving the memory of Thomas Mann in Lithuania?

VENCLOVA: In May 1955—my first year at university—Father was sent to Weimar, in the Soviet-occupied zone of Germany, to represent the USSR at Friedrich Schiller's 150th anniversary. Thomas Mann came to the festivities. He had some ties with Lithuania: as I have previously mentioned, in 1930–32, he vacationed with his entire family in the village of Nida (Nidden), not far from Klaipėda. Seated next to Mann at the official dinner, Father took the liberty of inviting him to Lithuania, "where his old house awaited him." A visit by Mann to the USSR at that time would have had strong political overtones; therefore his answer was noncommittal, although he was rather touched by the proposal. After returning to Lithuania, Father discovered that Mann's house was in very bad shape and was actually being used as an unofficial outhouse. He addressed a request to the Soviet Lithuanian government for immediate repairs, which were done. Thomas Mann never came (he died in August of the same year in Switzerland), but his house was transformed into a small museum, which it has remained. Nida is an unusual place with high sand dunes, as popular today with German tourists as it was in Mann's time. The Thomas Mann House now regularly holds conferences and concerts.

HINSEY: During this period your father also traveled to China—

VENCLOVA: In the fall of 1954, Father visited China, which was in its initial stages of Maoist transformation and was considered "an eternal friend of the USSR." He brought home a fragment of the Great Wall, and wrote an entire book about his journey, which had taken him from Beijing to Guangzhou. He made friends with some Chinese people (fifty years later, I encountered people in China who still remembered him). As for Western countries, he only visited Sweden and Iceland, and that was much later. But he frequently traveled to other Soviet Republics, in particular to Ukraine and to the most colorful parts of the USSR—Georgia and Armenia. My mother could accompany him on these journeys. I went with him once to Kyiv, Odessa, and Crimea. The trips were officially dubbed missions to "consolidate the brotherly ties between Soviet nations." In reality, this was tourism supplemented by meetings with local writers, which were not entirely devoid of purpose. Many Ukrainian, Georgian, and other authors—and here we are speaking not only about Soviet literature but also the classics—were translated at that time into Lithuanian, and vice versa. I still believe this was useful work. All non-Russian republics experienced the same problems as Lithuania, including that of ethnic survival, so one might say this reflected shared interests. On the other hand, it was a part of the great and sustained Soviet campaign to shift Lithuania's cultural orientation away from Western Europe and toward Eurasia.

HINSEY: You have frequently mentioned the role of your father's library in your development. What was the scope of his collection?

VENCLOVA: At that time, there were probably only two private libraries of consequence in Vilnius: one belonged to Kostas Korsakas, a Marxist literary critic (a sort of Lithuanian György Lukács and a former member of the *Trečias Frontas* group), and the other was my father's. The latter was not very large—around three thousand volumes, I suppose—but it contained many of the principal works of Lithuanian and world literature, as well as a number of rarities. Father's prewar library survived only in part. He supplemented it with books bought in Moscow during the war, and continued to visit secondhand bookshops in Vilnius and Kaunas, which for a time sold literature that was "suspect" from a Soviet point of view. Many members of the intelligentsia had reasonably good libraries, but at the height of Stalinism most of them destroyed anything that might cause them trouble. Neither Father nor Korsakas—whose library was much more extensive—did this. Both believed that their official standing protected them from searches (this may well have been an incorrect assumption, but nevertheless their libraries were spared).

Father's collection filled his workroom, and surrounded his desk on all sides except one. It overflowed into other rooms as well, including my bedroom. There was a small rotating bookstand on his desk with books for everyday use—the most visible of which was a one-volume Larousse encyclopedia brought from Paris in the thirties. Several lower cabinets remained locked, since they contained books my parents deemed unfit for a child, but over time I learned how to open these as well. There was a clay figurine of Bernard Shaw on one shelf, tattered portraits of Baudelaire and Edgar Allan Poe cut out of an old magazine from Father's student years, and a yellowing vertical sheet of paper depicting Pushkin's monument in Moscow. Father had saved it from

1937, the centennial year of the Russian poet's death (and, incidentally, the year of my birth). All this is still in our old Vilnius flat, where Father's study has been preserved, and during visits to Lithuania I can see it as it was at that time. My father's library looked a bit chaotic; in fact, it was well-organized. Books were shelved according to language and in chronological order, as well as by subject matter; therefore it was easy to find whatever one was interested in. The only small problem was that sometimes, due to a lack of space, books were shelved two deep. Also, many of them were in German and French, languages I could not yet read (with the help of the Latin taught to me by my grandfather, I later learned to understand French, but never really mastered German). There were practically no books in English, as this was a language that my father did not speak, but Shakespeare, Dickens, Thomas Hardy, Mark Twain, and others (even Chaucer and Smollett) were amply represented in adequate Russian translations. Most of the books were either in Lithuanian or Russian, languages that I could easily read.

HINSEY: In what specific ways did this collection influence your thinking?

VENCLOVA: Before entering university I was already acquainted with world literature from nearly all periods, and had developed a feeling that it was a sort of living organism, where the individual parts influenced each other and could not exist in isolation. This concept of culture as an organic and constantly evolving unity was perhaps the most precious part of my early education. For some reason, I was especially interested in ancient and medieval authors. These were present in Father's library in solid scholarly editions, mainly put out by the prewar Soviet publishing house Academia. For some time, Academia was headed by Lev Kamenev, a well-known Communist leader and one of the first victims of the Stalinist purges. Kamenev was, of course, a typical Bolshevik, but nevertheless he had relatively broad intellectual horizons, and many less than politically "reliable" translators and scholars (including, for example, the aforementioned Piotrovsky) found temporary employment under his wing. Of course Academia was destroyed by Stalin, and most of its contributors were imprisoned or executed, but the books were generally available in Moscow bookshops where Father used to purchase them. I believe that my interest in mythology and a certain fondness for Classical imagery, perceptible in some of my verses, date from these volumes, a tendency later reinforced by Osip Mandelstam.

Chronologically, my knowledge of world literature ended more or less with Nietzsche, Ibsen, Maeterlinck, and Chekhov. The Modernists were less present (Father possessed the first volume of Proust in Russian translation, a book of Hemingway's stories, and poems by Rilke, but that was about all). Excerpts from Joyce, T. S. Eliot, and their contemporaries had appeared in Russian before the war, but these were soon suppressed and removed from libraries or, at best, kept under lock and key. In the thirties, Juozas Miltinis, the stage director, had translated some stories from *Dubliners* into Lithuanian, and Juozas Keliuotis had promoted Kafka, yet these attempts had by and large been forgotten. In any case, Father's library did not contain these works, and he himself was not particularly interested in them.

HINSEY: What about the visual arts?

VENCLOVA: There were also books on the fine arts. Both my parents, partly under the influence of Aunt Maria, adored the Impressionists and the post-Impressionists, and therefore, early on I had become acquainted with Monet, Cézanne, van Gogh, and Matisse. In addition, there were two large volumes of general art history in French, bought in prewar Paris. These taught me there was a unity in the visual arts as well, similar to that of world literature.

HINSEY: This library was also important as concerns your relationship with your father—

VENCLOVA: Father did not prevent me from rummaging through his books—on the contrary, he rather encouraged it and from to time attempted to direct it. During his student years, he was very interested in François Villon and French Symbolism (he wrote a small book on Villon, with prose translations of his poems, and Symbolism was the topic of his senior thesis). Thus, he shared with me quite a bit about Villon, Baudelaire, Verlaine, and Rimbaud, and sometimes read aloud from their works in the French original, explaining the difficult points. He also recommended Whitman, who (in Russian translation) did not make a great impression on me. I remember these sessions of studying poetry with my father as moments of genuine friendship, when distinctions of age and family position did not play a significant role. At other times, our relationship could be quite tense. In my poem "For an Older Poet," I tried to convey these ambivalences; that said, as we will discuss later, the "older poet" in the poem represents not just my father, but his entire generation.

HINSEY: Would you expand on the banned books you were able to discover in your father's library?

VENCLOVA: There were quite a number. First, there were the Lithuanian émigrés: stories and historical dramas by Vincas Krėvė, poetry collections by Bernardas Brazdžionis and Jonas Aistis (two Modernists active in the thirties, who had rivaled Salomėja Nėris in popularity and influence, but who were now absolutely unmentionable), and so on. Of course, Father also kept the works of imprisoned authors like his friend Boruta. All the writers of the National Movement era, branded "reactionary" by the party, were in the library as well: for example, Adomas Jakštas, a critic of strictly Catholic persuasion, who was witty and insightful (a sort of provincial G. K. Chesterton, one might say). Incidentally, lots of authors were in the "gray zone." Although one could easily be arrested for keeping Brazdžionis, this was not necessarily the case with Jakštas. The same applied to Russian and world writers. In the case of a search, much depended on the knowledge, zeal or just whim of the officer conducting it (Viktoras Petkus, the future head of the Lithuanian Helsinki Group, was imprisoned in Stalinist times for possessing stories by the Swedish Nobel laureate Selma Lagerlöf—Nils Holgersson's trip with the wild geese and all that—which were deemed to be anti-Soviet).

In the locked cabinets, Father even kept the collected works of Smetona, Lithuania's prewar president (in the thirties, each person employed by the government, including teachers—which is to say Father as well—was required to buy them). There were also books and magazines printed during the Nazi occupation era, which, like Smetona, were totally forbidden. These were not necessarily just Nazi materials. There was, for instance, the literary magazine *Kūryba* (Creative Work), edited by Juozas Keliuotis. Its last issue, which appeared in 1944 just before the Soviets came, was dedicated to Oscar Miłosz—and Oscar Miłosz was Jewish on his mother's side. Of course Keliuotis did not discuss Miłosz's unmentionable lineage, but to mislead the German censorship in this way was extremely dangerous. This did not help Keliuotis during Soviet times: one of the causes for his arrest was "collaboration with the Nazis." (I will come back to *Kūryba* later, since it has some relevance to my own literary life.)

HINSEY: Let's speak a bit more about this "gray zone"—

VENCLOVA: Many Russian and Western authors in Father's library belonged to the "gray zone." As for veritable "enemies of the people," there was probably only Nikolai Gumilev, Anna Akhmatova's husband, executed by the Bolsheviks in 1921. Pasternak was not expressly banned, nor was Alexei Kruchenykh, a radical Russian Futurist whom Father had met during the war and who gave him a booklet with his signature—a great and costly rarity nowadays. Strangely enough, we did not possess any of Akhmatova's books, although my father had an immense anthology of modern Russian verse, published in the twenties, which featured many of her poems (more than once, he read them aloud). From this same anthology, I was able to form my first and very vague idea of Mandelstam and Tsvetaeva. Strictly anti-Communist Western writers, such as Koestler and Orwell, were entirely absent from the library, and completely unknown. Father had heard quite a bit about Czesław Miłosz (who defected from Poland in 1951, but prior to that had been employed by the Communist diplomatic service). After I emigrated, I learned that Father's name was also not unknown to Miłosz. We did not have Miłosz's books, but other Polish authors were reasonably well-represented—classics as well as contemporary writers, some of whom, like Julian Tuwim, Father knew personally. Father spoke satisfactory Polish and could read it, and Polish was virtually a native language for my mother.

Father raised no objections if I read Krėvė or Boruta: actually, he considered it a sort of a duty. But there was a gentlemen's agreement between us that I'd remain silent about such reading outside of the house. I must confess I sometimes violated this pact (while conversing with Romas Katilius, for example). And once or twice Father scolded me when he found me putting my hands on something really dangerous.

I understood (and Father knew for sure) that Lithuanian émigrés were continuing their literary production abroad, but these works only started to leak back into Lithuania after Stalin's death, around 1957–58. At that same time, other previously unknown literature became more or less available as well.

HINSEY: Would you talk about your family's everyday life and dynamics during this period?

VENCLOVA: Let's start with the fact that in the early fifties my father became seriously ill. He was a chain-smoker who went through at least forty cigarettes a day. (This habit started during the first week of the war when he was unexpectedly separated from his family and, on top of that, survived a ten-hour bombardment in Minsk.) One day, after climbing the hill to our house, he collapsed on the entryway floor. That was a close call: he was only forty-five and he had suffered his first heart attack. At that time doctors—in the USSR in any case—had very little information about how to treat such cases. Father had to spend several months in bed virtually motionless, and to quit smoking, which he did. Thanks to Mother's care, he lived another twenty years and continued to write. Several attacks followed, and he died of a final one in 1971. He was sixty-five. Today, I am more than ten years older than he was when he died.

In my life, I have witnessed close up two cases of serious heart disease. The second was Joseph Brodsky. With an uncanny sensation of déjà vu, I observed in him the same symptoms as my father—bouts of almost unbearable chest pain, progressive shortness of breath, weakness aggravated by anxiety. Brodsky lived in the era of bypasses and transplants, thus he had a better chance of survival, but he never quit chain-smoking, however emphatically his friends, including myself, attempted to persuade him. (I never smoked—I could not find the slightest trace of pleasure in it, although I discovered the joys of drinking relatively early, and was a heavy drinker for a time.) "An ape took a stick and became a human being; then, a human being took a cigarette and became a poet," Brodsky used to say. "Well, that's bullshit," I used to counter, "Dante didn't smoke, since in his time there was no tobacco in Europe." "That is the strongest counterargument I have ever heard," Brodsky answered, "but I'm not going to quit." He died at fifty-six.

HINSEY: Did your father limit his activities because of his illness?

VENCLOVA: Yes, to a degree. He had to curtail most of his trips outside Lithuania despite the fact that he was very fond of travel: he dreamed of seeing Egypt but had to renounce this plan. Father was still an official person and, in 1954–59, chairman of the Soviet Lithuanian Writers' Union (a capacity that, by that point, had no repressive functions), and in the last years of his life he became a freelance writer once more. He wrote a propagandistic novel about the events of 1940, but also managed to produce several short stories in the vein of Thomas Mann, and a number of fairly good if traditional verses. The main character in one of his stories dies of a heart attack—and the description testifies to an intimate knowledge of the subject. Perhaps it was an attempt to cheat fate. Some (though not much) of Father's work is being reprinted in independent Lithuania, even if he is frowned upon by many because of his official political role.

HINSEY: Was he able to make his living exclusively by writing?

VENCLOVA: Lithuania is a small country with a limited market, but in Soviet times the honoraria were relatively high and food and clothing prices (though for the most part basic) were relatively low. Monthly rents were negligible, but one was usually assigned a modest apartment only after many years of standing in line. A certain number of authors were able to survive by their writing, although they were expected to pay for this with unswerving loyalty to the party. Royalties, in general, did not depend on the number of copies sold, but on the number of printed pages. If one's work was translated into Russian and published in Moscow or Leningrad, one's income could double; one might also receive royalties for translations into, say, Ukrainian, Belarusian, or Kirghiz. Those times are now remembered with nostalgia by many writers, especially the older ones. In those years, the average number of copies for a

Lithuanian book of fiction was twenty-five thousand, and for poetry, up to ten thousand copies. Many, if not all, of the books sold out quite quickly. Today, fifteen hundred copies for fiction and five hundred copies for poetry are considered a success. Virtually all authors have to look for supplementary income.

Father was a productive author, translated into Russian and other languages of the USSR; he also received the Stalin Prize in 1952 (it came in three different degrees; his was the second—Salomėja Nėris was awarded the first degree Stalin Prize posthumously). Therefore our family was quite comfortable by Soviet standards. Mother did not have a job (which was far from the rule), although she translated several books from Russian into Lithuanian and was remunerated for it. As I have said, we employed a housekeeper.

HINSEY: If I am not mistaken, your family also had a car, which was considered unusual—

VENCLOVA: For a time, we owned a car (produced, of course, in the USSR, which meant it broke down quite frequently), but after several years Father sold it, and we started to use public transportation again. A car was a rarity in Vilnius during that era, and an unquestionable mark of status. Father never learned to drive and used a driver. Father and I often visited small towns and villages in Lithuania or in its immediate vicinity, sometimes covering hundreds of kilometers on bad roads. I remember trips to Belarus's western regions. These areas were the subject of Lithuanian territorial claims before the war, something that was never forgotten, though unmentionable. Territorial problems in the USSR had supposedly been solved once and for all. In certain Belarusian villages, one could easily find Lithuanian speakers. More depressing were our trips to former East Prussia, Donelaitis's birthplace: the Kaliningrad region now lay in ruins, inhabited by a relatively small number of impoverished-looking Russian newcomers. There were also certain Lithuanian patriots who claimed this area for Lithuania, albeit discreetly—as one could be arrested for such "imperialist" sentiments. Once, our car got stuck in sand in a remote southern Lithuanian forest. This was a dangerous situation, since partisans were still active in the area (their struggle was nearing its end and, as frequently happens, they were therefore very determined). They could easily have executed a known figure from the Soviet establishment, along with his son, and probably the driver as well as an unnecessary witness. But after several hours, we managed to dig ourselves out.

HINSEY: Was your family entitled to any other privileges?

VENCLOVA: No. Only the highest echelon of the party lived totally isolated from the people. I have heard of the so-called *dvadtsatka* (the "twenty families"), who were provided with villas, servants, armed guards, chauffeured cars, and meals on the government's account, but that was not our case. There were rumors about special shops that inexpensively sold hard-to-find food and liquor, but neither my parents nor I ever saw these. Justas Paleckis, the nominal head of Lithuania, a former leftist and Communist fellow traveler whom Father knew well from the prewar period, presumably belonged to the "twenty families." Once or twice, we were invited to his house. His family lived more than comfortably, but still far from what would now be considered upper-middle-class Western standards. (His son, also named Justas, was a bit younger than me, and was sent to Moscow to study international affairs; later he was employed by the Soviet diplomatic service in Switzerland. In today's Lithuania, he is a high-ranking member of the Foreign Office.) Incidentally, my father joined the party only in 1950, at the explicit urging of Paleckis, who had already done so in 1940.

We usually spent our summers in Palanga, a Baltic Sea resort north of my native Klaipėda. This is where the prewar, as well as postwar elite used to— and still do—gather. At first, we rented an apartment there, but later Father bought a modest summer house (some private property was allowed, although it was never called "private," but rather "personal"). It was a wooden structure, and consisted of a large common room, two glass verandas, a kitchen, and a bathroom: there was also a small piece of land attached, with an apple tree and one or two pine trees. Much later, at the time of my first marriage, I used to invite my friends there when my parents were absent. Sometimes up to ten people slept in the house, but that definitely led to considerable (if merry) overcrowding. Such dachas (although, as a rule, considerably larger ones) were typical of the Soviet cultural elite—whether it was Fedin or the less-than-loyal Pasternak. But this was much less the case with Lithuanian writers: at best, they spent the summer in their native villages. Father loved Palanga dearly and felt most at ease socializing with artists, actors, and all the others who gathered there (in 1935, he had spent his honeymoon near the resort). I remember the Palanga house as fondly as Freda. This fondness may be colored by the fact that neither place belongs to my family anymore.

HINSEY: Was there any serious political debate among the members of your family?

VENCLOVA: Not until 1956. Up until that time, I tended to agree with my father in most, if not all, respects.

HINSEY: Did your family speak about your father's brother Juozas? When did you learn about his fate?

VENCLOVA: This was not an unmentionable subject, but discussion of it was generally avoided, since it wouldn't do any good. His fate and death were considered a result of force majeure. I believe we learned about his passing soon after it occurred, but the full circumstances surrounding it only became known when his family returned from Siberia. Father supported his brother's widow and daughter after they resettled in their native village. I met them there several times. They were generally silent about what they had lived through.

HINSEY: Did you ever discuss the role of the Soviet secret police?

VENCLOVA: Usually not, though I was aware of its existence. Its founder, Felix Dzerzhinsky, was inordinately praised in our school and elsewhere. He was born into the Polish gentry in the Vilnius region and spent his formative years in the city. The authorities therefore did their best to establish a cult around him, which rivaled that of Stalin. There was a memorial plaque to Dzerzhinsky, and a central street was named in his honor (ironically, its former name was Calvary Street). But I knew—and had learned from my family—that secret police informers were a less-than-praiseworthy bunch. I remember a writer named Aleksys Churginas. He was an unusual figure, a polyglot educated in France before the war, who had been close to the ruling circles of the Smetona regime. In the Soviet period, he was attacked as being a "cosmopolitan," but not too harshly, and dedicated himself to translation work (although he also wrote some propagandistic doggerel). He translated the entire *Divine Comedy* and almost all of Shakespeare's plays into Lithuanian, along with Lope de Vega, *Faust*, and so on. Many of his translations were not bad, and are still in use, especially in Lithuanian theaters. Father liked to talk with Churginas, since the man was unquestionably erudite and rather witty. But Father did not conceal his disdain when it came to light that Churginas was an informer.

HINSEY: You have just mentioned the notorious campaign against "cosmopolitanism." How did it affect Lithuania? Could you also speak a bit about how this relates to the "Doctor's Plot" that was conceived just before Stalin's death?

VENCLOVA: The campaign against "rootless cosmopolitans" began in 1948 and was, in part, a continuation of the Akhmatova-Zoshchenko case. It was also linked to the secret trial of the Jewish Anti-Fascist Committee. Thus it was largely (though not exclusively) anti-Semitic. "Cosmopolitans" had to be found in all of the republics. In Lithuania, the campaign was directed not so much against Jews, as against people of European education and outlook, regardless of their background. Therefore Churginas, who was not Jewish, found himself among the accused (his name was thought to be suspect, but his ancestry was Russian—as far as I know, he was descended from Orthodox clergy). Father avoided taking part in the campaign (to tell the truth, he was also a cosmopolitan of sorts).

In January 1953, the newspapers printed an article about a group of doctors, almost all of them Jewish, who had allegedly poisoned several high-ranking party figures and had presumably plotted to murder the Leader himself (although this was never explicitly stated). For two months, the general mood was extremely tense. There were no pogroms in Vilnius, but I remember a grim joke from the time: an individual strikes a Jew during a private quarrel, and a large crowd immediately begins to do the same. When asked to explain its aggression, the crowd answers: "Well, we thought it was already permitted." A leading Lithuanian Communist Party member (Mečys Gedvilas, if I'm not mistaken) ordered an investigation into Petras Cvirka's death, which had occurred six years earlier. People quoted his words: "We'll show these Jews how to behave." Cvirka died in a hospital, the head of which, Dr. Preisas, was Jewish, as were several of his subordinates. Luckily, all of them escaped what was no doubt imminent arrest (many years later, I met Dr. Preisas in Israel, where he had become chief of Jerusalem's health services). Two months later, Stalin died, and within a month everything was over. An announcement was published, informing the public that the doctors were innocent, and their avowals of guilt had been obtained by "inadmissible means in total violation of Soviet law."

HINSEY: It turns out that these events reflected internal power struggles—

VENCLOVA: Yes—that was something new and incredible, and a portent of things to come. More precisely, they were the result of a complicated power play by Lavrenty Beria, the head of the Soviet secret police, who was maneuvering to obtain full control over the country. Recently historians have found that at approximately the same time, Beria ordered Jonas Žemaitis, the commander in chief of the Lithuanian partisans—who had been arrested a year or so earlier—to be brought to the Kremlin, where Beria made him some vague promises. Nobody knows what might have happened if Beria had prevailed (some say he was a closet reformer, a sort of pre-Gorbachev, though personally I don't believe it). But Beria did not succeed. At the end of June 1953, less than four months after Stalin's death, I awoke in my family's summer rental in Palanga to the sound of two people talking in the courtyard. One of them said, in Russian: "A Beriia-to okazalsia vragom naroda" (Well, it has come to light that Beria is an enemy of the people). Information about his arrest appeared in the morning newspapers. That was yet another sign of times to come, which coincided with my university years.

Hᴉɴsᴇʏ: This episode was then followed by the usual "erasures"—

Vᴇɴᴄʟᴏᴠᴀ: Soon after, my father—and all subscribers to the *Great Soviet Encyclopedia*—received a letter with several enclosed pages and instructions to cut out Beria's portrait along with his entry (which was quite extensive). These were to be replaced with new pages that, as far as I remember, included an entry on a scholar named Beritashvili and several photos of the Bering Sea. Father simply placed the new pages next to the old ones. He hardly felt any sympathy for Beria—it was just a small gesture of independence, which I appreciated.

Hᴉɴsᴇʏ: What happened to Jonas Žemaitis?

Vᴇɴᴄʟᴏᴠᴀ: After Beria's arrest, Žemaitis was executed. His death signaled the end of the partisan war in Lithuania, although individual fighters survived in the forests for a few more years.

Hᴉɴsᴇʏ: Stalin's death marked the beginning of a new period in the USSR and Lithuania, as well as in your personal life. Would you like to add a few more words about the atmosphere in your family and your own mood at this time?

Vᴇɴᴄʟᴏᴠᴀ: My last year of high school was 1953–54. It ended with final examinations for the so-called *brandos atestatas* (school-leaving certificate), which were required for university studies. This preoccupied me more than politics, although I closely followed that year's unusual developments.

The atmosphere in our family was one of cautious anticipation. Some memoirists say they feared the worst in the wake of Stalin's death, but my parents did not share this sentiment (nor did I), and in the end it did not come to pass. Father wrote several poems commemorating the Leader's demise, as many other authors did, but also produced some lyrical poetry. Not much changed in our family's routine, or in my school routine.

Hᴉɴsᴇʏ: At this junction, though, you were beginning to feel a distance from your family—

Vᴇɴᴄʟᴏᴠᴀ: Like many young people, I experienced bouts of rebelliousness. They mainly had to do with typical—and rather banal—crises related to maturing. My experiences at school were not always easy, even after I had joined the group where I felt less like an outsider. My feelings of uncertainty and lack of self-confidence were aggravated by a general—and vague—sense that the world was "out of joint," which I described previously. I attempted to assert my independence by various means, including escapades in the company of street ruffians (among whom I never felt fully at home). Later, when

I discovered hitchhiking—which became popular in Lithuania and the USSR in the fifties—I frequently left Palanga for several days. I explored its immediate and more distant environs on passing trucks: this provided me with an understanding of life not found in books. I'm not inclined to interpret my (or anyone's) life in Freudian terms, but there may perhaps have been an Oedipal component in this. While there was much love and trust in our family, Father had affairs, and these caused my mother to suffer; once, things came close to divorce. I was aware of this, though I did not necessarily know all the details, and took Mother's side. Perhaps I also somehow intuited the direction my life was going to take. I versified a great deal, but did not take it seriously: these were either pseudo-poetic pieces for a wall newspaper, or epigrams making fun of my friends (and myself). But the landscapes of my hitchhiking, the bell towers of Vilnius, the bouts of loneliness with which I could barely cope—all this sent me signs I had yet to decipher.

The examinations for the *brandos atestatas* lasted nearly a month. They were exhausting: we were given six hours to write a literary essay (with the inevitable Soviet references), then had to take a grueling math test, then pass at least ten oral exams in physics, biology, and so on. One was given a hundred or so topics to prepare and was expected to discuss three of them in detail chosen at random from a list. The history of the USSR was the final and most nightmarish exam. In three days, we had to refresh our memories of the three volumes of facts (and propaganda) about Russia, its princes, emperors, and revolutionaries. From a pile of examination questions, I drew one concerning, among other things, Rasputin and his assassination as a prelude to the collapse of tsarism. The textbook had stated that Rasputin was a horse-stealer in his youth, and I repeated this sacred formulation, but I do not remember how I proceeded from there to the collapse of tsarism, since I was on the verge of collapse myself. In any case, I got a "five" (which corresponded to an A) and, after a two-month break, began my university studies.

8

Vilnius University

HINSEY: We have now come to your university years. What kinds of entrance examinations were there, and what role did political loyalty play?

VENCLOVA: There were entrance examinations, and rather difficult ones at that. These tested not just a prospective student's knowledge and abilities, but first and foremost his or her political reliability. *Komjaunuoliai* activists were clearly favored; an ill-prepared person from a provincial school could be given precedence over a brilliant applicant, since social origin, demonstrable pro-Soviet views, or a good recommendation from the local authorities were taken into account (as far as I recall, this was never an official policy, but everybody knew it to be the case). It was very helpful if one's family had been victimized by the partisans, and even more so if, as a high school student, one had already distinguished oneself as an informer. Still, anyone who had received his or her school-leaving certificate with distinction was exempt from taking a second set of examinations. There were seven such individuals in our class, including Romas Katilius and me (this high number corresponded to the solid educational level of our school). Thus, I had two free months before my studies began. My mother and grandfather decided to offer me a car trip to Leningrad (my cousin Andrius, who was still in high school, came along as well). The journey also became the occasion to acquaint ourselves with the other two Baltic countries, Latvia and Estonia. Andrius, who had inherited artistic talent from Aunt Maria, drew sketches of the places we saw, while I tried to observe and remember.

HINSEY: Both Latvia and Estonia shared Lithuania's fate in 1940. Though collectively called "the Baltics," these countries have different histories—

VENCLOVA: Yes, and the differences were palpable. Latvia and Estonia did not experience independent statehood prior to 1918, and had virtually no history of uprisings against tsarist power. In the thirteenth century, both were conquered by the Teutonic (strictly speaking, Livonian) knights (Danes and Swedes were also colonizing the region). This might in certain respects be considered a misfortune, but it ultimately resulted in a relatively peaceful and civilized way of life. Latvians and Estonians were converted to Christianity much earlier than Lithuanians, and they became Lutherans in the sixteenth century, whereas Lithuanians remained Catholics. Incidentally, Latvian is as close to Lithuanian as, for instance, Portuguese is to Spanish (we could read signs and even some newspaper articles), but there was never any real feeling of kinship between our two countries. Estonian, on the other hand, is a totally different language, similar to Finnish. Nevertheless, there is a greater affinity between Estonia and Latvia than between either of them and Lithuania. (Only my native Klaipėda had something in common with the other Baltic countries, but that similarity has now faded.)

HINSEY: What languages did you use during the journey?

VENCLOVA: In Latvia, we tried to speak broken Latvian, but without much success. In Estonia, one might try German. But the lingua franca was, of course, Russian. The local people were decidedly reluctant to use it: one had to start the conversation in Lithuanian, then they would smile and switch to the hated language of the occupier. But there were also lots of Russians everywhere—more so than in Lithuania.

HINSEY: After your experience of Vilnius, what were your impressions of the other two Baltic capitals?

VENCLOVA: I was in love with Vilnius and therefore I was upset—almost enraged—by the fact that the two other Baltic capitals looked more impressive, Sovietization notwithstanding. At that time, Vilnius was a provincial backwater, full of ruins and wastelands, a sort of big village where one might come across a goat in the street. Riga, the Latvian capital, had a certain grandeur, and looked like a sort of minor Hamburg or Stockholm (which I had not yet seen, thus the impression Riga made on me was that much stronger). It bore traces of its Hanseatic past as well as its early twentieth-century prosperity. Tallinn, the capital of Estonia, was much smaller (the same size as Vilnius), but quaintly medieval and picturesque. After I emigrated, I discovered these same qualities in German cities along the Romantic Road. Of course there were also ruins in Tallinn and Riga, the same Soviet shabbiness and Soviet customs, and a palpable tension between the native populations and the Russian newcomers. Still, both countries were undoubtedly more European than any of the other Soviet republics. The small towns we encountered along our way were usually clustered around a castle or a Gothic church, and were less impoverished than those in Lithuania. One of them—Tartu in Estonia—subsequently played a role in my life.

I would later say, half-jokingly, that this 1954 vacation was a poor man's Grand Tour, like those undertaken by educated English men and women during the Victorian era. By the way, in post-Stalinist times, such trips to "palliative Europe" became popular among Russian youths. They used to come to Riga and Tallinn in droves—one finds rather vivid descriptions of this in the novels and stories of the "Thaw generation." In time, Vilnius began to compete with the two other capitals—even eclipsing them among connoisseurs, Joseph Brodsky for one.

HINSEY: After the "Grand Tour," you joined the ranks of the students—

VENCLOVA: From Tallinn, we went on to Leningrad, with which I was already acquainted, and returned to Vilnius in August, just in time for the start of the academic year. I was only sixteen, perhaps the youngest student in the university. I celebrated my seventeenth birthday on September 11.

HINSEY: This was also the university that Czesław Miłosz attended, then called Stefan Batory University. By 1954, following the war and Sovietization, it was a very different place, though it still contained a number of fascinating, hidden parts—

VENCLOVA: The university was on the same street as our high school, and not far from it; however, for a long time the former remained virtually unknown to me. I was a bit shy about visiting places where I did not belong. Only infrequently did I catch glimpses of the university's courtyards (usually behind closed gates), and I never entered its halls. Now, I could explore it to my heart's content. By the way, this was far from an easy task. In fact, I was not entirely correct when I said it was "on the same street" as my high school. The university occupied a very large parcel in the middle of the old town, surrounded by four streets, and three squares for good measure; the street our high school was on barely intersected with its back part. The wasteland that had replaced the former ghetto stood nearby, but the university—though dilapidated and uncared for—remained intact.

At one end of the university quarter stood a massive white bell tower—a veritable Italian campanile, the highest in Vilnius. Next to it was a church with an exquisite Baroque facade (I used to call it "non-Euclidian"), which was visible only from the main university courtyard. In Polish times, this courtyard was named after Piotr Skarga, a Catholic preacher, and the school's first rector. Of course the church was closed and shabby, and it was considered inappropriate to mention Skarga, who was a Jesuit (and a Pole at that). The courtyard now carried the not particularly inventive name, "the Main Courtyard," but a cracked memorial plaque to Skarga with a Polish inscription had survived on the church's wall. In an old book on Vilnius, which I read with Romas Katilius, the Skarga courtyard was compared to Piazza San Marco. This was an apt comparison, since the church and campanile formed one of its sides, and the three other sides consisted of Italianate arches. The plaza looked quite southern, even when drowning in snowdrifts.

HINSEY: Let's continue walking through the courtyards—

VENCLOVA: Through a low archway, you could enter the next courtyard, named after the astronomer Poczobutt, but now renamed "the Observatory Courtyard." True, there was an old observatory (established by Poczobutt immediately after those in Greenwich and Paris). It had two cylindrical towers with an inscription in hexameter verse, *Addidit antiquo virtus nova lumina coelo*, and elegant bas-reliefs of the signs of the zodiac. A third courtyard, very large and unconnected to the first two, had a dry fountain in its middle and pillars clad in cheerful red brick. It was known as "the Philology Courtyard," even though its patron was Sarbievius, a seventeenth-century poet who wrote in Latin and whose verses were illustrated by Rubens. A plaque with his marble profile also adorned one of the walls.

In all, there were thirteen courtyards: a massive and chaotic labyrinth that seemed endless. Certain of these courtyards could be glimpsed through the auditorium's windows, but it was impossible to discern how to gain access to them. There were also ancient halls and chambers: in one of them, Copernicus's book *De revolutionibus orbium coelestium* was displayed—the very copy that was allegedly presented to the author on his deathbed. I will not speak at length about all the mysterious and atmospheric nooks of the university; I have done so on numerous occasions, and have never exhausted the topic. I once said that these heterogeneous, asymmetric, and extraordinary buildings kept us from forgetting the very idea of civilization: I still believe this.

In fact, it was the university that finally taught me the essence of Vilnius. During my first year there, I understood that my city was far from inferior to Riga and Tallinn (or St. Petersburg, for that matter). Though perhaps lacking in Hanseatic polish and imperial grandeur, it nevertheless possessed a magic that was inimitable.

HINSEY: And Vilnius University is itself venerable, despite the numerous struggles imposed on it—

VENCLOVA: The university was by no means as old as Oxford or Salamanca, but established in 1579, it was the oldest university in the Soviet Union. (Well, the university in Königsberg, now Kaliningrad, was founded in 1545, but was destroyed during World War II.) This disrupted the pecking order of the Soviet empire. Naturally, the most honorable university had to be in Moscow—therefore, it should also have been the oldest (whereas it was the fourth oldest, after Vilnius, Tartu, and Lviv). Another problem was the fact that Vilnius began as mainly a theological collegium directed by the Jesuits (considered by the Soviets to be the least acceptable monastic order). For two centuries, instruction was given in Latin: the faculty and the student body were international, and included not only Lithuanians (part of whom were actually Belarusians) and Poles, but many others, from the Irish to the Finns. After 1781, the language of instruction changed to Polish and it became a prominent locus of Polish culture. This created a third problem: as the city belonged to Soviet Lithuania, Polish cultural ambitions (to say nothing of territorial ones) were most unwelcome. This brings me back to two of the greatest Polish writers of all times, who were among its students. As I have mentioned, the first was the nineteenth-century Romantic poet Adam Mickiewicz. One might call him the Polish Byron, though that would be a sort of depreciation, since his work is not in any way inferior to Byron's. In my first year at university, I wrote a paper on him and presented it at a student conference, which gave me the opportunity to learn some Polish. At the time, Mickiewicz was referred to rather infrequently but he was not on the list of banned authors: the Soviets accorded some value to him, calling him a revolutionary and a friend of Pushkin's (which was in fact an overstatement in both cases), while Lithuanian nationalists considered him one of their own, since his most famous poem began with the line "Lithuania, my fatherland." The second poet was Czesław Miłosz, but of course he was never mentioned. There were people in Vilnius who remembered him as a young man—some even used to be on friendly terms with him—but they were predictably reluctant to talk about an anti-Communist émigré.

There were several hiatuses in the university's history. After the 1831 uprising, it was closed by the tsarist authorities, and only reopened in 1919. (During that period, its buildings were occupied by a Russian high school, which was attended by, among others, Felix Dzerzhinsky, who was honored by the aforementioned memorial plaque, located on the gate of the main courtyard.) The government of independent Poland, which after 1919 resurrected the university, gave it the name of its sixteenth-century founder, King Stefan Batory. After Poland's downfall in 1939, the university became Lithuanianized, then Sovietized, then was closed by the Nazis, and finally reopened as a Soviet university after World War II. While I was still a student, it was rebaptized with the name of a Lithuanian Communist leader, Vincas Kapsukas. Luckily, this honorific title is now a thing of the past (along with the plaque for Dzerzhinsky), but the name of Stefan Batory was never reinstated.

HINSEY: Did Lithuanian remain the language of instruction?

VENCLOVA: Yes—this status was assigned to it in 1939, when Vilnius became the capital of Lithuania—though there were some exceptions. While I was a student there, one day of the week, namely, Monday, was entirely dedicated to military training, conducted in Russian. The students were exempt from military service but were expected to attain the rank of junior lieutenant after five years of study. This was the case for boys (the girls, I believe, underwent a sort of parallel medical training). There were certain groups of Russian-speakers who were given instruction in their native language, but they were not numerous and, as far as I remember, disappeared before my graduation. As for the Poles, they never received any instruction in Polish and were generally unwelcome. One of the university's rectors, considered by many to be a true Lithuanian patriot, used to proudly state (though not publicly) that he considered the "eradication of Polishness" to be his special service to his country.

HINSEY: We have previously discussed how you considered going into a branch of science, as such fields required fewer political compromises. Finally, however, you stayed with your decision to study Lithuanian language and literature—

VENCLOVA: As I mentioned, it was Romas Katilius who persuaded me to choose literature—he was fairly sure I would have been totally unfit for any other vocation. For some time, I thought about going to Moscow and studying Russian literature there. But my parents disagreed with that idea quite strongly. Both insisted that my place was in Lithuania. In Mother's case, there was perhaps an additional motivation: she preferred to keep me under subtle supervision as I matured. In that, she failed.

HINSEY: How did your university classmates differ from those you had met in high school?

VENCLOVA: First of all, compared with high school, the class was much larger. There were around twenty boys in my high school group, and more than seventy students in my freshman class at university. Our system differed from the Western model in that a student's major was selected at the very beginning: freshmen in a given subject area were required to attend mandatory classes together (optional subjects were introduced later, though they were not numerous). The second and most important change was that girls now made up half of our class. The mores were quite restrained, but after some time, couples formed, and some of these resulted in marriages. For me, it was a totally new experience—and, needless to say, a fascinating one, my initial shyness and awkwardness notwithstanding. Third, my former schoolmates had generally been townies, whether from working-class or intellectual backgrounds. Now, townies were in the minority. Most of the students came from the countryside, bringing with them vestiges of traditional village culture. Some were religious, although they did not reveal this openly, as that would have meant expulsion from the university (the preliminary screening process resulted in a considerable reduction in the number of ardent Catholics). Nearly everyone remembered the partisan warfare in which their relatives had often taken part, sometimes on the side of the "forest people," but more frequently on the side of the destroyer units (*stribai*). The war in the countryside was dying out, and generally one did not discuss it. There was one student who had spent several years in Siberia as a deportee, but who had managed to return. He was older than everyone else, perhaps over thirty. We never talked about his experiences—such talk could be dangerous, but first and foremost it was considered impolite. He was also a gifted and assiduous philologist, but never managed to have a career.

HINSEY: Now that your fellow students included women, did you form any significant attachments?

VENCLOVA: Yes, I should mention two girls who were close friends. They were from the city and felt a bit isolated—even lost—among their new colleagues. One of them, Judita Vaičiūnaitė, whose uncle was a poet, became a fine poet herself. She went on to write many books that conveyed the Romantic atmosphere of old Vilnius. The second, Aušra Sluckaitė, married a rebellious stage director and emigrated with him to New York: they tried to establish a niche for themselves off Broadway, then returned to Lithuania. Of course, all that happened much later. During our university years, they were nicknamed "bourgeois intellectuals" by some of our more zealous classmates (it was considered an innocuous gibe, but could easily turn into a denunciation). Since my background and character were rather similar to theirs, I became friendly with both of them. We met frequently, mainly at Aušra's Bohemian flat, drank cheap wine together, and imagined that we were in Paris (or prewar

Lithuania). They were also among the first readers of my early poetic attempts. Judita had already published some of her work, and Aušra wrote verse as well, though she did not pursue this.

HINSEY: What about the literature department? What were the various forces at work there?

VENCLOVA: The Lithuanian language and literature department was a rather particular part of the university. Contributing to the field of Lithuanian studies, or simply teaching the topic in a provincial school (which was the presumed fate of most graduates) was considered a patriotic task, and not without reason. It helped to maintain the separate identity of a country occupied by a brutal foreign power. At the same time, however, the authorities attempted to use our department to train the future ideological leaders of Communist Lithuania. The latter were expected to be totally obedient and prepared to follow even the most disgraceful orders. Both tendencies interwove in unpredictable and frequently grotesque ways—often even in the consciousness of one and the same person. All this was reflected in the makeup of the student body: there were clandestine patriots and bald-faced careerists, and all possible shades in between. The Young Communists were much more visible and active at university than they had been in high school, since now they could count on concrete promotions (after several years, they usually joined the party and were given good jobs among its ranks). Generally, one could distinguish between decent or inoffensive people and those who should be approached with caution. Still, there were informers who went undetected (some were victims of political blackmail, others simply attempted to supplement their meager student income). Only the unexpected career of a mediocre student following graduation provided some proof of involvement with the secret police.

HINSEY: Your first year at university was 1954—the year following Stalin's death. Were there any perceptible changes?

VENCLOVA: Though not immediately, the times gradually became, to use Akhmatova's expression, a bit more "vegetarian." A semblance of stability set in. The deportations and random arrests ceased; there was less fear of nighttime visits from the KGB. On the other hand, everyone understood that the new rulers were here to stay, most likely for several generations. This meant making peace with our circumstances. Few people supported the regime openly, but any remonstration against it became a rarity. In post-Soviet times, this period was—and still is—characterized as one of "silent" or "passive" resistance. The term soothes the conscience of the conformists but, in my opinion, muddies the picture: there was lots of Orwellian dou-blethink or just ignoble hypocrisy mixed with hidden nationalist feelings that were not necessarily benign. The regime soon learned how to co-opt these sentiments, at least to a degree.

HINSEY: As you had feared, the study of literature involved a considerable amount of Soviet class requirements and subject matter—

VENCLOVA: As I mentioned, a significant part of our time—one-fifth of it, to be precise—was taken up with military training. This was carried out by old officers of the Lithuanian division, many of whom had served in the army of prewar independent Lithuania and were therefore considered untrust-worthy for any military task except teaching. In general, they were likable men. Another time-consuming task was the study of Marxism (or Marxism-Leninism, to use the official term). It didn't have much in common with genuine Marxist doctrine, but good grades in "Marxism-Leninism" and the good opinion of your teachers were mandatory for receiving your diploma and embarking on a career. But this was something that students in all departments had to cope with.

During my first year of studies, we had to read *History of the All-Union Communist Party (Bolsheviks): Short Course*, known to everybody as the *Short Course*. The book, more or less forgotten today, was a sort of Soviet *Mein Kampf*. Produced by Stalin himself and written in his inimitable style, full of invectives against enemies of the people, it bore no official signature (though Stalin's authorship was not a big secret). We were expected to memorize Stalin's most pointed criticisms of his opponents: for instance, Syrtsov and Lominadze were characterized as "leftist brawlers and political degenerates." (I had no idea who they were, nor did I know that both perished during the Purges, but I remember the formula to this day.) I must confess that in 1954 I did not fully understand the toxic quality of the *Short Course* and read it with some interest as the story of an adventurous revolutionary group.

There was also a seminar in Marxism conducted by Mira Bordonaitė, the wife of Antanas Sniečkus, the first secretary of the Lithuanian Communist Party. She was herself a party member with a prewar record, that is, she took part in the underground movement during the twenties and thirties. Both Sniečkus and Bordonaitė knew my parents well. During the seminar, we read Lenin and Marx and presented short summaries of their ideas. I was less than impressed by Lenin, who seemed quite boring and almost unintel-ligible without a good knowledge of old interparty and intraparty squabbles, but I immediately liked Marx's *The Eighteenth Brumaire of Louis Bonaparte*, which I still consider an exemplary piece of sociopolitical analysis. Later, we had to study Marxist political economy (I mastered the initial chapters of *Das Kapital*, but most students did not even do that), and Marxist philosophy, which amounted to Lenin's primitive and virtually unreadable volume *Materialism and Empirio-criticism*. But all this occurred after my political turning point, that is, after 1956.

HINSEY: This did not leave much time for your actual area of study. Further, regarding the teaching staff: were there any professors left from the prewar period?

VENCLOVA: Even though there was not much time left for our area of studies, one could do considerable work in it. The teaching body was, of course, of varied quality. Those who had taught in the prewar Stefan Batory University had left for Poland en masse. Those who had lectured at the prewar Kaunas University (which was anything but bad), had usually emigrated, been deported, or simply perished. They had been replaced by former high school teachers (very frightened, as a rule), young careerists and sycophants or, at worst, by ideological zealots sent from Moscow. Therefore, the standards of the university dropped catastrophically. Well, there were exceptions, and gradually these became rather numerous.

I remember some of our linguists, however, warmly. The oldest of them, Professor Juozas Balčikonis, was one of the rare survivors from prewar Kaunas University. He was interested exclusively in preparing an immense dictionary of the Lithuanian language (comparable to the Grimms' *German Dictionary*). Although the Soviets had removed him from his post as editor in chief, he was still its *spiritus movens*—or rather *spiritus tutor*. An eccentric, he was also a courageous, if naive, person who did not believe in the longevity of Soviet rule and from time to time expressed that opinion publicly (strangely enough, he was never arrested—perhaps his reputation as a crank protected him a bit). Then there was Professor Zigmas Zinkevičius, a young, witty, and energetic man, who managed to teach the historical grammar of Lithuanian (a very difficult subject, even for an advanced linguist) in such a fascinating way that we eagerly awaited his lectures. Much later, when I was already an émigré, he developed into a scholar of European stature—and, unexpectedly, became a political figure of rightist persuasion. Indeed, the study of Lithuanian and Baltic linguistics, as well as Lithuanian ethnography and pagan mythology, frequently went along with nationalism. This mixture could become explosive. Perhaps the most talented linguist in Vilnius, Professor Jonas Kazlauskas, drowned under very mysterious circumstances: it was whispered that he had been murdered by the secret police, even though he was perfectly neutral politically, mainly interested in the development of the Lithuanian vowel system—or at least so it seemed.

HINSEY: Then there was language study, which you now undertook in a serious manner—

VENCLOVA: I already knew Russian very well, but that was not the case for many students who came from schools in the countryside. I continued English (the rudiments of which had been taught by "Mary" in high school) but I was still not particularly pleased with it, since interesting literature in English was not readily available. It was possible to study French and German, but I did not take any formal classes in these, preferring to leaf through texts on my own (I managed to understand Baudelaire and, to a degree, Rilke). After my paper on Mickiewicz, I realized that one cannot do any serious work in Lithuanian history or early Lithuanian literature without a good knowledge of Polish. Therefore, I enrolled in a small class taught by an elderly lady who had attended Stefan Batory University (I believe she knew Miłosz, though we never discussed it). She provided me with an introduction to Polish grammar, which proved to be very valuable in the years to come.

Finally, there was classical philology. The classics department was located in a beautiful old town lane, at some distance from the university quarter. Above the building's gate was a memorial plaque in Polish to Mickiewicz, who had lived there at the beginning of the nineteenth century (soon, it was replaced by another plaque honoring the same poet, except in Lithuanian and Russian). In the tiny cobblestoned courtyard, one could see blinds on the windows of Mickiewicz's apartment, as well as Vilnius's coat of arms depicting Saint Christopher—a primitive image that the authorities had neglected to remove. My grandfather was employed by the department as the oldest and most respected member of the faculty. Because it would have been inappropriate to attend his classes, I read Latin and Greek verse with other professors. These were my very best hours at university. In addition to both classical languages, I attempted to learn Sanskrit. Like all Lithuanians, I was proud of the fact that our language was said to be its nearest relative—but I soon found that this kinship was much overstated, and that Sanskrit was, purely and simply, too difficult for me.

HINSEY: Then there was the Lithuanian literature curriculum—

VENCLOVA: Yes, there was a rather primitive class on Lithuanian folklore. Classes in Lithuanian literature were given chronologically, starting with the sixteenth century. Probably the best scholar in this field was Jurgis Lebedys, who taught the earliest texts. In the fifties, there still was no printed text-book on Lithuanian literature that would have satisfied the Soviet authorities (prewar textbooks and surveys were banned, removed from libraries and frequently burned). Our main source of knowledge was our written notes from our lectures. Here I must also mention three female professors who taught nineteenth- and twentieth-century Lithuanian literature and formed a close-knit group—Meilė Lukšienė, Vanda Zaborskaitė, and Irena Kostkevičiūtė. All three had some pre-Soviet experience. All three were talented and honest, and never hesitated to express their views, which were fairly liberal and far from Communist (there was a sprinkling of Marxism in their lectures, but it never exceeded reasonable limits). One could not accuse them of nationalism or xenophobia, although they had a strong sense of their Lithuanian identity. Zaborskaitė was probably the best of the three. A lame and rather sickly lady, she was living proof that it was possible to work seriously in the humanities even under Soviet conditions. Of course, she as well as her two colleagues were helped by the early post-Stalinist "Thaw." In the later fifties, it became possible to speak about writers of the national movement, and even the pre-war Modernists more or less objectively, without incurring Zhdanovist abuse. Even some previously banned authors were no longer unmentionable (though living émigrés were).

All this was, however, a very precarious enterprise. The clear admiration the students had for these teachers only further aroused the suspicions of the authorities. After years of petty harassment, a big university pogrom came in 1958—I'll speak more about that later, since it was also a significant moment in my life.

HINSEY: What were the theoretical approaches at the time?

VENCLOVA: Needless to say, neither Lebedys nor the three female professors were particularly innovative methodologically speaking. Totally cut off from new trends in literary scholarship, they stayed within the limits of the so-called cultural-historical school that was predominant in Eastern Europe in the nineteenth and early twentieth centuries (only Zaborskaitė was interested in Russian Formalism). Yet the old methods still made sense when studying Lithuanian literature, which remained underresearched.

I remember my meetings with these teachers as highly enlightening and enriching. Very gradually, disagreements developed between us, since they were, in the final account, more "ethnocentric" and less cosmopolitan than I was. But that happened many years after graduation.

There is not much to tell about the other classes in literary history. World literature and Russian literature courses were mandatory, but these were taught by mediocre professors, and were at a high-school level at best. Greek and Roman literature was a sort of exception. I liked not only the ancient authors (whom I read in Russian translation and frequently in the original), but there was also a voluminous textbook on them written by the Leningrad professor Iosif Tronsky. This scholar deserves special mention because of his family name. Actually, he was Iosif Trotsky. When asked about his relationship to the famous Bolshevik leader Lev Trotsky, he used to answer: "We are not even namesakes!" (Lev Trotsky was a pseudonym for Lev Bronshtein). In the late thirties, such an answer became highly dangerous, and the professor had to alter his name a bit. As strange as it may seem, he survived, and his quite competent textbook remained in use in all Soviet universities for many years.

HINSEY: As a university student, how did you battle the "ideological deformation" around you?

VENCLOVA: In the beginning, I was a diligent student attempting to do my best in all classes including Marxism-Leninism and military training. Naturally, some courses (like Greek and Roman literature, which I just mentioned) were closer to my heart, while I considered others to be boring and tiresome obligations. To my parents' delight, I brought home mainly "A" grades. But my attitude started to change even before my political awakening in the third year of my studies. I was on friendly terms with some of my classmates who were Young Communist activists (yet not necessarily bad or unintelligent people). At the same time, I got to know the "bourgeois intellectuals" I previously mentioned, and one or two people of a markedly freethinking outlook.

I should say a word or two about one of these. In the last year of high school, I became acquainted with Zenonas Butkevičius. He joined our group for a very short time and was expelled because of his nonchalant attitude toward schoolwork (to put it mildly). Still, he had been talented enough to enter university, and in my first year I found him among my classmates once more. A tall, skinny, dark-haired young man, he cut a noticeable figure: girls were crazy about him. Zenonas was full of healthy skepticism toward the system and did not bother to conceal it. Besides, he was a born bohemian. His escapades impressed me enough for me to make friends with him. Soon we established a small group, which frequented bars in the old town for drinking bouts (of course the bars were shabby, the alcohol hardly first-rate, and the amounts consumed were rather modest). During one merry evening, we decided to call our group "the Schnapstrinker Party." This was an undisguised parody of the

Communist Party: we even stated that our main task was to write a *History of the Schnapstrinker Party: Long Course*. In Stalinist times, such jokes would have resulted in a long prison term at the very least. The fact that we were left alone (even if more than one person knew about the "Schnaptstrinkers") gives you an indication of the somewhat more liberal atmosphere of the early post-Stalinist era.

Zenonas never joined the Young Communist League. Later, he became a journalist focusing on ecology. Working in that area made sense under any regime. I remained a member of the league, yet I was hardly an activist.

HINSEY: During the period you are speaking about, directly after Stalin's death in 1953, there was a brief first period of liberalization in literature in the Soviet Union. This included the publication of articles by Olga Berggolts and Vladimir Pomerantsev, and Ilya Ehrenburg's novel *The Thaw*. Were the repercussions of this felt in Lithuania?

VENCLOVA: Not much. These publications appeared in Russian literary magazines but were never translated into Lithuanian. Since my father subscribed to these magazines, I read Pomerantsev's article "On Sincerity in Literature," which advocated some changes to the Socialist Realist paradigm, but not in a particularly convincing way. For me, decidedly more interesting was a long review that mercilessly and wittily demolished an ultraconformist book titled *Diary of a Writer* by Marietta Shaginyan. I knew nothing about the reviewer, Mikhail Lifshitz. Later, I learned that he was an old Marxist philosopher, and friend of György Lukács's, who had experienced considerable trouble in his life and had been expelled from the party precisely for that review. In the sixties, he became one of Solzhenitsyn's supporters. I found Ehrenburg's *The Thaw* rather boring, though it gave its name to the entire era. Father, who knew Ehrenburg personally, was a bit more taken by it. Liberal stirrings in Russia did not have any perceptible echo in Lithuania until 1956.

One change, however, was the partial rehabilitation of Vincas Krėvė, the best-known Lithuanian fiction writer of the interwar period, who passed away in a Philadelphia suburb in 1954. A book of his short stories appeared immediately after his death, in 1955. The press explained that Krėvė had been forced to make an anti-Soviet statement by the Nazis, then emigrated (although the Soviet people would have pardoned him); he then suffered terribly in the United States and died destitute. This was partly true, but Krėvė's case was much more complicated than that. I was already familiar with his work (amply present in Father's library) and chose it for my senior essay before graduation.

HINSEY: You spent a good deal of time during your university years in the library, reading on your own. However, much of the library consisted of "special funds," which is to say forbidden books. What did your reading consist of and was there any way to gain access to the special funds?

VENCLOVA: The old library of Stefan Batory University had remained mostly intact. Some books had been transferred to Poland, not always by legal means, but many were still in Vilnius, nominally available for professors and students. As I have said, there were several beautiful halls where one could leaf through ancient volumes in Latin, Polish, and Lithuanian (not many people did this, but I did from time to time while attending classes in old Lithuanian literature). In the library, there was a significant collection of nineteenth- and twentieth-century books and periodicals. Most of these were in Polish, which the students, as a rule, did not know. My Polish was gradually improving, so hypothetically I could take advantage of these resources. I quickly found out, however, that this was purely theoretical. About half of the library remained virtually inaccessible. Above all, this concerned press from the interwar period, whether in Polish or in any other language (there were also Lithuanian books and newspapers from the independence period, Russian émigré magazines printed in Paris, as well as English, French, and German books of non-Communist persuasion, but one hardly knew they even existed). To enter the "special funds" (and consult their catalogs, which were under lock and key as well), you had to have permission, which was bestowed only very reluctantly. When applying, you had to state your research needs, list the titles you were looking for, and provide a reference from the university administration, also obtained with difficulty. Professors usually managed to do this (party membership or general reliability helped considerably), but for students, work in the "special funds" was a sort of mission impossible. The same system functioned in all major libraries, even if amusing exceptions occasionally occurred (in Moscow, the volume of the *Encyclopedia Britannica* that included the entry on Lithuania was in the open stacks, while the volumes covering Russia and Ukraine were unavailable; in Vilnius, the opposite was true). In smaller public libraries, "unnecessary" books were simply burned.

HINSEY: There are quite a number of other stories about the funds—

VENCLOVA: Yes, one might tell lots of other comical yet undignified stories about the "special funds." To remain on the topic of reference works: an elder acquaintance, a professor of literature, received permission to use the Lithuanian émigré encyclopedia. In his application, he stated (truthfully), that he was studying Symbolism. Therefore, the volume covering the letter "S" was duly brought from the "special funds" and put on his desk. "The item on Symbolism was hardly enlightening," he used to tell his friends, "but the item on the Siberian camps was definitely informative." Later, when photocopiers appeared, only a copy of the requested article and not the entire volume was provided, thus preventing cases of misuse (needless to say, the machines themselves were under strict supervision).

After several humiliating setbacks, I resigned myself to the inaccessibility of the "special funds." There were some determined people who managed to make use of them by obtaining an extended pass. But that required far-reaching compromises, or a fair amount of hypocrisy at the very least. I had an aversion to this; moreover, I rather quickly found out that banned or semibanned books were often more easily available through informal networks.

HINSEY: Let's discuss those networks—

VENCLOVA: Some strictly banned literature was kept in various private libraries, of course in hiding. People shared it from time to time with utmost caution. As I mentioned, works by émigrés began to leak back into Lithuania after Stalin's death, although in negligible quantities (Krėvė was a big exception—everyone else was taboo). There were people who made handwritten or typewritten copies of various texts, which afterward circulated among small groups of friends. Around 1956 or even earlier, the term *samizdat* ("self-publishing") appeared: in Lithuanian it was called *savilaida*. All these manuscript copies formed early savilaida, to which our own uncensored work was sometimes added. In Anna Akhmatova's words, that was a regression to a pre-Gutenberg era—at times, even to the era of folklore, since poetry was frequently learned and recited by heart, of course with lots of unintentional changes and inaccuracies.

The king of savilaida was Juozas Tumelis, my student friend who entered the university a year or two after me. He managed to acquaint me and others with lots of forbidden texts, not just literary, but philosophical and political ones as well. Naturally, that was a perilous activity, and later Tumelis paid for it.

HINSEY: This is when someone who would become a close collaborator joined you at the university—

VENCLOVA: Yes, our small group was joined by Pranas Morkus, and that was a sort of qualitative leap. You may remember his name since it appeared at the very beginning of this book: in prewar Klaipėda, we were taken together in prams to a park by our mothers. After the war, Pranas's mother, a well-known actress, had remarried none other than the Lithuanian Zhdanov, namely, Kazys Preikšas. The stepfather sent Pranas to Moscow University where his stepson got out of hand (that was far from an exception among the children of party notables). Pranas made friends with people whose views were anything but Soviet, contributed to a samizdat magazine titled *The Phallus* (it was not pornographic, but certainly provocative enough), and published in the official student press an article on Pasternak, which the poet himself read and appreciated. For all of the above, Pranas was expelled from Moscow University and sent home to be reformed by his stepfather. This reeducation came to naught. Pranas continued his studies in Vilnius and finally became a screenwriter. From Moscow, he brought us hundreds of Russian samizdat and non-samizdat texts: Russian Formalists, poets, philosophers, and so on. It broadened our horizons to an incredible degree. Henceforth, we had two sources of samizdat: Tumelis supplied me (and others) mainly with books and manuscript copies in Lithuanian, and Pranas with materials in Russian.

But I am getting ahead of myself. Samizdat (or savilaida) networks developed mainly after 1956 (I believe Pranas came back from Moscow in 1957 or so). They really began to flourish about the time I graduated, which was in 1960. Today, it's difficult to unravel the entire story in its logical and chronological order. In any case, at the age of twenty or twenty-one I was already a member of a coterie to which Tumelis and Pranas, as well as my old friend Romas Katilius, belonged. Somewhere on the outskirts of the group was Zenonas Butkevičius with his "Schnapstrinkers," who did not disdain samizdat, but were more interested in a good time. There were also the "bourgeois intellectual" girls with whom we frequently shared banned texts. A bit later, two additional and exciting people arrived from Moscow. One of them was Virgilijus Čepaitis, a young man who had studied (with my father's recommendation) the art of translation at the Gorky Institute, where he rubbed shoulders with the celebrities of the "Thaw generation," including Yevtushenko and Akhmadulina. He brought along with him the pretty Natasha Trauberg, whom he soon married (her father, the famous movie director Leonid Trauberg, had suffered considerably during the forties after being stigmatized as "a nonreformable cosmopolitan"). Well, Natasha was another queen of samizdat of sorts, well-versed in English and Spanish literature, as well as being an ardent Catholic. It was she who acquainted me with religious philosophy up to Saint Thomas Aquinas. Her favorite author was G. K. Chesterton, but she supplied us with Orwell, Aldous Huxley, Borges, and Ionesco as well.

Our coterie survived for many years. Both Natasha and Zenonas Butkevičius died recently, but the others remain my close friends whom I always see when visiting Vilnius. To tell the truth, I would never again in my life have such a tight-knit group of friends.

HINSEY: Besides the discoveries you had made a number of years earlier in your father's library, what kind of poetry were you drawn to during this period?

VENCLOVA: I was very disappointed with Soviet poetry of the time, both Lithuanian and Russian. It was, to a large extent, graphomania (though there were certain stirrings among the younger poets, including those around me). Once I had access to Lithuanian *savilaida*, I became fascinated by the émigré poets, in particular by Radauskas, but also by a group that had formed in German DP camps and had continued its work in the United States—the so-called *žemininkai* (they took their name from the anthology *Žemė*—[The Earth]). Radauskas, as I mentioned earlier, was an aesthete in a somewhat old-fashioned vein, a follower of the French Symbolists, comparable also to the Russian Acmeists (and hardly inferior to them in the quality of his verse). On the other hand, the *žemininkai*, such as Alfonsas Nyka-Niliūnas, wrote in vers libre, in a style that was quite hermetic, full of metaphysical feeling and hidden yet recognizable nostalgia. One might compare them to T. S. Eliot, Montale, and in particular Czesław Miłosz (Nyka-Niliūnas translated *The Waste Land* into Lithuanian, and there was some contact between Miłosz and the *žemininkai*). After becoming an émigré myself, I made friends with poets from this group, although they were approximately twenty years older than me.

I knew something about Miłosz, but not much: only the prewar and émigré translations of his work into Lithuanian were available, and these were rather mediocre. Thanks mainly to Natasha Trauberg, I obtained some idea of modern English poetry, although post-Eliot poets such as Auden and Dylan Thomas remained largely inaccessible to me (well, I had heard their names). Juozas Tumelis, who read German, was a fan of Rainer Maria Rilke, as were many Lithuanians before the war. Yet it was Russian poetry of the so-called Silver Age that was the real discovery for me and became my greatest love. From 1900 to the 1930s, it was arguably the best poetry in the world. Pranas, Natasha, and others supplied me with small well-worn books by Mandelstam and Akhmatova. Tsvetaeva was available only in typescript (the same was true of Mandelstam's *Voronezh Poems* and Akhmatova's "Poem without a Hero"). And, of course, there was Pasternak, whom I had already tried to read in high school: now I knew virtually his entire oeuvre by heart after a trip to the Caucasus with Romas, but we will speak about that later.

HINSEY: Did you have a sense that you were building a personal philosophical framework at the time?

VENCLOVA: It's hard to say. In my university years, I attempted to study the history of philosophy in a more or less linear fashion, starting with Plato (translated by my grandfather) and including Spinoza, some of Kant, Fichte, and so on, but was never too successful at it. Hegel, for instance, remained beyond the scope of my comprehension. As Natasha had told me quite a bit about medieval—and modern—Catholicism, I discussed theological problems with her in a relatively in-depth manner. After 1956, we started to have some idea of existentialism, though this was mainly through word of mouth. Still, I managed to read Camus—not *L'Homme Révolté*, but *La Peste*, which was banned in the USSR but available in Polish translation. It made an immense impression on me (I had just undergone my political change, and I therefore learned the ABCs of resistance from it).

Just before graduation, I became fascinated—if temporarily—by something quite different, namely, Wittgenstein, Russell, Carnap, and mathematical logic in general. There was an old professor of philosophy, Vasily Sesemann, a very unusual figure. He belonged to a group of White Russian émigrés (he was also Tsvetaeva's friend) who had taught in prewar Kaunas. A specialist in his field, Sesemann corresponded with Husserl, Nicolai Hartmann, and God knows who else: it was therefore not surprising that after the war he was sent to a prison camp as an "agent of the world bourgeoisie." There, it is said, he managed to occupy himself with yoga and translating Aristotle (which he knew by heart) into Lithuanian. In Khrushchev's times, he was released, rehabilitated, and allowed to teach logic ("You were lucky to be proclaimed an agent of the world bourgeoisie and not, for instance, a Japanese spy," the investigator told him. "In such a case, we do not need to disprove the accusation, which can take years"). Sesemann immediately published his translation of *Peri psyches* with extensive commentary that he had produced in the camp, and acquainted himself with the newest trends in neopositivist and analytical philosophy. I had to pass an exam with him and was rather proud when he told me: "You might consider specializing in this area."

To return to my personal philosophical outlook at the time of graduation, it was a naive mishmash of Kant, Wittgenstein, and Camus. I believed that the transcendental world was noncognizable, and that one should avoid discussing it since such talk would lead only to antinomies and deadlocks. This did not mean, however, that Christian (or Judeo-Christian) ethical values were to be denied. I called this system of beliefs—hardly a system, to tell the truth—"heroic agnosticism." According to it, we were facing absurdity and nothingness, but nevertheless you had to do your very best in the face of it. Incidentally, one of the ways of "doing one's best," for me, was writing.

9

1956 AND KHRUSHCHEV'S SECRET SPEECH

HINSEY: Khrushchev's famous "Secret Speech" in 1956 at the Twentieth Party Congress denouncing Stalin sent shock waves across the whole of Eastern Europe. However, the first secretary of the Lithuanian Communist Party, Antanas Sniečkus, was relatively cautious about de-Stalinization, and waited a month to officially announce in the party newspaper *Tiesa* that the now-vilified "cult of personality" referred to Stalin. How was de-Stalinization first received in Vilnius?

VENCLOVA: Here, we have to go back a bit in time. The Twentieth Party Congress was held in February 1956, in the second year of my studies. That was before I learned to take advantage of the samizdat network. I was still a member of the Young Communist League, rather knowledgeable about the dubious nature of the regime and skeptical toward its practices, but still a member of the league. Like many Soviet people, I tended to believe that Lavrenty Beria, now executed, had been responsible for the deformities of the system to a considerable, perhaps even predominant, degree (in Lithuania, such beliefs were uncommon). Therefore, the Secret Speech came as a profound shock to me.

Antanas Sniečkus, a professional—and fanatical—revolutionary during the independence period, owed his career to Stalin. He understood perfectly that Stalin could destroy him at any moment, which only contributed to his zealousness. He fought the partisans with an unusual degree of hatred, was quite active during the deportations, and sent some of his own relatives to Siberia. At the same time, he was not devoid of political acuity, which helped him to survive and remain at the top not only under Stalin, but under Khrushchev and Brezhnev as well—a veritable exception among party leaders in the Soviet republics. Many, though not all, historians believe that he became a sort of closet separatist in his later years and attempted to work for the benefit of

Lithuania (as he understood it), shirking the demands of the Kremlin. In 1956, as on many other occasions, he displayed as much cautiousness as possible. It was far from certain who would prevail in the final account. Besides, I believe that Sniečkus held Stalin in a certain esteem (though the traits of a cunning, if narrow-minded, Lithuanian peasant finally prevailed over his Stalinist beliefs).

HINSEY: How and under what circumstances did you first learn about the Secret Speech?

VENCLOVA: In March of that year, Young Communists at the university—myself included—were told to gather in one of its big halls: not in the old medieval campus, but in a nondescript building erected during the so-called Polish times, that is, in the 1930s. We used to attend dances there. After everyone had passed through security, the doors were locked, and we were warned that spreading any information regarding what we were about to hear was strictly prohibited. No punishments were mentioned, but it was clear that the matter was quite serious. Then, a party official (I do not remember who he was, and doubt that he was part of the university system) read the Secret Speech, in Russian, from beginning to end. This took approximately three hours. The audience remained perfectly silent, and there was no discussion afterward. From time to time, the speaker read aloud indications that were noted in parentheses in the speech (for example, "A clamor of indignation"), and I was struck by the sharp contrast between these words and the total lack of reaction on the part of the students. As we were leaving, someone attempted a rather silly joke concerning the "cult of personality" of one of our activists, but it fell flat. For me, almost everything I heard on that day was new and unexpected. For most of the students, it was rather well-known, and only the fact that it had been announced more or less publicly was mind-blowing. I came home at dusk—perhaps I wandered a bit through the streets of Vilnius on my own, trying to come to terms with the event.

HINSEY: What was the reaction of your family?

VENCLOVA: Father was undoubtedly shaken by the Secret Speech, even if he knew much more than me about Stalinist practices. I saw a booklet with the text of the speech on his writing desk and asked for permission to leaf through it, since I wanted to check several sentences that had struck me particularly hard. Father answered that it was a top-secret document given to him for one day by the party authorities, and it was not to be shown to anyone else. Moreover, the very fact of the booklet's existence was not to be mentioned. I accepted this as self-evident, as I knew that the entire life of the Communist Party, from its very beginning, was based on conspiracy and I saw nothing wrong in that: the party was a group of revolutionaries, after all, and revolutionaries have to conform to certain prescripts of behavior. Then I took from his shelf the Russian translation of Henri Barbusse's biography of Stalin and started looking through it. To tell the truth, the book (published in 1936 or 1937) had also been banned: along with passages that praised the Great Leader in an unbearably rhetorical style, it included the names of some of Stalin's associates who were proclaimed "enemies of the people" several months after the biography's publication, and who therefore had become unmentionable. Suddenly I understood why I could find these names only in Barbusse and nowhere else. I discussed it with my father for some time. "Well, most of them were obviously punished without sufficient grounds," he said.

It took time for my father to adapt to the new situation. He had glorified Stalin in more than one poem and essay, and it was not easy to admit that this was tantamount to veneration of a monster. A certain (if poor) solace could be found in the fact that virtually everybody else had done the same. Once or twice, I heard him repeat a justification of Stalinism, which was rather popular at the time among older party members: "One cannot carry out the revolution in white gloves." In a word, he was somewhat ambivalent. Still, he did not belong to the group of Stalinists active in the Lithuanian Communist Party, and tended to support the more liberal wing, albeit quite cautiously. He also tried to maintain ties with nonparty intellectuals, especially with his old leftist friends (many of whom had become anti-Communist). In his later years, his profile in Lithuania reminded one to a certain extent of Ehrenburg's in Russia. As for Mother, I rarely talked about politics with her—that was definitely not her cup of tea.

HINSEY: For all of Eastern Europe, 1956 was a watershed year: what information was available to you about what was happening in the satellite countries in response to the Thaw?

VENCLOVA: We knew next to nothing about Czechoslovakia, Hungary, or Romania, except the fact that the system there did not differ much from ours. Poland interested us much more, because of old Polish-Lithuanian ties and the fact that Polish could still be heard around us. The memory of the Polish-Lithuanian interwar conflict was still very much alive. The authorities were not averse to maintaining this memory, as befits the maxim "divide and conquer," even if it was pursued in a roundabout way. The official line was simple: prewar Poland, a bourgeois and semifeudal country, a sworn enemy of the USSR, had done much harm to the Lithuanian people, including occupying its rightful capital, Vilnius. The bourgeois Lithuanian government had done nothing to correct the situation—on the contrary, it had actually conspired with Polish landlords, and its claims on Vilnius were pure demagoguery. Only the Communists had solved the question and ensured genuine friendship between the Polish and Lithuanian peoples by reconstructing both countries in the spirit of Leninist (and Stalinist) teachings. Well, however dubious that version of history was, it coincided with the Lithuanian nationalist paradigm, if only to a certain extent. On the other hand, promotion of "Polish-Lithuanian friendship" meant the preservation of some Polish schools in the Vilnius region, demonstrations of fake amity and, first and foremost, a relative abundance of Polish press on Vilnius's newsstands. There was a local paper in Polish, which did not differ from Russian and Lithuanian ones, but there were also newspapers and magazines brought from Poland itself, which around 1956 started to differ rather considerably from our own printed matter.

HINSEY: You have said that you started perfecting your Polish after 1956, as it was easier to learn from the Polish press about political events taking place, precisely because more Western literature was being translated into Polish. Would you speak a bit more about the impact of knowing Polish during this period?

VENCLOVA: My Polish had not been too bad even before 1956. As I mentioned earlier, I was interested in old Lithuanian literature, which required reading Polish (and also Latin) texts. My entire family knew the language, and that could only help. After the Twentieth Party Congress, very strong anti-Stalinist currents became visible in Poland, and in October 1956, following the Poznań protests, this led to serious changes in the composition of the Polish Communist Party's Central Committee. Under Gomułka, the party proclaimed a reformist course (called "revisionist" by the old-timers). This did not last long: still, it had an irreversible cultural impact. "Hot" reformist periodicals, such as *Po prostu* (Straight Talk), to which Leszek Kołakowski contributed, were not allowed into Lithuania, but even the official Polish Communist press, available at every corner in Vilnius, was quite informative. There was also *Przekrój* (Cross-Section), an immensely popular weekly promoting jazz, Picasso, and absurdist humor, which influenced the young Soviet generation mightily. Thus I bought and avidly read Polish papers, broadening my world outlook in the process. My student friends—Morkus, Tumelis, and others— did the same. We even started to talk among ourselves in Polish, partly out of snobbery, partly because we were grateful to the language we called "the most civilized in our unhappy corner of Europe."

HINSEY: Then there was the Polish bookshop in Vilnius, which became a sort of meeting place—

VENCLOVA: Absolutely: at approximately the same time, a Polish bookshop opened in Vilnius. It became a great center for social interaction. There, one could buy, or at least look through, books unimaginable in other shops, including works by Proust, Virginia Woolf, and Faulkner. These were in Polish translation, but that was much better than nothing. This is not to say that censorship had disappeared: neither Orwell nor Freud, Heidegger nor Nabokov were available. As for Kafka, several copies of *The Castle* reached Vilnius, but were withdrawn and burned (therefore, Lithuania became the only country in the world to have executed Kafka's will). Yet a copy or two escaped this fate, and one of them landed in my hands.

The first two books which I read in Polish in their entirety were *For Whom the Bell Tolls* and Gustav Meyrink's *The Golem*. This may be a reflection of the eclecticism of my tastes at that time. Hemingway's famous novel was banned in the USSR, since the head of the Spanish Communist Party, Dolores Ibarruri, who lived in Moscow, was offended by some passages and used all her influence to prevent its publication. As for Meyrink, he was a Prague author, fascinated by the Kabbalah and other esoteric teachings, which naturally marked him as a "mystic," and therefore inappropriate for Soviet readers. His novel had a tight plot, but impressed one mainly by its dark and enigmatic atmosphere (later, we used to look for "Golem-like" nooks in the ruins of the Vilnius ghetto). I remember reading both works in Palanga, under a tree, with a dictionary, sometimes asking my mother when I could not find a word. After finishing both books, I felt well-versed in Polish and never consulted the dictionary again.

This process of acquainting ourselves with Modernist literature in Polish translation lasted for years (out of habit, I still sometimes read Western books in Polish, though Lithuanian and Russian translations, to say nothing of the originals, are now readily available). In time, two important new developments took place. First, books such as *Animal Farm* began to reach us in Polish émigré editions that gradually leaked into Lithuania. Second, we found out that many Polish authors—Mrożek, a satirist, Lem, the author of provocative science fiction, Gombrowicz, and others—were no less fascinating than Western Modernist classics. Miłosz, as I have mentioned, was strictly forbidden in Lithuania—and in Poland, for that matter—but we began to learn something about him as well.

HINSEY: As 1956 progressed, what were the concrete effects of the Thaw on Lithuanian culture?

VENCLOVA: One visible change was the return of many cultural figures from prison or Siberian exile. Among these, Kazys Boruta was perhaps the most significant for me. He was released early, around the time of Stalin's death. During the Thaw, his situation improved even more, and his great book *The Mill of Baltaragis* ceased to be totally unavailable. It was published just after the war, but was immediately banned as nationalist and having nothing in common with Socialist Realism. *The Mill of Baltaragis* was a story about devils, ghosts, and sorcerers, based on folklore; it is quite funny and touching, a bit reminiscent of Miłosz's *The Issa Valley* (Miłosz translated Boruta in his youth and esteemed him highly, but neither he nor Boruta were aware that they had both produced similar books at the same time). Boruta, whom I have mentioned earlier, maintained a sort of friendship with my father and sometimes visited us in Vilnius and Palanga; I frequented his small flat as well, where I learned some things about poetry, but above all about politics. Another former prisoner was Petras Juodelis, also a family friend, and years earlier a deputy of my father in the Ministry of Education. A talented literary critic and leftist, he had been arrested and tortured by the Gestapo, and then by the Soviet secret police. After a stint in Siberia, he lived in a crumbling shack on the outskirts of the Old City, where he maintained one of the better private libraries in Vilnius. My friend Juozas Tumelis married his daughter and shared their home, which in the sixties became a focal point of our meetings (both Joseph Brodsky and Nadezhda Mandelstam spent time there).

HINSEY: In a student newspaper on October 17, 1956, you and your close friend Romas Katilius suggested that a society for the protection of cultural monuments be organized. Was this idea a response to greater liberalization? How did this initiative come about?

VENCLOVA: The society for the protection of cultural monuments was a typical idea from the period. A few public initiatives were allowed, although under the strictest of supervision. We were genuinely anxious about the state of old Vilnius. During the Stalinist period, some monuments had been torn down; there were plans for new boulevards in place of Baroque churches and the famous chapel of Ostra Brama. After 1956, these plans for Socialist development were largely forgotten, yet most of the churches remained closed and crumbling, the university's courtyards were shabby, and the former ghetto had become a veritable wasteland. Our coterie studied Vilnius's architecture intently. This was far from easy because of the lack of books (in the interwar period, Polish and Lithuanian scholarly books and essays about the city were rather numerous, but almost all of these had now been relegated to the "special funds," for fear of encouraging nationalist feelings or religious superstitions). Yet, a book by Mikalojus Vorobjovas survived in the private libraries of both my father and Romas's parents. We did not know who Vorobjovas was (his last name was Russian, with a Lithuanian ending): much later, we discovered much of interest about him. But his book was simply brilliant: a sort of Lithuanian *The Stones of Venice*. We learned it virtually by heart and used it as a guidebook during our walks, investigating every arch and column along our path. To tell the truth, for a while Romas and I even thought of entering the Department of Architecture (which Romas's younger brother did). Therefore, the idea of establishing a society for the protection of old Vilnius seemed quite natural to us. Nothing came of it, yet much later some measures for preserving Vilnius's monuments were taken by the official bodies, and the greater part of the Old City survived relatively intact.

HINSEY: On November 2, 1956, the yearly celebration of All Souls' Day took place in Rasos Cemetery in Vilnius, where many important cultural figures are buried. However, on this particular occasion, the event later turned into a demonstration, and the police intervened. Could you describe that day and the sequence of events?

VENCLOVA: Rasos Cemetery (Rossa in Polish) is perhaps the oldest, most prestigious and most picturesque burial ground in Vilnius. Now, it is closed and preserved as a sort of a museum, but in the early postwar decades burials still took place (in 1947, Petras Cvirka was laid to rest there). At the edge of the cemetery, a mausoleum was built by the Polish authorities in the late thirties for the heart of Józef Piłsudski. Although it was Piłsudski who ordered Vilnius to be taken from Lithuania by force, Lithuanian authorities had shown dignified restraint and protected his mausoleum, and the Soviets did not destroy it (which was a rare exception). Many Lithuanian political and cultural figures were buried in Rasos as well, including Jonas Basanavičius, the first signatory of the 1918 Act of Independence, and Mikalojus Čiurlionis, a famous painter (banned from being exhibited at the time, since his work showed an inclination toward Surrealism and abstract art).

One should remember that at the beginning of November 1956, the Hungarian uprising was in full swing. This boosted the spirits of many Lithuanians and Poles, who attended the All Souls' Day celebration at Rasos in much larger numbers than usual. Lots of students joined the event spontaneously. Hundreds of candles were lit at Basanavičius's grave, and there were several short speeches. Presumably, the same thing happened at Čiurlionis's tomb and at the Piłsudski mausoleum, although I did not see this myself; two or three candles were also lit for Cvirka. The mood was solemn and tranquil. One might have expected a Polish-Lithuanian brawl because of differing attitudes toward Piłsudski, but this didn't happen. The secret police did not interfere at the cemetery, limiting themselves to discrete observation. But large groups—mainly students—proceeded from Rasos toward the city center; the authorities feared this could develop into a demonstration. The students were attacked by KGB agents, and there were numerous arrests. Incidentally, a much more tumultuous clash took place in Kaunas, where the memory of independence fighters, buried in the city cemetery, was celebrated: there were rumors that young men, when assaulted by the police on the street, turned over several buses and built a sort of barricade.

HINSEY: Did the aftermath of the event have personal consequences for you?

VENCLOVA: I did not join up with any large group, and I was therefore not arrested. Naturally, however, my presence at the cemetery was noted, and a week or two after that I was instructed (like many other students) to appear before a board consisting of the university's Young Communist activists. I was sternly questioned: how was it that I, a Young Communist, had taken part in a religious celebration? I answered that no one should be forbidden to visit cemeteries on any occasion, and that my relative Petras Cvirka was also buried there. "Cvirka, an atheist, would condemn you if he were alive," replied one of the Young Communist chiefs. In response, I quoted a letter by Cvirka, published in his collected works, in which he warmly spoke about a Catholic feast. This caused consternation. In the end, I was given "a strong warning" that was inscribed in my personal file, which was the penultimate measure taken before expulsion from the Young Communist League. My parents never discussed it with me, though they were undoubtedly quite uneasy about it.

Not everyone was as lucky as I was. Several people were expelled from the league, which, as a rule, meant being thrown out of the university. A budding artist who was my age—the son of family friends—gave a speech at Rasos; he had to leave the School of Art and was immediately conscripted into the Soviet Army (only studies at a school of higher education guaranteed deferment of military service). He served in a polar region and his health was ruined there, perhaps as a result of handling radioactive materials.

HINSEY: You have stated that the suppression of the Hungarian Revolution was one of the turning points of your life—

VENCLOVA: As I have said, after the Twentieth Party Congress I understood very well who Stalin was, but maintained a modicum of faith in Socialism. And, as you know, most Lithuanians detested the regime and considered it to be a monstrous abomination forced upon them by "Asiatic" Russians. At the same time, almost everyone kept such feelings to himself or herself and tried to adapt to the system as best they could. I was aware of this, but for me it smacked of pitiable provincialism and a lack of dignity. Like many Russian and Polish intellectuals, especially younger ones, I thought that injustices might be corrected and falsehoods refuted within the system, and that the Twentieth Congress had given one a sense of direction, even if the evolution might be long and tortuous. Changes in Poland filled me with great hope. Moreover, there was a whiff of revolutionary Romanticism in all that: immense yet dignified crowds demanding their due on the streets of Warsaw could only impress one, especially a young man who had read Byron, Victor Hugo, and Mickiewicz as a schoolboy. In Warsaw, the authorities had been forced to yield, and that was a moment of triumph. In Budapest, Hungarians followed Poland's example: it seemed that all this was just the beginning of wide-ranging improvements. The inscription "Hurrah for the Hungarian Revolution" appeared on the wall of one of our university courtyards: I was in full agreement with its anonymous author. Yet things went terribly wrong. There were armed clashes between the Hungarians and the Soviet Army. It seemed Moscow was going to yield once more, but on the fourth of November, just two days after the All Souls' Day event in Vilnius, we learned that the Soviets had invaded Hungary in full force, shelling and destroying its capital, allegedly at the invitation of the Hungarians themselves, that is, of Kádár's government, which appeared out of nowhere. The hypocrisy was blatantly obvious.

For me, and perhaps others, it was the day of sudden awakening. In a split second, I understood that we still lived in a Stalinist universe, and that any attempt at "correcting its mistakes" in an evolutionary way was simply naive. The system had to be dismantled, period. One could—and should—contribute to its demise, if only modestly, but for that you had to place yourself as far as possible outside the system. Later, I often compared that moment to Zen Buddhist satori—a flash of awareness that changes one's worldview forever. Another simile that came to mind was connected to an experience from my early childhood. As you may remember, I was duped by our maid, who promised to show me nonexistent pigeons in the attic, and from that time on profoundly hated deception. Well, all the talk about the inalterable course of history, about a happy future, about the Bolsheviks' concern for the working class was just that—pigeons in the attic. There was nothing in it except the bald-faced selfishness of self-proclaimed leaders.

HINSEY: For a time, some activists in Poland and Czechoslovakia continued to believe in the idea of "revisionism" or "Socialism with a human face." As you have just described, this was not your case. Did this have to do with the specific situation in Lithuania?

VENCLOVA: Absolutely, and all this is more complicated than it seems. In Lithuania, Communist rule was considerably more oppressive than in the so-called satellite countries, where a measure of liberalism persisted, and one could still hope for gradual improvements. This was hardly our case. (The situation in Lithuania and the other Baltic countries was far from the worst in the Soviet Union: Belarus and Ukraine were even more hopeless.) Yet there were some who believed in "Socialism with a human face" in Lithuania—as well as in other Soviet republics or satellite states—especially among those who had achieved some level of education or status thanks to the regime. As a rule, they were around ten years older than my generation. Quite a few writers, for example, belonged to this group.

One should note here an important component of the Lithuanian mentality. In most of the satellite countries, there was a memory of democratic or semidemocratic times. Lithuania did not experience democracy after Smetona's coup d'état, that is, from 1926 on. Nationalism prevailed in the minds of common people, and even more so among the intellectuals. Virtually nothing except ethnic survival was of interest to them. Well, this is rather natural for a small group whose identity is perennially under threat of annihilation. For many, the existing system might have been more or less acceptable if Lithuanians, not Russians, were in power. Therefore, it was not so much "Socialism with a human face," but "Socialism with a Lithuanian face" that was the desired goal (it went without saying that the Lithuanian face would be more human than the Russian one). After 1956, there was a perceptible trend in joining the party. In Russia, intellectuals did it in the hope of bringing a measure of democracy to the system; in Lithuania, gradual elimination of the Russian cadres was the primary goal.

For me, this was not enough. The entire system, Lithuanian or not, had to be rejected. I felt more outraged by the mendacity of the system and by our isolation from the world than by ethnic oppression (which, in my eyes, was a bit less pervasive than it was in our intellectuals' presentation). And I had reasons to believe that a Lithuanian party cadre would not necessarily be better than a Russian one. Following my political conversion, this put me in a rather isolated position. My immediate circle of friends agreed with me, yet we were just four or five young people who had no influence at all. Boruta and Juodelis understood our stance, but they were also on the margins of society. In our total rejection of the regime, we were close to the position of avowed rightists (who had started to return from prison camps). But our vision of a desirable future—as yet a very vague one, to tell the truth—differed from their vision completely.

Rather, I agreed with the words of one Russian dissident who stated: "Socialism with a human face is as inconceivable as a crocodile with a human face." Joining a party that had murdered several million people was, for me, out of the question. Technically, I was still a Young Communist, but I considered the "strong warning" inscribed in my personal file to be a badge of honor. (After graduation, I ceased to pay membership dues and consequently terminated all ties with the league.)

HINSEY: Partly in response to these tumultuous events, you wrote a series of poems titled "Poems of 1956"—

VENCLOVA: This cycle of three short poems was written in November 1956 and a bit later, after the suppression of the Hungarian uprising. All of them were rather schoolboyish, that is, Romantic and rhetorical. The first one, "Hidalgo," was an imaginary monologue by Don Quixote: in accordance with a long, primarily Russian tradition, I treated him as an eternal revolutionary. The second was just a quatrain about "sleeping mausoleums and people who were awake" (naturally, I had in mind Lenin's mausoleum). The last was a sort of threnody for the fallen Hungarians. Of course, I did not think about submitting them to any magazine (even if the poems largely avoided references to actual events), but they received some currency in samizdat: a friend or two copied them, Judita Vaičiūnaitė liked them, and finally they reached Kazys Boruta. After Boruta's death in 1965, an excerpt from "Hidalgo" was found among his papers and almost made its way into his collected writings. Since my father was overseeing a multivolume edition of Boruta's works, I found the excerpt on his desk and luckily prevented an error that might have become a literary curiosity. Today, I consider the cycle very weak, but sometimes print it in my books as an opening text. In any case, it is a document of the time (among Lithuanian poets, only Henrikas Nagys, an émigré, wrote about the Hungarian Revolution). It was also translated into Hungarian and printed in Budapest in 2011.

HINSEY: We have discussed how Pasternak's poetry was already an important influence on you: how is this reflected in this work? How did you understand your poetic aesthetic during this period?

VENCLOVA: Well, "Hidalgo" was patterned, in part, after Pasternak's "Hamlet," his famous poem included in *Doctor Zhivago*. It was written in the same iambic tetrameter, had the same number of quatrains and employed the same device of a monologue. Moreover, there is a tradition (also mainly Russian) of juxtaposing Hamlet and Don Quixote. I read *Zhivago* in a clandestine edition only in 1959, but I most likely had already seen the poem thanks to Natasha Trauberg, who knew Pasternak well and was among the first to read his novel in manuscript. On the other hand, my last poem referred to the Lithuanian classic poet Maironis, quoting his words about the spring (presumably the "Spring of Nations") approaching us from the Carpathian Mountains. In general, the poetics and aesthetics of the cycle were traditional and nineteenth-century. Incidentally, Pasternak's *Zhivago* poems were much more traditional than his early Modernist work.

HINSEY: In 1957–58, you took an academic leave from your studies. What was the catalyst behind this decision?

VENCLOVA: As far as I remember, it was related to my political wrongdoings, yet technically the leave was for health reasons (which was not a total invention—I experienced a sort of slight nervous breakdown at that time due to some personal events). I had to face the possibility that, at this juncture, I might be leaving the university for a long time, perhaps forever. Therefore I decided to get a truck driver's license just in case I needed to be otherwise gainfully employed. I enrolled in a drivers' vocational school and graduated successfully. This never resulted in a job. (Moreover, even now I do not drive; following a serious accident, my wife Tanya prohibited me from ever driving again.) But I made friends with several young people in the vocational school, which helped me to better understand the situation of proletarians in the "proletarian state." On top of it, I had much more time to read: as I mentioned, I became well-acquainted with Mandelstam's and Tsvetaeva's poetry at this time. After my leave, I returned to university, joining the next graduating class, but still maintaining contacts with my former classmates.

HINSEY: During this period you made some of your first trips to Moscow—

VENCLOVA: I frequently visited Moscow with my parents. It was easy—no visa or permission was required. True, there was the question of a *propiska*: one had to register one's place of residence and report any trips to the police. But for short trips, it was rather a formality. We could stay in the building of the Permanent Representation of the Lithuanian SSR (formerly the embassy of independent Lithuania). It was downtown, and, as far as I remember, free of charge. The most memorable trip took place in 1955, when we visited the exhibition of the Dresden Gallery (it had been brought to Moscow as a war trophy, but was returned to Communist East Germany that year). There were enormous crowds milling around the museum, but Father was permitted, along with Mother and me, to jump the queue as he was a member of the Supreme Soviet. That was my very first encounter with outstanding European painting. I fell in love with Velázquez and Spanish Old Masters in general (today, I prefer the Prado over any other museum). After that, I began to study art history in a methodical way. There were other good museums in Moscow, and we visited several Moscow writers as well (Nikolai Tikhonov and Pavel Antokolsky had interesting stories to tell about literary life during the 1920s and early 1930s, when censorship was not yet all-pervasive). Tikhonov had known Mandelstam during this period, and Antokolsky had had a love affair with Tsvetaeva. I remained under my parents' guidance and did not make any acquaintances of my own, but I felt for sure that Moscow was a place well worth exploring.

HINSEY: At Vilnius University, in the fall of 1958, there was an initiative to publish an almanac called *Kūryba*, to which you contributed work. The almanac was suppressed by the authorities. You were forced to defend your views in public. Could you elaborate on the background of this event?

VENCLOVA: The initiative came from Juozas Tumelis, whom I mentioned earlier as the veritable king of samizdat or savilaida. At that time, students' almanacs were allowed and even encouraged, yet of course they were subject to censorship. Perhaps there was a degree of underhandedness on the part of the authorities in promoting these almanacs, since the KGB was eager to find unreliable persons among the students, first and foremost among their teachers.

In our preceding chapter, I spoke about three female professors of liberal persuasion—Meilė Lukšienė, Vanda Zaborskaitė, and Irena Kostkevičiūtė. For some time, they had been under close observation by the authorities. Moreover, there was more than a modicum of envy toward them among young careerists, who desired to take their positions as soon as possible. All three professors enthusiastically supported the idea of the almanac. One such almanac, *Atžalynas* (Undergrowth) had already appeared a year or two before, but in a single typescript copy; *Kūryba* (Creation) was to be printed by the official publishing house, in a thousand or so copies.

The choice of *Kūryba* as the name of the almanac proved to be unfortunate. *Atžalynas* had looked suspicious enough, since "undergrowth" brought to mind a young generation reappearing after the Stalinist disaster and continuing the work of their elders who had been wiped out. But this had gone unnoticed because *Atžalynas* had been read by the proverbial happy few. But *Kūryba*, as you remember, had been the name of a magazine edited by Juozas Keliuotis under the Nazi occupation. It was far from being a pro-Hitler review—on the contrary, it had printed some texts that could easily have brought the Gestapo's wrath down on both its publishers and authors. But, of course, it was nevertheless considered criminal and was strictly forbidden. I had read it in my father's library, and Juozas Tumelis also possessed some copies. Incidentally, he never thought about the fatal resonance with our new almanac, but the state censors became alerted to it and, after careful scrutiny detected lots of questionable material in the manuscript. This provided a marvelous opportunity for a big political showdown, and a pretext for the dismissal of our teachers for their intolerable lack of vigilance.

HINSEY: What were your contributions to the almanac?

VENCLOVA: Tumelis included in *Kūryba* several of my poems, which were subsequently declared "decadent," and an article (originally a term paper) about two early twentieth-century Lithuanian writers, Žemaitė and Vincas Krėvė, whose story I mentioned earlier. Officially, Žemaitė was considered an exemplary Realist, while Krėvė's case was more delicate: although he had been partially rehabilitated several years before, his Modernist leanings were still very much frowned upon. In my article, I did not conceal the fact that Krėvė looked like the more interesting of the two. This was definitely unacceptable and, what was worse, smacked of nationalism.

The almanac was suppressed, and a meeting of all the professors and students was announced for a "discussion of some errors in the work of the Lithuanian literature department." It was a classic witch hunt. In the official lingo of the period, "errors" meant punishable wrongdoings that more often than not resulted in a prison term or even execution. Well, the times were post-Stalinist, that is, more "vegetarian," yet the announcement sounded quite threatening. As far as I remember, the meeting lasted eight hours without a break. It took place in the beautiful eighteenth-century university aula (a large ceremonial hall), partly destroyed by a bomb in World War II, but rebuilt. Five busts of professors who had taught in Mickiewicz's times looked down on the proceedings—without much astonishment, one might say, since Mickiewicz and his friends were punished for similar offenses in the 1820s. A highly placed party functionary read a long report accusing Tumelis, me, and several other students of non-Marxist attitudes, presumably instilled in us by our teachers. His talk abounded in classic Zhdanovist insults. (The functionary lived in our house on the second floor and, as I've said, heartily disliked my parents, which could have contributed to his zeal.) Unexpectedly, the discussion that followed his speech was not unanimous. He was opposed by a professor of Marxism, an old leftist who had joined the party in Soviet times but preserved much of his decency and, moreover, his faith that Marx was a prophet of human freedom. Several toadies and stool pigeons rebuffed that unsuitably liberal pronouncement without delay. In any case, it was a small sign that the times were changing.

According to the unwritten laws of such meetings, we were expected to make repentant speeches, which might or might not help us in the final account. Tumelis, to his credit, did not speak at all. I took the floor, but my speech was far from contrite—it followed the line of the aforementioned professor of Marxism, who believed that genuine Marxism accepted at least some freedom of inquiry. For a corroboration of my views, I even quoted Marx's letter to Joseph Weydemeyer, which was hardly known to the functionaries in the room. As far as I remember, our teachers' speeches were rather bland, but dignified.

HINSEY: What were the final ramifications?

VENCLOVA: As a result, Tumelis was thrown out of the university. He found employment as a bibliographer, and much later, after the collapse of the Soviet regime, became editor in chief of the encyclopedia—a position that ideally suited his skills and interests. We remained close friends, though I frequently felt pangs of conscience when I thought about his case (I had escaped expulsion). The three female professors were summarily dismissed. They expected arrest, which however did not take place. Then, not without difficulty, they found jobs in their field and retained at least part of their influence. I met them on many occasions: one of them told me that my grandfather Merkelis Račkauskas was of great help to her during that period. They never reproached me, but I felt, and still feel, morally responsible for their misfortune, even if in my speech I did my best to shield them.

Part Two

10

Boris Pasternak

HINSEY: In 1958, *Doctor Zhivago* was published in Italy. How did it come to pass that you and a few fellow students wrote Boris Pasternak a letter of congratulations regarding his nomination for the Nobel Prize? How did you first hear this news?

VENCLOVA: Everyone in our small group loved Pasternak's poetry. His nomination for the prize was a joyous occasion (I believe we learned about it on the radio, which in 1958 was less jammed than before). During one of our meetings, quite spontaneously, we composed a short letter that Juozas Tumelis, Pranas Morkus, Romas Katilius, and I signed. In it, we expressed our faith that Pasternak would receive the well-deserved prize, and wished him good health and productive work.

HINSEY: How was this letter of congratulations transmitted to Pasternak?

VENCLOVA: While attending Moscow University, Pranas Morkus had established contact with some people close to Pasternak. As far as I know, the letter was transmitted via Irina Emelyanova, the daughter of Pasternak's last love, Olga Ivinskaya, who was the prototype for Lara. After the poet's death, Irina and her mother spent time in prison camps. I became acquainted with Irina after she was released.

HINSEY: On October 23, 1958, the Nobel Committee awarded Pasternak the Nobel Prize. After first accepting the award, he came under intense pressure from the Soviet leadership and was forced to renounce it. How did you learn about these events?

VENCLOVA: Again, by Western radio. Then, the Soviet media informed us of "the reactionary uproar raised in the imperialist press" because of the prize. In my diary, I noted that I had eagerly joined the reactionary uproar. As it turned out, it was the Soviet response that soon developed into a sort of pandemonium. Several years earlier, Pasternak had attempted to publish the novel in the USSR. A group of highly placed writers wrote him a letter explaining that the novel was unfit for print because of its counterrevolutionary tendencies. Now the letter was made public. The phrase "an apology for treason" was among its milder invectives. Dozens of letters soon appeared in the press, condemning Pasternak in the harshest imaginable terms. This "voice of the people" was characterized by the repeated expression, "I haven't read the novel and have no intention of reading anything so abominable, but . . ." The phrase "I haven't read the novel, but" soon became an ironic catchphrase. One such letter was signed by the employee of a Vilnius bookshop, who stated that she would refuse to sell *Doctor Zhivago* (to tell the truth, such a situation was inconceivable). My father, who was visiting Moscow at the time, recounted the reaction of some of the Russian writers he knew—for example, Kornei Chukovsky, who supported Pasternak, and Konstantin Fedin, who denounced the writer's actions. General meetings of writers were assembled everywhere with the express goal of condemning Pasternak. This happened in Lithuania as well. Although the common consensus was, "this is a Russian affair; settling the occupier's accounts is of no interest to us," virtually everyone cursed the Nobel Prize winner publicly, either out of fear or from indifference. This even included people who were considered to be honest, like the old Symbolist Vincas Mykolaitis-Putinas. Kazys Boruta was the only writer who stood up and left such a meeting. Incidentally, nothing happened to him.

HINSEY: Your father was among those who condemned Pasternak—

VENCLOVA: Yes. Perhaps he actually considered Pasternak's stance to be harmful. In any case, that was definitely a black mark on my father's biography. In his defense, I remember an incident from 1965. Father was telephoned by a correspondent from the Moscow newspaper *Izvestiya* and was asked to express his disapproval of Andrei Sinyavsky and Yuli Daniel, two writers who had published their work abroad under pseudonyms and were put on trial. He politely refused, saying, "I condemned Pasternak, and I regret it."

HINSEY: The storm around Pasternak did not abate and the writer was forced to make a public statement refusing the Nobel, which was published in *Pravda* on November 6, 1958—

VENCLOVA: I understood that the pressure on Pasternak was unbearable, and that he felt responsible not only for himself, but for the people around him. More than one person, including Pasternak himself, believed that he could be executed or at least imprisoned for a considerable term—not long before, that had been the fates of Babel and Mandelstam, whose "crimes" were less serious than Pasternak's. Still, I was unhappy that the great poet had been forced to his knees. Actually, there were two public statements by Pasternak, only the first of which struck me as dignified.

HINSEY: At the height of the attacks against Pasternak, he was threatened with loss of citizenship. In his letter to Khrushchev, he asked that he not be exiled from the Soviet Union. In light of your own later experiences with exile, what are your reflections on this?

VENCLOVA: I'm not in a position to judge Pasternak. He asked to not be exiled for many reasons: perhaps the principal one was the fact that Ivinskaya would not have been able to leave with him and she would risk imprisonment after his departure, which, as I mentioned, did occur after his death. Further, there are writers who are unable to do creative work outside of their homeland, and Pasternak probably considered himself one of these. Of course, there are also writers who produce their best work in exile, Tsvetaeva, Brodsky, and Miłosz (also Mickiewicz) among them. To put it in the simplest terms: there are as many cases as there are people.

HINSEY: You once wrote that "unpublished, and even unmentioned authors . . . can have a more important influence than those who are widely propagated." The impact of this paradoxical truth has no doubt diminished with the end of the Cold War—

VENCLOVA: As we have been discussing, samizdat was becoming the main focus of our reading at that time. This developed gradually, and the Pasternak affair was among the most significant catalysts in this. Naturally, we also read so-called *gosizdat* (texts printed by the state publishing houses), and these, now and then, were not without merit. But the uncensored typescripts fascinated us far more, not just because of their inherent value but also because they were "forbidden fruit." If such a typescript fell into our hands, it would be retyped, usually in four copies (the fifth copy was nearly unreadable) and distributed among friends. This was a dangerous pastime, but it did not necessarily result in serious problems: some caution was required, that's all. The number of copies could thus grow to hundreds, even thousands, which happened with texts by Mandelstam and Akhmatova and, a bit later, poems by the young Brodsky. Any method of duplication other than typewriter carbons was unavailable. If suspicious materials were confiscated by the police, the typist could easily be identified, as all typewriters in the USSR had to be registered. The large and lively samizdat subculture of the late 1950s and 1960s emerged mainly in Moscow and Leningrad, but also in provincial cities. In Vilnius we tried to emulate the Russian example, but our savilaida had local Lithuanian tinges (even if Russian texts also circulated in Lithuania). This gave rise to a good anecdote: a certain mother found herself in a predicament. Her son never read anything except forbidden manuscripts, and she was eager to acquaint him with the classics. Therefore, she hired a typist to produce a samizdat copy of *War and Peace*. The son was so delighted with Tolstoy that he retyped the novel in four copies.

Doctor Zhivago was half as long as *War and Peace*, so its typewritten copies were infrequent, although they did exist. An easier method was to attempt to obtain a copy printed in the West. Such books were nicknamed *tamizdat* ("there-publishing," in contrast to "self-publishing") and provided an important supplement to samizdat. I believe I read Pasternak's novel in the summer of 1959 in a Crimean village where I spent a month or so. Two small Russian volumes, which could easily fit in a pocket, were given to me by Natasha Trauberg who, as I mentioned in the previous chapter, was close to Pasternak. Sometimes, the émigré publishing houses used soluble paper for such books. In the case of a police search, all one had to do was drop them into a bucket, and they disappeared; yet I am not sure that was the case with *Zhivago*. To be honest, I was disappointed with the novel. It said many true things about the revolution, the Civil War, and human dignity, but its plot was confused, full of unbelievable coincidences, the love scenes smacked of a potboiler, and the discussions about religion were inserted into the text without adequate motivation. Only the poems, which make up the book's appendix—ostensibly written by Zhivago himself—fascinated me. They were much simpler than Pasternak's early verses, which I had already come to love, but absolutely perfect.

At this point, I can tell you a rather nice story. The *Zhivago* poems also circulated as a separate samizdat booklet. Once, I carried this with me to a canteen in Moscow and left it on a table. Twenty minutes later, realizing what I had done, I ran back to the canteen and asked: "Did you find a booklet, by any chance? It's a manuscript of my verses . . ." A waitress brought it to me and said with a sly smile: "How beautiful your verses are!" Most likely she had noticed the title *Poems from Doctor Zhivago*, but did not report it to the police.

HINSEY: In January 1959, an event was organized between two poets—yourself and Vladas Šimkus—at the Writers' Union in Vilnius. You were twenty-two years old. The premise of the evening was to set two young poets against each other, and to expose the decadent nature of your work. You had previously publicly said that Pasternak was your favorite writer—

VENCLOVA: This was a typical Soviet affair: the work of budding poets was frequently discussed and evaluated by the Writers' Union functionaries. It was usually a prelude to their admission to the Writers' Union. Membership brought with it some privileges, the main one being the possibility of earning one's living without official employment, by royalties only. Brodsky, as we will discuss, was arrested as a "social parasite," because he was unemployed and not a member of the Writers' Union. People were sometimes allowed to make their living as translators, but then they had to belong to the Writers' Union's parallel bodies: all of this was mind-boggling bureaucratic stuff that aggravated my life, and the lives of many others, for years.

Vladas Šimkus was a rather popular young poet studying at the university; I did not know him personally at the time. His verses were written in a manner that did not unduly trouble the censors, but I liked them. Energetic, very well done technically, with modern touches. They were honest and moving. As for me, I was becoming known as a poet in student circles, but my work looked somewhat more suspicious, mainly because of the all-pervasive tone of alienation and solitude. Moreover, I did not conceal my views, which were becoming more and more unorthodox. Therefore the Writers' Union's authorities decided to pit us against each other as the "proletarian" and the "decadent." No doubt the fact that some young careerists were attempting to discredit my father (who had "brought up a spoiled brat who was less than trustworthy") also played a nonnegligible role. But that's another story.

HINSEY: Would you describe the scene at the Writers' Union?

VENCLOVA: The hall of the Writers' Union was full (the union was located in one of the most aristocratic buildings in Vilnius, a veritable palace). Not only were established writers in attendance, but lots of young people, including my friends Judita Vaičiūnaitė and Romas Katilius. (Father, perhaps understandably, thought it inappropriate to be present.) Šimkus and I read samples of our work aloud: I remember that I envied his technical deftness. Several rather bland speeches followed. Then, a budding critic said that my verses were perhaps talented, but individualist and therefore hostile to the spirit of Soviet society. "Such poetry could have been written by Doctor Zhivago," he concluded. After that, several older writers attacked me in less ambiguous terms. "The emperor has no clothes" was one of the milder phrases. To tell the truth, it was only then that I fully understood that I was popular among young people, and that the authorities were determined to undermine that popularity.

When I was given the floor to reply, I started by quoting the humorous proverb, "We are all naked under our clothes." After that, I said that no one present in the hall, including myself, had actually read *Zhivago* and therefore was in a position to discuss it. (It was an obvious truth, but a blasphemy at the same time, since it went against the Soviet custom of slandering books one was strictly forbidden to read.) I continued: "So now let's forget about Pasternak's fiction. As for his poetry, I cannot deny that I love it and have learned much from it, as well as from Mandelstam and Akhmatova." That created total consternation, and the meeting was immediately cut short.

HINSEY: Were you at all concerned about the implications of such an act?

VENCLOVA: Not immediately. I simply felt that it had to be said, otherwise I would have been ashamed for the rest of my life. After the crowd dispersed, Romas and I headed toward his house, discussing the event. I told him: "Well, it has something to do with the meaning of life." Of course, I understood that I had jeopardized my admission to the Writers' Union at the very least, and was probably now blacklisted for many jobs, but somehow that did not worry me. A more complicated problem was the eventual conflict with my parents, but neither of them discussed the event with me, even if both of them could not have been very happy with its implications.

By the way, Vladas Šimkus was admitted to the Writers' Union soon after, and published several collections of rather good poetry. He never tried to ingratiate himself with the authorities, but remained within the limits of semi-Modernist psychological verse, which was considered inoffensive by them. One might compare his position with, say, that of Bella Akhmadulina (he was much more honest than Yevtushenko or Voznesensky). I sort of made friends with him: when Brodsky visited Vilnius I introduced him to Šimkus, among others. Still, ten years or so later he had virtually ceased writing, became a heavy drinker, and died prematurely—the fate of more than one person who could not endure the system's hypocrisy. His poetry is still read today. (The young critic who compared me to Zhivago became an influential figure during the Brezhnev years. In independent Lithuania, he organized a sort of private performance, burning all his works from the Soviet period, and became a nationalist.)

HINSEY: You have said that the event at the Writers' Union was the beginning of your "private war" with the system—

VENCLOVA: Yes, it was. It more or less coincided time-wise with the *Kūryba* almanac affair and some other events. I believe it was on that day that the authorities understood that they were unlikely to find modus vivendi with me.

HINSEY: Despite the events that had unfolded in connection with Nobel Prize, on December 14, 1959, you decided to visit Pasternak with Natasha Trauberg—

VENCLOVA: By that time, Pasternak's hounding had somewhat subsided. He was able to work as a translator. Ironically enough, he was asked to render into Russian Pedro Calderon de la Barca's *The Constant Prince*, a play about a heroic Christian who refuses to abandon his faith in the face of persecution. Pasternak's versions of *Hamlet* and other Shakespearian plays were still being staged, which ensured his personal and financial survival. He did not lose his country house in Peredelkino just outside of Moscow. People continued to visit him, although the house was no doubt under surveillance. As I have said, Natasha Trauberg was an acquaintance of Pasternak. When she offered to introduce me to the poet, I was only too happy to accept.

HINSEY: Regarding the visit, how did you travel to Peredelkino? Could you describe the surroundings, the time of day, and what the house looked like on that occasion? How were you greeted by Pasternak?

VENCLOVA: Peredelkino is a village ten or fifteen miles west of Moscow, with a small Orthodox church, next to which Pasternak was buried in 1960. It consists mainly of writers' houses, so-called dachas, usually wooden and sometimes quite spacious. Pasternak was assigned his dacha in the 1930s, when he was still hailed as one of the "leading Soviet poets," and it was here that he spent the last decades of his life.

To get to Peredelkino one takes a suburban train. The day of our visit was clear, the landscape reminded me of provincial Russia (it was difficult to imagine that the capital was so close by), and there was snow on the ground. Pasternak's two-story dacha, with a glassed-in porch, was surrounded by a rather large courtyard. The walkway had been cleared of snow by the poet himself (he liked to perform domestic chores and, as far as I know, did not employ any help). There was a sign on the gate: "Beware of the Dog." Such signs were commonplace in Russia and generally meant "Do not disturb," but here it had an ambiguous ring, given the epithets with which Pasternak had been tarred in the official press. I believe we rang the bell, and a slender, youthful-looking man came to the door and motioned for us to enter. He greeted Natasha cordially. We sat in the spacious vestibule, where one or two paintings by Pasternak's father Leonid hung (Leonid was a famous painter in his time, a friend of Leo Tolstoy's, and Pasternak insisted that he was a much better artist than himself). The poet apologized, saying that he had to go to Moscow in an hour or so to attend a theater performance. I think it was *Faust,* to which he had been invited by a troupe of East German actors. "What do you think—will I be executed afterward or not?" he asked half-jokingly. "We don't think so," we answered.

HINSEY: If I remember correctly, one of the points you had wanted to bring up with Pasternak was your admiration for his early poetry, which he had renounced. What was the substance of this exchange?

VENCLOVA: Natasha introduced me as a young poet who was attempting to translate Pasternak's verses into Lithuanian. "Don't do it," he said. "It's not worth it. My early verses are rubbish—mannered, pretentious, and incomprehensible. If I have written anything sensible in my life, it is my novel. Now I'm working on a play. I hope it will be something that really makes sense—of course, only if I try with all my might."

I did not agree with his judgment, above all because I was not a fan of *Doctor Zhivago*. Yet I was too shy to argue and just mumbled something registering my objection. (As for the play, *The Blind Beauty*, it remained unfinished. The first half of it, printed after Pasternak's death, proves beyond any doubt that it was destined to be a failure.)

HINSEY: What were your other impressions of Pasternak during that visit?

VENCLOVA: We talked for perhaps forty minutes: that is, he talked animatedly and incessantly, and we listened, interrupting him from time to time. I remember his words: "There are two kinds of literature. Take, for instance, Thomas Mann: very wise, learned, witty, even profound, but it remains what it is—just literature. Now take Dostoevsky or Hemingway. They manage to create a universe that works according to its own rules. And this is the point. My early poetry belongs to the first domain; hopefully, my novel [he never said *Zhivago*] belongs to the second." His high opinion of Hemingway probably had something to do with the fact that *The Old Man and the Sea* had just been translated into Russian, and was immensely popular among intellectuals.

There was also some discussion regarding Pasternak's situation vis-à-vis the authorities. "You know," he said, "it doesn't matter to me that some people denounced me and others refrained. No hard feelings, in any case. Everything that has happened has brought me to a place where such matters seem totally insignificant." He also mentioned his correspondence with English-language writers. "Some of my answers are published, and the critics complain about 'awkward translations,' not knowing that they are my original responses." (His English was a bit shaky, even though he had translated Shakespeare.)

When we left Pasternak's house, I told Natasha: "He is so young and energetic—he'll live at least another twenty years." I was wrong. He already had terminal cancer although no one, including Pasternak himself, was yet aware of it.

HINSEY: Pasternak died on May 30, 1960. You were present at his funeral. Did you travel to Peredelkino from Vilnius?

VENCLOVA: No. During that period I visited Moscow frequently, and I was at Natasha Trauberg's flat when, as far as I can remember, someone telephoned and told us about the poet's death. For me, it was a veritable shock. There was a strange coincidence, however, the full meaning of which only became clear much later. On May 30, unaware of the poet's death, my friend Volodya Muravyov and I visited the underground painter Oskar Rabin, who lived in a distant Moscow suburb. We looked at Rabin's work (it was more or less Expressionist, and critical of Soviet life, to put it mildly). We then drank some vodka, and Volodya read aloud several verses by a young Leningrad poet named Joseph Brodsky, including his famous poem "Pilgrims." I considered them to be rather weak and melodramatic, but felt that Brodsky—previously unknown to me—possessed a sort of poetic charisma. Thus, on the very day of Pasternak's death, I was introduced to a different great Russian poet and future Nobel Prize winner. The next morning, I visited Natasha and got the sad news. I went to the post office and sent a telegram to Romas Katilius, thus informing our Vilnius circle of friends about the event. In the telegram, I used only the poet's first name and patronymic, Boris Leonidovich, to avoid any hitches in sending it.

HINSEY: Information about Pasternak's death was largely suppressed, but thousands of people came to Peredelkino to pay their last respects—

VENCLOVA: For the authorities, Pasternak's death created a sort of predicament. Obituaries of Writers' Union members normally appeared in the press, yet Pasternak had been expelled from the Union, and his name was virtually unmentionable. On the other hand, passing over the event in silence was also inappropriate: it would have been natural under Stalin, but Khrushchev insisted on a modicum of "liberalism," however hypocritical that might be in reality. Therefore, a small notice was printed on the last page of a literary periodical about "the demise of B. L. Pasternak, a member of the Litfond (Literary Fund)." The Litfond was a relic from the tsarist period—a self-supporting charity organization. It used a percentage of its members' royalties to help impoverished colleagues and their families (also incurable drinkers, as was stated in the original charter). Incidentally, all the dachas in Peredelkino technically belonged to the Litfond. Pasternak was never expelled from it; the

Litfond was the only Soviet collective body that sheltered him from becoming an "unperson," to employ Orwell's term.

This unconventional obituary was just a formality, since the news spread instantly by word of mouth. Someone put a handwritten note about the upcoming funeral in the hall of the Kiyevsky railway station, from which suburban trains ran to Peredelkino. As far as I remember, the police did not remove it. Natasha's husband Virgilijus Čepaitis and I went to the station and boarded the train (Natasha was too upset to go). All the carriages were full, and we ran into more than one of our Moscow friends.

HINSEY: Could you describe the scene in Peredelkino?

VENCLOVA: The crowd was immense. It assembled spontaneously and was made up of people from every walk of life. Many writers attended, even if literary functionaries (many of them with dachas next to Pasternak's) were conspicuous by their absence. Voznesensky, a young poet considered to be Pasternak's protégé, also did not appear. The event was a sort of litmus test. Without any prearranged plan, it developed into a dissident demonstration, the first in many, many years. There had been nothing like it in Russia since Leo Tolstoy's funeral, in 1910. The comparison came naturally to mind since Tolstoy was also a dissident in his time, and attending his funeral was considered a sign of defiance. Pasternak himself, twenty years old at the time, was present at Tolstoy's coffin. The throng that filled the large field between Pasternak's house and the cemetery was exceptionally dignified and silent.

HINSEY: Pasternak's body lay in state in the parlor and people filed by the coffin. Was this part of the day for close family members, or for all who came?

VENCLOVA: We did not try to enter the parlor, and I saw Pasternak's body only when the coffin was carried out. I noted, somewhat thoughtlessly, that he was gaunt and much smaller than half a year earlier, when he had seemed so full of life. Some marks of decomposition, caused by the early summer heat, were already visible on his face. Earlier, at the parlor window, I saw a young girl: she was Irina Emelyanova, with whom I was not yet acquainted. An uninterrupted stream of flowers passed through her hands from outside in the direction of the poet's coffin.

HINSEY: Sviatoslav Richter defied the Soviet authorities with his attendance and played the Bechstein piano in the parlor. Do you have any recollection of this event or remember hearing about it?

VENCLOVA: I did not hear the piano, but learned about it later. There were three pianists who played in turn—Richter, Maria Yudina, and a much less well-known person who is rarely mentioned, Valentina Lass. Valentina was among the people I met on my last evening in the USSR, in January 1977. She was instrumental in transferring my archive from Moscow to France—a rather risky undertaking.

HINSEY: The funeral procession did not make use of an official car that had been made available for the occasion. Instead, there were pallbearers—

VENCLOVA: Neither I nor, I think, anybody else in the crowd had heard about an official car. At one moment, the coffin was simply brought out of the house and slowly carried in the direction of the church. It was probably a mile (a kilometer and a half) between the dacha and the uphill cemetery; therefore the procession lasted a long time. I was rather far from the coffin's path and did not see the people who were carrying it. There were, I think, a dozen or two pallbearers, mainly the poet's close friends, taking turns in their duty. I remember the person who was standing next to Virgilijus Čepaitis and me in the crowd. It was Susanna Mar, an elderly lady and minor poet, who was a radical Modernist in her youth. Like many former Modernists, she made her living translating poets from the non-Russian-speaking republics into Russian. This was done without any knowledge of the respective languages— word-for-word translations rendered by someone else were transmogrified into regular verse patterns, which provided income and, moreover, proof that one was involved in "socially useful" work. For that reason, Susanna Mar visited Lithuania frequently and made friends with our family. She was astonished that two young Lithuanians—one of whom she knew well—were attending the funeral.

HINSEY: The literary critic Andrei Sinyavsky and the writer Yuli Daniel carried the coffin lid. Five years later—as we will subsequently explore— they would both be arrested, tried, and sentenced for crimes involving "anti-Soviet propaganda." Is it too much to say that there was a strange portent at the funeral?

VENCLOVA: Almost all of the coffin-bearers later became leading figures in the dissident movement. Andrei Sinyavsky and Yuli Daniel were not well-known at the time, but they belonged to the broader-minded intellectual milieu and, I believe, knew the poet personally. Several years after the funeral, Sinyavsky contributed a preface to a volume of Pasternak's poems that had received official permission. I met Sinyavsky and his eccentric wife Maria the next year, in 1961. I followed his trial closely and, after I emigrated, we frequently communicated.

HINSEY: After Pasternak's coffin was lowered, the crowd refused to leave. What was the mood at this point? What speeches and texts were read?

VENCLOVA: I remember a dignified if bland speech at the graveside by one of the poet's friends, the philosopher Valentin Asmus. Perhaps two or three other short speeches followed, but I have no memory of these. Then, somebody shouted: "Glory to the deceased! He was the most honest person in Russia!" A commotion followed: the self-proclaimed speaker was silenced by people next to the grave, but some young men and women (as far as I know, Irina Emelyanova among them) requested that people be allowed to say what they wished. Then, someone began reciting Pasternak's famous poem "August," written in 1953 and included in *Zhivago*. It addresses the poet's anticipated death and has strong religious overtones. Many more poems followed.

HINSEY: How was the crowd finally dispersed? What are your other memories of the day?

VENCLOVA: The crowd started to thin after an hour or so. Finally, Virgilijus said to me: "Let's go. Now, there are only KGB agents left, reciting poems to other agents." However cynical that might sound, there was probably a modicum of truth in it. We left for the station and returned to Moscow. I never heard that the crowd was broken up by force: it dispersed on its own.

At Natasha's flat, we held a sort of a wake with some of her friends. We drank wine and vodka and recited Pasternak's poems—from memory or from his books, which were abundant in her apartment. I was already a drinker at the time, and therefore drank heavily, trying my best to retain my composure. The next day, I made a very long entry in my diary, but did not save it since it seemed chaotic and unreadable. (For some time, I had been keeping a diary, but I stopped on that day—I experienced something like "writer's block," or, to be precise, "diarist's block" for several years afterward.)

HINSEY: At the end of his life, in his memoirs, Khrushchev said that he was sorry about how he had behaved toward Pasternak: that he hadn't supported him and had banned *Doctor Zhivago*. He wrote, "My only excuse is that I didn't read the book"—

VENCLOVA: Khrushchev was not a reader and formed his opinions about books on the basis of information provided by his entourage. (In this, he differed from Stalin who read widely, not necessarily to the benefit of the authors he acquainted himself with.) It is generally believed that Khrushchev was not without human feeling and could regret his decisions. I have reason to believe that he was sincere in his memoirs about Pasternak. There is a legend that, after

Pasternak's death, he asked Tvardovsky, a fairly talented and popular writer: "How about that Pasternak? Is it true that he was such a great poet?" "Do you consider me a good poet?" Tvardovsky responded. "Oh yes," Khrushchev said. "Well, my work isn't worth a penny in comparison with his." "Oh my God, what an error I have made!" Khrushchev supposedly exclaimed.

HINSEY: When you look back on these events what is your reaction? How has time changed your perception of them? Given the ongoing state of censorship in the world, is there anything we can learn from this?

VENCLOVA: My opinion on the Pasternak affair has never changed, though perhaps I am now slightly more forgiving toward the people who condemned him out of fear, ignorance, and other reasons. One should not judge them too harshly: the totalitarian system was still quite strong at the time, and perfectly capable of mutilating human souls. But the entire affair—the poet's funeral included—represented a watershed in the history of the USSR and cultural resistance in the Communist world. Such situations are bound to recur, since tyrannical regimes of various stripes will be present on Earth for the foreseeable future. Still, resistance always pays off, if not immediately, then sometimes in unpredictable ways.

Study Group and the KGB

Hinsey: What was your situation after you graduated from university in 1960?

Venclova: I graduated in the spring. In addition to earning all the required credits and writing a senior paper, we had to undergo two months of full military training—one month before the start of our final year (in my case, the summer of 1959), plus one month after graduation (the summer of 1960). After that, every male student was given the rank of junior lieutenant as a mandatory supplement to his diploma. We spent our first month of training as privates in the Kaunas barracks, and the second month as sergeants in the so-called Kaliningrad region. The experience was, on the whole, comical, bordering on the absurd. Our superiors, mainly officers who had served in the Lithuanian division during the war, were Lithuanian speakers, but all the training was conducted in Russian. They had orders to harass everyone and work us as hard as possible, thus giving us a taste of combat; in reality they were less than demanding and turned a blind eye to many of our escapades. It was rather like *Good Soldier Švejk* with a touch of *Catch-22*. Actually, we even produced a wall newspaper with the title *Twenty Švejks*, which caused an extraordinary scandal because of its ideological incorrectness. We would sometimes go off base for an entire day, drinking heavily and acquainting ourselves with the local prostitutes who tended to flock around the barracks. I boasted that I was a record-holder in such *samovolkas* (absences without leave), especially in Kaunas: there, I could easily reach my grandfather's house and change into civilian clothes, which made me less conspicuous on the street. Perhaps that means at least some of the various military techniques I learned, such as camouflage, weren't wasted on me. In the Kaliningrad region, we served in the old, completely ruined city of Insterburg (Cherniakhovsk); each of us had to give orders to a detachment of Russian privates, which led to new farcical adventures.

HINSEY: What happened after the end of your military training?

VENCLOVA: Our training ended in August 1960. Following graduation, we were each assigned a job. As a rule, this involved teaching Lithuanian language and literature in a remote village, which was viewed as repayment to the state for the generosity of our education. Many remained in these positions for life; after a couple of years, those who were more ambitious managed to get back to Vilnius or Kaunas. There, they found work at a newspaper, in a publishing house, or elsewhere (if one had distinguished oneself by one's political loyalty, one might embark on a party or government career). I escaped being sent away to teach, and was assigned to the Lithuanian Soviet Encyclopedia, which was just then being organized. Yet that same year, the project was abandoned altogether (the *Great Soviet Encyclopedia* was deemed to be sufficient for Lithuania), and I found myself unemployed. This was propitious for further self-education and therefore not necessarily a bad thing—later, I made friends with many such "philologists without definite employment," who were, as a rule, enlightened and colorful types. That said, total *far niente* was frowned upon in the USSR (and soon became a punishable offense); moreover, I needed an income. Translating proved to be a good solution. I got a contract for a book of short stories by the Polish writer Jarosław Iwaszkiewicz (one of Miłosz's mentors), and thus became an acceptable member of society from the Soviet point of view.

HINSEY: After you graduated from university you decided to organize a study group—a bit in the tradition of the Polish "flying university," where people could meet to exchange information about "forbidden" subjects. How did you come to organize this?

VENCLOVA: I knew nothing about the tradition of the "flying university." That developed later, in the 1970s and 1980s, although two flying universities existed in Vilnius under the Nazi occupation. The Poles had already established underground university classes in 1939, and the Lithuanians did so in 1943, after Vilnius University was closed by the German authorities. Still, none of us knew much about this. The idea of creating a "self-study" group to discuss topics not covered by the official syllabus, had already been germinating in our coterie for several years. Romas Katilius and I were among its most fervent supporters.

There were underground groups (unknown to us) that studied mainly Lithuanian history—prewar independence, Stalinist crimes, the partisan war, and so on. All that was supposed to be the first stage in anti-Soviet resistance. As a rule, this first stage often proved to be the last, since the groups were soon uncovered by the secret police, and arrests and prison sentences followed (if there was no serious "counterrevolutionary activity," the end result might be severe intimidation and the conversion of some transgressors into stool pigeons). Naturally, we were also interested in such topics, but we were fully aware of the risks involved—in the place of systematic study, therefore, scraps of information from samizdat or savilaida had to suffice. Yet an immense field of semibanned cultural topics remained, which were less risky. There were large gaps in our knowledge about the latest developments in world literature, painting, music, theater, and so on (and not just Western trends, but Russian Modernism as well). Now, a veritable treasure trove of information could be opened, mainly thanks to, as I have mentioned, the Polish press. Even some Western books were no longer strictly banned—for example, the albums of Picasso, Matisse, and Dufy printed by the publishing house Skira could be bought in official bookshops, albeit for exorbitant prices. And we were most eager for knowledge—it was, in part, a matter of snobbery, but also due to genuine fascination.

In the autumn and winter of 1960, I found I had a great deal of spare time. Translating Iwaszkiewicz was not an exhausting job, and I spent many days reading less-available authors. Moreover, I was literally consumed with the desire to share my newfound knowledge with friends. Of course, there were my daily talks with Romas (his Polish was worse than mine, and I could therefore share lots of information with him). We decided the time was right to establish the long-awaited study group. Its members were expected to prepare and present papers on semibanned writers and cultural figures, read excerpts from their texts, and lead a general discussion.

HINSEY: How many people were involved and what topics did you cover?

VENCLOVA: As far as I remember, there were twelve people in all, boys as well as girls. The number "thirteen" was thought to be dangerous because of its Gospel connotations; of course, this was said in jest. In Stalinist times, people used to say that Judas might be found in any group of three people: now the situation was not as bad. Romas and his younger brother Adas invited their closest friends, who in turn invited their friends, and so on. Among these, I remember best Gediminas Baravykas, a budding architect with a lively disposition, and Kama Ginkas, a Lithuanian-speaking Jewish boy who, as you remember, was a survivor of the Kaunas ghetto. We met at Romas's flat, or sometimes at mine (if my parents were absent). It wasn't really a conspiratorial gathering, but everyone was supposed to be silent about the meetings, just in case. After the discussions, and frequently during them, we drank Hungarian

Tokay. Drinking Soviet vodka was deemed to be in bad taste, to say nothing about its possible aftereffects.

HINSEY: Were the other members of your college group involved?

VENCLOVA: Strangely enough, most of my coterie (Virgilijus Čepaitis and Natasha Trauberg, as well as Pranas Morkus, Juozas Tumelis, Aleksandras Štromas, and Judita Vaičiūnaitė) never joined the group, or even knew about it. Perhaps they were already sufficiently enlightened, and the group's main goal was pedagogical: we wanted to inform less knowledgeable people, thus preparing, so to speak, our successors.

As for the discussion topics, the very first paper addressed Hemingway, whose selected works had just appeared in a two-volume Russian edition (*For Whom the Bell Tolls* was not included). I prepared papers on Joyce and Kafka, whom I had read in Polish. We attempted to discuss Saint-John Perse, who was in the news, since he had been awarded the Nobel Prize in 1960. I translated and read aloud one or two parts of his *Anabase*. (Later, I completed the entire poem, which was printed in Lithuanian several times. I even sent the printed excerpts to the author himself, and many years later found them in his library in Aix-en-Provence.) One paper was dedicated to existentialism, then very much in vogue. Ionesco's *The Lesson* was read in Natasha Trauberg's Russian translation. We planned to stage it with Gediminas Baravykas (who was definitely male) in the role of the Maid. It wasn't only writers who were discussed, however, but composers as well (Hindemith, for example). At that time, Kama Ginkas was in a sort of predicament: he was uncertain about his future career; he was drawn almost equally to architecture as to the theater. I suggested that he give two presentations—one on Frank Lloyd Wright and another on Vsevolod Meyerhold (the great Russian stage director and innovator who was executed by Stalin). In the end, Kama thought Meyerhold looked more interesting, and he subsequently became a stage director himself, and a good one at that.

HINSEY: In the spring of 1960, Alexander Ginzburg visited Vilnius with the intention of editing a Lithuanian issue of his magazine *Sintaksis*. He had already produced two issues, one with poems by Moscow poets, and another with Leningrad poets, including writers such as Joseph Brodsky and Bella Akhmadulina. You met with Ginzburg and gave him some of your poems. However, after he returned to Moscow he was arrested and your poems were found during a search. Subsequently you were interrogated by the KGB—

VENCLOVA: Alexander Ginzburg was one of the earliest Russian dissidents. His *Sintaksis* was probably the first uncensored publishing venture in the

USSR since the time of the Bolshevik Revolution. Every issue consisted of fifty poems (ten authors, each represented by five texts) and nothing else: no prefaces, no articles, and no biographical notes. Ginzburg produced one hundred typewritten copies and mailed one to the KGB, in order to prove that he was not involved in a conspiratorial activity and had no counterrevolutionary intentions. That was a discovery as simple and brilliant as Columbus's egg. The poems were indeed not anti-Soviet, although, as a rule, they would not have made it past the censor for various reasons: radical formal experiments, individualist or anguished moods, erotic content, social criticism, and so on. Some poets like Akhmadulina, who were already well-known, gave their unpublished work to *Sintaksis*, and Brodsky made his debut there (he never failed to mention that Ginzburg was his very first publisher).

I met Ginzburg sometime around April 1960, before Pasternak's death. He had come to Vilnius because he was planning to publish a number of bilingual issues of the work of non-Russian poets, accompanied by Russian translations. To begin with, he wanted to prepare Georgian and Lithuanian issues, since Georgians and Lithuanians were, according to him (and many knowledgeable people) the strongest among the poets of the non-Russian republics. We were introduced to each other by Aleksandras Štromas, who had many contacts in Moscow and knew Ginzburg well. I remember walking one spring evening with Ginzburg and Romas Katilius along the banks of the Neris, next to Vilnius castle and cathedral. We talked quite openly about the situation in the country and the prospects for changing it. Ginzburg insisted that Lenin was, on the whole, right, and defined himself as a Leninist who rejected Stalin's perversion of the doctrine (several years after that, he became one of the most ardent anti-Leninists I ever met). Romas and I had already ceased to believe in Leninism, but agreed that uncensored publications like *Sintaksis* were undoubtedly useful.

We attempted to find Lithuanian poets who might submit their work to *Sintaksis* (Judita Vaičiūnaitė and Vladas Šimkus were the first who came to mind), but that project failed. The enterprise was, of course, risky. Juozas Tumelis, who also met Ginzburg and made friends with him, allowed himself a bon mot: "Before studying syntax, one should study phonetics and morphology; afterward, one will study geography" (he was hinting at imprisonment, which proved to be right in Ginzburg's case). We next thought about using texts by the émigré poets for the Lithuanian issue; and in the end this was done. My poems also remained for consideration. Virgilijus Čepaitis made word-for-word translations into Russian, and Ginzburg left for Moscow, promising to find Russian underground poets who would do the final versions.

HINSEY: However, it was not long before the authorities took action—

VENCLOVA: Yes, several months later, Ginzburg was arrested. His case was of course strictly political, but Khrushchev had just announced that there were no political prisoners left in the USSR. Therefore, the authorities had to find a different article of the criminal code for him. That was readily done. An old story was dredged up: Ginzburg had once tried to help a friend who was too lazy or too dimwitted to pass an exam. He went to the examination hall, forged his friend's signature and passed the exam with distinction. That kind of prank deserved some sort of punishment, but hardly two years in a prison camp. Nevertheless, that was the sentence—the first of several such sentences in Ginzburg's life.

My poems were apparently confiscated along with other *Sintaksis* materials. But I did not feel any repercussions of this until early 1961. Then, the plot began to thicken. One winter evening (was it December 1960 or January 1961?) a member of our study group ran into me on the street. He was slightly intoxicated and extremely upset. "I must tell you something about the KGB," he said. "Today, they invited me to their offices and asked me various questions about the group and about you." I brought him to Romas's flat where we got more information. His feeling was that he might have harmed us with his answers, about which he was rather distressed. We did not reproach him for his behavior, yet understood that interrogations might follow—perhaps even a trial: the KGB was still a ruthless and dangerous force, even if its methods had changed somewhat since Stalin's death (physical coercion, that is, torture, was no longer practiced, at least systematically). A trial could result in prison sentences, not necessarily long ones, but still changing our lives forever. Well, it was good to be warned in advance.

HINSEY: How soon after this did you hear from the KGB?

VENCLOVA: Several days later, I was summoned to the KGB building. As far as I remember, I received a phone call: the tone of the voice on the other end of the line was perfectly neutral, even friendly. In fact, this was unlawful: technically, a summons had to be presented in written form, otherwise the recipient had the right to ignore it. At that time, however, none of us were aware of such legal niceties, and the KGB did not care either—most people simply obeyed automatically. Much later, dissidents learned to insist on legal procedures.

HINSEY: Your friend Aleksandras Štromas later wrote that you went so far as to not shake the hand of your interrogator, which could have been considered a provocation—

VENCLOVA: Well, I arrived at the KGB building, which was known to everyone. It stood on Vilnius's main street, three or four hundred meters from our house. Secret services tend to occupy the same premises, despite regime changes (if only for the fact that the rooms have already been adapted to their needs by the previous owner). Therefore, it had been the Gestapo headquarters during the Nazi occupation; I believe that it served a similar purpose in Polish and even in tsarist times. After my papers were checked, I was taken to the fourth floor. It was early morning. Through the window, I could see a large square with a statue of Lenin on it. That was Lukiškės (then Lenin) Square where insurrectionists were executed in 1863. At its far end, one could make out the old Vilnius prison—still in operation—where my mother had spent a month or two with Jewish women in 1941. All that put me into a slightly Romantic mood. The interrogator greeted me politely and extended his hand in a friendly gesture. Quite spontaneously, I hid my hand behind my back. He was visibly offended, but above all astonished. Then, I explained my gesture, in a perhaps too-sophisticated way: "You know, one shakes hands with people in a situation of equals. We are, however, in an unequal position: you are supposed to interrogate me, and I am supposed to answer your questions." After that, we started to talk.

HINSEY: Could you describe the interrogation in detail?

VENCLOVA: The interrogator introduced himself as Captain (or Major?) Sprindys. His family name was perfectly Lithuanian, and our conversation was conducted in Lithuanian. (Several years after this took place, he approached me in one of Vilnius's bars and said: "Well, I'm Sprindys, perhaps you remember me?" This time, he did not extend his hand, and no talk followed.) His questions focused on our study group; then he suddenly turned to my meetings with Ginzburg. I gave answers as short and noncommittal as possible, trying to shield my friends. The study group's activities were hardly criminal, even from a Soviet point of view: studying Joyce, Kafka, or Meyerhold was, of course, ideologically incorrect, but it differed from writing leaflets or producing anti-Communist manifestos (the authorities now differentiated between such things, which was not the case during the Stalinist period). Nevertheless, the very fact of holding semiclandestine meetings was highly unacceptable. At one point, Sprindys said that he knew about the group sex sessions we had after reading bourgeois authors, but that made me laugh (our meetings were quite Victorian, even too Victorian for my taste), and his accusation fell flat.

Here, one more matter emerged. At that time, we had produced three or four samizdat booklets (with several copies of each), which contained my poems, an article about modern poetry, Natasha Trauberg's translation of G. K. Chesterton's essay "A Defence of Nonsense," and, as far as I remember, her translation of Ionesco's *The Lesson*. Some of the booklets had humorous illustrations, and all of them included, at the bottom of the title page, the notation Eglutė Publishing House (*Eglutė* means "Fir tree" or, sometimes, "Christmas tree"). That had been a playful, kitchen-table enterprise, without the slightest political overtone, but it was still samizdat, that is, uncensored literature, banned by definition. The booklets somehow fell into the KGB's hands. Sprindys asked me which pseudonyms I used for producing such materials. "I always write under my own name," I answered. "Are you sure?" "Yes, I'm sure." "Well, then whose pseudonym is Chesterton?" Once more, I laughed loudly and said: "Someday I'll tell my grandchildren that I was once mistaken for a classic British author." This line of investigation was also curtailed.

HINSEY: But there was still the matter of your relationship with Ginzburg—

VENCLOVA: Yes, my relationship with Ginzburg appeared to be a more serious affair (I already knew Ginzburg had been arrested and was facing a prison term). I said that I had met him several times but had no knowledge of any impermissible activities on his part, and had never given him any poems. Sprindys did not insist on proving the opposite.

Then, a second interrogator arrived, a Russian who introduced himself as Kapustin. He did not extend his hand and spoke much less politely. This was the classic "good cop/bad cop" routine (because I grasped this immediately, the effect was lost on me.) Kapustin took over until evening, at which point I was allowed to go home, but was told to return the next morning. The interrogation continued in a similar vein for two or three days. To tell the truth, it was not a standard interrogation, in which the accused would have remained in detention while it was being carried out. At the time, the KGB had started practicing so-called prophylactic talks with unreliable persons whose activities bordered on transgression, but which did not cross the line. As I have said before, these talks boiled down to attempts at intimidation and, more often than not, recruitment. Well, this was one of those prophylactic chats, but they never suggested that I become an informer: perhaps my behavior was not conducive to such a proposal. Finally, I was told that I was being released from further investigation, but was strongly advised that things could end much worse if I continued my misconduct. "You cannot hide from us: we'll always know what you are doing," were the last words of my interlocutors (at the very end, there were three or four of them, including, I believe, the head of the Lithuanian KGB, Alfonsas Randakevičius).

Hinsey: Were your friends interrogated as well?

Venclova: I think the KGB was only interested in those who had had direct communication with Ginzburg. Virtually all the members of our study group (as well as Natasha Trauberg and, I believe, her husband Virgilijus) were spared. Aleksandras Štromas and Pranas Morkus were, however, invited to KGB headquarters and questioned in rooms adjoining mine, but I only learned about this when I met them in town afterward. The worst fate befell Juozas Tumelis who, perhaps not without reason, was considered "the most inveterate" among us. His premises were searched, and a significant part of his library was confiscated. The KGB spread rumors that it had found a stack of Nazi pamphlets there, which was patently untrue. Nevertheless, Tumelis was left at large; his life had already been damaged by the *Kūryba* case and, as I mentioned earlier, he was eking out a living as a bibliographer.

Hinsey: It is clear that by 1960–61 you already had a personal sense of your direction regarding both art and resistance to the Communist system. Can you speak about this, and also how it changed the dynamic within your family?

Venclova: The Pasternak affair, my experience with the KGB, and the other events we have just discussed were akin to an initiation ritual. Many people my age—in Lithuania, Russia, Poland, and elsewhere—underwent similar initiations at the same time, and later became my friends. I understood very well that the system would most likely survive me and even my offspring. But trying to adapt to it was out of the question. This meant, at most, a modest life without any attempts at a career. The best way for a philologist to survive was translating—one might work on Charles Dickens, Mark Twain, or even Shakespeare, for that matter, which was useful work and did not involve any moral compromises. I knew a number of people who had chosen this path— Natasha Trauberg above all—and they were far from unhappy. One had to resist the authorities, but exactly how to resist was not entirely clear to me. Certainly not by armed struggle (but who knows . . .); a more likely method was to attempt to increase the scope of the permissible, educating yourself, and instilling non-Soviet values in those around you. As for my own poetry, at the time it was mainly therapeutic and auto-nurturing; I was not yet sure that it would become the central focus of my life.

I believe my parents understood all this to a significant degree. They were, of course, upset by the KGB episode and worried about my future (alas, it could only have contributed to my father's heart trouble), but they reacted to the situation tactfully. We never had any harsh discussions concerning the events and they never attempted to control my activities or friendships. Father held out some hope that he could convince me of the validity of his own values: here, both of us tried to remain reserved and rational, even if our conversations sometimes took a bitter turn. Gradually, it was agreed that I should separate from the family and live on my own, as most men of my age did, perhaps even away from Vilnius. I was only too eager to do it.

12

Moscow

1961–1964

HINSEY: In January 1961, you moved to Moscow. Let's speak about your decision to move there—did this have to do with the consequences of the independent study group in Vilnius?

VENCLOVA: Yes, I thought that in a big city it would be somewhat easier to escape KGB surveillance. That proved to be the case: my troubles with the authorities were an intra-Lithuanian affair, and it seems that the Moscow KGB, which already had its hands full, was not much interested in my humble person. In any case, I was never again invited to their premises for interrogation or any questioning. But of course there were other causes for my decision to move, which had to do with entering adulthood.

HINSEY: What was Moscow like as a city at that time—what were your impressions of it when you arrived in the winter of 1961?

VENCLOVA: I already knew Moscow, including its museums and theaters that were, and are, among the best in the world. But I had never fallen in love with it, as I had with St. Petersburg/Leningrad. The city was simply too big and chaotic. In one of my poems, I compared it to the Cretan labyrinth, which, in turn, was an allusion to Hades. The premodern architecture was either Byzantine (though most of the churches were in a shabby state, if not totally destroyed), or tasteless nineteenth-century, or, at best, Jugendstil, of which I am not particularly fond. One could find pleasant provincial lanes and nooks here and there—for instance, Kadashevskaya Quay not far from the Kremlin, where I lived for a couple of years—but these were usually overshadowed by Stalinist or grimly Constructivist buildings. There was a great deal of noise and dust, and dirty snow in winter. Most of the apartments I saw were extremely cramped, the stairs were foul-smelling and creaked, and people were generally poor and provincial-looking. One definitely felt the hand of the totalitarian system everywhere: there were lots of police, as well as quiet and frequently apprehensive faces. Many were fearful; on the other hand, boorish behavior and drunken quarrels were rather common and many parts of the city were dangerous at night. The shops—including bookshops, which interested me the most—were poorly stocked, and if some better goods (once more, including books) appeared, these sold out in minutes. There were fairly good restaurants in the city center—and not too expensive, incidentally—but to enter, you usually needed so-called *blat*, that is, connections. The general mood was one of deficiency and grayness, though not crude poverty. Well, I had experienced much of this in Vilnius. What was special about Moscow was its people—if one managed to find the right ones.

HINSEY: At the start, you didn't have settled accommodations, and you stayed in a hotel. Where was this located and would you describe what this experience was like?

VENCLOVA: As we've discussed, in order to live legally anywhere in the Soviet Union (and especially in Moscow), one had to register with the police. Of course there were thousands of illegal inhabitants, even if that was a bit risky (my *Schnapstrinker* friend Zenonas Butkevičius was caught on the street without proof of registration; he was taken into custody for a day and given seventy-two hours to leave the city. In detention, he spent some time in a cell with young criminals and managed to smuggle out lots of notes for their girlfriends, which we delivered to the addressees, receiving vodka from them every time). Staying in a hotel automatically solved this problem. Hotels in the city center were generally unavailable and at any rate quite expensive; but there was a cluster of guesthouses around the so-called Exhibition of Achievements of the National Economy, in the northern part of the city, where a bed in a room shared with others cost one ruble (most people made 100–200 rubles a month). Obviously, this is what I chose. From there, I could easily reach the center by subway (the famous Stalinist marble Metro, the pride of Moscow and of the entire country). I had one companion in my room. The only inconvenient aspect of this was caused by the fact that he used to invite his bride or lover to the room on certain nights and then would shyly ask me to "sleep peacefully without paying attention," which I attempted to do with mixed success. The first month passed uneventfully, but during the second month the guesthouse's staff began to look at me suspiciously; finally, they informed me that, after the first month, I had to pay two rubles a night in accordance with the guesthouse's rules. This was beyond my means; moreover, such a long stay was suspect in itself. I tried another guesthouse, but they had already been warned about my case. Therefore, I had to rely on the kindness of my Moscow friends. Thank heavens, I had some.

HINSEY: Did you develop a routine during these first weeks in Moscow?

VENCLOVA: I visited Natasha Trauberg almost every day. At the time she was living in Moscow with her husband and parents (I believe she already had a baby son). Her father, Leonid Trauberg, who I mentioned earlier, possessed a first-rate library that I zealously investigated. I spent my evenings with other friends, either on my own, or accompanied by Natasha or Virgilijus. The most interesting meeting place was Grigory Pomerants's flat, a tiny room in a god-forsaken lane next to the Moscow River. It contained the barest of furnishings: there was only a bed on which everybody sat, a table (usually with a bottle of vodka and homemade sandwiches), and a bare electric bulb hanging from the ceiling. Grigory Pomerants had studied at the IFLI (Institute of Philosophy, Literature, and History) before the war. This was a somewhat liberal establishment, which had managed to impart a modicum of knowledge and critical skills to its pupils even at the very nadir of the Stalinist era (György Lukács was among its professors, and Solzhenitsyn took courses by correspondence). During the war, Pomerants served in the Red Army and afterward was arrested for anti-Soviet conversations. He spent five years in a prison camp, was released after Stalin's death and now eked out a living as a librarian. A pedagogue by vocation, he used to bring young people together in his flat to discuss Hegel, Hindu philosophy, contemporary arts, and current events: it was an informal "study group," reminiscent of our group in Vilnius, though without prepared presentations (and perhaps at a higher intellectual level). Grigory's wife Irina and his stepson Volodya Muravyov, who did not conceal his anti-Communist worldview, played a huge role in the discussions (Volodya was a friend of Alexander Ginzburg's). Natasha and Virgilijus knew them well, and Pranas Morkus also attended meetings in Pomerants's flat during his Moscow stint. I met many of my future companions there.

One evening, Natasha brought me to a different *cénacle* or salon, which gathered in a flat on Pushkin Square, next to where she was living. It was led by two physicians, Vladimir Finkelstein and his wife Susanna, very likable people of advanced age. (Several years later, when Vladimir died of heart disease, Susanna committed suicide.) A rather unusual group attended these meetings: mainly young people born in France into émigré families. Their parents had returned to the USSR, as a rule, after the war, as they believed that the regime had changed for the better (which, of course, proved wrong). The children were given Soviet citizenship and were thus stranded in a country they heartily hated; they dreamed of *la douce France* where they had spent their childhoods and had received their primary education. All of them spoke good Russian, but their French was better. (Years later, all of them managed to leave for their beloved Paris.) The most visible among them was Andrei Volkonsky, the heir of an aristocratic family and an avant-garde composer, already well-known in musical circles. Another was Oleg Prokofiev, son of the world-famous Sergei Prokofiev. Oleg was an art historian who painted and wrote poetry in his spare time (several of his poems had found their way into Ginzburg's *Sintaksis*). A third individual, Nikita Krivoshein, the son of a French Resistance hero, had spent time in a Soviet prison because of his article in *Le Monde* concerning the fate of these naive people who had left France for the USSR. Finally, Dimitri Sesemann, who was considerably older than the others, was a friend of Tsvetaeva's family and came to Moscow with Tsvetaeva's husband and daughter. They were arrested almost immediately by the secret police. (Tsvetaeva's husband, Sergei Efron, perished; her daughter spent many years in prison and exile, and Dimitri was released during the war). What was particularly interesting for me was the fact that Sesemann's father, whom I have already mentioned, was a professor of philosophy in Vilnius. As you see, links between my native city and Moscow were rather numerous and unexpected.

There were several young women attending Finkelstein's salon as well, including Marina Kedrova, a lecturer in English language at Moscow University. Right from the start, she made a strong impression on me. The attraction proved to be mutual. I visited her flat several times, where she maintained a sort of permanent exhibition of avant-garde art produced by Moscow underground artists, most of whom she knew personally. It was a risky enterprise, of course, since abstract and Surrealist painting was frowned upon by the authorities, to put it mildly. In March, I moved to Marina's flat. After some time, we married, which legalized my status in Moscow.

I was twenty-three, and Marina was my first real love. We divorced in 1966, yet we remain friends to this day.

HINSEY: Could you describe Marina's flat in more detail?

VENCLOVA: It was a rather spacious room in the so-called Shalyapin House on Sadovoe Kol'tso (Garden Ring), not far from the city center and, incidentally, from the American embassy. The famous opera singer had owned the single-story house before the revolution. After he emigrated, the house was divided into several apartments (one room each) and became a sort of "communal flat," inhabited by several families. Marina inherited her room from her former partner, an art critic who had died some time earlier. Her connections to the underground art world and the collection she kept were related to this relationship. It was nice, if a bit strange, to live among several dozen large paintings, which were quite unusual for the USSR. The canvases covered all the walls, leaving almost no gaps: there were strange sea creatures, Primitivist still lifes, patches of color in the style of Jackson Pollock (the last word in avantgarde art at that moment), squares *à la* Mondrian (Oleg Prokofiev excelled in these), and so on. I have written several poems about that room, which was, in a sense, crucial to my life. It was frequently visited by painters, who sometimes brought new canvases or repainted old ones, and generally it had the air of an artist's workshop. Connoisseurs came as well, including Georgy Kostaki, a semiunderground art collector (though Marina did not trade in paintings and made her living exclusively by teaching English). After perestroika, the entire house was transformed into a Shalyapin museum. I visited it once, lingering for a while in our old room, now full of very different paintings, which had belonged to Shalyapin himself.

HINSEY: How long did you live on Sadovoe Kol'tso?

VENCLOVA: Only a month or so. Once, we burned something in an old stove from Shalyapin's times, and it exploded, filling the entire house with smoke. The neighbor appeared who was responsible for the communal flat. He saw Marina's collection for the first time and understood immediately that it was something illegal. We left in the morning to do some shopping, and when we returned, we found a padlock on our door: the neighbor informed us that he had invited the police to come confiscate the degenerate art, and was not going to let us in, as we had transformed our room into a den of bourgeois decadence. Well, it was a typical Soviet scene from Khrushchev times. We found ourselves on the street, without any possessions except our shopping bags. Luckily, we contacted Oleg Prokofiev, who lived nearby. A *fortochka* (a small ventilation window on the upper part of the frame) was open: Oleg, who was skinny and lithe, managed to squeeze through it and to open the entire window from the inside. Since the window was almost at street level, it was easy to remove our possessions, as well as all of the paintings, which we wrapped in linen and brought to the flat of another friend two or three blocks away. I can only imagine the expression on the face of the law-enforcing neighbor when he arrived with the police and found the room totally empty. He never looked for us—in any case, we heard nothing more about it. The paintings remained stored in our friend's flat for an indefinite time, and we moved in with Marina's mother on Kadashevskaya quay. She had a very cramped room (twelve square meters) at the end of a nineteenth-century courtyard; the three of us lived there together off and on—Marina and I moved to a rented flat from time to time, but sometimes came back.

A rather comical side to the story of the saved paintings was the fact that it happened on April 12, 1961, the day of Yuri Gagarin's flight. The streets were packed with enthusiastic crowds who carried banners and portraits of Gagarin. (The enthusiasm was significantly more authentic than on May Day or other, similar occasions.) At one point, two small boys pointed to one of our Mondrianesque canvases concealed in linen, and exclaimed: "Look, another Gagarin!" A slightly older girl, quite correctly, retorted: "How do you know? Perhaps it's not Gagarin at all!"

HINSEY: Along with your wife, you continued to meet people from the artistic underground. You just mentioned gatherings at the Pomerantses' and Finkelsteins' flats. Would you speak more about these underground artists?

VENCLOVA: Yes, many such people gathered at both Grigory Pomerants's and Vladimir Finkelstein's homes. These two groups overlapped to an extent, though they were rather different: the first was bohemian, the second more closed and reserved—we nicknamed it "Verdurins" (after a snobbish salon in Proust's novel). At the Pomerantses', there was, in addition to my friend Volodya Muravyov who wrote underground poetry, his brother Leonid who painted, and Nikolai Kotrelyov, also an underground poet, who later became a well-known philologist. At "Verdurins," in addition to Volkonsky and his friends, I met Andrei Sinyavsky. Marina introduced me to Dmitri Plavinsky, Lydia Masterkova, and other figures of Moscow's avant-garde, as well the sculptor Ernst Neizvestny, who was becoming rather famous at the time.

Two other significant individuals should be mentioned here. First, there was Gennady Aygi, a poet of Chuvash origin (the Chuvash are a small, Turkic-speaking group on the Volga River). He attended Gorky Institute with Yevtushenko and Akhmadulina, but was expelled because of his radical Modernist verses. At first, he wrote in his native Chuvash, but soon switched to Russian. He was the only well-known practitioner of vers libre in the entire country (even the underground poets used traditional meters and rhyme—which sounds somewhat more natural in Russian). After leaving Gorky Institute, Aygi found employment in the Mayakovsky Museum, a rather modest enterprise in the flat where Mayakovsky spent his final years with Lilya Brik. The most important part of this museum was its archive, which contained a considerable amount of material about Russian Futurism. Aygi was an admirer of Futurism (less that of Mayakovsky than his friends Velimir Khlebnikov and Alexei Kruchenykh), and considered himself their successor. Indeed, his poetry had something in common with the Futurists' vision, though it was devoid of their aggressiveness and urban imagery, and was mainly religious in spirit. Kruchenykh was still alive—an old man who eked out a living trading books and manuscripts; fortunately, the authorities did not pay much attention. Aygi organized private poetry readings for Kruchenykh. I remember one such reading at Andrei Volkonsky's apartment: it was a happening that bordered on the incredible. Kruchenykh was not just a poet who broke all the rules of grammar and common sense, but was a talented actor as well. (He visited us at Kadashevskaya Quay more than once and gallantly courted Marina.) On another occasion, Aygi managed to arrange a one-day exhibition in a certain *dom kul'tury* (house of culture) titled *Mayakovsky's Illustrators*. Among these artists were the Modernist giants Kazimir Malevich and Pavel Filonov, who were banned in the USSR but well-known in the West (and whose works were starting to fetch high prices there). Marina and I helped to hang one of Malevich's paintings, proud of the fact that Malevich was being shown in Moscow for the first time in thirty-odd years.

HINSEY: Aygi, if I remember correctly, became well-known in France—

VENCLOVA: Volkonsky was on quite friendly terms with Aygi and helped him make contacts in France, where Aygi soon became a rather famous poet. Of course, he could not visit Paris, but his books were printed there and had many admirers, since his work—part Dadaist, part Surrealist—struck a familiar note. Generally such things were impermissible, but the authorities seemingly decided to turn a blind eye. In any case, Aygi's poetry was perfectly apolitical. He also managed to edit and publish a large book of French Modernist poetry in Chuvash translation that included Mallarmé, Saint-John Perse, René Char, and dozens of poets that had never been translated into Russian. Prior to this, the only French poem to have appeared in Chuvash was "L'Internationale." Joseph Brodsky (not a fan of Aygi's work) once said that this French anthology was a supreme example of history's absurdity: while one or two Chuvash might have been interested in the Surrealists and Dadaists, thousands of Russians were passionate about them, but could not read them.

HINSEY: The other particularly significant person you met at this time was Natalya Gorbanevskaya—

VENCLOVA: Yes, Natalya (Natasha) Gorbanevskaya was a female poet who later became one of the most famous Soviet dissidents. She was Marina's university classmate, and they were old friends. Marina was one of the first people to listen to Natalya's poems when she was still too shy to recite them to a larger audience. I met Natasha for the first time at the Pomerantses': she was an acquaintance of both Volodya Muravyov and Alexander Ginzburg. This group was significantly more politically oriented than Volkonsky or Aygi, who disliked Communism of course, but maintained an "art for art's sake" stance. Natasha's poems were subtle and poignant, rather Romantic in spirit, addressing subjects such as music, tragic love, and memories of war. Soon, however, she began writing about the destruction of the Russian countryside and culture in the Soviet Union, as well as about interrogations and prisoner trains. She learned Polish and became passionate about Poland, especially its heroic wartime history—Monte Cassino, the Warsaw uprising, the Home Army, and so on. (We not only perceived Poland as "a window to the West," but were fascinated by the Polish ethos of resistance, which was noble yet nonchalant in style, as depicted in many novels and in the films of Andrzej Wajda. Oppositional writers of the older generation, such as Bulat Okudzhava and Boris Slutsky, also appreciated the Poles.) Soon, Natasha's poetry gained a wider audience. Dozens, if not hundreds, of people knew by heart her beautiful (and very musical) poem about Bartók, as well as her poetic credo: "I am a maker of verses who, sad as it might be, is unable to lie." For a time, her popularity rivaled Brodsky's, who was just then becoming known. Brodsky was on friendly terms with her and valued her poetry highly. Anna Akhmatova, a supporter of Natasha, talked with her frequently and attended her readings; she encouraged Brodsky and his friends to invite her into their circle. "Every poetic group should include at least one woman," she used to say. "Such was the case with the Acmeists—Gumilev, Mandelstam, several other men, and myself. You should invite Gorbanevskaya." That was never formally done, perhaps because Natasha lived in Moscow and not in Leningrad. Still, she was close enough to Brodsky's circle, which was later called "Akhmatova's orphans."

Marina and I possessed and read thin samizdat booklets of Natasha's poetry. This was a bit risky due to their decidedly nonconformist content. Of course, Natasha was much more at risk than her readers. She did her best to help Ginzburg and many other political prisoners. Later, in 1968, she distinguished herself as one of a handful of individuals who demonstrated in Red Square against the Soviet invasion of Czechoslovakia. In the next chapter we will return to this, and to the invasion of Czechoslovakia. As a result, she endured forced incarceration in a psychiatric hospital, but finally emigrated to Paris. Abroad, we remained as close as we were in the USSR. Incidentally, I dedicated "A Poem about Friends" to her in 1968. It was printed the following year, with the cryptonym "For N.G."; luckily the Lithuanian censors understood neither the meaning of the dedication nor the symbolism of the poem itself. (It would have been more easily deciphered in Russia.)

HINSEY: Let's back up a little. You arrived in Moscow during a period of momentous change in the Soviet Union, especially in the arts. For example, in August 1960, *Novy Mir* had begun to serialize works like Ilya Ehrenburg's memoirs *People, Years, Life*. Did you begin reading these memoirs in Lithuania or when you arrived in Moscow?

VENCLOVA: I had already begun to read it in Lithuania. My father knew Ehrenburg well, and was as interested in his book as I was (I believe he began to write his own three-volume memoir following Ehrenburg's example). The book now strikes me as superficial and full of glaring omissions ("internal censorship" was definitely at work in Ehrenburg's case), but at the time it resonated greatly with readers and had a positive influence on cultural life. Ehrenburg restored to the public realm hundreds of suppressed figures, Russian as well as Western (Guillaume Apollinaire, André Malraux, and even Pablo Picasso were almost as unmentionable in the USSR as Pasternak and Mandelstam). There were extensive essays on many writers and painters virtually unknown to the general public, as well as a rather frank description of the atmosphere during the Stalinist purges (though Ehrenburg could only allude to his friend Nikolai Bukharin, or Lev Trotsky, for that matter, in roundabout ways). While I was reasonably informed about many aspects discussed in Ehrenburg's work, including many of the names he resurrected, his memoirs gave me a much better understanding of the 1920s and 1930s. Much later, of course, Ehrenburg's memoirs were eclipsed by those of Nadezhda Mandelstam, which were written without any "internal censor."

HINSEY: In 1958, a monument to Vladimir Mayakovsky was erected in Moscow, and it became a place where public poetry readings and gatherings were held. In the winter of 1960–61 these meetings started up again. Did you attend these events?

VENCLOVA: I never attended, no doubt I was too busy with my love affair that winter. Marina's flat was not far from Mayakovsky's monument (which stood on the same Garden Ring, approximately a mile from our place). I passed it on my walks, but never saw any gatherings there. Perhaps by early 1961 they had already been suppressed; I heard about them later, when they were a thing of the past. Some friends of friends were active at Mayakovsky Square: Gorbanevskaya was a close acquaintance of Yuri Galanskov, the leader of the meetings who ended up in prison and perished in the Gulag. I never met Galanskov, and read his poetry only after these events had taken place. While his work, which was rebellious if somewhat naive, did not make much of an impression on me, there was no doubt that Galanskov was a heroic man. I think Volodya Muravyov also took part in the Mayakovsky Square activities, though I'm not 100 percent sure. During that period, that part of Moscow life escaped my attention. The meetings in which I participated were semiclandestine, but remained private gatherings.

HINSEY: Did you meet Vladimir Bukovsky at this time?

VENCLOVA: No. To tell the truth, I didn't yet know who he was. Of course, fifteen years later, I attentively followed the attempts to free him and his exchange for Luis Corvalán. We met only as émigrés in Paris (at the offices of the Polish émigré periodical *Kultura*).

HINSEY: Previously you talked about the origins of samizdat and your early experiences with it in Lithuania. This period in Moscow saw a significant flowering of this "self-publishing agency"—

VENCLOVA: In Moscow, samizdat circulated more freely than in Vilnius, and among a wider audience. First of all, there was underground poetry: it was read by almost all of my friends, many of whom contributed to it. In addition to the "established" samizdat poets, such as Aygi and Gorbanevskaya, we were introduced to dozens of lesser-known writers. Sometimes this kind of verse bordered on graphomania, but there was a sort of natural selection mechanism at work: as samizdat was based on duplication, no one except the authors themselves cared about copying and distributing amateur work, therefore it never reached the general public. One highly valued poet was Stanislav Krasovitsky, an eccentric individual who later became a Russian Orthodox monk (Marina knew him, and I met him once). Leonid Chertkov and Andrei Sergeyev, whom I will talk about in a moment, belonged to the same group— later, they became my close friends. Their poems were influenced by Western verse, following English patterns. Krasovitsky was the most original among them; he was irrational and weird, and influenced young Brodsky significantly. Another group consisted of the so-called bunkhouse poets—Igor Kholin, Genrikh Sapgir, and several others. They were also nicknamed the "Lianozovo School," as most lived in Lianozovo, a far-flung suburb also inhabited by underground painters of a similar world outlook (it was in Lianozovo that I heard Brodsky's name for the first time, on the day of Pasternak's death). These poets were mainly satirists, targeting the Soviet way of life and especially the Soviet mentality, often employing the persona of a dimwitted "loyal citizen." Kholin, a stout and rather coarse man who used to crack bawdy jokes, visited Marina and me from time to time (we even met him in Vilnius). There was also samizdat prose. Aleksandr Kondratov, a friend of Volkonsky's, excelled in this: his pieces were somewhat ahead of their time, in a style that much later became celebrated as Postmodernism.

After Ginzburg's arrest, several samizdat magazines appeared that attempted to carry on the tradition of *Sintaksis* (one of them was called *Phoenix*). I anonymously contributed a short story to one such magazine: it dealt with my experiences in the Kaliningrad region during my military training. That said, most of these initiatives were short-lived.

HINSEY: In addition to literary samizdat, other genres were also clandestinely published—

VENCLOVA: Yes, there was a different kind of Russian samizdat, namely, philosophical and political journalism. Grigory Pomerants was one of its best representatives: in his essays, written in a very civilized manner with an elegant touch of humor, he demolished not only the prevailing ideology but also any attempts to establish a final and definitive worldview. We read Zhores Medvedev's underground essay concerning the fate of Russian genetics during Lysenko's times. Natasha Gorbanevskaya even provided us with a contemporary memoir from a Soviet prison camp, titled *Reportage from the Nature Reserve Named after L. P. Beria*. It began with a story of a Lithuanian prisoner, which made it particularly compelling for me.

HINSEY: What about the practical aspects of how the works were passed around your group? How much danger did reading and circulating these works place you in?

VENCLOVA: The authorities did not care much about strictly literary samizdat, although one might be blacklisted or harassed if caught circulating it. Of course, the content and general tenor of the works did play a role: art for art's sake pieces were considered decadent, which incurred mostly "moral condemnation," while satirical pieces or poignant poems about the absurdity or tragedy of life (such as those written by Brodsky or Gorbanevskaya) could be defined as counterrevolutionary and therefore punishable. Political samizdat was another matter. One had to be extremely careful when copying, distributing, or even having it in one's possession. That could easily result in a prison term. Still, we had no run-ins with the authorities in Moscow: perhaps we were sufficiently cautious.

HINSEY: What were some of your other literary discoveries from this period?

VENCLOVA: As I mentioned, quite a number of unusual books were available in Leonid Trauberg's (Natasha Trauberg's father) private library, including *1984*, which I read in English with the help of a dictionary, and which left a lifelong impression on me. Volodya Muravyov provided me with English-language twentieth-century fiction—for example, Faulkner's *The Sound and the Fury* and Norman Mailer's *The Naked and the Dead*. I also read these in the original, though with considerable trouble as my English was not fully adequate at the time (both Volodya and Natasha Trauberg were fluent in English). By and large, these books reached the USSR in tourists' suitcases and then found their way to the black market.

In 1962, Marina and I moved to the flat of Elena Vasilyeva, a friend of Leonid Trauberg's. She leased us a room. (Elena was a samizdat typist and widow of one of the directors of the film classic *Chapayev*.) Her son, Alexander (or Sasha), who was the same age as I, owed his fame to two things: first, he was the most inveterate drunkard I have ever met in my life—and my experience in this area was not insignificant—second, he was a mighty black marketeer who dealt in books, which provided vodka not only for him but also for droves of his friends. Sasha knew everybody who counted in the Moscow underground and semiunderground. His alcoholism notwithstanding, he was a reserved and reasonable man with an impeccably perfect sense of humor, and we immediately made friends. Book dealers gathered not far from the Kremlin, around the monument to Ivan Fedorov, a sort of Russian Gutenberg. It was also the meeting place for Moscow's gay community (though Sasha was straight, and very much so). Black-marketeering was a punishable offense in the USSR, but Sasha Vasilyev never encountered any trouble: I believe there was a sort of secret understanding between habitués of Fedorov Square and the police. Hundreds if not thousands of rare and banned books passed through Sasha's hands; I managed to read many of them. From that time on, I deepened my knowledge of Russian Modernism (the so-called Silver Age), which was not just an immense pleasure, but also helped me later during my years at Yale.

HINSEY: What were your other experiences related to art?

VENCLOVA: Marina was not herself an artist, but possessed discerning taste and intuition, which under different circumstances might have led her to be an art critic. We visited underground painters' workshops and had access to Georgy Kostaki's collection of early Russian avant-garde art, one of the best such collections in the world.

Then there was music. I was not a big fan of jazz or rock, though my entire generation was extremely fascinated by these. Instead, I was interested in serious twentieth-century music; here, our friendship with Andrei Volkonsky was of course beneficial. He was one of the first proponents of twelve-tone serialism in Russia, knew a lot about Webern, Stockhausen, Nono, and Boulez, and possessed their recordings. This kind of music was very much frowned upon by the authorities (almost as much as Mondrian and Pollock), therefore Volkonsky created an ensemble of medieval and Renaissance music, Madrigal, which was not only a brilliant artistic enterprise, but provided him and other musicians with a decent living. We did our best to attend every one of Madrigal's performances.

I had no theatrical connections, but Marina soon left the university and became a lecturer in English language at VGIK (the Cinema Institute), where future film directors and actors received coaching. Our friend Sasha Vasilyev studied there, or rather pretended to study. There were lots of innovative trends in the world of film, which we tried to follow closely. All in all, my stint in Moscow was a sort of second university, perhaps more significant than the first.

HINSEY: During this period you earned your living as a translator for the Lithuanian State Publishing House. Which works did you first translate?

VENCLOVA: I primarily translated fiction from Polish. Once, I tried my hand at translating from Italian—Curzio Malaparte's *Kaputt*, a powerful book about World War II and the Holocaust, unknown in the USSR at the time. For day-to-day expenses, we relied on Marina's salary, but roughly once a year I received an honorarium that equaled or even surpassed her yearly income. Therefore, our partnership was on an equal financial footing, which more or less assuaged my macho vanity, such as it was. Of course we lived very modestly.

HINSEY: During this period, you wrote two books of popular science on astronomy and cybernetics—

VENCLOVA: I wrote these books at the suggestion of the Lithuanian State Publishing House, mainly for pecuniary purposes. That said, astronomy was one of my many interests, and cybernetics even more so—in Stalinist times it had been labeled "bourgeois pseudoscience," along with genetics, but by the early 1960s it was very much in vogue. I am still a bit ashamed of the first book, since it contained several nods to "Socialist ideals" in which I no longer believed (though I considered Gagarin's flight and astronautics in general, both Soviet and non-Soviet, a significant enterprise for all mankind). Such nods were expected from virtually all authors of published books, and most performed them automatically and without reflection. But for me it was a serious compromise, which I felt could easily result in my full surrender to the regime. After the book appeared, I was quite worried and did my best to avoid that slippery slope. There were no nods in my second book, nor, for that matter, in anything I subsequently wrote or published.

HINSEY: You also traveled quite a lot—can you speak about these journeys?

VENCLOVA: While living in Moscow, it made sense to visit other Russian towns and cities—Rostov, Uglich, Vladimir, Vologda, and so on. Sometimes I traveled with Marina, other times with Andrei Volkonsky and Oleg Prokofiev. I often went to the Caucasus in the summer, joining a group of hikers who crossed the passes between Russia and Soviet Georgia. Incidentally, Georgia—and, to a lesser degree, Armenia—was a part of the country where daily life was noticeably freer and more animated than in the rest of the USSR. I had visited Georgia and Armenia for the first time at the age of nineteen or twenty, along with Romas Katilius, and fell under their spell. A number of my early poems address that experience, which I will discuss a bit later.

HINSEY: You continued to visit Lithuania frequently: were Khrushchev's reforms felt there? Was there any rehabilitation of writers or painters? What about Mikalojus Čiurlionis's work?

VENCLOVA: It was just an overnight train trip from Moscow to Lithuania. We usually visited Vilnius in the summer when Marina was on vacation (I went even more frequently because my job did not require my physical presence in Moscow). My parents liked Marina and had welcomed our marriage. We might spend a month or so in the small Palanga house, usually in their absence. Vilnius and Palanga were becoming fashionable destinations in the USSR. Volkonsky and other friends visited there as well (Madrigal, for instance, was popular in Vilnius).

There was a certain measure of freedom in Lithuania in the early 1960s. Of course, the Soviet occupation and the KGB remained in place, but a new generation had appeared that was less inclined to conform to a Soviet worldview. Socialist Realism was virtually dead. In addition to Judita Vaičiūnaitė and Vladas Šimkus, an entire new group of poets and fiction writers had appeared—Marcelijus Martinaitis, Sigitas Geda, and others. I was acquainted with almost all of them and valued their work, even if our aesthetics diverged. They were "agrarians"—of village origin, fascinated by nature, folklore, and an ancient ethnic world outlook, which they opposed to the Soviet *Gleichschaltung*. I believe we will speak about this in more depth in a coming chapter. That said, nonconformism united us; this included not only young writers but also young painters, graphic artists, architects, composers, theater people, and filmmakers. The rehabilitation of cultural figures was extensive. In 1961, in part due to my father's efforts, Čiurlionis's work—banned during the

Stalinist period—was once again accessible to the public. This meant at least a partial rehabilitation of the entire avant-garde, which was henceforth less frowned upon in Lithuania than in Russia.

HINSEY: By the summer of 1961, over 3.5 million people had fled to the West through checkpoints in East Berlin. Khrushchev recommended resolving the East Berlin refugee problem through the construction of the Berlin Wall, which began on August 13. While this act was condemned by the West, no military action was taken, and the wall remained a symbol of the division of Europe. How did you view these events from Moscow—or from Vilnius, for that matter?

VENCLOVA: This was an ominous event, yet at the time we did not perceive it as a watershed moment in history (which it undoubtedly was). The construction of the Berlin Wall did not change our daily life: at any rate, the West had long been off-limits to us. It was only after I emigrated that I began to more fully understand the wall's role and symbolism. Later, we will touch on some of the poems I have written about this.

HINSEY: From October 17 to 31, 1961, the Twenty-Second Congress of the Communist Party was held. During this Congress—following the Twentieth Party Congress where Stalin's crimes were revealed for the first time—Khrushchev pushed for even greater reforms and de-Stalinization. This resulted in Stalin's body being removed from the Lenin Mausoleum. What were your impressions of these political events?

VENCLOVA: Throughout the 1960s and even after, there was a certain rhythm of "thaws" and "freezes." I did not allow myself to become too despondent over the freezes (though many people did), as I noticed that each one—though it might be quite severe—was nevertheless followed by an even more marked thaw. This gave me some hope that the system would finally collapse, even if I did not anticipate this happening in my lifetime. The Twenty-Second Congress of the CPSU (Communist Party of the Soviet Union) was a sensational event, and we followed its proceedings closely.

As for the removal of Stalin's body (I had visited the mausoleum in the late 1950s out of a morbid curiosity to observe two dictators' corpses), I can recount an interesting story, which I believe has not found its way into the history of the period. The evening following the announcement that Stalin would be evicted from the mausoleum, I was returning from the center of the city to Kadashevskaya Quay. My path home, as usual, passed through Red Square. A small crowd had gathered next to the mausoleum, creating a sort of "Hyde Park Speaker's Corner," which, during the days following the

Twenty-Second Congress, spontaneously formed in several parts of Moscow (in particular, around the Marx monument close to the Bolshoi). I stopped to listen to the discussion that was quite open and fascinating (Stalinists verbally abusing anti-Stalinists, and vice versa). The scene reflected the political tensions between old hardliners and those supporting Khrushchev's reforms. An hour later, when I looked around, the entire large square was so full of people that it was next to impossible to leave. Later, I was told that leaflets had been distributed by unknown people, on which was written, "We must not allow the Leader's remains to be desecrated," but I did not see any myself. In any case, the assembly smacked of danger. Soon, loudspeakers announced that everyone was ordered to leave the square as the rehearsal for a military parade was imminent (the celebration of the October Revolution, always accompanied by such a parade, was coming up), and uniformed officers appeared on the walls of the Kremlin. My feeling was that it was not out of the question that tanks or machine guns might be brought in. I did not have the slightest intention of dying for Comrade Stalin, but there was nothing I could do—the crowd was packed so tightly there was no way to escape. Then, a large detachment of police, accompanied by trucks, succeeded in removing the crowd from the square, very gradually and without the use of truncheons. When the throng was finally dispersed and I reached Gorky Street, I breathed a sigh of relief: it might well have been a new Ninth of January in the making (the day in 1905 when tsarist troops fired into a crowd in St. Petersburg, killing some one thousand people).

HINSEY: In October 1962 the discovery of the construction of Soviet nuclear missile bases in Cuba shocked the West. Later, however, when describing the Cuban Missile Crisis, Khrushchev said that, from the Soviet side, this event had had less internal significance for the Soviets. How was this portrayed in the USSR? How much information was available to you?

VENCLOVA: All this was presented in the press in a very roundabout manner. People were able to get more information from Western radio broadcasts, but as far as I remember, the jamming was intensified at that time (as was always the case in moments of crisis). As a rule, Voice of America and the BBC were easier to tune into than Radio Free Europe and Radio Liberty (which represented the émigré point of view). Sometimes all the stations, however, were jammed to the same extent, and at that moment I believe this was the case. I did not buy Soviet newspapers, but usually glanced at a copy of *Pravda* that hung on the wall of a small lane next to Vasilyev's house. We felt this was a rather unpredictable situation, and we followed developments with a certain apprehension. Someone joked: "Well, if we wake up tomorrow in the shape of small radioactive clouds floating in the stratosphere, that will mean no agreement has been reached." Yet it soon became clear that Kennedy had prevailed in the standoff (a fact, of course, that was passed over in total silence by the Soviet media, which simply announced that the crisis has been resolved to everyone's mutual satisfaction).

Kennedy was our hero: we called him "Jack," were enthusiastic about his youthful dynamism and his charming wife Jacqueline, and were genuinely grieved at his death the following year. A number of us thought Lee Harvey Oswald's crime could have been Soviet or Cuban revenge (while not a fan of conspiracy theories, I was also inclined to believe it). It should be noted that, at the start of the Cuban Revolution, we experienced a modicum of sympathy for Fidel Castro, if only because he stood in stark contrast to the Soviet gerontocracy. But by the time of the Cuban Missile Crisis, any sympathy had evaporated (in a sense, we considered Castro "a traitor to our cause").

HINSEY: The rhythm of thaws and freezes was perceptible in culture as well. The fall of 1961 saw the publication of an anthology titled *Pages from Tarusa*. There was an initial effort to stop the distribution of the seventy-five thousand copies of the book. Why was this publication so important?

VENCLOVA: It was the first attempt at an official yet semi-independent publication. As the anthology had been printed outside of Moscow, it had escaped overly attentive censorship, though of course some supervision and "internal censorship" were still at work. Later, this became a sort of a rule: books published in godforsaken provincial towns often generated keen interest because poems or essays originally written in Moscow or St. Petersburg—yet dubious from the authorities' point of view—might make it into print by this route. Frequently, these risky publications were confiscated and their editors punished. They were sometimes still available in the larger libraries, but more often than not relegated to the "special stacks." We read and discussed *Pages from Tarusa* quite avidly, stimulated by the fact that copies were a rarity. Tarusa was a town where Tsvetaeva had lived in her youth before the revolution: consequently, some of her work was also included—it was, I believe, her first appearance in the official Soviet press since the early 1920s. This was definitely the most significant part of the anthology.

HINSEY: Despite the Cuban Missile Crisis, which was a setback for Khrushchev, in 1962 the publication of works dealing with the legacy of Stalinism continued. Appearing in the October issue of *Novyi mir* were Yevtushenko's poem "The Heirs of Stalin" and Viktor Nekrasov's *Both Sides of the Ocean*. The idea of a generation of "The Heirs of Stalin" or of "Fathers and Sons"—began to take hold. But Yevtushenko and your milieu in the underground didn't necessarily see eye to eye—

VENCLOVA: Neither I, nor my friends, were fond of Yevtushenko: he was considered a gifted and dynamic man who nevertheless had sullied his reputation by more than a touch of careerism and time serving. At that time, I hadn't yet met him, though we had common acquaintances. He moved in circles that intersected with our milieu only to a degree: his readers were mainly liberal members of the party and the Komsomol, or just middlebrow intellectuals. Of course he was genuinely popular—a widely published poet exploring risky subjects, whose work was sometimes blocked by the censor but was recited during poetry readings and found its way into samizdat. But for us, he was "one of them," a member of the establishment, and his "The Heirs of Stalin" was an event that above all reflected intraparty squabbles. These squabbles did not particularly interest us. We were sure the party was incurable. Liberalism—that is, attempts to cure it—was certainly better than Stalinism, but real freedom could only come when the system had collapsed entirely, once and for all.

In pure chronological terms, I was a typical "son" opposed to the "fathers'" generation. Many of the "sons" from the Liberal or even the Stalinist milieu coalesced into the so-called *shestidesyatniki* group ("children of the 1960s"). Today, I tend to agree that the *shestidesyatniki* played a generally positive role in the history of the USSR. Yet I never considered myself a part of the group, and in my youth was critical toward it. As a rule, people such as Volodya Muravyov, Alexander Ginzburg, and Natasha Gorbanevskaya disdained the *shestidesyatniki* and looked for inspiration elsewhere.

HINSEY: This period also saw the publication of a few poems by Boris Slutsky, who had been banned from publishing after 1940. Later in life, Joseph Brodsky cited him as having a creative influence on him. Were these poems important to you?

VENCLOVA: Yevtushenko was the very epitome of *shestidesyatniki*, though at the same time, one of the most ambivalent figures among them. Nekrasov and Slutsky were better writers and were less ambiguous people. To tell the truth, Slutsky had publicly condemned Pasternak—a painful episode that caused him much remorse. Still, his poetry, boldly mixing official language and soldiers' slang, sarcasm and high tragedy, was significant for many, including the young Brodsky. Like everyone, I read Slutsky, but my poetic interests were of a different nature.

HINSEY: In 1963 you made the acquaintance of Andrei Sergeyev, a translator and a friend and mentor of Joseph Brodsky. Where did this meeting take place?

VENCLOVA: It happened in Palanga. Sergeyev spent the summer of 1963 there with his wife Lyudmila, who had been Marina's classmate at university. They met on the street, and Marina brought the Sergeyevs back to our house. We immediately made friends. Andrei was interested in all things Lithuanian, therefore I did my best to explain to him many lesser-known details about my country's present and past. I also introduced him to Romas Katilius and Juozas Tumelis.

Leonid Chertkov also visited Palanga at that time, and even stayed at our place with several other people. He belonged to the same group of underground poets as Sergeyev. Later, they parted ways (though they remained on very friendly terms): Sergeyev became a well-known translator and, to a degree, a member of the literary establishment; Chertkov kept as far away as possible from any establishment. After serving time in a prison camp, he made his living by preparing entries for the literary encyclopedia. This afforded him the opportunity to spend a great deal of time in the "special stacks" of various libraries—a privilege he valued highly: he even managed to make copies of banned texts and distribute them among friends. Both Sergeyev and Chertkov knew Brodsky well, and both were among the formative influences of his life.

The summer of 1963 was one of the merriest and most seminal of my life. We had long and open discussions on the veranda of our Palanga house, touching on every imaginable subject: current events as well as literature and history. Not only Sergeyev and Chertkov, but Dimitri Sesemann and some other of my Muscovite friends were present.

HINSEY: If I remember correctly, Sergeyev had an influence on your choice of translations at this time—

VENCLOVA: He was very knowledgeable about modern—and not just modern—English-language poetry. His translations of Robert Frost were considered first-rate (though Brodsky's praise of them was perhaps a bit inordinate). In collaboration with Volodya Muravyov, he managed to publish a volume of T. S. Eliot's work in Russian, which was an incredible feat, since Eliot was considered by the authorities to be as pernicious as Kafka—the very epitome of "bourgeois decadence." I started to translate the same poets into Lithuanian under Sergeyev's influence—and not without his help, but that happened later.

HINSEY: Let's return to your reading. During this period, people speak of "*Novy Mir* watching"—that is, keeping track of works that appeared there—

VENCLOVA: *Novy Mir* was the most influential liberal literary monthly, edited at that time by Aleksandr Tvardovsky, whom I mentioned earlier. He was a famous poet of peasant origins, accepted in party circles and close to Khrushchev himself, but undoubtedly an honest man. Tvardovsky did not belong to the "children of the 1960s," if only because he was considerably older. He believed as they did, however, in "Socialism with a human face" and made his monthly into the mouthpiece for their generation. Consequently, lots of bold writing, at times even exceeding the moderate program of the *shestidesyatniki*, appeared in *Novy Mir*'s pages. This was still Soviet literature, following Realist precepts and employing "internal censorship," yet often quite interesting. By the way, the fiction and criticism published in *Novy Mir* were better than its poetry (in that area, Tvardovsky's taste was limited—for instance, he never accepted Brodsky).

HINSEY: In November 1962, *Novy Mir* published of one of the most important works of this period, Aleksandr Solzhenitsyn's *One Day in the Life of Ivan Denisovich*. The book would have an immense impact on readers all over the world. Do you remember where you were exactly when you first began reading this work?

VENCLOVA: I was in Sasha Vasilyev's flat. All of us—Sasha, his mother, Marina, and myself—read *One Day*, almost tearing it out of each other's hands. Incidentally, the book's fame somewhat preceded its publication: a week or so before, I had heard (perhaps at Vladimir Finkelstein's) that "something really exceptional is going to appear in *Novy Mir*." And Volodya Muravyov quoted the last sentence of the story several days before the issue of the monthly reached us. It spread by word of mouth.

HINSEY: What were your impressions of the work, and how was it received by friends and those around you?

VENCLOVA: One of Akhmatova's friends did not consider it very good from a strictly literary point of view. "That does not matter at all. Two hundred and fifty million people must read it," retorted Akhmatova. (Brodsky, who was present at this exchange, often repeated her words.) Of course, the story's subject was shattering, but I believe *One Day* was a first-rate artistic achievement as well. At that time, many perceived Solzhenitsyn as a latter-day Tolstoy. This first work was, at the very least, on par with Tolstoy's early, but brilliant, *Sevastopol Stories*. It was concise and detached, devoid of any sentimentality. After reading it, I told Marina: "Well, this is prison camp cultural anthropology" (she agreed, though she considered my definition too dry). Moreover, Solzhenitsyn's feeling for the Russian language—its stylistic registers and sentence rhythms—was next to infallible. One might even have anticipated something equal to *War and Peace* from the unknown author. (Solzhenitsyn later tried to do this, and failed. Even his use of language went astray when he undertook his unconvincing linguistic experiments. *One Day* remains his acme).

One Day in the Life of Ivan Denisovich signaled a veritable sea change in Russian culture: it simply nullified Socialist Realism, which the "children of the 1960s" never managed to do. The expectations of the reading public, which longed for truth about the past, were finally met in full. The story became an immediate runaway bestseller—that is, the issue of *Novy Mir* that included *One Day* sold for exorbitant sums on the black market. (Perhaps only Tsvetaeva, whose book of poems appeared at approximately the same time, could rival it in that respect.) I may be mistaken, but I believe our landlady Elena Vasilyeva retyped *One Day* for a samizdat edition.

Akhmatova met Solzhenitsyn and asked him whether he was ready for world fame, which would be a hard trial. "I am used to hard trials," he answered. She had in mind the Nobel Prize (which she expected also for herself). There were rumors about the Lenin Prize as well. That would have put Solzhenitsyn in the somewhat ambiguous position of a "genuine Soviet author," but it never materialized.

HINSEY: While all books had to pass the Soviet censors, Khrushchev had personally approved the publication of this work. While the book had an immense impact on readers, Khrushchev also saw it as a means to support his reforms. Were any aspects of this strategizing apparent to readers at the time?

VENCLOVA: Not for me, in any case. Perhaps it was not so much a question of strategy but rather of Khrushchev's personal emotions and whims. We have heard that Tvardovsky convinced Khrushchev to approve the story. As legend has it, Tvardovsky was given the typescript of *One Day* by an employee at *Novy Mir*. He started reading it in bed, yet after several pages he stood up, put on his clothes and even his tie, and finished his reading fully alert. The next morning, he brought the typescript to Khrushchev and had a long talk with him.

HINSEY: Despite the publication of works such as *One Day*, this was a volatile period. In December 1962 Khrushchev and four Politburo members attended an exhibition titled *Thirty Years of Moscow Art* at the Manezh Gallery. During this visit, Khrushchev issued a public attack on abstract art, part of a more general backlash. Did you see this show, and how was Khrushchev's response understood at the time?

VENCLOVA: I did not see the show myself (as far as I remember, it was closed after Khrushchev's visit), but the event was widely discussed among my friends, especially at the Finkelsteins' flat, which was frequented by several art critics. Khrushchev's caddish behavior and remarks brought to mind the Zhdanov era, but also gave rise to much ridicule (unimaginable under Stalin). Still, the fates of the more innovative artists, to say nothing of the underground ones, hung in the balance, and we were well aware of it. I remember an illustrative anecdote from the time: finding myself and Marina in some financial straits, I tried to sell a volume of Hieronymus Bosch published by Skira at a second-hand bookshop (such sales were usually reasonably lucrative). The bookseller said: "This is abstract, and we can no longer accept it." My attempts to prove that there was no abstract art in the fifteenth century were less than successful.

HINSEY: In March 1963, six hundred writers, artists, and intellectuals were summoned to Sverdlov Hall, where Khrushchev called for a halt to de-Stalinization and liberalization. A number of writers were forced to recant their views. Were you at this meeting, or did you hear about it?

VENCLOVA: I did not attend (only established people were invited, and I was neither established nor known), but I heard about it. Several such meetings marked the end of this relatively enlightened cultural moment—they are now somewhat merged in my memory. However, certain signs of vacillation remained: for some time, Solzhenitsyn continued to publish new works, such as *Matryona's House*, and the Grand Prize was awarded to Fellini's *8½* at the Third International Film Festival in Moscow. These might have reflected either the continuation of intraparty struggles, or the inconsistency of Khrushchev's character and judgments, or both.

HINSEY: How did artists interpret these party declarations? Can you speak about the coexistence of "official party discourse" and the "artistic under-ground"? In 1963, how had the underground scene evolved since your arrival in 1961?

VENCLOVA: The reactions of the artists at the Sverdlov Hall meeting were extremely varied: Ernst Neizvestny held his ground in the verbal conflict with Khrushchev, and Andrei Voznesensky, another celebrated "child of the 1960s," did not. Khrushchev publicly offered to provide him with an exit visa and throw him out of the Soviet Union. To prove his loyalty, Voznesensky subse-quently wrote and published a servile poem dedicated to Lenin under the title "Longjumeau." Volkonsky, who was not invited to that meeting, remarked: "If I were in Voznesensky's place, I would have told Khrushchev: 'Nikita Sergeevich, you are just trying to intimidate me.' Then, with a grand gesture, he would present me with an exit visa, which would not be unwelcome." "We should not be forced to emigrate. We'll live until better times," someone contradicted Volkonsky. "Better times will never come. The Lord's curse is on this country," the composer retorted. I believe these words reflect the viewpoint of the entire artistic underground. If the "children of the 1960s," in large part, still cherished some hopes for "Socialism with a human face," the underground did not. In 1963, this difference became decidedly more pronounced than in 1961.

HINSEY: In 1964, Khrushchev's position in the Central Committee and the Politburo was weakened due to a number of factors including the Berlin Wall episode, the Cuban Missile Crisis, and the USSR's troubled foreign relations with China. In mid-October, while on vacation in the Crimea, he was forced to resign and pushed into retirement. How did you and your friends view this event at the time?

VENCLOVA: When Khrushchev was pushed out, I was in Vilnius. Incidentally, a day or two before his retirement was announced, my father hinted that it was imminent. At first, I did not believe him.

However strange it may sound, many (though not all) of us felt a modicum of pity and even sympathy for Khrushchev. His rudeness and comic stupidity notwithstanding, he was the only Soviet dictator who had preserved traits of a simple but not excessively evil human being. One had to wait until Gorbachev before there was another such case. Khrushchev not only released millions of political prisoners and reduced his country's isolation, but indirectly saved his own life in the process: due to his reforms, he was not executed and could spend his old age in relative peace (becoming more and more of a dissident with the passage of time). We could hardly expect anything as good from his successors.

13

Anna Akhmatova

HINSEY: I would like to now turn to a significant encounter from this period. When did you first meet Anna Akhmatova?

VENCLOVA: I believe it was in 1963. Our landlady, Elena Vasilyeva, knew Akhmatova personally, although she did not belong to the poet's inner circle. Once, Akhmatova asked Elena to type the manuscript copy of her essay "Pushkin and the Banks of the Neva." For several decades, Akhmatova had been seriously researching Pushkin's life and work. After Soviet censorship had blocked any publication of Akhmatova's poetry in the 1930s, she became a professional Pushkin scholar (Brodsky considered her among the best, and the only specialist on the same intellectual and artistic level as Pushkin himself).

HINSEY: What was the impetus behind her Pushkin scholarship?

VENCLOVA: To a certain degree, it helped her prove that she was engaged in "socially meaningful" work. But she also admired Pushkin more than any other Russian (or foreign) poet, and had a good eye for parallels between their two eras. She scolded me when I took the liberty of saying that Pushkin was not necessarily relevant to my generation.

HINSEY: And the essay—

VENCLOVA: "Pushkin and the Banks of the Neva" was not, strictly speaking, a samizdat affair (it was published shortly thereafter), but it had something Akhmatova liked to call a "triple bottom," like hidden compartments in a smuggler's suitcase. Its topic was Pushkin's lonely wanderings in the Vasileostrovsky district of St. Petersburg—unpopulated islands in the Neva where the poet looked for the unmarked graves of his executed friends, leaders of the failed Decembrist uprising. Exactly one hundred years after Pushkin, Akhmatova used to wander in the same part of the city, since her husband

Nikolai Gumilev, a great poet executed by the Bolsheviks, was also presumably buried there. Only a few people close to Akhmatova understood the analogy, which escaped the censors.

Elena Vasilyeva asked me to bring the typescript to Akhmatova, which I did happily, if timidly.

HINSEY: Where was Akhmatova residing at this time?

VENCLOVA: In Leningrad she lived mainly with the family of her ex-husband Nikolai Punin, to whom she had been married in the 1920s and 1930s. Punin was an avant-garde art critic who also perished at the hands of the Soviet authorities: he died in a labor camp a few months after Stalin's death. Akhmatova visited Moscow frequently, usually staying with her friend Nina Olshevskaya, whose husband Viktor Ardov—a minor satirist and a witty man—was appreciated by a number of nonconformist writers including Bulgakov and Pasternak. (It was Ardov who recommended that Akhmatova be reinstated in the Union of Soviet Writers in 1951.) Incidentally, Ardov's family were among the few permitted to call her "Acuma," which means "witch" or "hag" in Japanese—a nickname Punin invented. Everyone else, including Brodsky and myself, called her "Anna Andreyevna." Ardov's residence on Ordynka Street became a semilegendary address in post-Stalinist Moscow. It was only a short walk from Elena's flat to Ordynka.

HINSEY: What happened during your first meeting?

VENCLOVA: Akhmatova was alone in the Ardovs' rather large apartment—a stout lady with aristocratic bearing (she was sometimes compared to Catherine the Great), looking a bit older than her age, which was seventy-four. We talked in the hallway, perhaps for five minutes—she apologized for not inviting me in, stating that her room was in disarray. I was invited into the various rooms she occupied only during our later meetings. Regardless of whether it was in Moscow or in Leningrad, her living space generally looked the same: a cramped room with a writing desk and sofa, and practically nothing else. There were several drawings on the walls—above all, Modigliani's famous portrait of Akhmatova in her youth. I believe I saw it in both cities; it may have always accompanied her, though I could be mistaken on this point.

HINSEY: Brodsky said that after his first encounter with Akhmatova, it took him three or four meetings to fully understand with whom he was dealing. But this wasn't your case—

VENCLOVA: I knew very well with whom I was speaking. Needless to say, I felt extremely uneasy, almost paralyzed with timidity. For me, it was akin to visiting Pushkin, or Shakespeare for that matter. Akhmatova was much less amicable and communicative than Pasternak, at least at first. She kept her distance, although she was perfectly polite.

HINSEY: You had become acquainted with other Silver Age poets through your father's library, and your study of Mayakovsky—and had heard Akhmatova's name in connection with the 1946 Zhdanov speech condemning her and Zoshchenko—

VENCLOVA: The very first lines of Akhmatova that I ever saw were quoted in Zhdanov's famous speech: he said the poem was written by a "half harlot, half nun"—a qualification that had to be learned by heart by all Soviet schoolchildren. (It was plagiarized from the prewar Soviet *Literary Encyclopedia*.) I read more of her work following Zhdanov's assault, that is, in the late 1940s, because I was intrigued by his vituperative words (as were many others). A forbidden fruit, as a rule, attracts attention. At university, I managed to get my hands on a collection or two of Akhmatova's poetry printed before World War II: small-format books, dog-eared by generations of readers. Father did not conceal—at least at home—his appreciation for Akhmatova's work. As I mentioned earlier, he sometimes read her early poems aloud and his library contained an old anthology where many of her poems could be found. He was pleased when the Zhdanov decree was lifted and a new book (albeit a small selection, crudely censored) was published in 1961. By 1963, I was already well-acquainted with almost all of her work—in part through samizdat.

HINSEY: During this first visit you exchanged thoughts on translation, about which Akhmatova had some strong opinions—

VENCLOVA: Elena Vasilyeva had introduced me to Akhmatova over the phone and had told her something about my interests. After taking the Pushkin typescript, Akhmatova said to me: "I have heard you are translating Pasternak. No doubt that is difficult, he's so surprising. Generally, if one is able to write one's own poetry, one should avoid translating. However, it sometimes happens that a poet finds his vocation in it—for example Zhukovsky. Or Shengeli, whose version of Byron's *Don Juan* sounds better to my ear than the original. But Byron, I believe, is not the best of poets."

Akhmatova herself could not avoid translating as it was the only means of survival open to her for so many years. But, unlike Pasternak, she was rather loath to do it. Much of it was done with the help of word-for-word translations prepared by someone else. She even worked on Chinese and Korean classics (assisted by scholars of those languages); these were academic projects about which she could be proud. But at other times, she was a bit careless:

in certain cases, she put her name to translations by beginners who wouldn't otherwise have been published. Akhmatova merely provided her signature and handed over the royalties to the actual translators.

HINSEY: Among her poetic commissions, Akhmatova had translated Lithuanian poets—

VENCLOVA: Akhmatova told me: "I have translated your country's poets as well." I answered, "Yes, you have worked on Saloměja Něris." Lithuanians were proud of this fact, and her friend Lydia Chukovskaya recorded in her diary an occasion when Akhmatova had recited a moving poem by Něris. "But not only," said Akhmatova, "another poetess as well: a nineteenth-century one." She was referring to Eglě, a minor author (and, by a strange coincidence, a close friend of my great-uncle Karolis). I suspect that the translations of Eglě's old-fashioned ballads were another of Akhmatova's charitable gestures—that is, actually done by someone else.

HINSEY: Did you discuss other matters having to do with Lithuania? Had she visited Lithuania before or after the revolution?

VENCLOVA: Later, when I began to visit Akhmatova regularly, she told me, "You are the second Lithuanian in my life." The first was Vladimir Shileiko, whom she married after Gumilev's death. Shileiko was a poet and brilliant Assyriologist, who translated Sumerian texts into Russian and—fortunately— died a natural death in Stalinist times. He was indeed of Lithuanian origin, though from a Russified family, and did not speak the language. Akhmatova used to call him "one disaster of a husband."

Akhmatova visited Vilnius only once, in 1914, at the age of twenty-five. It was Christmas, and she was accompanying Gumilev, who had been con-scripted into the army and was going to be posted to the Russian-German front. They stayed in a hotel next to the chapel of Our Lady of the Gate of Dawn (Aušros Vartai in Lithuanian) with its icon of the Madonna, which was—and still is—considered miraculous. Akhmatova prayed at the icon for her husband's safety during the war. Gumilev was indeed spared death, and was not even wounded by German bullets, but was murdered by a Soviet one in 1921.

HINSEY: Did you speak to her about your father? Did they know each other?

VENCLOVA: We never spoke about my father. Most likely his name was not unknown to her, since he was a visible literary figure. They never met, but Father, upon hearing about my acquaintance with Akhmatova, sent her a present—his book of poems about Italy with Modernist drawings by a young Lithuanian artist, Stasys Krasauskas, who was fashionable at that time throughout the Soviet Union. Perhaps the book is still in her archive.

HINSEY: Akhmatova was born in 1889 and by the time of the revolution, her ethical and aesthetic beliefs were already firmly established—

VENCLOVA: Akhmatova was a living link to a different era, not just the Silver Age, but the entire tradition of Russian culture. First of all, she represented St. Petersburg and its heritage extending back to Pushkin—even to Kantemir, the first professional Russian poet under Peter the Great. It was a poetic as well as an ethical legacy: namely, loyalty to one's friends, stubborn yet calm resistance to the violence of the state, and, last but not least, irony and self-irony. Here, one might even go further back—to the archpriest Avvakum and his follower Morozova, two seventeenth-century martyrs whom Akhmatova mentioned more than once. In short, she stood for a hierarchy of values: good and evil had to be called by their names, period. Through communicating with her, one became aware that this ethical hierarchy was intimately—if not necessarily directly—connected with authentic poetry. These convictions were a potent antidote to the moral collapse during the Soviet period—as well as to Soviet or semi-Soviet literature.

HINSEY: Nadezhda Mandelstam says that she and Akhmatova were very concerned with the question of "what constitutes courage." They came to the conclusion that "courage, daring, and fortitude were not synonymous." What do you think was the source of Akhmatova's strength?

VENCLOVA: I would say its distinguishing feature was fortitude. Courage and daring are morally neutral qualities—they were also found in many revolutionaries whose actions, in the final account, promoted evil. Fortitude, on the other hand, is usually a sign of moral strength. Soviet dissidents were courageous by definition—and daring more often than not—but many of them lacked fortitude, leading to breakdowns, which at times discredited the cause. This was not the case with these two old women who were brought up according to the prerevolutionary tradition with its Judeo-Christian roots. Brodsky said once of Nadezhda Mandelstam that she was one of the very few people for whom the Ten Commandments were still in force. Akhmatova possibly even surpassed her in this respect.

HINSEY: Having reflected upon the subject for many years, why do you think that Akhmatova was never arrested?

VENCLOVA: The Stalinist terror was a sort of lottery: one might be completely loyal and perish nevertheless. Conversely, one might be considered an "enemy of the people" and survive. I believe this arbitrariness was part of the strategy: no one could be sure of his or her fate, which worked perfectly to Stalin's advantage. Moreover, Stalin was rather well-informed about literature, and generally understood the relative value of various authors. Figures such as Pasternak, Bulgakov, Akhmatova, or Platonov were preferable to hack writers, particularly if they could be transformed into bards for the regime (in the cases of Bulgakov and Pasternak, Stalin very nearly succeeded). Finally, there was also a sadistic element. Akhmatova lost her husband and several people she loved. Her son was imprisoned, then released, only to be imprisoned again. She was vilified in the official press and school textbooks, and for decades she was forbidden to publish her work. This was perhaps worse than execution— or a prison camp—where one might be more quickly put out of one's misery.

HINSEY: Akhmatova was sought out by younger writers for advice about their poetry, and she was always very tactful. However, it became known that she had a series of prepared answers with which to respond. Could you explain how this worked?

VENCLOVA: Akhmatova was a good storyteller and possessed numerous real-life anecdotes that she would recite verbatim. She liked to call these her "gramophone recordings." In the 1960s, she was literally besieged by young people who wished to acquaint her with their scribblings and hoped for encouragement from her. (Once, my friend Evgeny Levitin, an art critic, was introduced to her. After exchanging preliminary courtesies, Akhmatova said: "Well, go ahead and read your poems." "What poems?" Levitin replied, "I have never written a line of poetry in my life!" "Glory to God Almighty!" she exclaimed, "at last a normal person!") However, she took pity on young artists and had a fixed set of polite answers with which to respond to their efforts. These were also a type of "gramophone recording." If she said, for instance, "Your rhymes are astonishing," or "You are a master of metaphor," it meant that your poems left much to be desired, after which you would consider throwing yourself into the Neva. If, however, the writing was good, she would remark: "There is some mystery in these poems." That was what she said to young Brodsky, and to Natasha Gorbanevskaya as well.

HINSEY: In the preceding chapter, we spoke about Akhmatova's admiration for Solzhenitsyn's prose. But there is the famous story about him showing her some of his poetry—

VENCLOVA: Solzhenitsyn started out as a poet while in the Gulag—his verses (some of which have now been published) were straightforward and principally political. He was already a celebrity when he came to visit Akhmatova.

While she highly valued his prose writings, she could not conceal her disappointment in his poetry. She said: "Well, your poems are somewhat lacking in mystery." Solzhenitsyn retorted: "Well, Anna Andreyevna, perhaps your poems have too much mystery in them."

HINSEY: In the spring of 1964 you collaborated with Judita Vaičiūnaitė on a book of Akhmatova's poetry. Can you say how this volume came about?

VENCLOVA: After 1961, Akhmatova's poetic work was no longer entirely banned—the small book I just mentioned had appeared, and a larger selection was in preparation. At this time, the Vilnius State Publishing House began a series of books by Soviet Russian poets in Lithuanian translation—this was in line with an official "friendship of nations" policy. Still, there was a touch of liberalism about it. Although some of the chosen poets, like Zabolotsky, were not exactly Soviet in their outlook, the books (usually five in a boxed set) were carefully produced. My old friend Judita Vaičiūnaitė, already a well-known and widely published poet, was a natural candidate for translating Akhmatova, particularly since Lithuanian critics used to compare the two. (Much later, under Gorbachev, Judita translated "Requiem" as well.) The bulk of the translations were hers, but I was offered the chance to translate eighteen poems. This was perhaps a gesture by the publishing house, suggesting that I was not yet an incorrigible enemy, and could still perhaps become a normal Soviet man of letters.

This was my first major literary project, and I applied myself seriously to the task. I knew Akhmatova's work by heart and I translated her while walking the side streets of Vilnius, trying to match the movement of her poetry with the rhythm of my steps. After finishing the first poem, I stopped in a courtyard along my way, and was rewarded by an unbelievably beautiful view of Vilnius's church spires—one that I had never seen before. That remains one of the most memorable moments of my life.

HINSEY: You brought these translations to Moscow for her to read—

VENCLOVA: The book appeared in the shops, and I brought the first copy to the author as a gift from Judita and myself (Judita, unfortunately, never met Akhmatova; she rarely left her flat in Vilnius). By then, I had already been introduced to the poet a second time—Andrei Sergeyev, who belonged to Akhmatova's inner circle, took me along with him for a visit. I spent several hours listening to their conversation, once more in state of virtual paralysis.

HINSEY: What were Akhmatova's initial responses to your translations?

VENCLOVA: Akhmatova began by saying, "Lithuanian is extraordinary—I am proud that my poetry has been published in this language. Please read to me a poem or two." This I did, but not without considerable anxiety. After the second poem, she said, "You have correctly conveyed the intonation." As I had been warned by Sergeyev about Akhmatova's "gramophone recordings," I understood very well that she considered the translations unsuccessful. Therefore, I mumbled something, left the book on her desk, and quickly said good-bye. As a young poet, this plunged me into a nearly suicidal state.

HINSEY: However, on the same day, the Russian philologist Vyacheslav Ivanov came to see her—

VENCLOVA: Yes. At that time, Vyacheslav Ivanov was still a relatively young man, considered one of the most erudite and enlightened people in Russia (he is now a famous scholar, and a full member of the Russian Academy of Sciences). He was also a person of strict and unwavering liberal views, connected to the dissident milieu. Nadezhda Mandelstam used to say that his good education was due to sheer luck—because of health reasons, he never attended Soviet schools and therefore could read whatever he liked. A son of the well-known fiction writer, Vsevolod Ivanov, he had been acquainted with Pasternak and Akhmatova from childhood, and was their close friend and confidant. His nickname, used by almost everyone, was "Koma"—this helped to distinguish him from another Vyacheslav Ivanov, a Symbolist poet and philosopher, who died in Rome as an émigré in 1949.

Koma Ivanov visited Akhmatova frequently, and happened to stop by immediately after I had left. The book was still on her desk, open to the page with my translation. Koma is fluent in approximately fifty languages including Hittite and Ainu, and his Lithuanian is as good as mine. He read the translation and informed Akhmatova that he considered it quite accomplished. Following this, Akhmatova telephoned Elena and invited me to visit her "as often as I liked." She also inscribed the second copy of her Lithuanian book in Russian as follows: "For Tomash Venclova—my own verses which are nevertheless a mystery to me." ("Tomash" [Tomasz] was the Polish version of my first name—she was not necessarily aware of such linguistic details.) Akhmatova's keyword, "mystery," was there, to my elation.

HINSEY: Following this, you had a series of meetings with her. What kind of pattern did they take?

VENCLOVA: From time to time, I would telephone Akhmatova, and we would set a convenient hour and date. Sometimes I brought wine, or even vodka, with me. She was not averse to having a drink or two; according to her, vodka was preferable to wine at her age, since it expanded the blood vessels, while wine contracted them. Frequently, others were present: Anatoly Naiman, who acted as her sort of personal secretary, Punin's granddaughter Anya Kaminskaya, or my old friend Dimitri Sesemann, whom Akhmatova liked. We talked about everything, from Pushkin and the Silver Age to current events. She was very much au courant regarding the political and literary scene, and had strong opinions about both. Of course, she had no illusions regarding the regime, but she was capable of an occasional good word about Khrushchev ("say what you like, he released millions of prisoners"). Very quickly, an element of humor would creep into the discussions. I remember one time, Natasha Gorbanevskaya arrived at Akhmatova's flat unannounced, a habit she had. Akhmatova told Anya with a crafty smile: "Please tell Natasha that I cannot receive her immediately—I am busy with a young man."

HINSEY: Akhmatova knew that she was being shadowed by the KGB, and feared that her apartment was extensively bugged. Since the end of the Soviet Union, what kind of information has come to light regarding the extent of her surveillance?

VENCLOVA: There is no doubt that Akhmatova was under surveillance. However, the extent of the bugging is unclear, as almost all the Russian intelligentsia were prone to a sort of persecution complex (though the younger generation generally paid less attention to it). I believe the KGB preferred more traditional methods: shadowing Akhmatova and many others. Some of her female confidants were actually KGB informers: that came to light when the regime collapsed and certain archives were opened.

HINSEY: Did Akhmatova recite her poems for you, or the work of other poets she admired?

VENCLOVA: She did, though not frequently. Once, I was present at a special occasion—Moscow radio came to Akhmatova's apartment to record her reading five or six poems aloud. She did so in the deep, intense voice of a tragic actress. Another time, she recited to me several previously unknown poems by Mandelstam that had been found in archives by friends; afterward she gave me the texts. A poet she mentioned and recited more than once was Gumilev: Akhmatova considered him an undervalued figure, who had never really been appreciated by the reading public or the critics. She admired Blok, though with a modicum of reserve ("he had no real following"). As for Pasternak, she talked about him in a friendly way and always called him "Boris," but clearly disliked *Doctor Zhivago* and his poems from the 1930s and 1940s.

HINSEY: In addition to Russian, Akhmatova read fluently in Italian, French, German, and English—she had begun reading Shakespeare as a girl, and knew the great Modernist works. Did she speak to you about her reading?

VENCLOVA: Yes. She admired Kafka and found much in common between their respective works. However, she was not able to find a copy of *The Castle* in the USSR. I had to summarize it for her since I had read it in Polish. Unlike most of her contemporaries, she was not a Francophile, but an Anglophile: I believe Joseph Brodsky inherited this characteristic from her. She used to say that French Modernist painting had edged out French Modernist poetry, and was not a fan of Surrealists such as Max Jacob or Paul Éluard ("It is not freedom, it is arbitrariness"). But she was extremely knowledgeable about Shakespeare and, for instance, Shelley. She read *Ulysses* in English four or five times and confessed to having understood it fully only during her last attempt; such endeavors helped her to endure the worst of Stalinist times. She was also very interested in T. S. Eliot and she knew his entire oeuvre, indeed some of it by heart. Together with Nadezhda Mandelstam (an opinion not shared by Pasternak) she considered Hemingway a nonentity and much preferred the work of William Faulkner.

HINSEY: Akhmatova was quite concerned about errors in scholarship about her life—

VENCLOVA: In the sixties, certain émigré memoirs that discussed Akhmatova started to leak back into the USSR. She was profoundly displeased with them, especially with those by her acquaintances from prerevolutionary times such as Georgy Ivanov and Sergei Makovsky, which she considered particularly slanderous. I frequently heard stern words from her about these memoirists. Andrei Sergeyev attempted to rehabilitate Ivanov in her eyes, saying that his book was not strictly a memoir, but rather an epic saga about Russian writers who opposed Bolshevism. That said, Sergeyev's attempts were not successful. She collaborated with the young British scholar Amanda Height, attempting to respond to some of these memoirs. The result was a good, if modest and elliptical, book titled *A Poetic Pilgrimage*, which appeared after Akhmatova's death. It presents an image of Akhmatova that was, to a large degree, created by the poet herself.

HINSEY: Not all of Akhmatova's works have survived, including her verse drama *Enuma Elish*. This was written in Tashkent in 1942, where she had been evacuated during the war—

VENCLOVA: In the 1960s, when I visited her, she was very much concerned with this verse drama, especially since a Düsseldorf theater had approached her about staging it. The drama (which she preferred to call a tragedy) was a complicated, partly satirical work dealing with her experience of the totalitarian universe—a sort of prophecy regarding Zhdanov's assault and everything that followed. The exotic title was taken from a Babylonian poem, the oldest extant cosmological text of mankind predating the Book of Genesis: it means "When above . . ." (Akhmatova's interest in such texts derived from Shileiko.) She destroyed the manuscript, presumably in 1944, though perhaps for more strictly private than political reasons. Around 1964, she started to recreate *Enuma Elish* from memory, transforming it in the process, though she never brought it to completion.

HINSEY: Did she ever read you sections from this work?

VENCLOVA: More than once, Akhmatova read to me and to others excerpts from *Enuma Elish*—monologues or dialogues in verse that could also have been considered stand-alone poems (some of them were similar to poetic texts I already knew). The main plot line concerned the trial of a female poet; it was somewhat in the manner of Kafka. She also liked to say that her contacts with the German theater were insinuating themselves into the text and becoming part of it. Incidentally, the theater rated the fragments sent to it extremely highly and considered them "ten steps ahead of any play written today."

HINSEY: In 1963 "Requiem" was published in West Germany in Russian. What were the conditions under which you first were able to read this poem?

VENCLOVA: I believe I read it in samizdat before it found its way into print. The 1963 Munich edition lay on Akhmatova's desk when I visited her for the second time with Andrei Sergeyev—that is, before the Lithuanian translations appeared. The Soviet authorities decided to refrain from any response to this "criminal" publication. After the Pasternak affair, they tried to prevent scandals involving famous authors. Akhmatova was visibly happy that the book was finally available to a wider audience, and with the government's forbearance—though she still considered her situation to be precarious. The only thing she strongly disliked was the use of Savely Sorin's drawing as a frontispiece.

HINSEY: What insights did she share with you into her art as a poet?

VENCLOVA: She was reluctant to speak much about the art of poetry: for her, it belonged to the sphere of sacrum and enigma, which was best passed over in silence. Still, one could intuit her attitude from her remarks about individual authors and poems. She considered traditional poetic technique, going back to Pushkin, as an integral part of any work of value. For her, this was connected to a sense of harmony and order—and taste; for

Akhmatova, impeccable taste was inseparable from ethics. Therefore, one had to be a master of craft, well-versed in everything concerning rhythm, sound patterns, and so on. But this was just the foundation, so to speak. In this, poets were best served when their intuition was guided by language itself. On a higher level, the poem was dictated by a certain indescribable power—perhaps by the Lord (she was religious, though never ostentatious about it), or by the spirit of an entire people. She grasped that inspiration was the hardest part—one had to reckon with the possibility of failure, that a poem might remain a technical exercise (even if a brilliant one). She was extremely skeptical of "Thaw generation" celebrities such as Yevtushenko, Voznesensky, and Akhmadulina: for her, they looked superficial, too concerned with immediate success and perfunctory innovation, and lacking in ethical backbone. In connection to that, she frequently mentioned Balmont and Severyanin—two Silver Age figures who were incomparably more popular than Mandelstam or Tsvetaeva but proved to be minor poets in the final account.

HINSEY: Over the gates of Fontanka House where Akhmatova lived in Leningrad, there is the motto *Deus conservat omnia* (God preserves all). This appears in your poem "After the Lecture," which is, in many ways, a tribute to her—

VENCLOVA: The poem you have mentioned attempts to give an idea of Akhmatova's views on creative work. The monologue I created for her is imagined, but I hope its assertions would be acceptable to her.

The words *Deus conservat omnia* were consonant with Akhmatova's profound belief that memory is a higher form of justice, which can provide retribution for everything—good or bad. Memory was the axis of her philosophy. In her opinion, preservation of the world—if only of its details—in poetic lines made a human being virtually equal to God.

HINSEY: Akhmatova believed all poets were to some degree clairvoyant, and she had a tendency to communicate with them "through the ether"—did this enter into your relationship as well?

VENCLOVA: It never entered our personal relationship, but we discussed it sometimes. Once, I said that Gumilev, in his later works, was a mystical poet. "Well, every poet is a mystic," Akhmatova replied, "but Gumilev was also a clairvoyant, he literally saw the future. For instance, he knew that the planes would in time become extremely heavy, as they are today, although in his time they were flimsy and weightless."

HINSEY: While Akhmatova is known for her profound and masterful poetry, those who met her were struck by her marvelous sense of humor and of the absurd. On one occasion, a Swedish professor who was working on her poetry came to see her. What impressed her most about the meeting was how white his shirt was. She said, "We have lived through revolution, wars, and all sorts of blood, and the Swedes have been washing and ironing that shirt . . ."—

VENCLOVA: Most of her witty sayings were recorded in Mikhail Ardov's book (Mikhail was Viktor's son who became a Russian Orthodox priest), but some escaped his attention. There was a story about a Soviet editor who requested that she delete the word "angel" from one of her poems. He justified his request by the perfectly Marxist statement: "Angels do not exist." "Well, what does exist?" asked Akhmatova. Another story, known to the happy few, concerned her relationship with Pasternak. Once, they were walking in the evening on a Moscow street, talking about the minor writer Sergei Spassky, whose poems Pasternak praised inordinately. All of a sudden, Pasternak fell to his knees and proposed to her. "Dear Boris," Akhmatova said soothingly, "I'm not Spassky."

HINSEY: In December 1964 Akhmatova was allowed to travel to Italy to receive the Etna-Taormina Prize, and on June 4, 1965, she received an honorary doctorate from Oxford. Did she speak to you about these trips? What did she feel about her fame?

VENCLOVA: When Dimitri Sesemann asked her: "How did you like Italy, Anna Andreyevna?" she answered: "It was too late." (She had visited northern Italy—and Western Europe in general—as a young girl, before the revolution.) Still, her trips to Taormina and Oxford were among her favorite topics. She was happy to see Rome (I believe she had never visited it before), but called it a "suspicious city where God most likely competed with Satan." On the other hand, she did not manage to see Venice, and recounted, with a touch of humor, that her only impression of Venice was water splashing at the wheels of her train at the station. She was well aware of the fact that the Etna-Taormina Prize was a sort of rehearsal for the Nobel, and was undoubtedly proud of it, but nevertheless treated it lightheartedly.

HINSEY: In 1961 an antiparasite law was enacted, precisely as a way to handle artists and freethinkers who did not have permanent employment. In November 1963 an article appeared in *Vechernii Leningrad* accusing Joseph Brodsky of being a literary parasite. Brodsky was arrested on February 13, 1964, and his trial began five days later. Akhmatova was very close to Brodsky. Did she speak to you about these events?

VENCLOVA: As I mentioned earlier, I first heard Brodsky's name in 1960, on the very day of Pasternak's death. I did not meet him until 1966, but knew and admired many of his samizdat poems given to me by Andrei Sergeyev and others. His trial was a shocking event, very widely discussed in Moscow and Leningrad, and in Lithuania as well. Akhmatova mentioned Brodsky on every occasion—his fate was among her main concerns at that time.

HINSEY: She tried to support Brodsky—

VENCLOVA: Yes, she did her best, arranging petitions on his behalf and soliciting help from people with strong official standing, such as Dmitri Shostakovich, Samuil Marshak, and Aleksandr Tvardovsky. She also tried, by various means, to neutralize the harmful actions of Aleksandr Prokofiev, an influential Leningrad literary figure and one of Brodsky's principal enemies. During our talks, he was always nicknamed "Prokop." Once, Akhmatova arranged a small party, where we drank wine to Brodsky's freedom and "Prokop's" downfall. (Anatoly Naiman, who was a very close friend of Brodsky's at that time, was present as well—he managed to visit Brodsky in internal exile, in Norenskaya, a village in Northern Russia, but the party probably preceded his trip.) Incidentally, she felt pangs of conscience concerning Brodsky, since she believed (without the slightest grounds) that he had been arrested primarily because of his friendship with her, a proverbial "enemy of the people."

On the other hand, Brodsky was not well-informed about Akhmatova's attempts to support him, and felt a bit abandoned. However, when he came back to Leningrad she was still alive, and he learned the truth.

HINSEY: Did she share any of Brodsky's poems with you?

VENCLOVA: Yes, she recited a well-known Brodsky poem that was dedicated to her ("Roosters will start calling and bustling about . . ."), which she called "marvelous." (Brodsky considered it unsuccessful.) She also gave me several poems he had written in prison, which were smuggled out of his cell by means unknown to us.

HINSEY: When was the last time you saw Akhmatova?

VENCLOVA: It was perhaps in the late fall or early winter of 1965. I accompanied her to Andrei Sergeyev's flat. He lived on the outskirts of Moscow—in a five-story apartment building totally indistinguishable from all the others, which stood in long rows and were devoid of numbering. Such blocks were commonly known as *khrushchoby* (Khrushchev slums). Predictably, I brought her to the wrong flat in the wrong building. It was hard for her to climb the stairs because of her heart condition (there were no elevators). Thank God, it was only the second floor. Akhmatova was less than pleased, but we finally found Sergeyev's apartment and spent a long evening together. Then, I accompanied her back to Moscow, to the flat of her old friend Lyuba Stenich, which was, alas, on the sixth floor, and also without elevator. We climbed the stairs for half an hour or more. The next day, Lyuba telephoned to say that Anna Andreyevna had pardoned my error, and that I was still welcome to visit her. But that was the last time I saw her. I left for Vilnius directly afterward, and did not return to Moscow until early March.

HINSEY: Akhmatova died on March 5, 1966, at a sanatorium in Domodedovo outside of Moscow. There were a range of memorials for her, including in Moscow at the Sklifosovsky Institute, in Leningrad at the Saint Nicholas Naval Cathedral, as well as a graveside service at Komarovo, where she had her tiny dacha and was buried. Could you describe the scene of the event you attended?

VENCLOVA: Just as in 1960 when Pasternak died, I happened to be in Moscow; someone telephoned and told me Anna Andreyevna had passed away. On March 9, I attended the rites in the morgue of the Sklifosovsky Institute, a shabby place besieged by hundreds or even thousands of people. I believe Andrei Sergeyev and his wife Lyuda helped me to approach the coffin. I did not hear any official speeches (though I imagine these were delivered). At that time, my personal life was in such disarray that I considered suicide. I had a strange feeling that Akhmatova was watching over me and knew about my predicament, and I derived comfort from that. I was not in Leningrad for the service at the Saint Nicholas Cathedral, or the graveside service in Komarovo, where Brodsky and his friends said farewell to her. It was the genuine end of the Silver Age.

14

SIGN OF SPEECH

HINSEY: I would like to discuss your poetic work during this time: in the spring of 1972 you were allowed to publish a single volume—your only officially sanctioned book of poetry in Soviet Lithuania—*Sign of Speech*—

VENCLOVA: During this period, the censorship situation had somewhat improved. After 1968, the prevailing atmosphere was one of a "freeze," but there were some unexpected fluctuations in the party line, which were duly reflected in the editorial policy of the Lithuanian State Publishing House. For a time, experimental verse was permitted (or benevolently overlooked), especially if it possessed a "life-affirming," that is optimistic, quality or had a folkloric aspect. Several such books by Sigitas Geda and others appeared at this time. Usually, a "locomotive" was required: the very first poem in a book by a first-time author had to mention Lenin, or Fidel Castro (or, preferably, both) with due enthusiasm. Everyone consented to this demand, which was unspoken, or only discussed in private between an editor and an author. For me, it was out of the question. After my experience with my science book, I scorned the system and had enough respect for poetry to reject these "rules of the game." Brodsky faced a similar dilemma. After his exile, a book of his poems was being prepared in the USSR, but Yevtushenko told him it needed a "locomotive"—a piece about Lenin or, at, least, about the great Russian people. Brodsky had a poem on people and their language, and quite a good one (Akhmatova admired it), which could perhaps have been construed as "patriotic" and therefore adhering to the official line. Romas Katilius persuaded him this would have been a gesture of capitulation. Brodsky refused to include it in the book; it was subsequently rejected by the publisher. To my astonishment, *Sign of Speech* appeared without any mandatory "locomotive" or "lightning rod"—perhaps the first such case in Soviet Lithuania, or possibly in the entire Soviet Union.

HINSEY: You had previously published under a pseudonym in small samizdat editions, including *Pontos Axenos* (1958) and *Moscow Poems* (1962)—

VENCLOVA: *Pontos Axenos* was a slim booklet of ten or twelve poems, a typical samizdat enterprise printed by Eglutė, the kitchen-table publishing house I mentioned earlier, whose *spiritus movens* was Natasha Trauberg. I can still see the book's yellow cover, soft paper, and pale typescript. In retrospect, I should have titled it *Axenos Pontos*, as this word order is more common in Greek. As far as I remember, I used the semipseudonym Andrius Račkauskas (Andrius is my middle name, and Račkauskas—my family name on Mother's side). Four or five copies were produced, and one or two of them were quickly confiscated by the KGB. I don't know if there are any surviving copies; there may still be one in Pranas Morkus's archive. This volume was also a "first," namely, the first unofficially published book of poetry in Soviet Lithuania (as we have discussed, Lithuanian samizdat did exist, but it mainly consisted of political pamphlets and leaflets). Some people read and even transcribed *Pontos Axenos*, including Judita Vaičiūnaitė and Bronė Katinienė, my former teacher. Still, it never went beyond a small circle. *Moscow Poems* (Maskvos eilėraščiai) was a considerably larger booklet of typewritten texts, with a hard cover, which I prepared myself. It included poems written during my first years in Moscow and my first love affair. Juozas Tumelis once told me that its copies were eagerly sought by the KGB (but never found). When I left the USSR, I managed to bring a copy with me, but in the end it was lost. Most of the texts from both samizdat booklets found their way into my *Collected Poems* (2010), though they are obviously juvenilia.

HINSEY: *Axenos pontos*, "the inhospitable sea," is the name the ancient Greeks gave to the Black Sea—

VENCLOVA: Early in their history, the Greeks called the Black Sea "inhospitable," as they feared crossing it. Later, it became *euxeinos pontos*, "the hospitable sea," as Greek colonization spread along the Crimean and Caucasian shores. For me, the title had strong Homeric overtones. Beginning in early youth, I had read Homer, especially the *Odyssey*—mainly in the good Lithuanian translation by Jeronimas Ralys, or in the magnificent Russian translation by Vasily Zhukovsky; I also read parts in the original, thanks to the lessons given to me by my grandfather. Odysseus became not just one of my favorite heroes, but a sort of a personal myth. I subscribe to the notion that a significant part of one's life patterns are defined by such personal myths that arise during one's formative years (for Brodsky, it was a less popular epic hero—Aeneas). I entertained the idea—at one time current in Lithuania—that Odysseus might have visited the Baltic Sea, thus becoming part of our tradition, and I even wrote a poem about it, one of two texts about Odysseus that appeared in *Pontos Axenos*.

But my real passion for the classical world, as we have discussed, really began at university: my best hours as a student were spent in the old building that faced the cobblestoned courtyard and windows of the apartment where Adam Mickiewicz once lived. After that, there were my trips to the Caucasus (with Romas Katilius) and to Crimea. I perceived both of these places as extensions of the ancient Greek world (which they were). In Armenia, we found an authentic Greek temple, and I could touch its battered reliefs with my own hands—the Parthenon itself could not have left a stronger impression on me. At that time, I also started reading Mandelstam, who never had the chance to visit Greece (or Rome, for that matter), but who grasped Antiquity better than anyone else via the same lenses of the Caucasus and Crimea.

My generation shared the common belief that we had a task to fulfill. The chain of cultural memory had been broken and needed to be restored. To do so, we had to reestablish our foundations: this was the best way to overcome the disastrous legacy of Soviet rule. Thus, *Pontos Axenos* consisted primarily of verses on Classical (and even pre-Homeric) topics—a direction I continued to follow for several years after this first attempt at a poetic book.

HINSEY: In the context of Soviet Lithuania, *Pontos Axenos* could also have political implications—

VENCLOVA: Even before *Pontos Axenos*, I had written several pointedly political poems. One was "Hidalgo," which we have discussed. There were also two allegorical poems, whose action took place in revolutionary France: one described a Jacobin facing execution (presumably Bukharin or László Rajk); the second poem alluded to the well-known painting by Delacroix *Liberty Leading the People*—and, like "Hidalgo," dealt with the Hungarian Revolution. I managed to publish both in the official press, which testifies partly to their weakness, and partly to the illiteracy of Lithuanian censorship. I did not include these, however, in *Pontos Axenos*. The "inhospitable sea" could also, of course, be construed as "the hostile system." What I had in mind, however, was a general feeling of alienation, shared by many young men and women at that age regardless of where they lived. The title poem, written in Sapphic verse, depicts an Odysseus who never returns to Ithaca. (At that same time, I also attempted to write a full-length play in which Odysseus does come back, only to find that numerous pretenders have visited his native island; he is taken for yet another impostor, even by Penelope and Telemachus.) Another topic that fascinated me at the time was the destruction of earlier generations of gods (Uranus vanquished by Cronus, Cronus unseated by Zeus). This progression leads back to extremely ancient events predating Homer—most likely the destruction of Mycenaean culture by the more primitive Greek tribes. Subliminally, I associated that prehistoric catastrophe with the social changes in twentieth-century Eastern Europe. Another poem, obviously influenced by Mandelstam, was a monologue by a Mycenaean warrior who faces the end of his gods and his own demise; he cherishes the hope that Aphrodite will emerge from the disaster (but a tragic goddess, "foam and ice, ashes of the sea"). "Laocoon," which I gave to Alexander Ginzburg for publication in *Sintaksis*, dealt with the unhappy consequences of the Trojan War. "Taman'" referred to the myth of Iphigenia in Tauris and hinted at the plot of the *Oresteia* (Taman' is a peninsula facing the Crimean shore and Tauris is the Greek name for Crimea). "Alpine Meadows" was built on an extended metaphor equating the Caucasian mountains with the theater in Athens where Aeschylus was staged. And so on. In a word, it was youthful and naive Romanticism. There was nothing strictly anti-Soviet in it, but the general spirit was entirely a-Soviet—cosmopolitan *poiesis docta*, unrelated to any topics prescribed by the party and, what was worse, it lacked any "life-affirming" or "patriotic" qualities.

HINSEY: Before we go on to speak about other poems, I'd like to ask about poetic inspiration. In her book *Hope against Hope*, Nadezhda Mandelstam says that for poets "auditory hallucinations" are a recurring occupational hazard, and that Osip Mandelstam experienced poetic inspiration as a musical phrase insistently ringing in his ears. Early on, did you notice any particular sensations that heralded the onset of a poem?

VENCLOVA: I'm not a very musical person. My imagination is more visual than aural: I admire (and, I hope, understand) architecture and painting, and I love Bach, Handel, and Purcell primarily because they remind me of architecture. Thus, the phenomenon of auditory hallucination described by Nadezhda Mandelstam comes to me not so much as musical phrases sensu stricto, but rather as rhythmic units that can also be understood in spatial terms. But yes, I experience an insistent and intrusive, even irksome feeling of something constantly repeating itself and demanding a liberating effort. It is frequently preceded by a general feeling of unease and a bout of bad mood. In my youth, I learned to understand this as the signal: "A poem is coming."

HINSEY: During the period preceding the publication of *Sign of Speech*, how did the stages of writing a poem generally unfold? Did poems emerge all at once or over an extended period? Was there a recognizable pattern in their composition?

VENCLOVA: As a rule, my very early poems were short, consisted of a few quatrains (sixteen lines were the usual format) and they were generally composed in one day. Following the Acmeists and young Pasternak (also Henrikas Radauskas, who was their admirer), I strove for an epigrammatic quality—naturally, with limited success. Later, during the period of *Moscow Poems*, this structure was supplemented by lots of technical innovations (including vers libre with insertions of prose), which I considered, somewhat naively, to be an antidote to Socialist Realism. These poems, many of which luckily did not survive, bordered on incomprehensibility; nevertheless, my goal was that they be succinct and aphoristic. Marina Tsvetaeva, a paradigmatic poet of the aphorism, once said that an entire poem should be written for the sake of its last line. Well, I devised my own version of Tsvetaeva's formula: a poem should be written for the sake of its last quatrain—*and* its opening line (which was, in my case, the most difficult one, and frequently came at the very end of the writing process).

In those years, I generally did not produce poems at a writing desk, but during long walks through the deserted lanes of Vilnius or Moscow. This working method applied equally to translation, as I previously mentioned regarding my first translation of a poem by Akhmatova. While walking, my steps matched the intrusive rhythm of the "auditory hallucination," which gradually crystallized into iambic, anapestic, or other metrical patterns. Similarly, vague amalgamations of words would begin to swirl in my mind, exchanging places and finally crystallizing into sound patterns, rhymes, images, and lines (preferably, but not necessarily, starting with the final quatrain). There was usually a certain general idea for the poem (along the lines of "landscape in October," "short love encounter," or "river Lethe") that clarified itself in the process. Since I usually hummed and mumbled during such walks, this may have contributed to my reputation as a "slightly unhinged" person among the (luckily not numerous) people I met along my way. I only wrote the poem down after it was completed in my mind. Later, there would be corrections and changes (which might take weeks or months).

HINSEY: Anna Akhmatova, as we discussed in the preceding chapter, considered traditional poetic technique an integral part of any work of value. Early on you began writing sestinas, sapphics, and employing intricate metrical forms—

VENCLOVA: In my youth, traditional poetic technique was as natural to me as breathing. In Lithuania, classical rhymed stanzas following iambic, trochaic, and similar patterns were introduced by Maironis at the end of the nineteenth century. He did his best to eliminate syllabic versification in Lithuanian verse, which was derived from Polish models. Maironis's verse proved to be extremely influential, because he wrote well, per Auden's dictum. Moreover, his versification was better adapted to the inner structure of the Lithuanian language. Maironis patterned his metrics on Pushkin and Schiller. My head was full of these traditional patterns, since I knew hundreds of Lithuanian and Russian poems by heart, and most if not all of them followed Maironis and Pushkin, respectively—sometimes with slight variations. Last but probably not least, these patterns were employed by my father as well, who admired Maironis and translated Pushkin.

There were other reasons I preferred traditional rhymed stanzas. As we just spoke about, I strongly believed that the threads of memory, severed by brutal historical events, had to be gathered up anew. That meant referring back to old topoi and mythical motifs, as well as to traditional forms. To our minds, these represented harmony—and therefore value—amid our chaotic world deprived of such values. We learned much from Akhmatova in this respect. Further, our cult of Mnemosyne, the goddess of memory, was also a cult of mnemonics: Akhmatova's "Requiem" was memorized by a small group of people and then reconstructed on paper much later, word by word and letter by letter. This would have been much more difficult if "Requiem" had been written in free verse. It is rare for poems to be written under conditions as extreme as the height of the Stalinist terror, but this link between form and ethos—between form and victory over adversities—was significant for our entire generation.

Thus we valued the Acmeists, who were masters of poetic craft, over the Futurists, whose aesthetics consisted mainly of épatage and destruction. Later, when we learned some English and French, we preferred Frost to Pound and Valéry to the Surrealists. The world around us was unstable and cataclysmic, but the most effective artistic approach was not to imitate this chaos, but rather to confine it within a formal framework.

Gradually, however, I also came to understand the dangers of traditional poetic techniques: if not well-handled, they can result in clichés and repetitions that choke meaning. The authorities also understood this and exploited it, in their own way: they used such forms to manipulate or "discipline" human consciousness. Half of Socialist Realist poetry was written in impeccable quatrains; the other half used quasi-Modernist sloganeering in a poor imitation of Mayakovsky. In an attempt to avoid these pitfalls, I increasingly began to use varied and unexpected forms. One method involved disrupting metrical patterns by adding or omitting syllables—metrical "substitution" in English—a method well-known to many early twentieth-century Lithuanian (and Russian) poets; another was to employ intricate stanzaic models. From time to time, I also made use of vers libre. As a rule, however, these latter poems still contained hidden patterns, visible perhaps only to me, that nevertheless restricted their disorder to a degree.

HINSEY: Your early engagement with form is particularly striking in a poem such as "To the squares on our walls and floors"—

VENCLOVA: This is probably among my most popular early poems—at various readings, I'm frequently asked to recite it, and some people know it by heart. This is somewhat embarrassing, as it is nothing more than a technical tour de force (it has become the butt of a certain number of parodies as well, and rightly so). It is written in the "toast" genre, popular in Russian Silver Age poetry. A poet drinks to various phenomena—even unexpected ones—as in the famous poem by Mandelstam where he defiantly lists elements of the inadmissible prerevolutionary past ("I drink to soldiers' star-flowers . . . to lush furcoats, to asthma, to Petersburg days and their bile"),[7] or painful, as in Akhmatova's poem of 1934 ("I drink to the ruined house, / To the evil of my life").[8] In my poem, I strove for concision (even going so far as to omit the verb "to drink"), and attempted to create a feeling of isolation bordering on claustrophobia. Naturally, the poem referred to our secluded totalitarian world cut off from the wider universe by the Iron Curtain. All the images (for instance, "amputated shores" or "keys tested long before") pointed to that overarching theme; locomotive wheels threaten, and only maps studied in solitude provide an illusory way out. The poem's versification itself becomes a sort of cage: four iambic quatrains making sixteen lines, with a single dominant rhyme. The narrator and his audience are locked together in a cramped space consisting of squares and straight lines; everyday rooms are transformed into prison cells. The repetition of the numbers "two" and "four" correspond to the idea of that oppressive quadrate. Of course, this is an attempt to interpret the poem in rational terms, which is by and large a hopeless enterprise. To a certain extent, it was an exercise in *écriture automatique*, that is, it is a rather incomprehensible text, whose effect on the reader is achieved primarily through its strangeness. The ending is ambiguous. Does it mean that all human relationships were doomed to fail in that isolated—and isolating—universe? Or is it a sign of resistance, a statement that some rules simply cannot be changed by coercion? In the original, the penultimate line was "two and two do not make two." In the English translation (by Diana Senechal) the element of resistance is emphasized ("two and two still making four, / And two times two—still four").[9]

HINSEY: As we are speaking about formal patterns, one might also mention your poem from this period, "Desist, desist. The crumbling sentence dies." This villanelle is also characterized by an atmosphere of alienation—

VENCLOVA: This poem was written in December 1975 and therefore not included in *Sign of Speech*. In fact, it could never have been printed in the Soviet Union, due to its evocation of a concentration camp—not a Stalinist one, which one might perhaps have been able to mention, but the Gulag camps that were still in operation. The year 1975 was a difficult one for me. As we will speak about later, in May of that year I had requested the right to emigrate. This appeared to be highly improbable. That winter, I had to seriously face the possibility of imprisonment—and even if this didn't happen, my prospects looked rather grim. Poetry was a sort of self-therapy.

The villanelle is a poetic form practiced mainly in English-speaking countries. For me, it represented a challenge. As far as I knew at the time, no Lithuanian poet had previously employed this form. I was less certain about its use in Russian poetry, though I couldn't recall any in that language either (the Symbolists may have tried their hand at it, but I didn't know of any concrete examples). I took as my model Dylan Thomas's emblematic "Do Not Go Gentle into That Good Night." Several years earlier, I had translated it into Lithuanian, along with five other of Thomas's poems, including "And Death Shall Have No Dominion." After emigrating, I read villanelles by Auden, Elizabeth Bishop, Seamus Heaney, and others, and wrote another villanelle myself, although for this second poem I allowed for some variation in the refrains.

While my translations of Thomas were no doubt awkward, I was thunderstruck by his verbal expressiveness and the symbolic weight of his lines. A slightly altered version of Mandelstam's famous dictum came to mind: "It doesn't exist in *Lithuanian* and yet it must."

I started my first villanelle with the line: "Sustok, sustok. Suyra sakinys," which in literal translation means "Stop, stop. The sentence falls apart." I remember that it suddenly came to me; only afterward I noticed that it was strongly alliterated, perhaps under the influence of English verse. The main theme of the poem—that is, the breakdown of communication—was already apparent. Subsequent motifs emerged, first of all snow (Siberian winter, perhaps) and fire (in contrast to the cold, but also deadly). The fire and snow motifs were echoed in dawn's light and the rooftops, respectively. Everything else was dictated by the rhythm, the sound, and the inner logic of the imagery.

Reflecting on this poem now, it strikes me as tightly structured, as befits a villanelle. Its subject is the same daunting and oppressive world we discussed earlier. At the same time, it depicts a gradual vanishing of time and space. In the second tercet, this is evoked by the image of the clock's pendulum, which comes to a halt in the earth. In the third tercet, the universe's outline recedes into a mirror's reflection. In the middle of the text, a prisoner appears. For him, time is equal to his rounds of exiting and returning to his cell, and space is reduced to the "fenced-in zone." All that is left for lovers is "a grain of time, a splinter of the skies" that encloses their bodies, although they are abandoned by the angels—and by God himself. In short, everything shrinks to a single point. It is undoubtedly a tragic poem, but its frankness and exactitude represented a sort of catharsis for me.

"Desist, desist . . ." embodied two of my poetic aspirations at the time. First, its technique was derived from an old tradition; second, that tradition was Western and unknown in Lithuania—and as such, could serve to shift and enrich our cultural paradigm. Of course, I did not formulate such aims theoretically in advance—all that took place on a subconscious level.

HINSEY: When we spoke about your visit to Peredelkino, you cited Pasternak's influence on your early work. Czesław Miłosz described his verse as "inventing incredible assonances" and "weighting every line to the breaking point with metaphors"[10]—

VENCLOVA: In my father's library there was a volume of Pasternak's verse, published in the late thirties in Moscow, which contained nearly all his poetic work up to that time. Early on I read selections from it but, as I've mentioned, I found it almost incomprehensible. Nevertheless, I brought it with me on my first trip to the Caucasus. There, suddenly, everything fell into place: I fell in love with every poem I read. During the course of that summer, I explored the entire book, and afterward was rarely parted from it. Pasternak was unique. Similar to nearly all of his Russian contemporaries, he used Pushkinian verse patterns, but he achieved a level of density of meaning unlike anyone before him. The first thing that caught the eye (or, rather, the ear) of the reader was his incredible mastery of sound, of instrumentalization. Clusters of consonants were repeated and continuously transformed, giving his lines a fugue-like quality (before becoming a poet, he had trained as a composer, and a gifted one at that). Moreover, he drew words together that in the process became strangely linked simply because they shared similar sounds. There was also a complete lack of clichés in his poems. The sheer number and inventive quality of his metaphors left one speechless. Further, they were never elevated— rather, they often referred to the humble, everyday world (for instance, in his sequence "Waves" he compared the chain of the Caucasus mountains to a bed with rumpled sheets). Incidentally, Roman Jakobson insisted that Pasternak's poetics were not in fact based on metaphor, but on metonymy: it was as if spatially adjacent objects exchanged their traits and qualities in his stanzas. The result was a whirling, constantly shifting universe that Romas Katilius and I nicknamed "corpuscular" (as opposed to Tsvetaeva's "quantum" universe). A nook in a forest, an urban landscape, a railway car, or a momentous meeting between two people were transferred to the written page in their entirety, accompanied by all their attendant dynamics.

I tried my hand at least at some of these techniques in my awkward attempts to describe drifting ice on the Neris (clouds and water, in flux, exchanged places), a distant view of Klaipėda from a boat (the city fell into the sea from its quays, like Venice in Pasternak's poem, but with a heightened theme of suicide), or a thunderstorm on the Ukrainian steppes (with alliteration based on the sounds "zh" and "r"—"žaibų žiema, dangaus ruožai ir aidas ritosi žeme" (lightning's winter-white, wisps of sky and echoes rolled over the earth). In technical terms, my goal was not to describe natural phenomena, but rather, to create synonimical effects equivalent to the qualities that arose from such phenomena. All this was schoolboyish at best, though it afforded me some experience in the craft of verse.

HINSEY: We have mentioned Mandelstam a number of times, but I'd like to now speak more in depth about your interest in his work, which you translated into Lithuanian in the 1960s—

VENCLOVA: I read Mandelstam somewhat later than Pasternak. In a sense, they were opposites in the Russian poetry of their time—Mandelstam was a classicist, while Pasternak's tendencies were on the Romantic side. Pasternak belonged to Moscow, a multilayered and disorderly city, while Mandelstam was the very epitome of the Petersburg poet. They appealed to different tastes (Akhmatova jokingly divided all her friends into two groups: those who liked dogs, tea, and Pasternak, and those who preferred cats, coffee, and Mandelstam). Both suffered tragic fates: Pasternak survived into his later years, but then was hounded to death, while Mandelstam perished in a Stalinist transit camp at the age of forty-seven.

Even as a child, I knew about Mandelstam, though he had been relegated to the Orwellian status of "unperson." However, I really became interested in him when Pranas Morkus brought copies of Mandelstam's late work from Moscow to Vilnius. In addition, Natasha Trauberg gave me his collection *Tristia*, published in 1922, whose absolute brilliance was immediately apparent to me—"perhaps the best poetic book of all time and all countries," as

I used to say. My fascination with Pasternak remained, but I drifted over into Akhmatova's second group of poetry lovers (where I remain to this day). Poems in *Sign of Speech* frequently bear "a Mandelstamian mark." Here the term *influence* is inadequate (in the same way it would be absurd to speak about being influenced by Shakespeare, Goethe, or Pushkin); rather, the early poems are suffused with his invisible presence and fate.

HINSEY: One of these poems, "Shoots of grass pierce one's face and hands," directly addresses Mandelstam's exile—

VENCLOVA: That short poem, written in summer 1963, refers to Mandelstam's internal exile in Voronezh. After his first arrest, as a result of his famous "Stalin Epigram," he was sent to Cherdyn in the Ural Mountains, where he suffered a nervous breakdown. Later, thanks to the protection of some highly placed party figures, including Nikolai Bukharin, the poet and his wife Nadezhda were given permission to live in Voronezh, a fairly large city south of Moscow. There, he was employed by a local theater and wrote several dozen brilliant poems, today known as *The Voronezh Notebooks*. Nevertheless, life there was the prelude to his final imprisonment and death (Bukharin was executed by Stalin in 1938, and Mandelstam perished soon thereafter).

I visited Voronezh in the early 1960s; as far as I remember, I went there two years in succession searching for Mandelstam's traces. (Voronezh has its place in Lithuanian letters as well: a significant Lithuanian community was active there during World War I.) With the help of a local literary scholar, Anya Kolesnikova, I located Mandelstam's close friend and Platonic love Natasha Shtempel, and we talked for days on end about him and his work. Voronezh was totally destroyed during World War II, but some vestiges of the poet's exile survived—the streets and parks where he used to walk with Natasha (as well as with Akhmatova, who visited him there), the steep narrow lane where he rented a miserable flat, and, above all, the surrounding steppes. My poem was built on my experiences of these places. It abounds in quotes by Mandelstam and hidden references to his biography, although his name is never mentioned.

HINSEY: Would you describe some of these allusions?

VENCLOVA: Thus, "shoots of grass pierce" is a reference to the steppes' vegetation, upon which the poet probably rested, and an allusion to his imminent death. The phrase "glory to poverty" hints at Mandelstam's quality of life in Voronezh, which he described as being practically Franciscan. "The earth is made of roses" (in the Lithuanian original, "the earth turned into roses") is an inverted quotation of his well-known line, "The rose was earth; time, ploughed from underneath." The beginning of the second quatrain ("Some umpteen planets lie beneath the heart, / And Dante's circles press against the windows")[11] refers to the fact that Mandelstam read Dante in Italian during his exile in Voronezh—which was comparable to Dante's Ravenna—and wrote about Dante's heavenly circles in *The Voronezh Notebooks*. The end of the same quatrain speaks of "an ominous ringing" (Stalin rang Pasternak up and discussed Mandelstam's fate with him—a trial that Pasternak passed, though hardly with flying colors). The phrase "embittered bread," in the third quatrain is, of course, a Dantean concept.

In one of his poems, Mandelstam played with the name of the city: "Voronezh—voron, nozh" (Voronezh—a raven, a knife). This was impossible to replicate in Lithuanian (or in English, for that matter). Still, I attempted to produce a similar, though inverted, play on sounds: "*varža, Voronežo* dir*vožemis*" (resistance, the soil of Voronezh).

HINSEY: You once said that "Shoots of grass pierce one's face and hands" also contains a system of rhymes closely tied to the poem's content—

VENCLOVA: The last quatrain has a triple rhyme, while the final line remains unrhymed. The poem ends on the word "šeima" (family). I evoke the "family of world capitals" (in English, "family" was translated as "clan"), that is, Rome, Florence, and Paris for which Mandelstam longed his entire life, particularly when he was in exile. In his imagination, these cities were related like brothers and sisters. The taboo, yet easily guessed rhyme for "šeima" was "Kolyma": (the very antithesis of that family) the prison camp region in the Far North, to which the poet was sent in 1938, but never reached.

"To the Memory of a Poet. Variation" also deals with Mandelstam—with his shade, let us say—appearing in contemporary St. Petersburg. This poem is also full of quotations from his work. This is true of many of my early texts: for instance, the symbol of the "blind swallow" in "A Poem about Memory" is taken directly from "Tristia." I tried to learn the art of intertextuality from Mandelstam himself, who was the unsurpassed master of hidden and not-so-hidden quotations, covert references, and secret reminiscences (many consider this to be the defining trait of his poetics).

HINSEY: Lithuanian poetry is also essential to your formation as a poet. We have just been discussing the work of Henrikas Radauskas, for example—

VENCLOVA: Radauskas was an aesthete who advocated an "art for art's sake" philosophy in the face of historical disaster, stating that perfect amalgams of words have a far greater chance than anything else to survive such disasters. He often expressed his disdain for nineteenth-century-style civic and patriotic poetry, practiced by older émigré poets such as Brazdžionis. Among the younger Lithuanian writers, he possessed the broadest cultural horizons: he was not only familiar with Esenin and Mayakovsky, but also Pasternak (whom he translated) and Mandelstam, to say nothing of the French Symbolists and other significant Western poets. His poetry, frequently epigrammatic and written in traditional formal patterns, had a playful quality that fascinated me, but was somewhat at odds with my temperament. His pronounced dandyism sometimes struck me as a bit provincial, almost snobbish. Still, he was a good poet, during his period perhaps the best in Lithuania. His cult of memory and *le mot juste* reflected my own concerns only too well. (Brodsky read Radauskas in Randall Jarrell's English translations, and admired him.) Another émigré author who evoked my lively interest was Alfonsas Nyka-Niliūnas, who I mentioned earlier: a hermetic *poeta doctus* comparable to, say, the Italian poets of the postwar generation (and, perhaps, to Czesław Miłosz in part). If I do not enumerate other Lithuanian poets, including the classics, it is because they were simply part of the air I breathed.

HINSEY: This brings us to the question of language itself. Your poetry is written in Lithuanian—not Russian—a language that, due to its archaic structure, possesses its own specific wealth of resources, including a large number of cases and therefore word endings—

VENCLOVA: This is the reason I did not experience much "anxiety of influence" when dealing with Russian poets (although I felt it acutely with Radauskas or Nyka-Niliūnas). An image, a stylistic gesture or a technical device, when transposed into the context of another language, begins to function in a totally different way and is therefore altered beyond recognition. Borrowings and imitations in one's own language are much more dangerous and can result in a loss of identity. Pushkin borrowed a great deal from the French poets, and Donelaitis from Virgil, yet both remained unique.

For a poet, Lithuanian is a tough nut to crack. For example, its nouns have endings that were lost in other Indo-European languages, and are consequently at least one syllable longer than in Russian or German. It is almost impossible to squeeze a Russian line of, say, iambic tetrameter into Lithuanian iambic tetrameter (although I gradually learned how to do it—incidentally, my father attempted to master it before me when translating *Eugene Onegin*). Lithuanian has an incredibly complex system of accentuation that reminds one a bit of Greek prosody. The very texture of its phonetics is rough as stone—as feldspar, I would say. At the same time, sibilants are frequent in Lithuanian—perhaps too frequent. But it is a good and versatile material, and I am still exploring its immense resources.

HINSEY: However, to return to the question of poetic influence, this is quite complex, and it is perhaps more accurate when evoking this topic to speak about "elective affinities." Which is to say, that something in another poet's Weltanschauung corresponds to one's own philosophical, emotional, or political preoccupations. On a deeper level, how did the work of these poets correspond to your own inner creative and intellectual world?

VENCLOVA: Yes, "elective affinities" is the right term. And there is also the question of taste. I was drawn to the Russian poets (or to Radauskas and Nyka-Niliūnas, for that matter) because of their ability to de-automatize our perceptions, to present reality transformed by the impact of emotion, as Pasternak said once. This is an innate characteristic of any genuine poetry, but these writers brought it to an extreme—almost to the breaking point, but never beyond. They avoided sentimentality, melodrama, stereotypical poetic constructions, and approached each poetic task in a fresh way, while managing to maintain a link with tradition. There was an inimitable mix of freedom and discipline in their work. I was also deeply impressed by their stance toward their disastrous era (in which we all continued to live): the poet's resistance consisted of disdain, stoicism, and the ability to sustain the memory of the values that distinguish us from our prehuman ancestors. On the other hand, this was very far from *littérature engagée*, that is, the defense of specific social causes, without considering the price. Yet their approach was, I believe, the only serious answer to the challenges of our—or any—century.

Yet there were significant differences between the poets I liked. Thus, Pasternak was a poet of "yes," accepting reality as God's gift and yielding to it, something that could lead to attempts to conform to history. Mandelstam, who loved the physical world no less than Pasternak, was nevertheless a poet of the "no," of resistance. I preferred Mandelstam's attitude in the final account.

HINSEY: Not only poetry, but philosophy, prose works, and other texts are important in a poet's development. Pasternak's philosophical studies in Marburg brought him in contact with works by Bergson, Novalis, and the German Romantics, among others. Would you speak about your philosophical influences during this period?

VENCLOVA: As for philosophy, my knowledge of it at the time remained rather embryonic. Thanks to Natasha Trauberg, I had some idea of Christian Personalism—Mounier and others—as well as Russian philosophers such as Berdyaev and Shestov. I was familiar with disparate texts by existentialists such as Jaspers and Camus (Heidegger was very hard to obtain, and the style of the few pieces I attempted to read was simply too dense). Sartre—primarily his plays, but some of his theoretical works—could be found in Polish translation, yet I frequently felt irritated and antagonized by him.

As we mentioned earlier, I was busy forming a sort of personal ethics, borrowing precepts from diverse and sometimes contradictory sources. There were all sorts of ideas that appealed to a young person: strict individualism mitigated by empathy, transcendental values upheld by one's behavior, and so on. A rather naive composite Weltanschauung, which reflected my poetic tastes and preferences.

HINSEY: There is a strong current in Lithuanian verse—as in many countries' poetic traditions—that is pastoral, rooted in the countryside and landscape. You previously described this group as "agrarians." Your aesthetic affinities, however, put you at a distance from this current—

VENCLOVA: My Lithuanian friends often looked for their roots in the local soil—native history and (mainly imagined) prehistory, pagan mythology, idealized rural customs, landscapes, and so on. In so doing, they continued in the line of early Mickiewicz and Maironis—albeit in a transformed and updated manner. As I remarked at the start of our conversations, a good parallel in the West would be the Gaelic revival. This search for roots also had much in common with Heidegger's "quest for true being" (which is still popular in Lithuania, with all of its potentially dubious sociopolitical implications).

I tried my hand at poems that incorporated Lithuanian folklore—even employing lines from folk songs—but without much success. I was a congenital town dweller (among the younger writers Judita Vaičiūnaitė was similarly disposed). Vilnius, and also St. Petersburg with its classical architecture, was more significant to me than villages, wooden crosses, and Mother Earth.

As my early verse was clearly lacking in "national spirit," it proved to be rather unacceptable to the authorities—and to most of my opposition-minded contemporaries as well. Yet to my thinking, good use of the Lithuanian language was sufficient to uphold national spirit and maintain Lithuanian identity. Moreover, since the time of the Grand Duchy a defining part of our culture was the Classical tradition—something I called, in one poem, "the dark well-spring of the Mediterranean." But that was debatable: ethnic themes and the "primordial vitality" of imagined archaic tribes were clearly preferred by a large part of the general public. Thus, *Pontos Axenos* and *Sign of Speech* remained somewhat "out of place" in Lithuania for years.

HINSEY: And yet, following World War I, Modernist aesthetics of urbanity had quickly become a dominant feature in world poetry, including in European poetry—

VENCLOVA: In the twenties, poetry addressing urban themes appeared in Lithuania, and was quite popular for a time. Since our native cities were few, and still rather provincial, poets such as Sruoga and Binkis depicted Western metropolises—primarily Berlin with its unconventional urban life—which they had visited as students or tourists. It represented a totally new world for those who had grown up in the countryside, somewhat intimidating yet fascinating. The next generation, which included Kazys Boruta and my father, saw the city as a locus of social conflict and satirized the mores of the bourgeoisie. Here, my native Kaunas (and Riga, the much larger Latvian capital) could serve as models. In short, Lithuanian literature faithfully followed the European and American trends of the period. After 1944, mandatory glorification of the proletariat notwithstanding, Lithuanian poetry turned back to the village: the alleged benefits of collectivization, idealized rural vistas with Soviet overtones, and so on. For me, a city—be it Vilnius or Klaipėda—was not a mere industrial setting, but rather a man-made, cultural landscape often preferable to a natural one; it was a place where human relations achieved new levels of dynamic sophistication. Moreover, this was a link to world culture and history (while the village represented isolation and repetitiveness). Such an attitude was an exception in the Lithuanian letters of my period; Vaičiūnaitė also attempted to convey a similar message in her numerous poems about Vilnius's lanes and alleys, which constituted a veritable Baedeker).

HINSEY: Could you speak about the similarity between your book's title—*Sign of Speech*—and that of Joseph's translated collection, published some years later, titled *A Part of Speech*?

VENCLOVA: Pranas Morkus proposed the title *Metelinga* for my book. *Metelinga* was a Lithuanian distortion of the Latin "nota linguae": a punishment sign teachers used to hang around the necks of pupils who spoke Lithuanian instead of the mandatory Polish (or later, Russian). "You speak a sort of improper poetic language, therefore this would be a marvelous title for you," Pranas said. However, such a title had no chance of getting past the censors due to its political connotations. Therefore, I rendered the Latin as *Sign of Speech* (which also corresponded to my interest in semiotics, the science of signs). Joseph approved of the title, although he proposed, in jest, also the title *Vodka* (a parody of Guillaume Apollinaire's *Alcools*): as all of us drank rather heavily. When in 1977 Brodsky published his *A Part of Speech*, I asked him: "Is this a reference to my title?" He answered: "Yes, it is."

HINSEY: Thus, from the beginning, your work constituted its own specific universe. In his essay "Poetry as a Form of Resistance to Reality," Joseph Brodsky said that your poetry represented an alternative to the Soviet reality that surrounded you—

VENCLOVA: I think Brodsky had in mind not just Soviet reality, but reality as such. True, Soviet reality was grimmer than most. After the nightmare of the camps and executions, from which we were trying to awake (to quote Stephen Dedalus, whose experience was milder than ours), we were confronted by an ugly and monotonous present that promised no further change. We were surrounded by the absurd. And that was only a part—one of the worst parts, to tell the truth—of the chaos and nonsense of life. Poetry—and art in general—was a way of resisting that chaos, holding it at bay. This also had political consequences. Politics, seen from this perspective, was something transitory (even if one had to make decent choices in everyday life). That said, it would be an overstatement or even a distortion to assert that we were totally apolitical in our work. The stifling Soviet atmosphere aggravated by the smug audacity of the authorities provoked not only disdain, but resentment and indignation that could not help but find its way into our verses.

HINSEY: One of the techniques of resistance in your poems was a "filtering out" process. In your work from this period one senses that the human realm, with its usual range of activities and enterprises (with the exception of friendship), had become so deformed, that it no longer merited a place in authentic poetic utterance—

VENCLOVA: That's true. Everything mediated by the state or Soviet society was false. A certain level of inauthenticity is endemic to any society, but in the Soviet Union it reached extreme levels. Friendship—and love, which is (or should be) friendship to the second power—provided the only solid ground. In many of the East European countries, networks of friendships eventually crystallized into an "alternative society," which played an important role during the systemic changes of the eighties. But it was a slow process, and in Lithuania, the "alternative society" consisted of small islands almost to the very end.

HINSEY: In her work, Akhmatova frequently speaks about how the Soviet period robbed individuals of the chance to live out their own destinies. In your "A Poem about Memory," and elsewhere, you reflect on "such a shortage of authentic fate"—

VENCLOVA: In her magnificent poem, the fifth "Northern Elegy," Akhmatova speaks about all the things she was denied due to the circumstances of her era. She nevertheless states that she perhaps did everything that was possible in the only life left to her. I was stunned by these proud words. Naturally, our situations were not comparable, but in "A Poem about Memory," I attempted to understand the way to "do everything possible."

HINSEY: At times, this "filtering out" approach in your early work results in such a radical paring down that it is as if the poet can only find recourse in the reliable constants of time, nature, the elements, and the fact of weather—

VENCLOVA: Nature undoubtedly was a certainty in our uncertain and inauthentic world. Here, once more, Pasternak comes to mind. He was perhaps the greatest poet of weather in the entire history of literature (he maintained that the duty of an author is to first depict the weather in the place of action, and only then describe everything else). Cloudbursts, blizzards, summer heat, and thunderstorms were frequently more significant in his verses than any other object or fact. One might say that the unceasing movement of nature represented for him, paradoxically, an immovable Archimedean point that gave him strength. *Sign of Speech*—not without Pasternak's influence—takes a similar approach (not to mention the fact that the elemental world is a fascinating and challenging topic in itself, especially for a young poet).

HINSEY: All this creates, in your early work, a poetic environment that is reminiscent of a Platonic universe filled with absolutes. I think, however, this would misrepresent its specificity. There is something entirely pragmatic about the elemental phenomena that remain in your poems. One senses that this is a reflection of the fact that tyranny has been unable—at least as of yet—to corrupt the natural world's periodic table or the weather—

VENCLOVA: I was struck by a rather comical scene in Solzhenitsyn's *One Day in the Life of Ivan Denisovich*, where the titular hero is informed by the authorities that the sun would no longer be at its highest at midday. He scornfully thinks to himself, "As if the sun would obey their decrees!" This nonsensical scene points up the obvious: decrees cannot change the natural processes. Well, it gives one a modicum of hope.

HINSEY: Time, on the other hand, is a more complex issue; as you discussed in your essay "Czesław Miłosz: Despair and Grace," "Totalitarianism . . . threatens the temporal dimensions of humanity first of all; if we wish to have a future we must have a past"[12]—

VENCLOVA: Twentieth-century tyrannical regimes propped themselves up with eschatological myths (a trend continued by present-day regimes that emphasize nationalism). The perfect and happy future was understood as a continuation of the happy present, at best with minor modifications. Meanwhile, the past had to be continually cleansed, in accordance with Orwellian precepts. Time had to stop: in the sixties and seventies, we were still living somewhere around 1945, and we were supposed to have no knowledge of the changing world beyond our borders, or of the world that had preceded ours. One of my generation's main concerns was the restoration of a normal past and, consequently, a normal future.

HINSEY: This feeling of deformed time is particularly present in your poem from this period, "The twenty-four hours cross the middle, silence grows louder"—

VENCLOVA: This is a long poem written in regular anapestic lines; it bears traces of Romanticism and the influence of Brodsky's early verse, which I was reading extensively at the time. The poem was prompted by one of the defining experiences of my youth—lonely travels through the Lithuanian countryside. As we have discussed, I loved hitchhiking and covered considerable distances on passing trucks, spending days and nights away from home. These were times of complete solitude; they were taxing, but nevertheless had their ecstatic moments. It was our version of Jack Kerouac (*On the Road* had appeared ten years earlier, but we were not yet aware of the book).

That said, this poem mainly addresses the question of time. First, there is the twenty-four-hour cycle: the poem starts at midnight, followed by the dawn, then day's onset full of frantic movement, and finally returns to the evening, which symbolizes disappearance and oblivion. Second, the text addresses the annual cycle. The poem is set during the moment of almost imperceptible change at the beginning of autumn—understood to be late August or early September. These two cycles are echoed by a key's circular movement at the end of the second stanza. I tried to convey the bitter, yet intoxicating atmosphere of the changing seasons—reflections on water, clouds, the voices of birds, a frozen spring next to an abandoned farmhouse. This was not exactly the redeeming landscape of most of the poets of my generation. The poem's journey starts somewhere in an uninhabited part of Samogitia (in an empty homestead that perhaps once belonged to a deported family) and it ends at the seashore, in Klaipėda. In 1967, when the poem was written, the latter was still a destroyed city: "the white postwar dust, . . . / The fortresses' empty ditches, the beacon in ruins, / And, behind the cracked walls, and open to all, the rooms."[13] It is partly a return to my early childhood—so early, that it is barely contained in memory, represented only by the hulls of half-drowned ships. Low tide has left driftwood and glass bottles with Cyrillic letters on them.

Time, even if it continues its habitual cycles, has stopped, like the "age-old night" in the first stanza.

> And childhood is easy, and youth completely bereft
> Of meaning. Our souls are nearby, our felling was recent,
> The clock of noon is ticking somewhere in the present,
> And an arrow halts in the air, having strayed from its line,
> Since the world is the same, while solitude changes each time.[14]

Incidentally, the arrow is a hidden reference to Henrikas Radauskas's poem, "An Arrow in the Sky," which provided the title for one of his books written in exile. I believe Radauskas was referring, in turn, to Longfellow's well-known poem, "The Arrow and the Song." Well, such is the circulation of the lifeblood of culture (all three texts are different, and are even at odds with each other in their symbolism). No one in Lithuania picked up on the reference, but an émigré critic, Pranas Visvydas, caught it: his analysis of it reached me much later.

If there was something worth lending one's ear to in this universe of stasis and absence of time, it was the voices of multiple generations that had been felled by history. This is, perhaps, the meaning of the lines "voices, once lost, return from the world to their place / Inside us." Still, even that amounted to "oblivion, a well, / The outskirts of others' nonbeing."[15] In short, an elegiac piece.

HINSEY: Which poem in *Sign of Speech* still has the most resonance for you?

VENCLOVA: Perhaps the poem "I was welcomed by twilight and cold," written in March 1971. Its composition includes a change of tempo and semantics in its middle section, signaled by a slight shift in the rhyming pattern, and it comes to a close with an anticlimactic quatrain. The poem draws upon a specific episode in my life. At the previous year's end, I was stranded in Moscow for several days, as the airports were all closed due to fog, and the trains were sold out (a fact duly mentioned in the second stanza). After a long separation, I met my former wife Marina, whom I had not seen for five years. She now had a son (he is a well-known Byzantologist). Let's say this was a complicated experience. Moscow appears in the poem as a kind of underworld, yet with all the characteristics of a large modern city: it is a place of memory, and a site of exile, portrayed from an emotional distance. The capital is a maze of brick lanes, with nine railway stations—"the realm of Ariadne and Minos." The circular layout of the city prompted me, in part, to employ one of the geometric metaphors associated with John Donne: "Only memory, as the days pass, /

Widens itself like a compass, / Until a straight line is the past." At the poem's end, I tried my hand at aphorism: "The highest power, or the void / Sends the angel down: rhythm and language."[16] Was it God or a feeling of total loneliness that sent that priceless gift? I don't know, but that became my credo. The émigré philosopher Vytautas Kavolis, who later became my friend, once told me that I was treading here—and in my entire poetry—the thinnest possible line between religious and atheist discourse. That might be so.

HINSEY: The power of language as a resource is, however, paradoxical. On the one hand, as you have just described in "I was welcomed by twilight and cold," it is one of our essential forms of recourse ("Thank God for the dictionary"). But, in the villanelle we spoke about earlier ("Desist, desist. The crumbling sentence dies") it is also fallible, and contains the eternal potential for corruptibility—

VENCLOVA: This ambiguous nature of language was acutely felt by the Romantics. As Fyodor Tyutchev, one of the best Russian poets after Pushkin, famously wrote: "A thought once uttered is untrue"; he nevertheless continued writing, even if it was, according to his dictum, senseless by definition. Language, and poetic language above all, hovers on the edge of truth and untruth: this is what makes it so fascinating and challenging.

HINSEY: Nevertheless, all these things we have been discussing point to something miraculous in the human faculty. This is that despite the best efforts of tyranny and indoctrination, individuals can still sense, as you previously described, that things are "out of joint"—and something in their spirit compels them to seek out the truth—

VENCLOVA: Perhaps there is a transcendental element of human nature that compels us to strive for truth. In the final account, the efforts of Big Brother—however successful they might seem—appear unable to extinguish the instinct for freedom. But this is difficult to prove—we can only believe it: here, we exceed the limits of verifiable thinking and border on theology. Still, something I would like to stress again is the immense role played by literature in this process. All literature of quality provides the reader with patterns and insights that enable him or her—perhaps not systematically but frequently enough—to resist false doctrines. Poetry, in particular, is somewhat mysteriously linked to ethics; and poetic discipline to the fortitude of the spirit. Many poets, including Zbigniew Herbert and Akhmatova—and her protégé Joseph Brodsky—insisted that refusal to succumb to evil is primarily a matter of *taste*. I was of the same mind.

HINSEY: None of this is achieved, however, without sacrifice. In the fall of 1972, only six months after *Sign of Speech* was published, there was a significant tightening of the ideological net. In the poem "Winter Dialogue," you speak about how there are moments when what can be positively affirmed is meager, but must nevertheless be cherished:

"This century is managing without
A sign; there's just statistics." "Gravity
Of death has fettered person, plant, and thing,
But sprouts burst forth from seed and sacrifice,
And then not all is over, or so I think."[17]

Thus the human quality of tenacity also becomes an important component of personal and poetic ethics. Or as you described in "A Poem about Friends," dedicated to Natasha Gorbanevskaya, and written after the 1968 demonstration against the invasion of Czechoslovakia in Red Square: "And those who live are chosen by the fog, / Deserted houses, journeys into the distance, / Their weapons are staunchness, abstinence from speech"[18]—

VENCLOVA: During this period, it seemed as though the course of events was governed by laws of raw power, that is, by statistics. The force of words and human solidarity were our means to counter this, even if this meant prison or exile, as was the case for many of my friends. Speech—or, at least, a silent refusal to lie—was the axis of their existence. I tried to convey this in the very title of my book.

JOSEPH BRODSKY

HINSEY: Let's return to the 1960s and your relationship with Joseph Brodsky. In late August 1966, following his return from internal exile in Norenskaya, in the Arkhangelsk region, Joseph Brodsky was in rather low spirits—

VENCLOVA: Brodsky was released from his internal exile in Norenskaya in the second half of 1965. In the end he served less than two years of his five-year sentence. We considered it an almost incredible success. For almost the first time since 1917, the state machine went into reverse due to international protests and, what was more important, to the pressure of mounting public opinion in the USSR. Brodsky returned to his parents' flat in Leningrad, met Akhmatova, who was instrumental in his release, and started to look for translation contracts (he made a very modest living as a translator before the trial). An old literary scholar Viktor Zhirmunsky (a friend of Akhmatova's and a member of the so-called Formalist school in the twenties) proposed involving him in a very promising project. A large book of English metaphysical poetry was to be published in the academic series *Literaturnye pamiatniki* (Literary Monuments), and Brodsky began to render John Donne, Andrew Marvell, and others into Russian, continuing his own poetic work at the same time. In Norenskaya, he had undergone a veritable transformation: he produced a hundred or so poems during his exile, which were much more original and powerful than most of his previous work. To tell the truth, they were on a par with Pasternak, Akhmatova, or anyone. He also managed to learn English in that northern village—friends had provided him with books by Auden and many others.

Therefore, Brodsky's situation in those years did not look too bad. By Soviet standards, it could even have been seen as enviable. Yet of course he was under strict surveillance by the KGB, and remained on the margins of "normal" society, shunned by all official bodies. The fact that he became the very epitome of

Leningrad's and Russia's literary underground, adored by hundreds of young people, lionized by opposition cultural figures, and frequented by Western students who managed to get into the USSR, only served to aggravate his predicament. After his ordeal, he was in rather bad nervous shape (well, he always had certain psychological problems, as befits a highly talented person). On top of it, his private life had collapsed. His great love, Marina Basmanova, spent some time with him in Norenskaya and had given birth to their son, Andrey, but they never married. Moreover, Andrey was registered under her surname, and she prohibited Brodsky from seeing him. That happened a bit later, but there were already signs of trouble in 1966. It is a complicated and sad story—much has been written about it already, in manifest violation of Brodsky's wishes. He hated any discussion of it among his friends.

HINSEY: Andrei Sergeyev and his wife Lyudmila were staying in your friends' Romas and Audronis Katilius's apartment in Vilnius and devised something that they thought might help Brodsky—

VENCLOVA: After I became acquainted with Sergeyev, I introduced him to Romas Katilius and his brother Adas (their full names are Ramūnas and Audronis, which perfectly corresponded to their characters—Ramūnas means "the quiet one" and Audronis "the stormy one"). By this time, Romas was already a budding physicist, and Adas an architect. (I've never spoken much about Adas, but he was and remains one of my closest friends. Together, we took a canoe trip that lasted twenty-three days, and once went to Moscow to visit Modernist architectural monuments: we even managed to locate a grand old man of Russian Constructivism, Konstantin Melnikov, who still lived inconspicuously in a round house he had built for himself in better times.) In short, these were the people with whom any Russian dissident could feel at home. Sergeyev and his wife Lyudmila became literally enamored of Romas and Adas and spent lots of time with them in Vilnius. Sergeyev, who was highly valued by Brodsky as a translator and a human being, was privy to Brodsky's troubles. He decided that a trip to Lithuania and making the acquaintance of some Lithuanians might be good medicine for Brodsky. Thus, he advised Joseph to come to Vilnius—that was in August 1966.

HINSEY: If I'm not mistaken, Joseph had a family connection with Lithuania on his mother's side—

VENCLOVA: Yes, his mother Mariya Moyseevna came from a Litvak (Lithuanian Jewish) family: both her parents were born in northern Lithuania and presumably spoke Lithuanian. Once I asked him whether that contributed to his interest in the country. "Not in the slightest degree," Joseph answered.

"My relationship to Lithuania is, first and foremost, my relationship to my Lithuanian friends."

HINSEY: This said, you once wrote that Lithuania played an important role for him, as Georgia did for Pasternak and Armenia for Mandelstam—

VENCLOVA: Joseph once wrote that for a person born in an empire it's better to live in a godforsaken province on a seacoast. Beyond any doubt, he had Lithuania in mind. Even if it was a country occupied by a foreign power, and therefore in some sense more constrained than Russia itself, it preserved a great deal of its historical and cultural individuality. There were memories of the interwar independence period, and a specific air—something nearly indefinable that smacked of civilized behavior and good taste. All three Baltic states gave a newcomer from Russia a whiff of "Western freedom." My experience with the Lithuanian KGB notwithstanding, even the Soviet authorities looked somewhat milder (the farther from the center of power, the better). As I mentioned earlier, post-Stalinist cultural policy was a bit less repressive in the Baltics than in Moscow or Leningrad. One could produce Impressionist, Expressionist, and even abstract paintings, stage theatrical experiments, play jazz, and live as a bohemian without too much trouble. Lithuania was perhaps a leading country in that respect (well, Estonia ran a close second). There were perceptible ties with Poland and with the Lithuanian diaspora: these also contributed to the general Westernization, even if the Soviets did their best to control all that.

This was a typical characteristic of the Russian Empire even in the tsarist (and Stalinist) era: some peripheries were preferable for freedom-seeking writers. Pushkin, Griboyedov, and Lermontov most likely felt better in the Caucasus (especially in Georgia) than in Russia itself. In the Soviet period, Georgia and Armenia (even Central Asia) provided a much-needed respite from the imperial mores. Stalinist terror was as severe there as elsewhere, perhaps even worse, yet after Stalin these countries became as lively as before. By the way, there were Russian-language magazines in Georgia, Armenia, and Uzbekistan where one could publish, for instance, works by Mandelstam or Babel that did not pass "central" censorship. Yet in the sixties and seventies, the penchant for the Oriental USSR was exchanged for the Occidental—that is, all things Baltic. Joseph used to say: "For a Russian, Lithuania is always a step in the right direction."

HINSEY: Joseph also took an interest in Lithuanian history, in the press ban and the partisan war against the Stalinist regime after the end of World War II—

VENCLOVA: Yes, very much so. He strongly preferred Lithuania to Latvia and Estonia since it was Catholic (not Protestant): Lithuania reminded one not of Germany, but of the Italy with which he had been enamored from early youth. I would even say that Vilnius was, for him, a palliative for Rome. Lithuania also had a much more impressive medieval and modern history than the two other Baltic states. Romas, myself, and other Lithuanian friends were fans of that history and could tell Brodsky a lot about it. Traces of our talks are quite obvious in his "Lithuanian" poems.

HINSEY: As you have just described, when Joseph arrived in Lithuania in August 1966, he met a circle of people who would go on to be his "Vilnius" group—

VENCLOVA: The group coincided, to a degree, with our self-study group of 1960. There were Romas and Adas, of course; also Kama Ginkas, Pranas Morkus, Virgilijus Čepaitis, several women including Ida Kreingold and Ina Vapšinskaitė (Joseph struck up a close friendship with the latter). The circle was rather exclusive. We maintained ties with lots of Vilnius's Bohemians, but, as far as I remember, virtually none of them ended up being close to Brodsky.

HINSEY: You were not in Vilnius when Joseph arrived, but in Estonia, though you returned soon after—

VENCLOVA: At that time, I became very interested in Yuri Lotman and his work. Lotman was a professor of Tartu University, and the founder of the Russian branch of structuralism and semiotics who soon grew into a figure of world stature. I felt his ideas might enable one to escape Soviet clichés and to study literary criticism in an uncommon and fascinating way. Lotman, his wife Zara Mintz, and his collaborators (in particular, Koma Ivanov, Akhmatova's friend whom I have mentioned), opened truly new vistas regarding Tolstoy, Dostoevsky, Blok, Pasternak, and literature in general. All of them were impeccably honest, devoid of any trace of toadying to the authorities. After reading their books, I decided that a translator's work is not necessarily the only way of avoiding moral compromises in the Soviet Union: one might also become a literary scholar and semiotician of the Lotmanian persuasion. For several years, I visited Tartu frequently (it could be reached from Vilnius by train in several hours) and became Lotman's student of sorts. In a sense, I still am, since my scholarly work at Yale was always grounded in Lotman's theory.

It was 1966 when my collaboration with Lotman began. Natasha Trauberg and I traveled to Kääriku, an Estonian village in the vicinity of Tartu, where Lotman's seminar on semiotics (the so-called summer school) was taking place. Around thirty scholars from Moscow, Leningrad, and Estonia participated in it. We presented two papers, one of them under two names; the other one, on G. K. Chesterton, belonged entirely to Natasha. That was in the second half of August, and when we returned to Vilnius, Joseph was there.

HINSEY: What were your first impressions of Joseph as a person?

VENCLOVA: After reading his mature work, I knew for certain that he was a poet of genius. That was the common opinion among the intellectual milieu. The old and respected art critic Aleksandr Gabrichevsky once said: "He is the most brilliant person I have ever met in my life." "Don't talk nonsense," somebody retorted, "you have met Kandinsky, Stravinsky, and Leo Tolstoy." "Brodsky is the most brilliant person I have ever met in my life," Gabrichevsky repeated imperturbably. Needless to say, I was somewhat intimidated by Joseph's presence. Yet in the first days of our acquaintance, I did not feel that he was a person of genius. A witty man of original mind, frank to the point of arrogance, and very vulnerable at the same time—that's all.

After meeting in the Katiliuses' flat, we went for a walk through the lanes of Vilnius's old city. He knew them rather well, as Romas, Adas, and Ina Vapšinskaitė had already acquainted him with the downtown area. Later, he produced several poems about the Saint Catherine and Dominican churches—located next to Liejyklos Street where the Katiliuses lived. By the way, Liejyklos (a street also described by Miłosz) means "Foundry": in the seventeenth and eighteenth centuries, the masters who cast Vilnius's bells lived there. It was a strange coincidence, since the Leningrad street next to which Brodsky (and Akhmatova) lived, was also called "Foundry" (Liteynyi). Still, we did not talk about history and architecture. The very first words with which Joseph addressed me were: "Why did you go to that semiotics seminar? That was a crazy idea."

HINSEY: So Brodsky took a dim view of your Kääriku adventure. Why was that?

VENCLOVA: At that time, he considered semiotics a snobbish enterprise—which it was, in part. He knew several semioticians personally, and they had not made a good impression on him (Koma Ivanov was an exception). He also disliked "exact methods" for studying literature. More than once, he said that a literary scholar must be equal in brilliance to the poet he or she is analyzing (as I said, he bestowed that status on Akhmatova as a Pushkin scholar, yet hardly on Lotman). Much later, he changed his views, or at least modified them: he met Lotman in Italy and was reconciled with him. "You know, the Lotmanian method is the only way of explaining poetry to nonpoets," he told me during one conversation. Moreover, his insistence on language as a force that dictates the poem, and the author as an instrument of language, sounds Lotmanian indeed.

HINSEY: What about the other topics of your first conversation—and other examples of Brodsky's forthrightness?

VENCLOVA: I mentioned the Polish poet Konstanty Gałczyński who lived in Vilnius in the thirties and wrote extensively about the city. "A bad poet," Brodsky said peremptorily. I was positively astonished, since I knew Brodsky's translations of Gałczyński that were popular at that time, and undoubtedly had been done with love and understanding. Therefore, our first meeting went a bit awry. Later, we went to Natasha Trauberg's flat. There, a sort of brouhaha developed. Joseph said something disdainful about Chesterton, whom Natasha adored to the point of idolatry. A nervous exchange followed, after which Joseph slammed the door and left. We had to calm him down at the Katiliuses', with the help of some vodka. Natasha and he never became friends, even though she loved his poetry.

As for me, we became rather close friends in several days. Perhaps it would not be improper to add that there was a private reason for this. I had just separated from my first love, and Brodsky was parting with his lover. Both ladies were named Marina, and probably had similar traits (though they did not know each other). I never met Marina Basmanova, and Joseph never met Marina Kedrova. We did not discuss these family problems, yet there was an undercurrent of common experience in our talks that helped both of us a bit.

HINSEY: During that first visit, Brodsky read his work—first to a small group, then later to a slightly larger gathering at the Katiliuses' apartment. He read poems such as "You Will Gallop in the Dark," "Two Hours in an Empty Tank," and "Verses on the Death of T. S. Eliot." What was your impression upon hearing him read?

VENCLOVA: He was very shy and reluctant to read: he asked me to start with my poems, but I declined the offer. Yet after reciting his first lines, the reading turned into an incredible performance. Some people have defined it as "shamanistic" or compared it to synagogal chant. I believe both descriptions are inaccurate. Throughout, Joseph was fully in command, which is atypical for a shaman, and he avoided a singing quality: his voice was very loud, rhythmic, and monotonous, but the emphasis was on the words, not on the sound or melody. Stanza breaks, as well as enjambments, were clearly marked by a sudden change of tone. Although the poems were long, he knew everything by heart. "He writes the poem anew while reciting it," Virgilijus Čepaitis said afterward. Joseph did not pay the slightest attention to his audience, but after finishing the poem asked, a bit fearfully: "Nu, kak?" (Well, how was it?). That was not an easy experience. By Joseph's own definition, he was just a mouthpiece for a certain higher power (be it God, or language, or anything). I wrote in my diary: "There is a limit to how long one can listen to an angel or a muse." We dispersed in awkward silence. A large part of Joseph's popularity was due to his immense gift as a reader.

At that time, Andrei Sergeyev used to tell a story about Joseph's poetic career. In the late fifties and early sixties, there were several dozen budding samizdat poets in Leningrad, including Brodsky's close friends Evgeny Rein and Anatoly Naiman. In Joseph's own words, he set a task for himself: he must learn to produce better verses than any of them. He achieved his goal in a couple of months. The next task was to learn to write better verses than any samizdat (or, for that matter, officially published) poet in Russia. That was done in a year or so. Then, a new goal appeared: to write better poems than Robert Frost. "Here, I never succeeded," Joseph said.

HINSEY: Your friendship involved a number of adventures and escapades—

VENCLOVA: Among the escapades connected with that first visit, I remember two trips—to Trakai, the medieval castle on a lake not too far from Vilnius, and to Sudervė, a godforsaken suburb. The first trip is a must for all newcomers to the Lithuanian capital, and for its inhabitants as well (as you may remember, my parents went there on the first day of the Nazi invasion); the second one is only for connoisseurs. In Trakai, Joseph sat on a tower's wooden parapet, some thirty meters above the earth, raised his arm and proclaimed: "I'm the Lithuanian coat of arms!" (The emblem of the Lithuanian state, banned during the Soviet period, is a rider on a white horse with a sword in hand, similar, though not identical, to Saint George.) In Sudervė, there is a beautiful round Classicist church built in the early nineteenth century. It is famed for its acoustics. We ascended its dome and stood opposite each other, separated by the entire space of the cupola. Then Joseph whispered two stanzas in Polish—it was Cyprian Norwid, a great poet exiled from his fatherland in 1842, whom both of us liked and translated. I heard his whisper very clearly.

By the way, Joseph had an intimate talk (not exactly a confession, but something close to it) with Sudervė's Catholic priest, Father Trusewicz. I believe Brodsky also visited Sudervė the next year with his friend Anastasia Braudo, a famous organist. She played the organ there, taking advantage of the church's acoustics, while Joseph worked the bellows.

HINSEY: After a week in Vilnius, Joseph headed off to Palanga—

VENCLOVA: Yes, and I could not accompany him because I had caught a bad cold. I believe Joseph stayed there under the care of Petras Juodelis, the father-in-law of our mutual friend Juozas Tumelis. Juodelis, a former political prisoner, a good interlocutor, and, generally, one of the nicest men in Lithuania, was employed by the art museum and therefore had access to Count Tyszkiewicz's magnificent palace in Palanga Park. Joseph slept in the palace's basement. He dedicated several poems to Palanga, and to Juodelis as well.

HINSEY: Did Joseph read any of his new poems to you during his first visit to Vilnius?

VENCLOVA: Yes, he did. On the very first day, he gave me a new long poem, "Podrazhanie satiram, sochinennym Kantemirom" (Mimicking the Satires Composed by Kantemir). It was a veritable tour de force. Antiokh Kantemir, the very first significant Russian poet, lived during the times of Peter the Great and his immediate successors. His work corresponded to the work of Dryden and Pope, though his language was perhaps more archaic and removed from modern standards than theirs. Joseph valued Kantemir's satires highly and considered him the founder of Russian philosophical poetry. According to him, Kantemir's line of writing was continued by Baratynsky and Tsvetaeva— the nineteenth- and twentieth-century poets whom he loved most of all. "Podrazhanie" was a sort of comic stylization, produced in highly old-fashioned language and using an extremely refined system of rhymes, yet quite serious in its message. Incidentally, I read it to Lotman (who was an authority on Kantemir). He was positively fascinated by the poem.

On every visit to Vilnius—there were at least ten of them—Joseph brought new work, which he generously shared with us. Once, he read us his translations of John Donne including "The Flea" and "The Storm." Our knowledge of Donne at that time was very limited (well, everybody could recite by heart his famous lines about the tolling of the bell, taken as the title of Hemingway's novel). Therefore, the translations simply overwhelmed us. He also supplied us with English poetry books: in my diary, I noted that he gave me a large volume of Wallace Stevens and a book of Cavafy in translation (he was very fond of Cavafy, and I fell in love with him as well—soon, I translated "Thermopylae," "Ithaka," and several other poems into Lithuanian).

HINSEY: Alexander Ginzburg had also asked Brodsky for poems to publish in *Sintaksis*, which, as we know, led to various difficulties for all involved. In 1968 you signed a letter of protest against Ginzburg's arrest—

VENCLOVA: That's correct. Joseph liked Ginzburg, though they were never close friends. In 1968, Ginzburg was arrested for the second time, since he and Yuri Galanskov had compiled and smuggled to the West *The White Book*, a four-hundred-page report about the Sinyavsky and Daniel show trial. He was sentenced to five years of hard labor. More than a hundred people, including myself, signed a petition on his behalf (I identified myself as "an author, an instructor at Vilnius University"). Strangely enough, I was left alone, though some other signatories lost their jobs.

HINSEY: Also, sometime during this period, Joseph and Virgilijus Čepaitis produced a sort of wall newspaper called *Pravda-matka*, to which you contributed. What did this involve?

VENCLOVA: It was a funny, school-boyish enterprise: a parody of the main Soviet official newspaper *Pravda* (Truth). One might roughly translate the title *Pravda-matka* as "Stark Naked Truth." Čepaitis enjoyed such ventures highly: he wrote absurdist comedies in the vein of Ionesco and even comic novels that have largely remained a family affair. Here, he found a kindred spirit in Joseph. *Pravda-matka* consisted of short poems and stories, as well as parodistic newspaper items, which made fun of official Soviet values. For example, there was a rhymed advertisement for a bordello, proudly boasting that it was frequented by Vladimir Ulyanov (that is, Lenin) himself. All of the poetic parts were produced by Brodsky, and some stories as well; my participation was minimal—at most, I proposed several newspaper items (I had some experience in doing such things from the time of my Schnapstrinker youth). Of course it was a risky business, but it never went beyond a very narrow circle of friends. Joseph was quite fond of *Pravda-matka* and remembered it to the end of his days. I believe this is an important part of his literary legacy and of Soviet samizdat in general. Today, it remains in Čepaitis's possession; he has not been in a hurry to publish it.

HINSEY: March 1968 saw unrest in Poland, and in August, the repression of the Prague Spring. Could you say something about how you saw these events? Did you and Brodsky hold the same views?

VENCLOVA: We followed the unrest in Poland closely, since Polish newspapers were still widely available. Naturally, these were censored and highly biased, yet while reading them one could reconstruct the events rather easily. The BBC, Voice of America, and Radio Free Europe also did their job, even if jammed. By the way, Lotman visited Vilnius at that time: I translated Polish newspapers for him, with my own comments. Everyone, including Joseph of course, was more than sympathetic toward the Polish dissidents. The Prague Spring put us in quite high spirits. Virgilijus Čepaitis even did something rather incredible: he managed to subscribe to a Czech oppositionist weekly

Literárni noviny (Literary News), learned Czech in a week or two, and gave us priceless information about everything that was going on. (No one else in Vilnius did this, since nobody knew Czech, and the very idea of subscribing to a Prague publication looked crazy.)

As is well-known, the Prague Spring was crushed in several months—on August 21, to be precise. At that time, I was on the Baltic seashore with Tanya Nikitina, now my wife of many years. We hitchhiked back to Vilnius. It was only in the morning after our return to Vilnius that we heard the news. Čepaitis proposed to arrange a demonstration on Cathedral Square: I was quite eager to participate in it, yet Tanya was strongly against it (needless to say, she did not want to see me imprisoned). Finally, I yielded to her, and the protest did not materialize. The day's heroes arranged a demonstration in Moscow. I wrote two poems on the subject—one of them in the fall of 1968, the second thirty-one years later: it deals with our trip to Vilnius and with the news we got at dawn.

Joseph was in Leningrad at the time. I went there a month or so later, and read his poem about the invasion where he compared Soviet rule in Prague to a Nazi protectorate. "The brotherly help" given by the Warsaw Pact troops to the Czechs was defined by him as the brotherly help given by Cain to Abel (soon, it became a commonplace saying). As far as I know, the poem is still unpublished—I saw it in an incomplete state, and perhaps it never went beyond a rough copy. At that time, we were fascinated by Auden's poem, "The Ogre does what ogres can," translated into Russian by an émigré poet (Ivan Elagin, I believe) and read on Radio Free Europe.

HINSEY: A bit later, you made a trip to Poland. What happened during this trip?

VENCLOVA: I visited Poland twice, in 1970 and 1971. Let me start with the first visit. At this time, I belonged to the category of *nevyezdnye* (persons not allowed to go abroad) due to my reputation as an "enemy of the people." The very existence of such a category of Soviet citizens was never publicly recognized, but many people, including some well-known writers and artists, simply couldn't get a Soviet exit visa, no matter how hard they tried. The ban might be revoked, or imposed again, depending on the person's behavior. Yet Poland was a bit different. There was a funny, politically incorrect Russian saying: *Kuritsa ne ptitsa, Pol'sha ne zagranitsa* (A hen is not a bird, and Poland is not a foreign country). This was truer in Lithuania than anywhere else, as there were long-standing ties between the Vilnius region and Poland: hundreds of old ladies from Polish-speaking families, for instance, would visit their relatives (usually in remote Polish villages), and were, as a rule, engaged in a lively smuggling trade. Lithuanian ham and Russian caviar were brought to Warsaw and Kraków; reciprocally, catchpenny fabrics, prayer books, and blue jeans found their way to Vilnius, sometimes appearing at open-air markets, but usually just smartening up the lucky bearers of exit visas. More than one party member, or even a liberally minded intellectual, followed the example of these ladies: the income earned from smuggling could be substantial by Soviet standards.

When a Polish theater, led by the world-famous director Andrzej Wajda, visited Vilnius, our group of Vilnius Polonophiles managed to make friends with Professor Jan Błoński, who was the head of the literary division. Błoński was a significant critic, an authority on Proust, and a very genial man: he immediately arranged invitations to Poland for several of us, including myself. Not yet believing my good luck, I got an exit visa (and a Polish entry visa, which was easier) and crossed the border by train in August 1970. As I've mentioned, I had a good reading knowledge of Polish—but I had never attempted to speak it. However, after crossing the border I had no other choice but to switch languages. To my astonishment, I found that I was able to speak Polish fluently: my companions on the train took me for a Pole from the Vilnius region because of my accent.

Poland might not be "a foreign country": still, its mores differed from the Soviet ones quite perceptibly. In Błoński's house in Kraków, I met Stanisław Lem, the celebrated science-fiction author who was as anti-Communist as they get; and in Warsaw, I made friends with Wiktor Woroszylski, a dissident poet knowledgeable in unofficial Russian literature (including émigrés). Everyone talked much more freely than in Lithuania, where distrust and fear prevailed—well, even more freely than in Moscow (Lithuania's cultural policy was a bit more liberal than Moscow's, but private discussions between Muscovites were more daring than in Vilnius). During a one-month stint, I managed to read literally dozens of very interesting books, including numerous works by Miłosz (they were banned yet easily available nonetheless). In all, it was an incredibly enlightening experience.

HINSEY: On December 14, 1970, workers from the Gdańsk shipyards began a strike in response to, among other grievances, an increase in food prices. On December 17, troops fired at unarmed workers and this led to nationwide protests—one of the most important crises of postwar Poland. You addressed these events in your poem "Winter Dialogue"—

VENCLOVA: This poem was a sort of internal monologue: in it, I tried to express my anxiety regarding these events and my hope that not everything in our part of the world was ruled by the laws of pure statistics, that is, by a supremacy of force. Outwardly, the poem described a Northern landscape, yet the stanzas were full of hidden symbolism. During the Gdańsk events, I was in Palanga, attempting—mostly in vain—to get news about Poland. It was only several months prior that I had visited Poland for the first time. I was anxious about my Polish friends' fates and worried that some of them might have perished in Gdańsk or elsewhere (which luckily was not the case). Gdańsk is not far from Palanga—only a hundred or so miles of sea separate the two cities: the narrator of the poem strains his sight, as if attempting to see the streets of Gdańsk, but of course he sees them only in his mind's eye. The poem was written later, in the summer of 1971 in Vilnius, yet it conveyed my December mood—and perhaps the mood of many people at that moment.

HINSEY: In 1972, after Joseph Brodsky had gone into exile, he showed this poem to Czesław Miłosz—

VENCLOVA: He showed Miłosz my entire book, *Sign of Speech*, which had appeared just before Brodsky's exile. Miłosz was interested in young poets from Vilnius; therefore he read the book (he had a reading knowledge of Lithuanian) and chose this particular poem to translate into Polish.

HINSEY: The poem would go on to have an important destiny, beginning in the United States—

VENCLOVA: In his translation work, Miłosz was helped by a classical scholar at Berkeley, Raphael Sealey, who knew Lithuanian well. As far as I know, they sensed the poem had hidden symbolic meanings, but did not yet connect them to concrete events—Miłosz said he was just impressed by its somber yet hopeful atmosphere. His translation was published in *Kultura*. Later, it became rather well-known because Miłosz reprinted it in his books on more than one occasion. Two lines from "Winter Dialogue" were chosen as a motto for one of Poland's underground periodicals.

HINSEY: Later you learned about the poem's fate from a friend in Poland—

VENCLOVA: *Kultura* was banned in Poland, but almost every intellectual there had copies: it influenced the country's public opinion and its political life to a degree quite unusual for an émigré enterprise. Some issues leaked to Lithuania as well (I had even seen one or two of them before 1972, but they were a rarity). I believe Jan Błoński wrote me a letter of congratulation, recounting that he had read my poem "translated by a great poet." I immediately surmised that he meant Miłosz, and answered in kind: "well, I guess I know the translator's name since there are not too many great poets around, but I'm interested in the place of publication—is it a certain *cultured* city?" (That, of course, was a reference to *Kultura* and Paris.) Błoński easily understood and wrote me back that my hypotheses were correct. Well, here you have an example of the rather funny Aesopian language we practiced at that time to avoid postal censorship—today, all that sounds quite far-fetched.

Several months later, one of my acquaintances, the liberal literary scholar Vytautas Kubilius, managed on a trip to Poland to smuggle out that issue of *Kultura* and presented it to me in strictest secrecy. Well, it was a badge of honor and an example of Polish-Lithuanian dissident collaboration, very rare in that period. Publication in an "enemy" press, as a rule, was punishable (at the very least, one had to print a statement explaining that it had been done without one's knowledge and against one's will), but the Lithuanian KGB was perhaps not following the Polish émigré press too closely.

HINSEY: Then there was the time in April 1971, when you arranged for Wiktor Woroszylski to meet Joseph in Vilnius during one of his visits—

VENCLOVA: I invited Woroszylski to Vilnius but he could not make use of my invitation since both of us, not without reason, were considered less than politically reliable. Then, he got another invitation from Estonia, which worked, and he made a stopover in Vilnius. He was accompanied by his wife and young daughter Natalia (she became a Polish cultural attaché in Moscow after many years and historical changes). Naturally, their visit to the Lithuanian capital was kept semisecret. Since Wiktor was very interested in Joseph's poetry (he was one of his first translators and promoters in Poland), and Joseph, in turn, displayed immense interest in all things Polish, I made a phone call to Leningrad. Just in case, I did it from the post office and not from my flat. I invited Joseph to Vilnius without any further explanation. "When should I be at your place?" he asked. "Today," I answered. "Well, tomorrow." The next day, I met him at the airport: he was sure that a surprise marriage party for one of our friends (presumably Adas Katilius) was being arranged. We took a long walk through Vilnius together with the Woroszylskis, and also went to Trakai, talking all the way about Robert Frost, Robert Penn Warren, and similar topics. The impressions of that meeting found their way into Joseph's well-known cycle of poems, *Lithuanian Divertimento*.

HINSEY: If I remember correctly, there also turned out to be a little problem with some midnight visitors—

VENCLOVA: I gave my flat (an attic in a modest house next to the main street in Vilnius) to the Woroszylski family, and spent the night at the Katiliuses', along with Joseph. That very night, several unknown persons rang the attic's bell:

they explained to Woroszylski's wife (who was in her nightgown, and frightened by the visit), that they were looking for me, since I was requested for a stint in the barracks as a reserve junior lieutenant of the Soviet Army. Well, I was absent, so they left. Such things used to happen in the USSR—people were taken for temporary army service without any warning—but it was more or less clear this time that the night visitors didn't belong to the army but to the secret police. In the morning, we nicknamed the event "a visit from the night milkman." (This was a reference to the famous maxim by Winston Churchill: "Democracy means that if the doorbell rings in the early hours, it is likely to be the milkman.") Of course I stayed in Katilius's flat for several more days, just in case.

When Woroszylski left by train for Poland, he told Brodsky: "Well, Joseph, we managed to meet anyway, though history did its best to prevent it." "We were helped by geography," Joseph replied. Incidentally, the entire Woroszylski family underwent strict body searches at the Polish border, yet nothing was found.

HINSEY: After your second trip to Poland, you were never again allowed to travel, and a series of professional invitations were refused—

VENCLOVA: In the fall of 1971, I was invited to Warsaw to take part in the Cyprian Norwid celebration (the 150th anniversary of his birth), as Norwid's translator into Lithuanian. Joseph was invited as well, since he had translated Norwid into Russian, but he, predictably, did not get an exit visa. I received one and therefore visited Poland for the second time. Perhaps my speech at the anniversary meeting (where I mentioned Joseph and expressed my regret that he was not with us) was a bit suspicious, yet the veritable faux pas occurred that evening. Together with Woroszylski, I went to a Warsaw theater to see a play by Witkacy, the Polish predecessor of Beckett and Ionesco who had committed suicide in 1939 after the Soviets, in a pact with Hitler, invaded eastern Poland. During the intermission, Wiktor told me: "Did you see that young man in the fourth row? He's Michnik, we should talk to him." "Well, who is Michnik?" I asked. "A serious person, you'll see," Wiktor answered.

Adam Michnik, fresh out of prison, happened to be the *spiritus movens* of the March 1968 students' unrest in Warsaw. He was ten years younger than me. After the play, we went to his flat: several of his fellow prisoners were also there, including Barbara Toruńczyk, a smart beautiful young woman. We sat together until dawn, drinking and talking about Poland, Lithuania, and Russia. That was the start of a friendship that lasts until today: Adam soon became one of the key figures of the Polish dissident movement (he is now the head of *Gazeta Wyborcza*, the main liberal daily in Warsaw, a sort of Polish *New York Times*). Joseph became a close friend of Barbara and Adam during his émigré years.

In 1971, things unfolded in a slightly different, yet predictable way. The day after our meeting, I was briefly detained by uniformed police on a Warsaw street (far from Michnik's flat). My passport was checked, and then the policemen released me without any explanation. After returning to Vilnius, I was never allowed to travel again (prior to my emigration).

HINSEY: Joseph, who was born in May under the sign of Gemini, often spoke of you as his "twin." Now, many years later, what are your thoughts on this?

VENCLOVA: First of all, my name, Tomas, means "twin" in Aramaic. We were both aware of that. Once, I showed him the bas-reliefs of the zodiac that adorn the eighteenth-century astronomical observatory at Vilnius University. Gemini is considered to be the most beautiful one. They are depicted as small children—strangely, with faces that remind one of Romantic poets. In *Lithuanian Divertimento*, Joseph describes a night in a Vilnius flat—presumably the very night when the secret police rang the bell—where the protagonist lies "alone and naked in your sack . . . fallen from the Zodiac."[19] It is definitely a reference to the Gemini relief. (My own sign, incidentally, is Virgo.) We also had in mind Thomas the Apostle, whose inclination for doubting is somewhat consonant with my character.

A unique human being, Joseph literally longed for people similar to himself. For some time, he looked for "twins" among the Leningrad underground poets, such as Rein, Naiman, and even Bobyshev who later became his adversary. Perhaps he considered my fate to be somewhat parallel to his own. Both of us could rarely, if ever, publish our work; both were skeptical of the powers that be (to put it mildly) and antagonistic toward the literary milieu around us; finally, our poetic tastes were rather similar. We did not always share our predilections, but we definitely shared our aversions—for instance, we disliked fashionable poets of the Yevtushenko and Voznesensky sort (as well as their Western counterparts) with equal vehemence. There was also the private reason I mentioned previously. I was luckier than Joseph in some respects (I never experienced poverty or imprisonment), but there were nevertheless certain similarities.

HINSEY: We have a tendency to remember poets by their mature styles. But like all young poets (you were twenty-nine years old when you met Joseph, he was twenty-six) in the early 1960s, Joseph's work was still in the process of developing and he was searching for an authentic style—

VENCLOVA: Like nearly everyone, Joseph began with unskilled poems of a traditional bent, full of clichés and sentimental pathos, which he later dismissed as "kindergarten pieces" and never included in his collected works. Still, even these were somewhat thrilling. There was an inimitable sharp and poignant quality to some of his lines. Also, he daringly introduced tragic, philosophical, and religious topics into his verse, which countered the officially permitted "life-affirming" poetry. Of course it was a reintroduction. Perhaps without even knowing it, Brodsky continued early twentieth-century trends, interrupted by censorship following the revolution.

At first, he read mainly the Soviet poets who were close to hand, preferring, as we have mentioned before, the less conformist ones, such as Slutsky. He was also influenced by some—not necessarily major—Western twentieth-century authors published in Russian translation by the magazine *Inostrannaya literatura* (Foreign Literature). Yet he developed very fast. In that, he was quite similar to Tsvetaeva who started with two weak and naive books and became a great poet literally in several months. Brodsky's "Christmas Romance" and "Elegy to John Donne" were magnificent works that struck a totally new note in Russian poetry—in the case of "Elegy," I would even say, in world poetry. Yet the watershed event was his exile to Norenskaya. After this, and during his émigré years, he developed his mature style, writing long and complicated poems that deal with metaphysical topics, primarily with time. These were essentially philosophical treatises, perfect in their poetic technique and strongly imbued with irony. These are one of a kind: nothing in poetry prior to Brodsky can be compared with them. However, I must confess that I especially like Brodsky's poems written just before emigration, for instance, "Conversation with Celestial," "Nunc Dimittis," and "Nature Morte."

HINSEY: In the years before you both went into exile, you were in regular contact with Joseph, exchanging letters and manuscripts. The mechanism of literary exchange and influence is very subtle, but it is clear that you and Joseph were able to share things that would go on to be important mutual influences—

VENCLOVA: As for me, I was fascinated by Joseph's work, purely and simply. I knew (and still know) much of it by heart. Needless to say, I was influenced by it, sometimes referring to his motifs, metrical and stanzaic patterns, quoting him, and so on. I believe it was not an imitation but a dialogue. I have noticed some hidden quotations from my poetry in his works—but all this is normal poetic exchange.

I was rather shy about sharing my poems with Joseph, but Romas Katilius made some word-for-word translations for him and read him the Lithuanian originals aloud without my knowledge or permission. Apparently Joseph liked them. Once, on a Leningrad tram, we talked about my poem "Night descended on us with a chill" for a long while. "Well, I stole the idea of the geometric metaphor from you," I said. "And I stole it from Donne," Joseph retorted.

HINSEY: Joseph had discovered, perhaps in part through Andrei Sergeyev, the work of Auden and Frost, which he began reading in exile. You both were interested in Mandelstam. Who were the writers you most discussed and shared?

VENCLOVA: In his early youth, with the help of his friends and later Akhmatova, Joseph had discovered the Russian Silver Age. Among its writers, he was most impressed by Tsvetaeva, whose poetic gift had much in common with his own. I believe that Brodsky's later inclination for logical and multilayered exposition of thought, his penchant for enjambments, and many other traits were related to his study of Tsvetaeva's work. Mandelstam came next, then Akhmatova. He liked Pasternak the least of the Great Four: Joseph was suspicious of his "facile pantheism," though he valued the *Zhivago* poems. For me, the hierarchy was different: Mandelstam, then Akhmatova, Pasternak, and Tsvetaeva. Moreover, Joseph disliked Gumilev and Blok, and positively hated Vyacheslav Ivanov, while I was a bit fonder of them. Among the nineteenth-century classics, he valued Baratynsky most of all. "To tell the truth, he's better than Pushkin." Joseph used to say. "But there are no hierarchies at that level." He also loved Lermontov yet virtually rejected Tyutchev and Fet. We discussed our preferences frequently, sometimes getting into arguments, which, by the way, were never too heated.

After learning English in Norenskaya, Joseph began to study English-language metaphysical poetry and Modernist classics quite assiduously. He was not particularly fond of Eliot (notwithstanding the fact that he dedicated a brilliant poem to his memory) and, I believe, had a limited knowledge of Yeats; but Donne, Auden, and Frost became his daily reading. More than once, he expressed his high opinion of Gerard Manley Hopkins, Thomas Hardy, and Wallace Stevens. "Among the pre-twentieth-century English authors, the only poets I'm not particularly fond of are Milton and Blake," I remember him saying. As for the French poets, he loved only Baudelaire: all the others, in his opinion, "lacked rage," and the Surrealists were his bêtes noires. He was also rather lukewarm toward Rilke, whom Tsvetaeva adored. Our preferences in Polish poetry were similar (Norwid, Szymborska) and, as I have said, we were equally fascinated by Cavafy.

HINSEY: While, as we discussed in the preceding chapter, your early work was already deeply reflective of classical sources, Joseph said that at the time of his exile in the North his classical education was relatively limited. Did your knowledge in this area have an impact on him?

VENCLOVA: That, I cannot say for sure. I could read Latin and some Greek thanks to my grandfather, while Joseph learned Latin only in his émigré years. Sometimes, we talked about mythology: once, I mentioned Telegonus (son of Odysseus and Circe)—a name that was unknown to him. Incidentally, the story of Telegonus is the subtext of my poem "The Eleventh Canto," which Joseph translated. There were other exchanges of information, concerning, for instance, the Greek lyric poet Archilochus. But, as a rule, Joseph studied ancient mythology, history, and poetry in a very independent way. In the United States, we frequently discussed Virgil, Propertius, and other Latin poets together: by that time, he displayed an ample and profound knowledge of the topic.

HINSEY: The literary scholar Viktor Kulle has written that the "neoclassical" period in Joseph's work was, in part, an outcome of his acquaintance with Lithuania—

VENCLOVA: It's possible. In our milieu, comparing the USSR to the Roman Empire during its decline and fall was a commonplace. Joseph's exile in Norenskaya was compared by many, including him, to Ovid's exile. It also had some similarities to Pushkin's exile (Pushkin had spent part of his youth in Bessarabia, the same place to which Ovid had been banished). Bessarabia and Lithuania possessed common traits: both were small countries leaning to the West yet occupied by Russia. That entire metaphorical web looked meaningful to us.

As I have mentioned before, Lithuania reminded Joseph of a Roman province, in a sense preferable to Rome itself. It is true that Joseph became especially interested in classical motifs in the course of his visits to Vilnius.

HINSEY: Both your and Joseph's work has been described as "rebellious classicism"—

VENCLOVA: That's correct. Still, one should keep in mind that Joseph was a "rebellious classicist" only at the beginning of his career. Generally, he was more of a Baroque than a Classicist poet.

HINSEY: You also both knew Akhmatova, and received from that encounter what Joseph called in his dialogues with Solomon Volkov a "tanning of the soul"—

VENCLOVA: As Joseph himself confessed, Akhmatova influenced him more by her moral and civic stance than by her poetry. She was a paragon of calm yet unflinching resistance to the totalitarian state, as well as of loyalty to the ethical values abandoned by most people around her. Joseph also said that one learned Christianity from the very fact of communicating with her, though she never insisted on Christian rituals and did not keep any icons in her room. I shared that experience of spiritual training (let us call it by that name), as did everyone who visited Akhmatova.

HINSEY: You have written about how Joseph favored "vast, large-scale constructions" as opposed to the Russian tradition of the "small-scale masterpiece." However, many of his early poems are indeed short. Corresponding with him and sharing work, can you say something about this evolution?

VENCLOVA: Joseph still produced short pieces until the end of his days, yet he opted for large and complicated philosophical poems early on: he felt that this was a virtually unexplored area in Russian verse. As I have mentioned, he considered only Kantemir, Baratynsky, and Tsvetaeva to be practitioners of that genre (well-developed in English-language poetry). It was not just a promising field of writing, but most likely corresponded most closely to his cast of mind and personality. Many people criticized him for his "boring long-windedness." He once said to Romas Katilius: "Long-windedness is just a poetic device, like metaphor or ellipsis." Akhmatova's straightforward and concise verse was the very opposite of his involved constructions. He loved Akhmatova's later poems, such as "Requiem" and "Poem without a Hero" (which were lengthy and many-layered) but not her early work. Yet interestingly enough, his poem in memory of Akhmatova consists of only twelve lines and has a powerful epigrammatic quality.

HINSEY: In the years after Joseph's departure and before your own in 1977, you wrote "The Shield of Achilles" and Joseph composed "Lithuanian Nocturne" (in 1973/74). While not "planned" can you discuss how this exchange came about?

VENCLOVA: I wrote "The Shield of Achilles" in Palanga and Klaipėda in the summer of 1972, under the immediate impact of his departure. At that time, I received a postcard from him from London in which he described his first experiences as an émigré, from which I concluded that nothing much had changed regarding Brodsky's state of mind: that gave a tonality to my first stanza. The title was, of course, a reference to Auden, but in the context of the poem it meant a sheet of paper on which verses are written. A bit later, Joseph started to compose "Lithuanian Nocturne," a long poem about Lithuania and our friendship, in the Hotel Wales in Manhattan: he abandoned it after writing several stanzas, and finished it only in 1984. That "exchange of poetic letters" was purely coincidental, even if one may see a similar image or two in both of them.

HINSEY: This is a period when you both were exploring the possibility of longer poems—

VENCLOVA: Following Joseph's example, I had switched to longer, not-so-epigrammatic poems around 1970, and found that it also corresponded to my sensibility. Still, my poems were never as long and complicated as his, and they tended to be narrative, while his works usually explored purely philosophical discourse. Once, I told him: "You know, I have a sort of format-feeling: that is, I know from the very beginning that a new poem will consist of, say, nine or eleven stanzas. Just like a painter who has to fill a canvas of some predetermined size." "I know this feeling very well," Joseph answered. "Still, it often happens that after writing the planned eleven or so stanzas, I must add a stanza or two."

HINSEY: Just before Joseph's departure for the United States, you were discussing Polish poetry, debating which poet deserved to be considered the most important poet. Joseph believed this title should go to Zbigniew Herbert, but you mentioned a poet he had never heard of, who would go on to play an important role in both of your lives—

VENCLOVA: That happened in Leningrad—on February 19, 1972, to be exact; Joseph did not yet know that he'd depart in a couple of months. We were in a restaurant with a view of the cruiser *Aurora*—the battleship that signaled the start of the October Revolution by a blank shot toward the Winter Palace (it was turned into a museum and still is one to this day). After a drink or two, Joseph asked me who, in my opinion, was the best contemporary Polish poet ("I would say Zbigniew Herbert," he added). "Well, Herbert is good," I replied, "but there is also Miłosz." That provided us with a chance to talk about Miłosz, whose poetry I already knew while Joseph did not. "Can you compare him to any poet I know?" Joseph asked. "Any great poet is beyond comparisons," I said. "But, if you will, he shares some similarities with Auden and you." "In that case, he must be good," Joseph answered. His knowledge of Miłosz amounted to that exchange until they became acquainted after Brodsky's arrival in the West.

HINSEY: Later that same year, Brodsky was forced to emigrate—

VENCLOVA: In early May 1972, Joseph was summoned to a KGB office and was asked why he did not request permission to go to Israel. He answered that he was a Russian poet and preferred to live in a country where Russian was spoken on the streets. His interlocutor said with a shadow of threat in his voice that he recommended Joseph apply for a visa for Israel—the sooner, the better.

HINSEY: Just before Joseph's departure you gave him a bottle of Lithuanian liqueur, in case he managed to find W. H. Auden in Austria when his plane touched down in Vienna. What did he tell you about completing this mission?

VENCLOVA: Yes, I provided him with a bottle of very strong Lithuanian liquor Malūnininkas (Miller), much liked at that time, and I asked him to drink it with Auden during their first meeting. By that time, I had translated into Lithuanian and published "In Memory of W. B. Yeats" and "September 1, 1939." I had sent the publications to Auden and had received a letter back from him. Joseph mailed me a postcard from Vienna with the information that he had accomplished the task. Many years later, in Auden's attic in Kirchstetten, I saw several empty bottles of liquor preserved as museum pieces, but the Lithuanian bottle was not among them. Still, I have reason to believe it was indeed consumed by two poets in 1972.

16

CIVIL SOCIETY AND DISSIDENCE

HINSEY: Let's now address some questions about the emergence of the Lithuanian and Russian dissident movements. To take a few steps back, you have written that, after the war, due to deportations, imprisonment, and emigration, civil society in Lithuania was particularly broken—

VENCLOVA: Even before the Soviet occupation, Lithuania had neither the time nor the opportunity to develop a mature civil society. There had been the autocratic tsarist rule, which had lasted more than a century, from 1795 to 1915. Independent public opinion and Western-style political life started to appear only at the end of that period, mainly in the final decade, but remained very rudimentary. (Poland was in somewhat better shape because part of it belonged to the Austro-Hungarian Empire where the political environment was incomparably more liberal than in tsarist Russia. Finland and, to a lesser extent, Latvia and Estonia, while occupied by Russia, still possessed a degree of autonomy that was denied Lithuania as a result of its antitsarist uprisings). After World War I, Lithuania's independence was established, but the country enjoyed democracy for only eight years, from 1918 to 1926. Antanas Smetona was the first president, but his party was not in power, and in 1926, the left won a parliamentary majority. Following this, his supporters (who were influential in the army), staged a coup d'état and dissolved Parliament. We have already spoken about this period of authoritarian rule, which lasted until 1940; Smetona took over the presidency and the Tautininkai (Nationalists) became the sole legal party. Smetona was not a Fascist, nor were the Nationalists Nazis; indeed, there was intense conflict with Hitler over Klaipėda. Hitler's racial policies were generally condemned. Yet, there was clear sympathy for Mussolini, whose style was considered more or less suitable for Lithuania. Later, certain young rightists looked to Franco, and especially to Salazar, the Portuguese Catholic dictator (just as some young leftists were fascinated by Lenin and Stalin). Arbitrary arrests and censorship became the norm, and a heavy-handed cult developed around the "nation's leader" (who was disliked even by many in his own party).

HINSEY: Then there were the Soviet and German invasions—

VENCLOVA: Yes, on top of all this, the Soviets invaded in June 1940. Smetona fled to Germany and then, through Portugal, to the United States. (He died in Cleveland in 1944, during a fire. Some suspect that the Soviets played a role in this, but that is, at least in my opinion, a typical "conspiracy theory": by that time, he no longer played a significant role in Lithuanian politics.) Quite a few people—and not only leftists—welcomed Smetona's removal from power. It was not long, however, before everyone understood that the new regime was far more brutal than the former, somewhat patriarchal dictatorship. Whatever shortcomings the Lithuanian Nationalists had, they certainly paled in comparison with the crimes of the Stalinist era. Earlier, we talked about the deportations and executions that became everyday occurrences. Censorship and ideological control were all-pervasive, and Stalin's cult was so monumental that the one that had surrounded Smetona began to look amateurish. After the invasion, the sentiment of national humiliation was unbearable, heightened by the fact that the Lithuanian army, pampered and glorified by Smetona, put up no resistance.

Less than a year later, the Nazis occupied Lithuania. Needless to say, this only contributed to the country's collapse and demoralization. When the Soviets returned in 1944, few vestiges of civil society remained. Most of the country's intellectuals, on both sides of the political spectrum, found themselves in DP camps; those who remained generally lived in fear. Some of them may have cherished naive hopes that Lithuania's civilized mores could resurface and even influence Russia, and some were not necessarily averse to Socialism, but in a couple of years all of these illusions had vanished.

HINSEY: Further, because of Lithuania's status within the Soviet Union—as opposed to the situation of the satellite countries—in the early years, the level of repression was particularly intense. The country had lost one-sixth of its population to deportation, war, and resistance—

VENCLOVA: One-sixth is the usual figure given in history books, although this may be on the high side. Although we don't know the exact number, the losses were horrible. Not all of them had been caused by the Soviets. As we discussed, nearly all of Lithuania's Jews—which had accounted for 7–8 percent of the population—had been exterminated by the Nazis. Klaipėda's Germans had mostly fled, war casualties continued to mount, and sixty thousand people emigrated. After the war, many of Vilnius's Poles were forced to relocate to

Poland. Deportations and the partisan war also took their toll—around two hundred thousand people, as far as I know. Lithuania only reached its prewar level of population in the sixties (incorporating many newcomers). The loss of the country's Jews (and Polish-speaking intellectuals) deprived Lithuania of important intellectual resources: these groups could have contributed significantly to a post-Stalinist democratic renewal.

Whatever pressure was brought to bear upon the Eastern European satellite countries, it was more bearable than in Lithuania. In Czechoslovakia and Hungary, for example, a measure of normality prevailed until 1948. Poland was in worse shape, but it was still formally a sovereign state: the currents of free thought and independent ethos, as we know, would prove to be quite resilient there. I suspect that the satellite countries in Southern Europe—say, Romania or Albania—experienced a level of brutality comparable to that in Lithuania. The Stasi in Berlin or Dresden were perhaps more omniscient and omnipotent in the seventies and eighties than the KGB in Vilnius or Kaunas. But Lithuania had been annexed by the USSR, and that meant that everything was controlled by Moscow. We therefore passed through the same stages as every other part of the Soviet Union: Stalinism, Khrushchev's Thaw, Brezhnev's stagnation . . . A total loss of sovereignty and the fear of losing one's ethnic identity created a depressive—and explosive—psychological atmosphere.

One should say, however, that the situation in Lithuania was more benign than in some of the other Soviet republics. I suspect that America's policy of nonrecognition of the incorporation of the Baltic states into the USSR played a certain role in that, though this is speculation on my part. Attempts at Russification in Lithuania were rather awkward—and reversible, to a degree; in Belarus it resulted in a near elimination of the local languages, while in Ukraine the same result was obtained in several big cities. By the way, in Latvia and Estonia the percentage of Russian newcomers was much larger than in Lithuania, but these local people were never assimilated. The partisan war in Western Ukraine was fiercer than in Lithuania, and incurred larger losses. The Central Asian republics were just colonies, as they had been in the nineteenth century, with a veneer of Sovietization added, which was hardly a blessing.

HINSEY: In 1953, with Stalin's death, things began to change, though there are those who have asserted that Lithuanian resistance at first mainly took the form of "organic work"—can you explain a bit about what this meant?

VENCLOVA: The concept of "organic work" became popular in Poland after the unsuccessful uprising of 1863. It meant striving for economic and cultural improvements within the limits of what was possible, which was believed to pave the way to some form of home rule, and then, *in spe*, to independence. People who practiced organic work collaborated, in a sense, with the tsarist Russian (or, for that matter, German or Austrian) authorities. The degree of such collaboration varied, from rather disgraceful compromises to a stubborn, if hidden, struggle for national goals. Lithuanians practiced organic work in the final decades of the tsarist regime as well. It helped to train the new elites who were later instrumental in securing the country's independence.

The post-Stalin stirrings in Lithuania took the same form of semicollaboration and semiresistance, though the term "organic work" was never used. The overarching goal was silently defined as "preserving the nation for better times." This meant, above all, the discontinuation of the partisan war (which, at any rate, was dying out) and taking advantage of any liberalization of Soviet rule. Educational institutions had to be Lithuanianized, the national classics reprinted, the clichés of Socialist Realism avoided to a degree, new Lithuanian theaters and museums established, sensible economic projects promoted (and harmful ones avoided), the landscape protected, and so on. All of that, of course, had to take into account the Kremlin's wishes and directives, which at times had to be borne (especially if they were not particularly noxious), and at other times cleverly circumvented. Just as in tsarist times, one could be servile to varying degrees, earning respect or disdain as a result. But people from quite different backgrounds ended up working for similar ends. Among them, there were Communists (including my father), who were prone to compromises by definition, as well as many closet anti-Communists, who tried to remain as honest as possible, even if they were not always able to succeed in that ambition. Hypocrisy was considered justifiable and even praiseworthy. To my young eyes, all this was an amusing, if at times sorry spectacle.

HINSEY: Your friend Aleksandras Štromas used the term "intrastructural dissenters" for those who attempted to change the system from within—

VENCLOVA: Aleksandras Štromas invented this term in the late seventies: he had in mind people who were involved in official Soviet structures—that is, virtually everyone, since the Soviet system was the only employer—but who nevertheless cautiously promoted their own non-Soviet or even anti-Soviet agenda. "Intrastructural dissent" was virtually synonymous with "organic work." There were also "extrastructural dissenters," who promoted their agenda—frequently the same as the agenda of the intrastructural ones—by illegal means. These were not numerous, though, at least for me, they merited more respect than their intrastructural counterparts.

The distinction between the two groups was a bit vague, and many crossed the line. Štromas himself was a case in point. He was one of the few survivors of the Kaunas ghetto. But his parents, who perished during the Nazi years, had been on friendly terms with Antanas Sniečkus, the head of the Lithuanian Communist Party; after the war he was adopted by Sniečkus's family. He was brought up as a Young Communist and sent to study Soviet law at Moscow University, where, by the way, Gorbachev was his classmate. There, Štromas became a member of the opposition, though for many years he remained an intrastructural dissenter, working as a lawyer in different Lithuanian cities, and even organizing a scientific institute. Later he met people such as Ginzburg and Sakharov, and established clandestine connections between the liberal-minded people in Moscow and Vilnius. It was then that he crossed the line, opting for extrastructural dissent, even if formally he remained employed in academia.

The *shestidesyatniki* in Russia were typical intrastructural dissenters. Brodsky was definitely extrastructural, not only because of his views but also due to his independent behavior and moral stature. Akhmatova, Nadezhda Mandelstam, and (to a degree) Pasternak were his counterparts in the elder generation, just as Ehrenburg was a counterpart for young *shestidesyatniki* like Yevtushenko. Solzhenitsyn was on the border for a relatively long time: after the publication of *One Day in the Life of Ivan Denisovich*, he became an officially recognized writer, but his subsequent work was banned, and a veritable war ensued between him and the Soviet government, which ended with his exile. Similar stories also took place in other Soviet republics, though they are much less well-known.

HINSEY: It has been argued that late in his career, the first secretary of the Lithuanian Communist Party, Antanas Sniečkus—through policies such as the gradual elimination of the Russian cadres and the sabotage of directives from Moscow—played a role in preserving Lithuanian nationhood. For example, before 1952, 30 percent of cadres were ethnic Lithuanians, and by 1957 this figure was 50 percent—

VENCLOVA: Later, the percentage of local ethnic Lithuanians in the Lithuanian Communist Party was even higher, which was a mixed blessing. Quite a number of these Communists were very cautious intrastructural dissenters. One should not forget that the first president of independent Lithuania, Algirdas Brazauskas, was a former Communist functionary—and he was not the worst president imaginable. Another such case was Justinas Marcinkevičius, who authored the antidissident novel *The Pine that Laughed*, yet later became a cult figure among those seeking independence for Lithuania. Such Communists played a role in preserving Lithuanian identity, but there was always the threat of servility and demoralization. Sniečkus himself was a very ambivalent figure. I have already mentioned that he was a zealous Stalinist, at least until the end of the partisan war. After Stalin's death, however, he managed to cautiously carry out a form of separatist politics, promoting the interests of his personal territory (that is, Soviet Lithuania) and permitting a degree of Lithuanian nationalism. Well, he was neither a tyrant nor a megalomaniac. But also not a liberal, like Dubček: rather a patriarchal authoritarian. We jokingly called him, "the most gifted Lithuanian politician since the Middle Ages," and predicted, also jokingly, that people would choose him as a president in free elections. This does not seem too far-fetched if one keeps in mind Brazauskas's case.

HINSEY: In the West, little is known about the early development of Lithuanian dissent. You have written that after 1956—following the return of political prisoners and deportees—"small islands" began to form around individuals, activist priests, and prewar intellectuals—

VENCLOVA: Extrastructural dissidents promoted their views by writing leaflets, organizing secret circles, raising the Lithuanian tricolor on factory chimneys under cover of night, and so on. Quite often they were schoolchildren, not only eager to express their patriotism but also looking for ways to rebel. Such things usually led to prison terms, or at the very least, harassment and pressure (frequently successful) to become a KGB informer. In the late 1950s and 1960s, clusters of dissenters began to crystallize around former political prisoners and Catholic activists. For example, there are a number of cases of priests who established secret religious circles, organizing prayer groups or simply teaching catechism—all of which was fiercely persecuted. People faithful to the memory of Lithuania's prewar independence tried to impart at least some of their beliefs to the younger generation. Of course, these were all clandestine activities with their own rules, discipline, and ethos; therefore not all such clusters ended up being exposed. Even some prewar intellectuals, who were generally loyal to the powers that be—say, Vincas Mykolaitis-Putinas, the poet, or Juozas Miltinis, the stage director—attracted clusters of admirers with dissident inclinations.

HINSEY: Lyudmila Alexeyeva has hypothesized that, paradoxically, certain Lithuanian traits connected with hard work, ethics, and perseverance endured in the camps, and were even preserved there—

VENCLOVA: I think she is right. The former political prisoners I met were, as a rule, people of high ethical standards. On the other hand, their opinions sometimes seemed a bit anachronistic. A person who has spent fifteen or twenty years in a camp remains, so to speak, hostage to his or her youth—that is, the worldview that was dominant before their arrest.

HINSEY: We have discussed the influence of your grandfather's prewar experiences and education—as well as those of a number of your teachers—on your thinking. Are there any other encounters of this nature that you'd like to mention here?

VENCLOVA: I have mentioned Petras Juodelis and Ona Lukauskaitė, both of them prewar intellectuals, survivors of camps, and people of the highest moral stature. One might also say several words about Justinas Mikutis. Mikutis was arrested immediately after the war, when he was still a high school student. After enduring beatings and torture, he spent many years in some of the worst corners of the Gulag. After returning to Lithuania, Mikutis became a sort of wandering mendicant philosopher, a guru for lots of young people, and a legendary figure. (During the Nazi period, it is said that, claiming that he was Jewish, he attempted to join a column of Jews being led toward execution, but was driven away by a guard.) I only met him once, yet he left an enduring impression on me. He was, without a doubt, a strange man, perhaps slightly unbalanced, but very knowledgeable, and his reflections on any topic were fascinating. Like Brodsky, he was not anti-Soviet, but rather a-Soviet. He knew even more of Pasternak's poetry by heart than I did. Dozens of people have told me that he was a seminal influence in their lives.

HINSEY: You previously described the importance of the 1956 All Souls' Day event. After that, young people in Lithuania became progressively involved in more outward signs of dissent. What type of acts of resistance were these?

VENCLOVA: There are many stories concerning Lithuanian dissent. In 1957, we were summoned to a meeting at the university where we were informed about an anti-Soviet student organization that had been unmasked. This information served as a warning for anyone who might have been tempted to take part in such foolhardy enterprises. We were informed of the names of the transgressors, to whom punishment, that is, prison sentences, had already been meted out. I didn't know any of them (they were seniors), but I immediately felt sympathy for them, since I had already undergone my political conversion. Much later, I met one (he was a polyglot, and after serving his term, he managed to find employment editing translations). The students' agenda had been strictly nationalist, and their activities clandestine. But there were other cases as well. For instance, the young poet Mindaugas Tomonis, an engineer by profession, was ordered to repair a monument to the victorious Red Army, which had started to deteriorate. He wrote an open letter to the authorities, refusing to honor the occupying power and proposing instead the erection of a monument to the victims of Stalinism. For that, he was subjected to psychiatric treatment. (One of the alleged proofs of his "psychosis" was that he studied Leibniz and Nietzsche in his spare time.) As a result of this treatment, he committed suicide.

HINSEY: Do you remember any other subtle signs of civic renewal from this period? Kitchen-table conversations, sayings, or even humorous expressions?

VENCLOVA: "Kitchen-table conversations" were quite common at that time. In almost any group of close friends things were discussed more or less openly. The general mood among Lithuanians was nationalist. Discussions could lead to problems if a secret police agent managed to infiltrate the group, but that did not happen very often (anti-Semitic remarks or opinions were not necessarily considered pernicious by the authorities). Such discussions provided an opportunity to vent one's emotions but they led nowhere. Literally hundreds of political jokes and anecdotes circulated in almost every milieu, including party circles: after Stalin's death, people were no longer threatened with execution or imprisonment for such things, although it could be harmful for one's career. Most people followed Western broadcasts. Radio Free Europe was assiduously jammed (three immense towers were built on the highest point in Vilnius exclusively for that reason), but one could listen to it in the provinces—people sometimes traveled outside the city for that sole purpose.

In 1959, the quasi-Modernist café Neringa opened in Vilnius. It became the watering hole for genuine and fake Bohemians (Brodsky liked it and wrote a poem about it, nowadays printed on Neringa's menu.) There was a table in a corner where prewar intellectuals and their younger followers used to meet over a bottle of Armenian cognac or the like. Conversations there were also rather free, though it was generally assumed that KGB agents were present as well.

With my friends, such as Romas Katilius, Natasha Trauberg, or Aleksandras Štromas, I exchanged all sorts of information and reflections, without the slightest hesitation. We used specific slang, for instance, *Sof'ia Vlas'evna* (a female name) instead of *sovetskaia vlast'* (Soviet power)—but this was more for joking among ourselves than for conspiratorial reasons. Sof'ia Vlas'evna, in our conversations, was an aged lady who had gone through numerous unhappy love affairs (for example, with Adolf Aloisovich, that is, Hitler) and was not expected to live very long.

HINSEY: As we have discussed, in the mid-sixties samizdat and other underground literary and historical projects gathered momentum. I'd like to explore a specific event in a little more detail: while books like *Doctor Zhivago* had seen publication in the West, some younger writers, having learned from the "Pasternak Affair," began to publish their books abroad, but under pseudonyms—

VENCLOVA: As you know, the publication of *Doctor Zhivago* resulted in the author being hounded, but the appearance of Akhmatova's *Requiem* in Munich (1963) was passed over in silence: the authorities were somewhat hesitant about a new international scandal. This encouraged several dissident authors (including graphomaniacs, like Valery Tarsis) to publish their work in the West, usually under pseudonyms. This happened not only in Russia but also, for example, in Estonia (though not in Lithuania).

HINSEY: In September 1965, a year and a half after Joseph Brodsky's trial, Andrei Sinyavsky and Yuli Daniel were arrested for transmitting their works to the West; they were charged with "anti-Soviet agitation and propaganda." What were your thoughts upon hearing about their arrests?

VENCLOVA: When I first met Sinyavsky and his wife Maria Rozanova, who later became an author in her own right, I had no idea of their clandestine activities. For me, Sinyavsky was a Pasternak scholar. Both he and Rozanova were interested in Northern Russian folk art, which they collected (examples of this type of art were rapidly disappearing under Soviet rule, thus becoming a prized rarity). That was the only topic of our conversations. In 1962 or 1963, my friend Volodya Muravyov gave me a copy of *Encounter* in which Sinyavsky's short novel *The Trial Begins* was printed under the name of Abram Tertz. God knows how Volodya got hold of it. I was not particularly impressed, but that was perhaps due to the fact that I was reading Faulkner's *The Sound and the Fury* at the same time, also given to me by Volodya (my English was still shaky, and I struggled through Benjy's babble and Quentin's divagations with excruciating effort, but I simply could not put the book down). In any case, *The Trial Begins* was a courageous and risky piece. Upon hearing that Abram Tertz was Sinyavsky, I was astonished, purely and simply.

HINSEY: In response to the arrests of Sinyavsky and Daniel, on December 5, 1965, Alexander Esenin-Volpin organized a protest at Pushkin Square in Moscow to demand an open trial. It is now considered by many to be the beginning of the Soviet human rights movement—

VENCLOVA: I heard about the gathering, and Esenin-Volpin was close to my Moscow milieu. He was a son of Sergey Esenin, and was himself a gifted mathematician who had produced several witty anti-Soviet poems. One of these was a pastiche of Edgar Allan Poe, in which the raven was asked, "Will I see the end of Terror and the start of Thermidor?" to which it predictably answered, "Nevermore." I knew the poem by heart but I never met its author, even though we both found ourselves in the United States in the late 1970s.

HINSEY: In December 1965 you were in Vilnius. If the Sinyavsky and Daniel trial was one of the signs of the end of the Thaw in Moscow, were there similar signs in the artistic milieu in Vilnius?

VENCLOVA: Many people in Vilnius discussed Sinyavsky's case and expected a tightening of the cultural policy in Lithuania, but as far as I remember, it did not materialize until 1968. My father, as you know, was asked to condemn Sinyavsky and Daniel but refused. After the trial, books by Sinyavsky and Daniel, printed abroad in Russian, started to circulate in some Vilnius circles. There was a humorous expression *Bibliotechka antisovetchika* (something like "Anti-Soviet Reader's Digest"), which was applied to these and similar texts.

HINSEY: Did you have any connection with the members of SMOG?

VENCLOVA: I knew about SMOG (an acronym that stood for "courage, thought, image, depth" as well as "The Union of Very Young Geniuses") but did not consider it a serious literary group—the *smogists* were known mainly because of their eccentric behavior. Still, some of my friends maintained contacts with the members of SMOG, who took part in protests or supported protesters.

HINSEY: In the previous chapter you mentioned how Alexander Ginzburg and Yuri Galanskov compiled notes on the Sinyavsky and Daniel trial, which became an important report called *The White Book* (a tradition that had begun with Frida Vigdorova's transcript of Joseph Brodsky's trial). Because of this, in 1968 Ginzburg and Galanskov were arrested and tried, along with two others in "the trial of four." You signed the letter protesting against their case. How was this organized?

VENCLOVA: As far as I remember, I was shown the letter by Yuri Glazov, an Orientalist scholar (a specialist in ancient Tamil literature, to be precise) whom I had first met in Tartu. There were a hundred or so signatures—I knew at least some of the signatories. Glazov said to me, intently: "Signatures are still being collected." Thus, I signed.

HINSEY: You have said that during this period there was a change in thinking about the viability of "organic work"—

VENCLOVA: That's true. Prior to this, like many people, I had participated in organic work, publishing translations, literary essays and, from time to time, my own poems in the official press. As you know, I also produced two books of popular science. Moreover, I was sporadically employed by Vilnius University (substituting for instructors who were either ill or on leave). I also thought about writing a doctoral thesis under Lotman's supervision: the topic was to have been Jurgis Baltrušaitis, a Symbolist poet who wrote in Russian and Lithuanian and left his mark on the Silver Age. That would have been "organic work" sensu stricto—the broadening of Lithuanian cultural horizons, since Baltrušaitis was a semibanned figure (he had served as the ambassador for independent Lithuania in Moscow in the 1920s and 1930, helping, among others, Mandelstam and Marc Chagall). Yet from the beginning, I was wary about such officially permitted work: it was very difficult to retain one's dignity, and that went against my disposition. My inclinations were toward samizdat: Brodsky's example proved that it was possible to do something significant without official approval. I also felt that work permitted by the Soviet authorities could not result in authentic changes—something else had to be done.

Around 1965–68, many people began to feel that organic work was becoming more and more difficult—at best, fraught with unavoidable compromises. Still, almost every cultural figure in Lithuania continued to practice it—there was simply no other way to survive in the arts or the university. A sort of philosophy regarding this developed: only "organic work," whatever the cost, allowed for the preservation of Lithuanian identity, which was the overriding task. This philosophy left me rather skeptical.

HINSEY: In the preceding chapter we spoke about 1968 and the momentous developments of the Prague Spring. In April of that year, Gorbanevskaya had founded *A Chronicle of Current Events*, an important publication, and the forerunner of similar human rights publications—

VENCLOVA: Gorbanevskaya initiated this project along with several other people. *A Chronicle of Current Events* was a clandestine publication that presented cases of human rights violations throughout the USSR. Such cases were numerous: arbitrary body and house searches and arrests, attacks, and beatings by the police (or, for that matter, by "unknown" assailants), blatant censorship and brazen interference with religious services; it also covered people who had been expelled from school for holding "incorrect political views," and so on. The particular strength of *Chronicle* was its unwavering objectivity: first, it meticulously verified all information (it was very difficult to accuse it of "slanderous inventions," which was a common tactic by the authorities when dealing with the underground). Second, it avoided any subjective commentary, even if this might have been more than justified. The publication was anonymous, supported by dozens of (also anonymous) people who provided news from various parts of the country. It appeared in several typewritten copies and gradually started to leak to the West, where it received some attention. There were people in Lithuania who maintained contacts with *Chronicle*. I was not one of them and saw the publication infrequently: I was unaware of the role of Natasha and her coeditors in this project. In our milieu, there was a general rule: the less you knew about clandestine activities, the better. No one was immune from breaking down during interrogation, or, for that matter, unwittingly revealing a secret during a private talk.

That said, I was perfectly aware of the fact that Natasha was involved in samizdat. In 1967, she came to Vilnius with an entire suitcase of forbidden materials. I remember that visit very well, as it coincided with a significant change in my personal life. Natasha had hitchhiked from Moscow, as was her custom—and, on top of it, arrived at four o'clock in the morning. I showed her around Vilnius, which she had never seen. We then went to a café and made the fortuitous acquaintance of a girl who knew Alexander Ginzburg's family. I fell in love immediately—one might say I was thunderstruck. At the time, I was single and rather unhappy after the dissolution of my marriage with Marina; after this encounter, my spirits rose. The girl was Tanya Nikitina. We are still very much in love. We parted in 1968, but met again many years later, and decided never to part again.

HINSEY: Of those who protested on Red Square the 1968 invasion of Czechoslovakia, Litvinov, Bogoraz, and Babitsky received sentences of internal exile, while Delaunay and Dremliuga were given terms in labor camps. Fainberg and Gorbanevskaya were sent to prison and psychiatric hospitals, although Gorbanevskaya temporarily remained at liberty because she had recently given birth. She was subsequently arrested in December 1969, and imprisoned until February 1972 in a psychiatric prison. During this period, were you able to get news regarding her situation? How was this possible?

VENCLOVA: I was not able to learn much about her situation, or the situation of other protesters, though some news leaked out of the courtroom and prison. In the psychiatric ward, she was held virtually incommunicado.

Incidentally, she participated in the Red Square demonstration with a baby in her arms. The protesters were attacked by a crowd (presumably, composed of secret police agents), beaten, and arrested—all that took just a couple of minutes. Natasha was set free, but only for a time. The baby remained with her mother. Later, Gorbanevskaya described these events herself, in her well-known book *Polden'* (Red Square at Noon).

I saw her immediately upon her release from the hospital, in Moscow, and was much comforted by the fact that her mood and character had not changed at all. Later, she visited Vilnius just before she emigrated, in 1975.

HINSEY: Do you know what her "diagnosis" was?

VENCLOVA: She was diagnosed with "sluggish schizophrenia." That was a quaint diagnostic category invented by a certain Professor Snezhnevsky and used mainly for political purposes (it is still considered valid in Russia, though it has never been recognized in the West). The symptoms could be minimal and almost unnoticeable: they included pessimism, a lack of social adaptation or holding reform ideas that led to conflicts with authorities. Gandhi, Martin Luther King, and Nelson Mandela could all rather easily have been diagnosed with "sluggish schizophrenia." Not only Natasha, but Fainberg and many others received that diagnosis. Brodsky was on the verge of it. The cure, as a rule, consisted of forced injections, which sometimes resulted in genuine disorders.

Were there genuinely unbalanced people among the Soviet dissidents? Here Chaim Weizmann's joke comes to mind: "You don't have to be crazy to be a Zionist, but it certainly helps." The Soviet system was so intimidating, that a modicum of craziness was sometimes a help. The percentage of such people among the dissidents was noticeable, but Natasha was not one of them.

HINSEY: Earlier, you described your evening at the House of the Writers' Union in Vilnius in 1959 with Vladas Šimkus as the start of your "private war with the system." How did your thinking regarding civic matters evolve as external events progressed, and your friends were arrested?

VENCLOVA: It evolved in stages. Once, Volodya Muravyov fantasized about a possible armed action in Red Square. "It would be something like the Decembrist uprising of 1825: a signal to the world that not everyone here submits to the damn system. Of course it would be better to avoid the possibility of breakdowns after arrest; therefore it might make sense to swallow slow-acting poison before anything starts." Obtaining the necessary poison and rallying enough people to challenge the Kremlin guards, if only for a short time, was the easy part of the project; but where one might find arms was another matter. Such ideas were of course Romantic and childish daydreams; still, my dislike of Communist rule at that point was so intense that for a split second I actually considered it. But this occurred during my early Moscow years. For a time yet, I more or less continued to subscribe to the theory of "organic work." Yet the acts of civil disobedience in Moscow and St. Petersburg practiced by people such as Gorbanevskaya provided an example of what could—and should—be done. Such activities were extremely risky, yet their repression resulted in new challenges for the regime: perhaps some hope lay hidden in this dynamic?

HINSEY: Other than what happened when the Woroszylski family stayed in your flat, were there other run-ins with the "midnight milkmen" that you'd like to mention?

VENCLOVA: I did not notice any, even after I switched to active dissent. Perhaps I did not possess a gift for observation; or maybe one of my friends was right when he said: "If you start to see black cars or men in disguise following you everywhere, it is most likely a bout of megalomania. The KGB is very busy nowadays and not necessarily all that interested in your person."

HINSEY: In Moscow in 1969 the first human rights association, called "The Initiative Group for the Defense of Human Rights in the USSR," was formed headed by Sergei Kovalyov. In November 1970, "The Committee for Human Rights in the USSR" was founded by Valery Chalidze. Among its first members were Andrei Sakharov and Andrei Tverdokhlebov. All three were physicists. In the years prior to the 1975 Helsinki Accords, was there any attempt to create a similar "formal" group in Lithuania?

VENCLOVA: No, there was not.

HINSEY: To put it otherwise: during this period—that is, in the late 1960s and early 1970s—the idea of a human rights movement extending across the Soviet Bloc was something that started to emerge as a viewpoint in the dissident community. Was this view unanimously held in Lithuania?

VENCLOVA: It was far from unanimous. I considered it then—and still do—a serious handicap for the Lithuanian human rights movement. Many people tended toward isolationism and were only interested in what was happening within their borders. All this became even more pronounced after Lithuania regained its independence; this is something that continues to hamper the civic development of Lithuanian society.

HINSEY: Did you have the feeling that Lithuanian freethinkers were developing in similar ways to their Moscow counterparts?

VENCLOVA: Well, it depends. Lithuanian intellectuals were interested in Moscow samizdat and developments in Poland: small groups crystallized that maintained contacts with the Muscovites (communication with Polish dissidents was next to impossible due to the strictly controlled state border). In particular, Lithuanian political prisoners easily forged ties with their Russian— and of course Ukrainian, Georgian, and Armenian—comrades in misfortune. Prison experiences, as a rule, helped one to overcome isolationist and radical nationalist prejudices. Yet there were lots of people, especially among those whose hatred of the system did not translate into any serious activism, who continued to repeat mantras such as: "All Russian dissidents are closet imperialists who will never consent to Lithuanian independence," or "Poland's overriding goal is to take back Vilnius, it will never change." A large part of the émigré community supported these views, which leaked back into Lithuania by various channels. This only served to harm the Lithuanian movement: the sentiment of being totally alone, surrounded by implacable enemies, implied that the situation was hopeless. According to that viewpoint, only a new war between the USSR and the West might be able to liberate Lithuania—and such a war was highly improbable, to say nothing of the moral side of the question if this resulted in substantial casualties. I suspect that the KGB did its best to promote isolationism among the population, paradoxically pushing it in the same direction as the émigré "hawks" did. But I also knew people who held different views, even if they may have been in the minority. The idea of an East European human rights movement (which would include the entire USSR) gradually made inroads.

HINSEY: Beginning with the immediate postwar period, the situation of the Catholic Church in Lithuania was particularly precarious—

VENCLOVA: Notwithstanding its pagan past and late baptization, or perhaps for that very reason, Lithuania was almost as Catholic as Poland or Ireland. We used to say jokingly that, as the last country in Europe to embrace Christianity, it will also be the last one to abandon it. Catholic churches were, and still are, the most obvious architectural features in any Lithuanian city, town, or village. There were also lots of wooden statues of saints and of Christ, the so-called *rūpintojėliai*, along all the roads, frequently of high artistic value. Around 1948, a ferocious atheization campaign started. It was, in part, due to the fact that a number of priests supported the partisans. But there was also a more general reason: Communism by definition could not tolerate competing ideologies, in particular religions, be it any Christian denomination, Judaism, Islam, or, for that matter, Buddhism. To tell the truth, Soviet Communism was a sort of religion itself, and anybody who subscribed to a different doctrine, or practiced it, was considered a heretic—with all the consequences of the Middle Ages. Catholicism was declared to be the most pernicious of all, since its seat of governance was outside the USSR and could therefore not be controlled.

Thus, most of the churches were closed and transformed into warehouses (or, at best, museums). There were more than forty Catholic sanctuaries in Vilnius, almost all of them architecturally valuable; as far as I remember, only nine remained open, and the rest were left to decay. (Russian Orthodox and Protestant shrines suffered more or less the same fate; as for the synagogues and the Jewish community, the Nazis had already taken care of that during World War II.) The wooden statues of saints disappeared, thus considerably altering Lithuania's landscape: that was due partly to the Komsomol campaign, partly due to patriotic intellectuals who took the opportunity to enrich their personal folk-art collections, justifying themselves by the rather reasonable notion that "otherwise these relics would disappear forever." Hundreds of priests found themselves in arctic mines or Siberian exile. In school, we had to learn by heart a long poem, "The Bats," by the former Futurist Teofilis Tilvytis; the text left no doubt that Catholic priests should be likened to weird nocturnal animals and must be eliminated like all other parasites.

HINSEY: And what about the situation after 1953?

VENCLOVA: After Stalin's death, the poem ceased to be forced on young minds, and those priests who had survived came back. Still, the closed churches remained off-limits, and the authorities tried to control religion to the best of their abilities. Quite a few priests were recruited by the secret police. Those who refused had a hard life. Two bishops, Julijonas Steponavičius and Vincentas Sladkevičius, who proved to be less than docile were exiled—not to Siberia, but to small local villages where they could not perform their bishops' duties. The monastic orders were abolished (though clandestinely active). The campaign of forcible atheization continued, even if in a somewhat milder way.

HINSEY: In March 1972 a publication titled *The Chronicle of the Catholic Church in Lithuania*—akin to Gorbanevskaya's *Chronicle of Current Events*—began to be published by the Lithuanian underground—

VENCLOVA: Yes. Like Gorbanevskaya's venture, it was an anonymous publication, consisting of several typewritten copies in the format of a notebook. It detailed cases of harassment of the Church or of individual Catholic believers, first in Lithuania, but later also in Latvia, Belarus, Moldova, and elsewhere. I saw an issue or two—of course I didn't know, and never attempted to learn, who its editors were (even today, some of its editors remain unknown, though the leading person was Reverend Sigitas Tamkevičius, now the archbishop of Kaunas, and the inspiration came from the two exiled bishops). *The Chronicle of the Catholic Church in Lithuania* was smuggled to the West, where it was reprinted by Lithuanian émigrés; it aroused the strong interest of the Vatican, particularly under John Paul II.

HINSEY: Did this Lithuanian publication address things in a different way than *A Chronicle of Current Events*?

VENCLOVA: It was patterned on *A Chronicle of Current Events* in a variety of ways. Overall, it followed the best traditions of its "comrade in arms," that is, careful checking of information and a lack of subjective commentary. But its scope was narrower, limiting itself to violations of religious rights. It was clear that those responsible for the publications were in contact with one another, and the circles of their contributors intersected to a degree. Moreover, the Moscow dissidents played a role in the transmission of the Lithuanian *Chronicle* to the West. Much later, we learned that Lyudmila Alexeyeva was instrumental in this, among others. Well, it was a case of Lithuanian-Russian collaboration that luckily surmounted narrow-minded nationalism and isolationism.

One should keep in mind that Lithuanian Catholics also had their own tradition of clandestine or semiclandestine work, which dated back to the Smetona era (he had banned the Christian Democrats, like every other party), and to the Nazi period.

HINSEY: In Lithuania in 1970 and 1971 there were trials of priests. For instance, Antanas Šeškevičius was arrested for teaching catechism to children—

VENCLOVA: Teaching catechism to children was formally forbidden, although many priests (as well as laypersons) did their best to circumvent this. If caught, a priest could be imprisoned. The case of Antanas Šeškevičius was widely publicized (I believe it was one of the first, if not the first case reported by *Chronicle*). He spent a year in a strict regime prison, yet his sentence was probably reduced due to indignation in the West.

HINSEY: The legacy of the Prague Spring continued to have implications for Lithuania. In Kaunas, on June 14, 1972, there was a case of self-immolation similar to that of Jan Palach—

VENCLOVA: A nineteen-year-old schoolboy, Romas Kalanta, went to the public garden that is in front of the Kaunas opera theater, poured gasoline over his body and struck a match. Actors who were rehearsing in the theater ran out of the building and tried to save him, but it was too late. Kalanta died in a hospital after several hours of intense suffering.

His act was unequivocally political. Some people heard his last words, "Freedom to Lithuania!" He also explained his decision in a notebook that survived. Incidentally, the very place of his self-immolation had symbolic value: in 1940, a puppet "People's Parliament" met in the Kaunas opera to vote in favor of joining the USSR. Thirty-two years later, Kalanta expressed his indignation about this.

Little is known about Kalanta. He had links to the hippie subculture, thus the authorities did their best to persuade people that he was mentally unbalanced. A group of psychiatrists, convened for the purpose, officially declared Kalanta a lunatic. The diagnosis had the same value as "sluggish schizophrenia" in Gorbanevskaya's case, and was formally revoked in 1989.

HINSEY: Romas Kalanta's funeral was scheduled in such a way as to prevent crowds from gathering. Nevertheless, people marched toward the city center and the square in front of the theater where the incident had taken place. A second day of demonstrations and arrests followed—

VENCLOVA: For two days, Kaunas was virtually in the hands of the people; the demonstrators were, as a rule, peaceful and disciplined. Such an event was unprecedented in the history of the Soviet Union, and foreshadowed things to come. The authorities attempted to disperse the protesters by nonviolent means, yet predictably, in the end, opted for violence. Many young people were severely beaten. The actors who attempted to save Kalanta, incurred their share of hardships—interrogations and so on (I knew some of them personally). Antanas Sniečkus reported to Moscow that the demonstrations had been "petty hooliganism," thus preserving his position—and, as some believed, helping Lithuania to avoid the worst.

HINSEY: You were in Leningrad at this time and discussed the event with Joseph Brodsky at length—

VENCLOVA: We were very moved by Kalanta's act, and understood it as a sign of the changing times. Romas Katilius said, not without pride: "Well, we, the Lithuanians, have become the second most significant group in the Soviet empire—after the Jews." (At that time, aliyah—the emigration of Jews to Israel—was gaining momentum.) Joseph said, half-jokingly: "If Lithuania secedes, the two of you might get stuck here in Russia without an exit visa—if I were you, I'd return as fast as possible." I indeed left for Vilnius as soon as possible, but the tension had subsided before I arrived.

HINSEY: In late spring 1971 there was a meeting of the board of the Lithuanian Writers' Union, and ten candidates were considered for admittance. Of the ten writers, only your candidature was refused—

VENCLOVA: That's true. I applied for the translators' section, as membership in it guaranteed that you could make a living by royalties only, without being employed in a Soviet office; in that way, as we've discussed, one could escape accusations of being a "social parasite." Still, my reputation as a person of unacceptable views was only too well-established by that time. A very influential Soviet poet, Eduardas Mieželaitis, reportedly said: "This young man does not conform to the first article of the Writers' Union statutes." (The first article stated that any Soviet writer should hold correct political views and struggle for Communism.) "Well, he's just a translator," somebody attempted to argue. "He does not conform to the first article as a translator either," Mieželaitis retorted. That was true, since I mainly translated poets such as Eliot and Pasternak. Be that as it may, my case was discussed and voted on at the meeting. My candidacy failed to garner the necessary number of votes—to be precise, a single vote was lacking for successful admission.

HINSEY: You have written that the refusal of your candidature to the Writers' Union was directed not only toward you, but also your father—

VENCLOVA: There were people in the voting body who had private scores to settle with my father. At the time of the meeting, he was hospitalized: his heart disease was in its terminal stage. The board's decision represented a much greater insult to him than to me (I applied for membership to the union for purely pragmatic reasons and not without reservations). He died three months later.

HINSEY: Your father died on June 28, 1971—for a certain period, his presence had afforded you some protection from actions by the authorities—

VENCLOVA: Well, maybe. I am sure that he never took any steps to protect me or promote my writing (although he generally liked it), but his official stature in itself might have had an impact. By the way, that stature did not suffer because of my dubious reputation. Father was given a state funeral attended by Sniečkus.

HINSEY: Up until this time you had been able to live on your translations, but following your father's death there was a change in official policy toward you, and you suddenly found you were no longer able to publish them. Did this happen immediately, or was it something that occurred over the course of a few years?

VENCLOVA: I noticed it in 1973 or 1974. To begin with, *Sign of Speech* was rather negatively reviewed in official Communist Party periodicals. To be precise, this was not only my experience, but was the case for an entire group of avant-garde poets—some were attacked even more ferociously. I prepared a large book of poetic translations, but the publishing house rejected it under the pretext that "the choice of translated authors was somewhat biased" (well, it was—poets such as Louis Aragon were not included). The Hungarian scholar Bojtár Endre, who knew Lithuanian, invited me to Budapest to collaborate on a Hungarian edition of my poems, but I was not allowed to go. The same thing happened with an invitation to a semiotics conference in Urbino, where I had been invited by a well-known French semiotician of Lithuanian origin, Algirdas Julien Greimas. These were not just signs of ostracism: in the long run, I could face problems of sheer survival (Father had left an inheritance that was considered substantial by the standards of the times, but it was rapidly diminishing). If I was not a member of the Writers' Union, I could eventually be accused of social parasitism. In short, the situation was difficult, and was aggravated by my feeling that I was living in a vacuum, since many people close to me had already left the Soviet Union.

HINSEY: You have mentioned that the poetic, dissident, and scholarly groups you were involved with overlapped in that they were all viewed as unacceptable to the authorities—

VENCLOVA: Well, that was typical for the era. Almost any serious author or thinker was a covert—and sometimes an overt—oppositionist. I remember a conversation I had about this with one of my friends. I made the remark that the most significant writer in the Soviet empire (Solzhenitsyn) and the most significant scholar (Sakharov) were both public dissidents—a situation rather infrequent in the history of mankind. "What we lack is the most significant politician," my friend sighed.

HINSEY: Alexeyeva has said that by the end of 1972, due to intense repression and arrests, the human rights movement had been dealt a number of serious blows. Despite important events, like the 1973 circulation of Solzhenitsyn's *Gulag Archipelago*, one would have to wait for the 1975 signing of the Helsinki Accords for the movement to regain momentum. How did this compare with your own personal situation and what was happening in Lithuania?

VENCLOVA: Lithuania experienced a similar dynamic, even if the number of arrests in 1972–74 were not yet extensive. I believe there was a general feeling that the dissident movement was approaching a state of deadlock. For me, the situation was exacerbated by a personal deadlock.

17

The Lithuanian and Moscow Helsinki Groups

HINSEY: During the 1970s, many people in the Soviet Union began to see emigration as one of the only possibilities for living a normal life, in which one might contribute and work productively—

VENCLOVA: In the 1950s and 1960s, emigration was not an option. The USSR's borders were hermetically sealed with watchtowers, barbed wire, and wide patches of raked earth to detect the footprints of Western spies. In reality, the authorities were much more interested in the footprints of would-be Soviet escapees who rarely, if ever, made it to Poland or Hungary (where they were tracked down as well). The armed border guards were under the same orders as prison camp guards. Privately among ourselves, we used to call our country "the big zone" ("zone" meaning "concentration camp" or Gulag in Soviet parlance). While the Berlin Wall is perhaps the best-known symbol of Communist force, one should keep in mind that the entire perimeter of the USSR—many thousands of miles—was essentially the same, even if, as a rule, there were no concrete slabs. Incidentally, the border guards, together with their heroic dogs, used to be praised in popular songs and movies as those on whom the peace and safety of the country depended.

To leave "the big zone," one had to be issued an exit visa. Permanent exit visas were virtually unheard of, and temporary visas were a privilege accorded the happy few, whose loyalty was beyond suspicion—people such as Ehrenburg or Yevtushenko (or my father, for that matter). Small, closely monitored groups of tourists traveled under surveillance, and had to conform to quite strict rules. Needless to say, defections were infrequent. While many people yearned for the West, most just hoped for a better standard of living (meaning, above all, cars, clothes, and appliances). That said, there were also those who cherished the idea of freedom, however vague that concept might be. In the late 1960s and early 1970s, a joke made the rounds: "What would you do if they opened the borders?" "I would climb a tree." "Why?" "I wouldn't want to be trampled."

Around this time, however, things started to change. The frontiers became somewhat more permeable. One might, for example, marry a foreign citizen, which accorded you the possibility of leaving the country: of course this was strictly theoretical, since such marriages were discouraged by every imaginable and unimaginable means (frequently, the visa for the foreign bride or bridegroom would be revoked a day or two before the established wedding date). Some nevertheless succeeded, but they were usually people who already enjoyed a celebrity status: the famous chansonnier Vladimir Vysotsky managed to marry the French movie star of Russian descent, Marina Vlady—moreover, he was allowed to commute between Paris and Moscow. (Brodsky dreamed about something like this for himself, but he was hardly a celebrity from the authorities' point of view, and therefore the idea failed.)

HINSEY: What about defections?

VENCLOVA: Defections were now much more commonplace. During the fall of 1970, Lithuania distinguished itself in this respect. On October 15, Pranas Brazinskas and his young son Algirdas seized a domestic plane that had just left the Georgian airport in Batumi, and after a shootout during which a stewardess perished, commandeered it to Turkey. Soviet air space was guarded even more closely than its land borders, yet the Brazinskases succeeded due to the fact that Batumi was only six or so miles from Turkish air space. The hijackers were tried and imprisoned but not extradited to the USSR; eventually, they made their way to the United States. All that created lots of commotion: people in Vilnius jokingly nicknamed the father and son "Daedalus and Icarus," and I once was present at a feast in the Georgian capital of Tbilisi, where the participants drank to the Brazinskases' health, as well as to the health of Solzhenitsyn. "They may be criminals, but they are real *dzhigits*," one Georgian exclaimed (*dzhigit* means a "brave equestrian"). Unfortunately, they indeed turned out to be common criminals, and the whole affair ended accordingly: in Los Angeles, the son murdered the father. The next incident, however, which occurred a month after the hijacking, was flawless from a moral point of view. The young Lithuanian seaman Simas Kudirka leaped from a Soviet ship that was anchored off the coast of Martha's Vineyard, and onto the deck of a US Coast Guard cutter. Kudirka asked for asylum, but the American commander, following the orders of his superior, allowed a detachment of Russian sailors to board his ship and take Kudirka back. This was a rather stupid decision that precipitated an all-American scandal (and later inspired several highly critical films and books, as well as in a change in US asylum policy). Kudirka was severely beaten in full view of the American sailors, brought back to Klaipėda and imprisoned. Luckily, a legal loophole was found that enabled Kudirka to leave for the States in 1974. It might be interesting to note that my future friend Viktoras Petkus—about whom I'll talk more later—was instrumental in his release.

Well, all that occurred in the context of the 1970s. Yet the really significant development was the Jewish emigration movement aliyah. In the Stalinist era, the situation of Soviet Jews had been particularly precarious. Now, even if things such as "the Doctor's Plot" were a thing of the past, their religious and cultural life was practically nonexistent. I was told by a number of Jews that Lithuanians were in a comparatively enviable position, as they had schools, a press, and a significant literature in their native language, while Yiddish was dying out and Hebrew was officially banned. After the Six-Day War, anti-Semitic attacks (under the guise of the "anti-Zionist struggle") increased, but Jewish pride and political activity grew as well. The authorities gradually yielded to the Jewish community's requests, with support from world public opinion, and began to allow people to emigrate to Israel, although this involved endless bureaucratic hurdles and harassment. Subsequently, in the 1970s, Jews left in the tens of thousands. People seeing off their friends at railway stations and airports used to quote Mandelstam: "Who can know when he hears the word goodbye / what kind of separation lies before us?";[20] this referred not only to the final separation of death but also to the simple fact that they might apply to leave as well.

Vilnius's Jews (who had retained some memory of their prewar stature and discipline) belonged to the avant-garde of the aliyah movement. It changed the entire atmosphere of the USSR and Lithuania: the country ceased to be hermetically sealed. Many Soviet Gentiles, including in Lithuania, supported these Jews seeking to emigrate. In fact, it was a golden age of Lithuanian-Jewish cooperation, when, unlike any time before or after, the grievances of 1941 were less pronounced.

The party and the KGB soon realized that issuing exit visas and one-way tickets to the West was a way of getting rid of troublemakers, and not necessarily just Jewish ones. Some people were encouraged to emigrate even if they were reluctant to do so (like Brodsky), or were forcibly expelled (like Solzhenitsyn). Of course such practices were reprehensible, but they also contributed to the change in climate, as there were quite a few people who felt, especially after 1968, that remaining in the USSR amounted to wasting one's life.

HINSEY: These waves of emigration involved a number of well-known intellectuals—

VENCLOVA: Many important Jewish contributors to Lithuanian culture left, including two highly visible writers, Icchokas Meras and Grigory Kanovich. Both of them continued their work in Israel: Meras, a survivor of the ghetto who was saved by peasants, wrote in Lithuanian, and Kanovich writes in Russian, but on Lithuanian topics. For Gentiles who wanted to take advantage of this unexpected possibility to leave the USSR, there were two ways to go about it. First, you could emigrate as the husband (or wife) of a potential Israeli citizen. This was the case with Vladas Žilius, a painter whose abstract works were frowned upon even in relatively liberal Vilnius. He married Ida Kreingold, a good friend of mine as well as of Brodsky and Natasha Trauberg. Both made their way to the United States where Vladas joined the New York scene. Jonas Jurašas's case was a bit different. He was a young and promising stage director; I have mentioned him before, as he is the husband of Aušra Sluckaitė. His work had been seriously hindered by the censors; finally, when his best production was banned outright, he became furious and wrote an open letter to the authorities telling them everything he thought about their incompetence. Naturally, he was thrown out of the theater and for some time made his living as a stonebreaker. Neither he, nor his wife, was Jewish (notwithstanding Aušra's reputation as a "bourgeois intellectual"). Jurašas therefore invented a sister, who was presumably married to an Israeli citizen, and concocted an invitation from her—a strategy also used by Jews who did not have Israeli relatives. After considerable trouble, Jurašas also left for New York, where he found a niche and even staged a play on Broadway; after 1990 he returned to direct theater in Lithuania. Both of these cases happened just before my emigration, and I was involved in both to a degree.

HINSEY: When and how did you start to think about emigration?

VENCLOVA: For many years, I believed that people involved in cultural work, above all poets, should stay in the Soviet Union and do their best, that is, attempt to widen the scope of the permissible and to promote genuine—that is, non-Soviet—values. That was the common point of view in my milieu. Even when their chances for emigration increased, many of my acquaintances remained faithful to this idea. A well-known Leningrad literary scholar— Brodsky's and Solzhenitsyn's friend and supporter Efim Etkind (whom I met more than once) wrote a samizdat essay stating that one should strive for changes in one's own country, rather than taking the easier option, namely, a way out. (As a result of this essay, he lost his job, his Writers' Union membership, all his scholarly titles and finally was forced to take "the easier option" against his will.)

Sometimes, I resorted to quoting Kant's "categorical imperative" to myself and my friends ("Act only according to that maxim by which you can, at the same time, will that it should become a universal law"). "The entire population cannot emigrate, therefore leaving one's country cannot become a universal law," I used to say. That was probably naive, and I doubt if Kant would have agreed with such an interpretation of his maxim, but for a time this standpoint satisfied me. And translating Pasternak and Eliot was sufficient to give meaning to one's life.

As I have mentioned, all that changed around 1973–74. I was no longer invited to give lectures at the university. My translations—not to mention my poems—were unanimously rejected by the state publishing house and journals (the publishers usually hinted that the quality of the work was adequate but there were some reasons for rejection that had to be passed over in silence). The most mind-boggling, at least for me, was the case of my Velimir Khlebnikov translations. He was a Russian Futurist poet, a companion of Mayakovsky, and rather pro-Soviet in his outlook, while at the same time being genuinely avant-garde. In Russia, his work was deemed acceptable for publication, even if this happened infrequently; in Lithuania, my translations of Khlebnikov proved to be utterly unacceptable. Besides, my application for membership in the Writers' Union had been rejected. All this made my situation precarious. I had to look for some type of official employment—before, I had done my best to avoid this, but now I needed a source of steady income and, even more important, proof that I was performing "socially useful work." I started to commute, twice a week, to the provincial city of Šiauliai, where I found a job as the literary director of a local theater. It wasn't the worst place in the world, even if my work was not particularly meaningful. I helped to establish the repertory (Goldoni, Lope de Vega, and so on), lectured to the actors, drank with them, and, in general, enjoyed a taste of theatrical life with its playfulness and improvisations. My other employment was at the Lithuanian Academy of Sciences: this involved producing abstracts of nineteenth-century philosophical or quasi-philosophical texts. All in all, emigration seemed preferable to this kind of life.

Thus, I started to contemplate leaving. But I was a Gentile, therefore my situation was more complex. An additional level of complication was my family background. While I could count on my mother's understanding, from the authorities' point of view, the emigration of the son of the late Antanas Venclova—one of the best-known official figures in Soviet Lithuania—was next to unimaginable.

HINSEY: Did your friends play any part in your decision?

VENCLOVA: In Brodsky's final days in the USSR before leaving for the West, he toyed with the notion that his entire circle of friends should join him abroad and create a "colony" in the United States. The idea never went further than that: almost everyone stayed in the USSR, even if many, at least theoretically, could leave. Nevertheless, I must confess I found the project not unattractive. Later, I had a long and important talk with Aleksandras Štromas. His case was an exception: he was allowed to join his relatives in London (they were well-known people who had influence among English and Soviet authorities) without losing his Soviet citizenship. From 11:00 p.m. until dawn, we walked through the empty lanes of old Vilnius, and Štromas did his best to persuade me that my life in the Soviet Union no longer made any sense, and that I should try to leave the country, in spite of the considerable effort that this would require. Whatever the case, I was aware that, if necessary, Brodsky and Štromas would do everything they could to help me.

HINSEY: Were you influenced by any discussions circulating in samizdat or elsewhere?

VENCLOVA: A strong impetus for me was provided by Andrei Amalrik—not so much by his famous book *Will the Soviet Union Survive until 1984* (I believed it would survive much longer), as by the entire tenor of his life and work. One of my most vivid memories concerns the moment when I was literally thunderstruck by a thought—"this is the paradigm to follow: a person who overtly speaks his mind in a servile society, without using Aesopian language or resorting to forms of conspiracy."

As for discussions about emigration, the most straightforward samizdat text I read at the time was by Igor Mel'čuk, a semiotician who later became a professor in Canada. I don't remember whether it preceded my decision, but during this period I subscribed to each of its sentences (only later, I began to have some reservations concerning Mel'čuk's argument). Mel'čuk started with the half-serious, but indispensable, notion that he only address people who thought along the same lines as he did. Then, he proposed three axioms. First, the Soviet Union, in the shape it was in at the time, was a criminal state that promoted a false ideology: it strove for world domination and planned military adventures that were dangerous for the very survival of humankind. Second, one couldn't live in the USSR and avoid participating in its crimes, if only for the fact that all individuals paid taxes. Third, Soviet intellectuals, particularly liberal and avant-garde artists, contributed to the system's crimes more than anyone else, because they created the impression that the USSR was a relatively normal country, which was definitely not the case. A theorem followed: there are only two ways to escape involvement in the nefarious activities of the Soviet state. The first: to be imprisoned by it. The second: to leave the country.

Well, I said to myself: this is a harsh but irrefutable argument. If I were to ascribe to it, I would be agreeing to the following: I would either land in jail, or have to emigrate, or both (a number of people, including Brodsky and Solzhenitsyn, emigrated only after a stint in a prison). There was no other way around it.

HINSEY: On May 9, 1975, you sent a letter to the Central Committee of the Lithuanian Communist Party explaining your views and requesting permission to emigrate. Where were you physically when you typed the letter? What was your state of mind?

VENCLOVA: I wrote the letter in the Vilnius flat where I lived at the time. This was no longer the attic where Woroszylski stayed and where the "visit from the night milkman" took place, but a slightly more comfortable apartment on the embankment of the Neris River. From its windows I could see the Baroque church of Saint Raphael, along with its reflection in the water. It was a place that was privately significant to me. One can sense the mood of that period in my "Two poems about love." Living there was tinged with a certain melancholy, which disappeared the instant my letter was deposited in the mailbox.

HINSEY: Before sending the letter you went to see your friend Romas Katilius—

VENCLOVA: Yes, I felt I should consult someone before taking such a step, and Romas was the person I trusted more than anyone else in Vilnius. I just casually dropped by his flat, as had been our custom for many years, and after some small talk I silently placed the letter before him. We could not exclude the possibility of eavesdropping, even if this was not particularly probable in Romas's case. That said, he was a friend of Brodsky's, my humble person, as well as other suspect individuals, and his views (like the views of many) were far from Communist, though he was never considered "an enemy of the people." He quickly read the text and, after a bit more small talk, proposed we take a stroll. We boarded a trolley, went to a far-off part of the city and discussed the situation in detail on an empty street. "Well, this is really serious," Romas said. "These days, various things can happen, and it is not totally impossible that you'll join Joseph and others in the West. Based on what I have observed, it appears that on average it takes a couple of years, perhaps less. Of course you understand that after sending this letter there will be no way back; therefore you must be prepared for any outcome." "Here is the essence of the problem," I answered. "I know I am high-strung, and I fear I might break down in the case of failure." "I've known you for a very long time, and there is one thing I know for certain: you are neurotic in minor matters, but strong in matters of principle."

HINSEY: In your letter you wrote: "Communist ideology is alien to me, and in my view, is largely false. Its absolute domination has brought our country a great deal of misfortune," and, "The informational barriers and repressions imposed on those who think differently are pushing our society into stagnation and the entire country into regression."[21] Your text is a condemnation of the system and your statements leave little doubt about your views—

VENCLOVA: Yes, of course. I also said that, notwithstanding my opinions—which I had never concealed from anyone—I had previously been able to contribute to Lithuania's cultural life, but now those opportunities were barred to me. Therefore, in accordance with the Declaration of Human Rights and the laws in vigor in the USSR, I was asking for permission to leave the country and to establish my residence abroad. The case of my friend Jonas Jurašas and others demonstrated that this was not impossible. (At that very moment, Jurašas was already in Munich; both he and his wife were being wildly reviled in the Vilnius press.) I also asked that the members of my family, who held other views than I did, not be persecuted and be allowed to remain in Lithuania (above all, I had my mother in mind).

HINSEY: A letter of this kind, which directly laid out your disagreement with the Communist system, was a dangerous undertaking—

VENCLOVA: Well, it was. I had heard about the case of Yury Maltsev, a Moscow translator from Italian, who had written a similar letter, perhaps as early as 1964, explaining his disagreements with the system and asking for permission to leave the USSR for Italy. Rather predictably, he was placed in a psychiatric hospital, but in 1974 finally received an exit visa. At the time I sent my letter to the authorities he was teaching in Parma (or was it Milan?). Needless to say, such stories evoked anxiety, but at the same time instilled hope.

HINSEY: Do you have any memory of the moment you posted the letter?

VENCLOVA: In my mind's eye, I can clearly visualize the moment, but to this day I can't remember where the mailbox was—perhaps on the corner of the main street? It was a nice May morning. Incidentally, May 9 was a symbolic date—during the Soviet period in Lithuania, it was the day the country commemorated victory over Nazi Germany. (In today's Lithuania, as in Europe and the United States, the anniversary is observed on May 8.) All offices were closed, and official buildings were decorated with red flags. Well, perhaps the date foreshadowed my personal victory.

HINSEY: You once described to me that you experienced a sort of surreal elation after you had sent it—

VENCLOVA: The elation was there, but it was hard to describe. In any case, I had the very clear feeling that it was a watershed day, when one of the most important decisions of my life had been made. The irrevocability of it gave one a unique feeling of carefreeness, or "lightness of being," as Kundera put it, even if his meaning is not necessarily the same.

HINSEY: Did you notice any intensification of surveillance after the letter was sent?

VENCLOVA: No, but that may have been due to my lack of observational skills. To tell the truth, I was a bit anxious about the possibility of being attacked by secret policemen. Such things happened in Lithuania and elsewhere. Konstantin Bogatyrev, a dissident and translator from German, whom I had met many times, received a blow to the head while opening the door of his Moscow flat. He passed away two months later. When I returned home in the evening, I carried a stick or a stone, to defend myself against any blows, just in case. No doubt that was an excessive reaction. The funniest part was that when my situation started to become well-known, several young Lithuanian dissidents, unbeknownst to me, began to follow me in order to help me out in case of an attack. One can easily imagine we could have ended in a scuffle due to a misunderstanding. My poem "Nel mezzo del cammin di nostra vita," dedicated to Bogatyrev's memory, is related to these events.

HINSEY: Can you speak about your concerns regarding the implications of the letter for your mother and your friends?

VENCLOVA: I was worried, but by that time, the parents and relatives of dissidents were, as a rule, left alone. Besides, I knew my mother's inner strength. Some protection was afforded her by the fact that she was the widow of a famous political and cultural figure. After I sent my letter, Eduardas Mieželaitis, the head of the Lithuanian Writers' Union, telephoned her and proposed a meeting, but she flatly refused. She was also visited by an employee of the secret police (who was evasive, but very polite). With my help, she wrote a courteous but indignant letter about the visit to the head of the KGB and received a sort of apology: she was informed that the visitor was an impostor, and she was asked to inform them if such visits continued (predictably, they did not).

As for friends, they could decide to avoid me or not. Those whom I valued chose the second option.

HINSEY: About a month after the letter was sent, at the beginning of June, you were invited to the Lithuanian Central Committee—can you describe your thoughts upon hearing this news? How did you feel as you walked to this appointment?

VENCLOVA: Writing letters to the Central Committee was not an unheard-of event. People usually chose that option as a last resort in the case of serious problems. (In Stalin's time, they addressed their letters in a very simple way: "Moscow, Kremlin, Comrade Stalin." As a rule, they stated that their arrested relatives were innocent, and petitioned for their release. The results were nil, though not without certain exceptions exaggerated by propaganda.)

Most likely there was some kind of formal rule that required that letters be answered in a month or so. The answer usually consisted of a piece of paper, which read: "There are no grounds for us to review your case." I did not expect any answer to my letter; therefore, the invitation was a sort of surprise. My only feeling as I walked to the appointment was curiosity. Permission to emigrate was highly unlikely; naturally, I was not counting on it. But what line would they take?

This, however, was a game in which I had a potential trump card. The letter was marked "open," which meant that it was intended not only for the Central Committee but also for the general public. It was not easy to reach that audience, of course, but just before mailing the letter I gave a copy of it to Juozas Tumelis. I had some grounds to believe that he had contacts with the Lithuanian underground, in particular, with *The Chronicle of the Catholic Church in Lithuania*. (Another copy, in a rather roundabout manner, went to Alexander Ginzburg in Moscow.) Tumelis read the copy in silence, just like Romas, and put it in his pocket. We did not exchange any words, but I was pretty sure the letter would find its way into *The Chronicle* and consequently be leaked to the West. That would create a stir among the Lithuanian diaspora and perhaps even beyond—and that kind of scandal was the very last thing the authorities wanted. In general, if your case was known in the West, it gave you a measure of protection. And what if the stir had already started?

HINSEY: Had it?

VENCLOVA: Not yet. That happened several months later, in fall or early winter 1975. This is when the Lithuanian émigré press published the letter. Thanks to Czesław Miłosz, it also appeared in *Kultura, Esprit*, and elsewhere. It provided my case with an extra-local dimension, which was most welcome given the circumstances.

HINSEY: Would you describe the office where you had your meeting with the officials?

VENCLOVA: It was a small room on the first floor (or was it in the basement?) of the building on the main street of Vilnius, just opposite the Central Committee. (This rather nice Le Corbusier-style building had been built in Polish times, when it housed Vilnius's local authorities.) In it, appointments with minor party officials took place.

HINSEY: You had a meeting with a certain instructor Kuznetsova—

VENCLOVA: She was alone in the room—a not bad-looking middle-aged woman who was reasonably polite. She introduced herself as Kuznetsova: this was clearly a Russian surname, but her Lithuanian was as good as mine. Either she had managed to learn Lithuanian, which was infrequent among Russian officials, or, more likely, was a native Lithuanian who had taken her husband's name. There was also the chance, however, that this was a pseudonym: who knows the mores of the secretive Central Committee?

"We received and read your letter," she said. "We believe it was written in a moment of despair. Therefore, let's forget about it, and act as though it never existed. We will pay no attention to it. Please continue with your usual activities—we do not intend to interfere with your work."

HINSEY: How did you respond to this obvious strategy on their part?

VENCLOVA: I simply replied: "I have been preparing to write such a letter for my entire life. Now that it has been written and posted, I have no intention of renouncing it."

HINSEY: Kuznetsova then suggested that you simply go to the Office of Visas and Registration and ask for a visa to leave the country—a logical sounding idea, except this obviously reflected the Kafka-like world of the time—

VENCLOVA: She told me: "Issuing visas is not the work of the Central Committee. As you may know, it is under the auspices of the Ministry of Internal Affairs and the OVIR. If you have sufficient grounds to leave the country, please address the OVIR, as everyone does in such cases."

Well, the Ministry of Internal Affairs was the regular, uniformed police—not the secret police. Its detachment, the OVIR (Office of Visas and Registration) accepted applications from people who wanted to leave for Israel or travel for tourism. After a waiting period, which could be quite long, the exit visa was issued or not. It was an open secret that all visas had to be approved by a group of officials including representatives of the Central Committee and the KGB. I visited the OVIR, just to make the point, but was predictably advised that I had no grounds for application since I had no relatives in Israel, and a simple desire to spend the rest of my life outside of the USSR was obviously not sufficient. Naturally, they had already been alerted to my case, which had begun to be generally known in Vilnius.

HINSEY: Now that your request at the OVIR had been denied, your situation began to seem rather hopeless. How did you live with this state of uncertainty? One can only imagine the tension of this period, not knowing if you would eventually be allowed to leave, or be imprisoned—

VENCLOVA: It was not particularly easy, but it was the lot of many people at that time—the so-called *otkazniki* (refuseniks). Most of them were Jewish scholars, engineers, and so on, who at some point in their careers had had access to information that was considered vital to Soviet national security. A sort of joke made the rounds about a refusenik who told the authorities: "It is ridiculous to speak about military secrets, since our technology is thirty years behind Western standards." "Well, *that* is the military secret," the official retorted.

Now, I became a refusenik, though not a typical one: a Gentile who never had any access to sensitive information. The very fact that one was not alone helped considerably. Many people felt sympathy for refuseniks (though others avoided them like the plague). Moreover, among the refuseniks there were networks of mutual help, and ways to communicate with the West. Once, I sent a secret letter to Brodsky through such a network.

HINSEY: Did this situation isolate you from others?

VENCLOVA: Yes, to a significant degree. Incidentally, the people who avoided me the most were writers. But Marcelijus Martinaitis, a very fine poet who was the same age as me, made a point of shaking hands with me in the street and engage in friendly conversation. "Aren't you afraid?" I once asked him. "Well, it's a matter of honor," he answered, no less straightforwardly.

At one point, however, I felt that I was on the verge of a breakdown. Here once again, I was helped by Romas. One summer day, I drove to Birštonas, a little spa town where he was staying (I owned a small Soviet car at the time), and I told him about my predicament. "You simply have no right to hesitate," Romas stated. "Your decision is too important, and not only to you personally. Besides, if you surrendered, they would never pardon you anyway."

HINSEY: At the time, you were still working at the Institute of Philosophy at the Academy of Sciences, and as the literary director of the Šiauliai theater. Following your letter, you left these jobs—

VENCLOVA: Neither of these positions was very meaningful but they provided me with some sort of income. Now, I felt that my presence there might be harmful to my colleagues; therefore, I filled out the necessary resignation forms. I did not experience any serious harassment at either job, which was by no means the norm: refuseniks and, in general, those wishing to make aliyah were frequently subjected to a veritable Gehenna (even if in Lithuania the mores were a bit milder). Instead, I was asked to stay on: the authorities obviously wanted to avoid scandal as much as possible.

After leaving both of my positions, I was on thin ice. Then, something unexpected happened. The grand old man of Lithuanian theater, Juozas Miltinis, suggested that I translate Shakespeare's *The Tempest* for his troupe. (This was his cherished project: he intended to play the role of Prospero and in so doing bid farewell to his art as he was already quite elderly.) I said: "You know that I have demanded the right to emigrate. I'm going to continue to push for that right until I succeed. I doubt you'll ever be allowed to stage a translation by an émigré." "That's crazy," Miltinis replied. "Nobody will ever let you out." "If not," I said, "I'll land in prison, and staging a translation by a political prisoner would no doubt be an even more questionable enterprise." The following day, I was invited to the Ministry of Culture where they reiterated the proposal, and I replied in the same manner. "Well, it doesn't matter if your translation is ever staged," I was told. After some deliberation, I signed the contract and received the advance—I absolutely needed income, and translating Shakespeare was the most decent job imaginable. I am pretty sure the entire project was coordinated by the Central Committee, perhaps even initiated by it: they were still hoping to avoid a scandal and thus were eager to show that I was still able to work as I had previously. In any case, I did the translation, which made life a bit more bearable. Miltinis staged *The Tempest* after I left for the United States, of course with my name omitted from the playbill (I don't even know if it was my translation or not). I published it as a book in 2003, in independent Lithuania.

HINSEY: Were there any other attempts to dissuade you?

VENCLOVA: Yes. Once, our family friend Mikalina Meškauskienė invited me for a visit. She was an interesting woman: formerly a Socialist-Revolutionary (like Kazys Boruta and Ona Lukauskaitė), she was sentenced to a long prison term under Smetona's regime and had been persuaded by her cellmates to join the Communist Party, which she did while still incarcerated. After the war, she performed minor government duties but had some influence due to her old friendship with Antanas Sniečkus. "Dear Tomas, stop this senseless behavior," she said. "Otherwise, it's clear you'll be imprisoned." I fully understood that my answer would reach the Central Committee, and therefore should be as decisive and to the point as possible. "You spent eight years in prison because of your views," I snapped. "Do you think I'm unable to endure an even lengthier term?" This may have sounded impertinent and a bit pompous, but my response was probably effective.

A very different story involved the émigré historian, Vincas Trumpa. After my letter to the Central Committee made its way to the diaspora press, he wrote an appeal addressed to me and published it in the liberal Chicago monthly *Akiračiai* (Horizons). His main message was: one has practically no prospects for cultural work in emigration, thus one should stay in one's native country. Trumpa quoted two ancient paradigms: Ovid's exile from Rome, which ultimately resulted in his creative collapse, and that Socrates was right to refuse to leave Athens, even if he had to drink poison in the end. A friend passed me a copy of this issue, which had leaked into Lithuania. In a single night, I produced an answer, saying, in effect, that my country had nothing in common with Athens and little in common with Rome, and that there also existed a modern paradigm of the émigré who manages to contribute to the development of his or her country, as Herzen and Mickiewicz had done. My answer reached Chicago and was printed in *Akiračiai* as well. All that took place in May 1976. This was the first uncensored public debate, between a diaspora Lithuanian and a person still living in the country, to occur in thirty-odd years (after 1944), and verged on the unimaginable.

HINSEY: At this point, there was a significant confluence of events. On August 1, 1975, the final act of the Conference on Security and Cooperation in Europe was signed in Helsinki, with its famous "third basket" concerning "Respect for human rights and fundamental freedoms, including the freedom of thought, conscience, religion or belief"—

VENCLOVA: At that moment, I did not feel it was significant, but my opinion changed soon enough.

HINSEY: While we now have a different understanding of the meaning of the Helsinki Accords, at the time, for the Soviet leadership, their importance lay in establishing the inviolability of the postwar borders in Europe. Because of this, there were some who felt that the Helsinki Accords were, like Tehran and Yalta, another form of appeasement with the USSR—

VENCLOVA: Yes, that was the feeling of many people. Helsinki proved, however, to be the very opposite of Munich, Tehran, and Yalta: instead, it was a brilliant coup that contributed to the victory of democracy in Eastern Europe. Still, an appreciation of the importance of the accords took time.

HINSEY: Still, for much of the Lithuanian diaspora, it was seen as a final abandonment—

VENCLOVA: There was extensive discussion in the émigré media about the meaning of the Helsinki Accords for Lithuania and the two other Baltic states. It ended in almost unanimous agreement: Helsinki was a disaster since it formally recognized the 1940 Soviet annexation of these territories. "The Western powers have betrayed us once again," people repeated. Predictions of immediate brutal Russification of the Baltics, the closing of their still-surviving embassies, and so on, abounded. Many were a bit surprised when these predictions failed to translate into reality.

HINSEY: You first heard about the Helsinki Accords when you were in Palanga. You discussed their relevancy, particularly for members of the Jewish community who wished to emigrate, with the translator Felix Dektor—

VENCLOVA: Felix Dektor was my old acquaintance who made his living by translating books from Lithuanian into Russian. At that moment, he was profoundly involved in the aliyah movement. I discussed the problems of the Jewish community (and of the entire Soviet Union, including Lithuania) with him quite frequently. Examining the text of the Helsinki Accords on the veranda of our Palanga summer house, he told me: "Well, the third basket may open certain new possibilities for emigration, even in your case, although that is not too likely. It says something about one's right to choose the country where one will reside." We did not continue to explore that line of thought and did not yet fully grasp that the third basket had serious potential for encouraging—and easing—opposition within the Soviet system in general. Today, I am convinced that the Helsinki Accords were a watershed event: by signing them, the USSR paved the way to its own demise.

HINSEY: In December 1975, you had not yet met Sakharov, but you were in Vilnius when he tried to attend Sergei Kovalyov's trial—

VENCLOVA: Sergei Kovalyov, a biophysicist, was a personal friend of Andrei Sakharov's and a member of his Initiative Group for the Defense of Human Rights in the USSR. He was also one of numerous Muscovites who maintained clandestine contacts with the Lithuanian dissident movement and helped to pass *The Chronicle of the Catholic Church in Lithuania* to the West. Because of that, he had been accused of "anti-Soviet agitation and propaganda" and was arrested in December 1974. After a full year of preliminary detention, he was submitted to a trial—not in Moscow, but in Vilnius where some of his "crimes" had allegedly taken place. The reason for such a decision was simple enough: there were no Western diplomats in Vilnius, and access for foreign journalists was severely limited. Nevertheless, the authorities miscalculated a bit. In October 1975, Sakharov was awarded the Nobel Peace Prize, but was not allowed to go to Oslo to receive it. Thus, he went to Vilnius instead. At the very moment that his wife, Yelena Bonner, was reading his acceptance speech (she had received permission to travel to Norway), Sakharov stood in front of the closed doors of Vilnius's courthouse, attempting to enter the hall where Kovalyov was being tried. Predictably, he was denied entrance; his vigil lasted four days (in the evenings, he tried to call Yelena Bonner from the post office, but was unsuccessful). During that week, Sakharov was surrounded and supported by Lithuanian dissidents, including Viktoras Petkus. At one point, he was attacked by "hooligans" on a Vilnius street, but Lithuanians managed to defend him. He stayed in the small flat of Eitan Finkelstein, a Jewish activist. In the end, Kovalyov was sentenced to seven years' imprisonment and three years of internal exile.

HINSEY: Your friend Ida Kreingold suggested that you lend your apartment to Flora and Mikhail Litvinov, who had come to the trial as witnesses for the defense.

VENCLOVA: Ida had been in communication with Sakharov, as she was seeking his help with her and her husband's demand for emigration. During that week, she was busy finding rooms for the people who had accompanied him to the trial. I did not meet Sakharov at that time, but naturally agreed to share my apartment with Mikhail and Flora. Their backgrounds were uncommon, as Mikhail's father was Maxim Litvinov, an old Bolshevik and colleague of Lenin who was Stalin's foreign minister in the 1930s. When Stalin decided to ally with Hitler, Litvinov, a Jew, was replaced by Molotov, an Aryan. Moreover, Litvinov was far from the type of person who would have automatically carried out every one of Stalin's orders. Although Litvinov died a natural death, he feared the very real possibility of arrest in his later years, and every night slept with a gun next to his pillow—suicide was the best way to escape imprisonment and torture.

HINSEY: You spent time with the Litvinovs during the trial—can you say a bit about what you discussed?

VENCLOVA: I stayed in my apartment along with the Litvinovs, thus our discussions were quite extensive. They mostly related to the trial itself, but we also discussed Mikhail and Flora's son, Pavel Litvinov, who was my age and who had participated in the 1968 Red Square demonstration with Natasha Gorbanevskaya. Following the protest, Pavel had been sentenced to five years of internal exile; after having served his term, he left for the West in 1974. I met and befriended him in Tarrytown, New York, where he still lives.

HINSEY: Did Sakharov's presence—and Kovalyov's support of Lithuanian human rights—help to create a feeling of solidarity between the Lithuanian and Russian dissidents?

VENCLOVA: Quite definitely so. One might also say that it strengthened the links between the Soviet and Lithuanian human rights movements and the Jewish aliyah movement, which was represented in Lithuania by activists such as Finkelstein.

HINSEY: In the Soviet Union, the year 1976—after the signing of the Helsinki Accords—was a watershed year for dissident activity. In early spring, the physicist Yuri Orlov approached Lyudmila Alexeyeva about forming the Public Group to Assist the Implementation of the Helsinki Accords in the USSR—

VENCLOVA: That was an idea that had taken time to mature. In the previous chapter, we spoke about how Alexander Esenin-Volpin organized the first demonstration at Pushkin Square. He was perhaps the first to discover something that was as simple and powerful as Columbus's egg. The Soviet Constitution formally recognized certain democratic rights, such as freedom of speech and free assembly, and so on, yet no one had ever thought of exercising them, as you knew that was a sure way to land in prison or, worse, a psychiatric ward. But what if one took the Soviets at their word and insisted that Soviet law be obeyed? If people were punished, this would mean that the authorities were themselves breaking the Constitution. Of course, to behave as a free human being exposes you to immense risks, but it also undermines the system, if only for a time. Vladimir Bukovsky once said: "If one out of 250 million Soviet citizens refuses to conform, he or she deprives the system of one 250-millionth part of its power." Such a fraction might seem insignificant, but it had a potential to grow exponentially. Sakharov took the same standpoint when he declared "the principle 'what is not prohibited is allowed' should be understood literally." The Helsinki Accords, namely, the third basket, opened new vistas in this respect.

HINSEY: On May 12, 1976, a press conference was held to announce the establishment of the Moscow Helsinki Group at Andrei Sakharov's apartment in Moscow—

VENCLOVA: The initiative emerged from Sakharov's immediate circle (though he did not join the group himself, as he was already busy with several other human rights associations). Yuri Orlov was the group's leader; Lyudmila Alexeyeva, Yelena Bonner, and Alexander Ginzburg were its most visible members; it also included Anatoly (or Natan) Sharansky, a young Jewish activist who represented the aliyah movement. The group announced that its purpose was to monitor violations of the Helsinki Accords in the USSR, and to inform all the signatories regarding such cases, including the Soviet government. (It is easy to imagine the scope of these cases: censorship, persecution of religious rights, restrictions on ethnic groups, arbitrary searches and arrests, obstructing emigration, and so forth—one could hardly complain for lack of work.) The group's philosophy was based on transparence. The names and addresses of its members were published in its founding manifesto. The group defined itself as an association working within the limits of Soviet law, and thus not involved in any clandestine activities. It was a stroke of genius: to persecute such a law-abiding body would only reveal to world public opinion the nature of the system, and no amount of demagoguery would be sufficient to hide this fact. For at least half a year the Soviet leadership was totally at a loss. The group prepared formal documents about violations of human rights, publicized them at press conferences to which Western journalists were invited, and went unpunished—even unhindered. Purely and simply, that was incredible.

The Moscow initiative was soon followed by a similar one in Kyiv: Ukrainian dissidents established their own Helsinki group. In fact, the legal right that concerned them above all was Ukraine's right to secede from the USSR. It was enshrined in the Soviet Constitution, but any attempt to put it into practice—or even any discussion of it—was treated as high treason. This was of course the same for all Soviet republics, including Lithuania, but Ukraine was considered the most sensitive case because of its size and significance. (The so-called autonomous republics, such as Chechnya, did not have such a right.) Later, the Georgian Helsinki Group was established under the leadership of the fierce nationalist Zviad Gamsakhurdia, who later became the first—and highly controversial—president of independent Georgia. In short, a kind of "socialist competition" started up between the different republics, as one Western diplomat described it in private.

HINSEY: Let's return to your personal situation, which was being followed by your friends and fellow writers in Europe and the United States—

VENCLOVA: After the publication of my letter to the Central Committee in *Kultura* and elsewhere, my case became internationally known. It was frequently mentioned by the Western media. At the time, as we touched on earlier, a sort of rule had emerged: there might be some hesitation on the part of the authorities to arrest or overtly harass a known person. Those who had no international profile risked perishing without a trace, as was the case with Professor Kazlauskas or Mindaugas Tomonis whom I mentioned earlier. Of course this type of protection was not infallible, but it could help, at least for a time.

My friends, above all Brodsky—who had benefited from the international stir surrounding his case—were well aware of this. Thus Brodsky issued a call for my safety in the *New York Review of Books* on April 1, 1976. In May or June of that year, someone knocked at my door. It was a foreign tourist, most likely a diaspora Lithuanian, whom I had never met. He silently handed me a clipping of Joseph's text and then disappeared. (Westerners were quite afraid of the KGB, and were therefore even more cautious than Soviet dissidents.) I read the clipping: in my opinion, Joseph had wildly overstated my merits, but perhaps that was understandable under the circumstances.

Brodsky also telephoned me, and at one point Czesław Miłosz did the same. It was the first time I had heard his voice. Luckily, by then my Polish was almost as good as my Lithuanian (and better than my English). Miłosz also wrote me a letter, which miraculously made it through postal censorship: it was written in a rather neutral tone, but it left no doubt that he knew who I was and was interested in my fate. Such letters were frequently opened by the KGB, photocopied and only then delivered to the addressee. When, during the post-Gorbachev period, I was able to have access to my secret police file, I found copies of dozens of letters, though Miłosz's was not among them. Miłosz had arranged an invitation for me to teach for a semester in Berkeley, California, where he was employed as a professor of Slavic literatures. This invitation established formal grounds for me to once again address the OVIR, but when I did so, I was predictably sent away.

HINSEY: Were others also involved in your case?

VENCLOVA: I also received the information that Algirdas Julien Greimas, the famous semiotician, was working on my behalf. Yet the most ridiculous story concerned Arthur Miller. His play, *The Price*, was being staged by the Vilnius State Drama Theater and was enjoying considerable success. Suddenly, without any warning or explanation, it was dropped from the repertoire. Neither the director nor the actors, to say nothing of the audience, had the slightest idea what had happened. Some of my friends and I suspected that Miller had perhaps supported my case. Years later, I met Arthur Miller at his house in Connecticut, and he confirmed our suspicions: he had indeed written a letter to Petras Griškevičius (the first secretary of the Lithuanian Communist Party following Sniečkus's death), requesting that I be permitted to emigrate.

HINSEY: In 1976, you began to work with Eitan Finkelstein—

VENCLOVA: As I have mentioned in relation to the Kovalyov trial, Finkelstein was a Jewish activist—a rather well-known physicist and refusenik who was not permitted to leave the USSR because of his alleged knowledge of military secrets. He moved from Moscow to Vilnius, as the attitude toward aliyah was a bit more liberal there; he also became involved in Lithuanian affairs. He helped dozens of potential émigrés—including Ida Kreingold, for example—by giving them practical and legal advice. He lived with his wife and their small daughter in a one-room basement flat, about two hundred meters from my parents' house. In 1974, Nadezhda Mandelstam stayed there for several days (I met her there, though her hosts were absent). The only decoration in the extremely modest apartment was a large map of Israel, which had been a gift from a tourist: Eitan knew every inch of the country. He had been symbolically appointed a professor at Jerusalem University by its administration, and always mentioned that in the various forms he had to fill out for the OVIR and elsewhere. Once, a policeman told him in all seriousness, "Oh, I didn't know they had established a university in Jeruzalė." (As you remember, Jeruzalė—meaning Jerusalem—was the rural suburb of Vilnius where I spent the first days of the Soviet-German war.)

Eitan's struggle for his family's right to emigrate lasted fourteen years, much longer than mine. He finally left in 1983. In the West, he became a journalist and a novelist. We remain close friends to this day.

HINSEY: Around this time you were asked by Felix Dektor to write an essay on the complex relationship between Lithuanians and Jews. You discussed this work with Finkelstein—

VENCLOVA: Dektor was editing an underground Jewish newspaper, in which he had printed the memoirs of a Kaunas ghetto survivor. The author described in detail the June 1941 Kaunas pogroms, which were mainly carried out by ethnic Lithuanians. "This is something that must be discussed by both sides," Dektor told me. "Would you be willing to write an article about these events, from the ethnic Lithuanian point of view?" As an open dissident and "refusenik" myself, I had no qualms about contributing to the underground press. Therefore, I wrote an essay titled "Jews and Lithuanians." The article's central theme was a call for repentance. At the time, my information about the events was limited, but I strove to be entirely honest, which was not necessarily the position of many Lithuanian nationalists. All this happened, I believe, as early as summer 1975. Eitan Finkelstein read the typescript. Both he and Dektor approved it and believed it could become a bridge between the two communities. Dektor left for Israel shortly afterward: in 1976, the essay was reprinted in the Israeli press, and then in the Lithuanian diaspora press (I was still in the USSR). The Lithuanian émigré response was mixed, but *Akiračiai*, which also printed my correspondence with Vincas Trumpa, supported my views without reservation.

HINSEY: Approximately a month after the establishment of the Moscow Helsinki Group in 1976, you were approached by Finkelstein and Viktoras Petkus who invited you to go for a walk—

VENCLOVA: Yes, they knocked at my door and proposed that we go for a stroll. Finkelstein had previously mentioned Petkus to me, describing him as "a serious guy, a tutor of the younger Lithuanian generation." When I saw Petkus, I remembered that we had briefly met many years before: he had been working in an office I visited during my student days because a certain pretty girl was employed there as well. But I knew next to nothing about him, and an outline of his life is well worth recounting.

Viktoras Petkus came from Samogitia, that is, western Lithuania, whose inhabitants are known for their reserve and stubbornness. (Petkus was a physically imposing man.) He was arrested immediately after the war, at the age of eighteen, for running a clandestine Catholic youth group in his high school. Such groups were abundant in prewar Lithuania and generally opposed the Smetona regime, but they were declared criminal by the Soviets. After Stalin's death, Petkus was released, but remained true to his convictions and never concealed this fact. His life was therefore divided between jail and occasional employment. After 1965, he enjoyed a period of relative freedom. He was able to resume his previous work, gathering together groups of young people to whom he informally explained Catholic teachings and subjects related to Lithuanian history. This was quite dangerous, but Petkus managed somehow to steer clear of trouble for a time. In addition, he was a bibliophile, and was able to put together the best collection of Lithuanian poetry in Vilnius.

During Kovalyov's trial, Petkus was one of the Lithuanians who shared Sakharov's vigil. Both he and Finkelstein were in contact with Yelena Bonner and other Russian human rights activists. I believe they discussed together the idea of establishing Helsinki groups as early as December 1975, when Sakharov visited Lithuania.

HINSEY: Where did your walk take place?

VENCLOVA: On Tauras Hill, next to Finkelstein's flat and very close to my parents' house (Petkus lived in the Old City). The hill is a large, green, mainly treeless expanse slightly to the south of Vilnius's central street—you can see a considerable part of the city from it, including, by the way, the KGB building. Information had circulated among Soviet dissidents—whether accurate or not—that eavesdropping was technically impossible beyond a distance of four hundred meters. On Tauras Hill, it was easy to detect the presence of anyone within that range, thus providing some assurance that one wasn't being overheard. There, Petkus and Finkelstein explained to me the idea of a Lithuanian Helsinki Group and invited me to join it.

HINSEY: Why did they believe you might be a key participant for the group?

VENCLOVA: "Your case is mentioned almost daily by Radio Liberty and other Western media," they said, "and we need people who are known in the press."

HINSEY: What was your answer?

VENCLOVA: My answer was more or less the following: "This is a brilliant idea, and I wish you every success. Helsinki groups are practically the first cases of de facto democracy in the Soviet Union, which up to now has been practiced only by individuals, such as Sakharov and Amalrik. In the long run, this will probably contribute to the downfall of the system—and, God knows, that is long overdue. But, as you are well aware, the system will do everything in its power to cut short these developments. I have already put in a request for emigration. If I join the group—which would only be natural for someone with my views—it is not impossible the authorities will throw me out of the USSR, while other members of the group may land in jail. From an ethical viewpoint, I am not sure this is acceptable, to put it mildly."

"Well," Petkus replied, "There is a good chance that we'll all land in prison. On the other hand, in the highly improbable case that one of us gets thrown out of the country, that person could become our representative in the West, which is something we badly need as well. Incidentally, Eitan has also asked for permission to emigrate—perhaps he will be the one who ends up abroad. But we all have to face the fact that this is serious: each one of us has to be prepared for a sentence of ten to fifteen years. Please take this book: read it, and then we'll meet again."

The book was Eduard Kuznetsov's *Prison Diary*, which had been published in Paris. In 1970, Kuznetsov had taken part in an unsuccessful attempt to hijack a Soviet plane and attract world attention to the plight of those in the aliyah movement. He was sentenced to death, but in the wake of strong protests this was commuted to a long prison term. (Brodsky—who was still in Leningrad at that time—wrote a letter to the Soviet authorities on Kuznetsov's behalf.) His prison camp diary was leaked to the West with Yelena Bonner's help. It graphically depicted prison conditions in the USSR. After reading the book I had to face what I might really be getting myself into; for a couple of days (and nights) I experienced acute anxiety. Then I managed to overcome this, knowing that I would not be at peace with myself if fear prevented me from joining the group. Perhaps this was facile reasoning on my part, but it led to my second most important decision of that period, and was accompanied by the same slightly surreal elation. I went to Petkus's flat and told him that I agreed to become a member. To avoid being overheard, we communicated by writing: Viktoras had a special notepad (made in the United States, I believe), where words disappeared after you lifted a filmy top layer.

HINSEY: You three decided that there should be at least five members in the group—how did you decide on this number?

VENCLOVA: The Moscow group had eleven founding members. I told Viktoras and Eitan that our group should unite people of various backgrounds and viewpoints—a sort of miniature parliament, if you like. I then proposed the candidacy of Ona Lukauskaitė, the elderly leftist poet, and Viktoras proposed a Catholic activist, the Jesuit priest Karolis Garuckas, also of advanced age. Lukauskaitė, whom I have mentioned before, was a Socialist-Revolutionary: she had spent ten years in the Vorkuta camps, had written a samizdat book about her experiences, and was now subsisting on a meager pension in Šiauliai where I had met her during my stint at the local theater. I went to see her, and we also took a stroll together. She told me: "Of course I will join you—I have waited for this kind of project for many years. I am used to prisons, but this time, given my age, it is perhaps internal exile that awaits me—maybe even within Lithuania's borders. Your prospects, however, may be worse." Garuckas's reaction was quite similar. We decided that five people were enough to begin with. In the case of arrests, other people might be needed to take their places (I thought about Romas Katilius in this respect, but I did not discuss it with him yet).

HINSEY: In October 1976, at the suggestion of Ginzburg, you went to Alexeyeva's flat in Moscow. You had hoped she would help you transmit a letter to Joseph Brodsky. Was this the first time you had met Alexeyeva?

VENCLOVA: Yes, it was. There was a popular joke from that time: "Revolutionaries in tsarist times arranged clandestine meetings disguised as drinking parties, and we, the Soviet dissidents, arrange drinking parties disguised as clandestine meetings." Well, I found just this kind of meeting at Alexeyeva's apartment. Several of my old Moscow acquaintances were there, thus I felt quite comfortable. (The letter to Joseph was transmitted later by a slightly different network.) After an hour or two, Andrei Sakharov stopped by for a short visit. I was introduced to him, and we had a very brief exchange. It was the only time I met the great man.

HINSEY: Later in October Alexeyeva came to Vilnius as a member of the Moscow Helsinki Group to investigate a case concerning the expulsion of a group of high school boys—

VENCLOVA: The KGB finally tracked down the circle of young people whom Petkus was instructing in Catholic doctrine and Lithuanian history. All of them were male (they were considering becoming priests) and were in their last year of the same Vilnius high school I had attended. All were summarily expelled, which meant conscription into the military somewhere in the Far North (frequently, people returned ill and broken). Expulsion from high school just before final exams was uncommon even in the USSR, and the fact that it was carried out without any formalities, made it a violation of the law. (The authorities also prepared a "smear case" against Petkus, accusing him of homosexuality—which was definitely not the case—but in the end this failed.) All that attracted the attention of the Moscow Helsinki Group, and Yuri Orlov sent Alexeyeva to Vilnius to investigate, as well as to establish closer links with the Lithuanian dissidents.

HINSEY: You and Petkus met Alexeyeva at the train station, along with Antanas Terleckas—

VENCLOVA: Terleckas, a middle-aged man, had been a political prisoner for many years (he was of nationalist, rather than strictly Catholic, persuasion); he was an associate of Petkus's. At least a dozen members of the secret police tailed us at the station, while other KGB agents had followed Alexeyeva and her husband from Moscow. After checking both of the Russian dissidents into a hotel and showing them some of Vilnius (which they were visiting for the first time), we started to carry out our work. I made an appointment with Antanas

Rimkus, Soviet Lithuania's minister of education, and Alexeyeva and I went to his office. The minister was impeccably polite and did not fail to mention that my father, whom he held in high esteem, had been his predecessor. He had never heard of the Public Group to Assist the Implementation of the Helsinki Accords in the USSR—perhaps he took it for a new meaningless invention of the Kremlin authorities. Consequently, he sent us to the high school itself to investigate the expulsion further; there, we were received by the director as "controllers from Moscow" who should be obeyed. "Well, you understand, the boys were practicing religion, that is, promoting superstitions; therefore, expelling them as quickly as possible was the only logical step to take," he said. Suddenly, the phone on his desk rang: apparently the minister of education had been apprised of the true nature of the Helsinki Group, and warned him to cut the meeting short, which he did at once. We had nevertheless collected enough material to prove that the Soviet Constitution (ensuring freedom of religion) had been violated. We drank some champagne in a nearby bar: this was the budding Lithuanian Helsinki Group's "baptism of fire."

Unfortunately we were unable to help the boys much then, but the story has some positive outcomes: today, one of them is a much-loved liberal Catholic priest, another an MP, and so on.

HINSEY: On the second day of the Moscow members' visit, you drove with Alexeyeva, Finkelstein, and Petkus throughout Lithuania—

VENCLOVA: The car was provided by one of Petkus's associates. We left Vilnius around 5:30 a.m.—according to Viktoras's information, which was considerable, the KGB only started working at 6:00 a.m., thus we could leave the city unnoticed. Our trip lasted exactly twenty-four hours—we returned at 5:30 a.m. the next day, presumably also unnoticed. Our itinerary included several small towns in Northern Lithuania, as far away from Vilnius as one can imagine. We, the men, drove in shifts and did not sleep at all. Thankfully, Lithuanian roads were usually good, if narrow. Our main, though by no means only goal, was to visit the two Catholic bishops, Julijonas Steponavičius and Vincentas Sladkevičius, who were in internal exile, that is, forcibly sent to towns outside their bishoprics without the right to leave. This had been carried out by a simple fiat of the authorities, without any due process; the length of the punishment was indeterminate. I mentioned the case before: at its origin was a conflict between the bishops and the government's Department for Religious Affairs over the right to give religious instruction to children.

We reached Julijonas Steponavičius late in the afternoon, and Vincentas Sladkevičius before dawn the next day. Petkus knew both of them very well.

After a short explanation about the group's goals—which they welcomed—we interviewed them at length. Thankfully, their situations were not dire—they had been assigned living spaces and could perform their priestly duties in small local churches. From a legal point of view, however, what had happened was in flagrant violation of Article 124 of the Soviet Constitution regarding the separation of church and state.

I was particularly impressed by Vincentas Sladkevičius, a very simple and friendly (one might even say, Franciscan) man of slight stature who prepared coffee and sandwiches for us in the middle of the night. Later, in independent Lithuania, he was promoted to the rank of cardinal, and Julijonas Steponavičius became the archbishop of Vilnius. Unfortunately, both of them have now passed away.

HINSEY: After this trip, the Lithuanian Helsinki Group prepared its first two documents—

VENCLOVA: Yes, they concerned the two cases I have just mentioned: one was about the young men who had been expelled, and the other was about the bishops' situation. We also publicized a secret government circular concerning religious communities, which was obviously in violation of the law. Releasing the circular could perhaps be compared to today's "whistle-blowers."

HINSEY: At the end of November 1976, you decided to officially announce the Lithuanian Group to Promote Implementation of the Helsinki Agreements in the USSR—

VENCLOVA: Because Western correspondents were rarely able to visit Vilnius, and then only under very strict surveillance, we decided to hold a press conference in Moscow to present the group's manifesto. We were careful when traveling there: Petkus, Finkelstein, and I took different trains, and out of precaution, carried no materials related to the group. Theoretically, the borders between the Soviet republics were open, and one's documents were not checked on trains (at airports, one had to present one's internal passport before boarding—a rule introduced after the Brazinskases' affair). Still, dissidents were frequently taken off trains without any explanation. Well, we thought, even in the case that one, or even two of us were prevented from making it to Moscow, the last one might be successful. This proved to be overprecautious: we met up in Moscow without any problem. Lukauskaitė and Garuckas could not come, but authorized us to use their names.

HINSEY: At the beginning were the aims of the Lithuanian and Moscow groups the same?

VENCLOVA: They were quite similar, but the Lithuanian group retained its independence from Moscow and preserved its specific goals concerning our country's situation. As you have seen, our first documents were related to the rights of Catholics, which was rather natural since they were a majority in Lithuania, but we were interested in the rights of all religions, be they Russian Orthodox, Lutheran, Jewish, Muslim—or Buddhist, for that matter; also in the rights of all the ethnic groups in Lithuania and of all individuals there. This covered all arbitrary arrests, all illegal limitations on choosing a place of residence, and so on.

HINSEY: Can you describe your mood on the morning of December 1, 1976, the day of the announcement of the Helsinki Group?

VENCLOVA: It was "business as usual." We had had the chance to observe the hectic and somewhat chaotic working method of our Muscovite friends in their apartments. "This is an example that should not be emulated—our Lithuanian group should act in a more orderly manner," Viktoras quipped, impressing Alexeyeva considerably.

As we had not brought our documents with us, they had to be typed in Lithuanian before the press conference, then translated into Russian and English. That meant we had to find a Latin alphabet typewriter, which was not an easy task in Moscow. Finally, this was provided by the dissident scholar Lev Kopelev, a specialist in German literature and a former cellmate of Solzhenitsyn.

Incidentally, the date given for the announcement of the group in history books is November 25, 1976, but this is because our manifesto was slightly backdated. The reason for this is because we outlined it at the end of November, but it was only written down on December 1. Such things are not uncommon in diplomacy, and also in conspiracy.

At 4:00 p.m. we headed over to Yuri Orlov's apartment to hold the press conference. There was a chance that the secret police might stop us on our way, but this did not happen: at that time, the KGB was still taking a "wait-and-see" attitude (which changed in early February 1977).

HINSEY: In your manifesto you stated that the Lithuanian Group would "concentrate on those articles which relate to human rights and basic freedoms, including freedom of thought, conscience, religion, and belief," but also that "We hope, that the participant states of the Helsinki Conference will consider that the contemporary status of Lithuania was established as a result of the entrance of Soviet troops onto her territory on June 15, 1940, and will pay special attention to the observance of humanitarian rights in Lithuania." This last sentence could be considered particularly damaging—

VENCLOVA: Alexander Ginzburg, who was present while we were typing the manifesto, made the following remark: "Look, guys, this might be considered 'an attempt to violate the territorial integrity of the USSR,' which, at least theoretically, could result in the death penalty." After some discussion, we decided to retain the statement: the chance of such grave consequences was rather negligible, and we believed our wording sufficiently cautious.

HINSEY: There were a small group of foreign journalists there—

VENCLOVA: I remember a Reuters correspondent and a correspondent from the *Chicago Tribune*, whose presence was probably due to the fact that Chicago was the home to the United States' largest Lithuanian diaspora community. We read the documents in Lithuanian as a matter of principle—and then switched into Russian. Orlov, Ginzburg, and Alexeyeva represented the Moscow Group. Natan Sharansky provided simultaneous translation into English, as his language skills were the best.

HINSEY: Was there a high level of tension at the press conference?

VENCLOVA: Overall, no. It was lively and businesslike. Immediately after it was over, some Asian-looking people arrived in Orlov's apartment—they were Meskhetians, that is, Georgian Muslims who had been exiled by Stalin to Central Asia, and were demanding the right of return. Thus, the transition to the next item on the day's agenda went smoothly. The end of our stint in Moscow was uneventful.

HINSEY: After the press conference you traveled to Leningrad, finally returning to Vilnius around December 7—

VENCLOVA: Yes, I decided to visit some friends in Leningrad, while Petkus and Finkelstein returned directly to Vilnius. I had no idea of the news that awaited me in Lithuania.

18

PREPARATION FOR EXILE

HINSEY: The Lithuanian Helsinki Group's press conference in Moscow had transpired without incident, but upon your return to Vilnius, you were informed that you had been invited to the Ministry of Internal Affairs—

VENCLOVA: The first thing my mother told me when I entered her flat was that I had been summoned by the ministry to appear the very next day. As I have said before, the Ministry of Internal Affairs, or MVD, differed from the KGB in that it meant "regular" rather than secret police. That said, both offices were sometimes merged, and at other times separated during the Soviet era. In any case, the reputation of the ministry was grim enough.

HINSEY: Can you describe your internal state before your meeting at the ministry?

VENCLOVA: It was not exactly radiant. I had to reckon with the possibility that they would arrest me in the MVD building, although at the same time that seemed somewhat abstract. Rather, I expected another intimidating talk that led nowhere. In any event, I felt very clearly that, for me, there was no way back. Later, I used to say that I took a "prison bag" with me, that is, a change of underwear, a toothbrush, and so on, but that was a joke. In fact, I didn't take any precautions.

HINSEY: What time was your appointment? Would you describe the room? Who was present at this meeting?

VENCLOVA: It was in the morning, perhaps around eleven o'clock. The building was well-known to me, and to everyone in Vilnius—it was a veritable palace on Cathedral Square, with security guards inside who checked your identity papers. The room where the meeting took place was quite large, much bigger than the interrogation room in the KGB building, which I remembered well. Perhaps the idea was to create the impression of one's insignificance in relation to the authorities. There were three or four people on the other side of the desk. I knew one of them, as I had met him before: a highly placed official, perhaps the minister of the interior himself, although I'm not entirely certain. It was he who had once advised me that I had no grounds to apply for emigration. On my right was a nondescript young man. Instinctively, I sensed he was from the KGB.

HINSEY: What did the authorities propose? Initially, what did you answer?

VENCLOVA: One of them said: "You have an invitation from the University of California, Berkeley. Why don't you go there?" "Well, I have neither a passport that is valid for foreign travel, nor an exit visa," I answered. "We will provide you with both, and we advise that you leave for Berkeley as soon as possible." "I must consult with my family and my friends concerning this matter." "We believe two weeks are sufficient for that."

Then, the presumed KGB representative asked me: "Do you have any questions?" "No," I replied. "In that case, we have something to tell you. We would like to give you the following advice: be cautious abroad and don't cut your ties to Lithuania, to which you belong. Various people might approach you there, posing as friends, though they might not necessarily be trustworthy. Please keep that in mind." I made no reply at all and I took my leave.

HINSEY: What happened next?

VENCLOVA: I contacted Romas Katilius who told me. "Congratulations. It took a year and a half, which is pretty close to average—even less, considering that your case was not exactly routine." Of course, before that I discussed the situation with my mother. She perfectly understood that my emigration meant separation—most likely forever—but she preferred this to my imprisonment. If she harbored hopes that things might change, she never dwelled on this. I remember her words, which at the time were a bit unexpected: "You have proved to be an upstanding young man; you have seen the situation through." Romas, who was present during one of our subsequent talks, complimented her, saying that her behavior throughout the whole ordeal had been exemplary. Thus, the only thing that remained was to discuss the situation with the Lithuanian Helsinki Group.

HINSEY: Where did your meeting with the other Helsinki members take place?

VENCLOVA: Petkus, Finkelstein, and I went to Šiauliai by car and had a long meeting at Ona Lukauskaitė's flat. My three friends were happy for me with respect to the developments. Viktoras Petkus, true to his passion for doing everything in an orderly fashion, prepared a special document that authorized me, if necessary, to meet and communicate with Lithuanian émigré groups. We did not meet with Garuckas, who lived in a remote village, but he was apprised of the news and had no objections to my departure. The Moscow Helsinki members were also alerted by Eitan Finkelstein, who phoned Sakharov's wife Yelena Bonner.

I received my passport on January 6, which was my father's birthday. Later, this gave rise to speculations among some Vilniusites about a "birthday present from the authorities," but no doubt it was pure coincidence.

HINSEY: While 1976 had been an annus mirabilis for dissident action in the Soviet Union, a period of brutal crackdown on the Helsinki groups began in early 1977—

VENCLOVA: That began in February, after my departure. I left the USSR on January 25.

HINSEY: In a document from November 15, 1976, Yuri Andropov, then the chairman of the Committee for State Security, detailed the "hostile actions" of the Helsinki groups where "the adversary's special propaganda services have been trying to create the appearance of . . . a so-called "internal opposition," and that the KGB was "undertaking measures to compromise members of the 'group' and put an end to their hostile activities"[22]—

VENCLOVA: This document was top secret and became known only during the perestroika years. Of course we guessed that something of the kind was being prepared—given the Soviet system, it could not be otherwise.

HINSEY: Another thing that you would only find out about later was that your personal case had gone all the way to the top of the Central Committee in Moscow—

VENCLOVA: I learned about this only when these documents were published, more than ten years after the fact. This explained, however, the Lithuanian authorities' sudden change of mood concerning my case. They would never have allowed me to leave the country without direct prodding from Moscow.

HINSEY: In another official document—dated January 20, 1977, and also signed by Andropov—the fates of four dissidents, Yuri Orlov, Alexander Ginzburg, Mykola Rudenko, and yourself, were decided upon. In the document it states that Orlov, Ginzburg, and Rudenko were to be arrested and imprisoned, while you would be allowed to go abroad, but that "your fate would be determined on the basis of [your] behavior while abroad."[23]

VENCLOVA: It is a bit strange that this document was dated January 20, while my case was decided on, or before, January 6. Still, such things happened. The Soviet bureaucracy sometimes gave its formal blessing to decisions made a bit earlier.

HINSEY: This document also reflects an important strategy of the Soviet system, which was that one could never know what fate would befall any individual person—

VENCLOVA: That's true. I suspect there might have been four factors that influenced the decision regarding my case. First, I had requested the right to emigrate before joining the Helsinki Group, while this was not the situation with Orlov, Ginzburg, and Rudenko. Second, the latter were more deeply involved in dissident activities than I was. Third, my case had already created something of a stir in Western intellectual circles (even if Ginzburg, for example, was much better known than I was). The fourth factor, and in my opinion the least significant, was my social background (this did not, in the end, help Pavel Litvinov, or numerous other people). I was not the only Helsinki member to be thrown out of the Soviet Union. This was also the fate of Alexeyeva and Petro Hryhorenko, the founder of the Ukrainian Helsinki Group. In both of their cases, they had also requested permission to go abroad.

HINSEY: There was also a fear that exiles might be assassinated abroad—

VENCLOVA: Many people considered this a serious threat. I must say, I never really took it into account. It happened rather frequently during the Stalinist era, but during the relatively "vegetarian" Brezhnev period only KGB defectors, who were privy to important state secrets, were in real danger. I used to comfort myself with black humor, repeating the dictum: if one is at war with the regime, perishing in battle is perhaps preferable to death by cancer or cirrhosis of the liver.

HINSEY: In addition to your work with the Lithuanian Helsinki Group, there were other serious personal considerations involved in your leaving the USSR. You were married at the time and had a young daughter—

VENCLOVA: Well, my private life was a bit chaotic after my marriage to Marina collapsed. In 1973, I married Natasha Oguy, a director at the Šiauliai theater. We had a daughter, Maria, who was three years old at the time of my departure. I had hoped that my family would accompany me, but Natasha was not in agreement—she wanted to continue her theatrical career. She understood, no doubt correctly, that it would have been next to impossible to do this abroad: she didn't speak English or any other foreign language and had no connections in the United States or elsewhere. Both of us understood that my departure from the USSR would be a handicap for her, but as I mentioned, in the Brezhnev era, such things were more manageable. She had received an invitation to join Yuri Lyubimov's world-known theater in Moscow, which was more or less exempt from troubles at that time. On my side, there was no way I could remain in Lithuania. Therefore, I left, which was taxing for everyone involved, to put it mildly. I loved my daughter, even if our family situation was already unstable. (Mutatis mutandis, Brodsky's case was similar—he wanted Marina Basmanova and their little son to accompany him into exile, but she refused.)

Against the odds, Natasha and Maria managed to join me in the United States in 1982, but by then our family ties were irreparable. After some time, Natasha married an American professor who was a friend of Brodsky's. I knew him rather well—we had become acquainted in Leningrad even before I met Natasha. By a stroke of good luck, as well as through hard work, Natasha found a niche in the theatrical world of New Orleans. (Yuri Lyubimov emigrated as well, and his theater subsequently fell apart, but that is a different story.) Maria, now a wife and a mother herself, lives in Florida, and we meet frequently. Thus, there was a happy ending of sorts.

HINSEY: Can you describe the process by which the authorities finally issued you a Soviet passport? How long was it valid?

VENCLOVA: I was given a passport by the OVIR, following their regular procedure. As was standard for Soviet foreign passports, it was valid for five years, while my exit visa, as far as I can recall, was only valid for three months.

HINSEY: Even if you were going to be allowed to leave for Berkeley, the authorities hoped that exile would be a form of "disappearance"—

VENCLOVA: They may have indeed hoped for something similar. I suspect they believed I would come to understand that my prospects in the West were nil, and thus I would keep quiet and return to the USSR before my visa lapsed—providing them with a sort of "moral victory." Of course I have no proof of this—it is just conjecture. Conversely, if I remained abroad (which they perhaps considered less probable) my exile would in time transform, as you put it, into a permanent form of "disappearance."

HINSEY: One of the authorities' other "disappearance" tactics was to remove all traces of a writer's work from bookshops and libraries—

VENCLOVA: Yes, that happened to almost all émigré writers and public figures. And it happened to me as well: my books were removed from libraries and destroyed. As for bookshops, this was unnecessary, as the books were already sold out. But that happened only a year or so later. There was a special censorship decree concerning my case. The Lithuanian samizdat press got ahold of the decree and published it in 1979. Needless to say, I was rather proud of it.

HINSEY: How did you react?

VENCLOVA: I published—and also read on Western radio—a short text that employed the often-quoted dictum by Mikhail Bulgakov, "Manuscripts don't burn." My only addition was: "Books don't burn either."

HINSEY: Apparently, some copies of your books that were in libraries were saved by people who took them out and never returned them—

VENCLOVA: Yes, I learned about that from several people who were directly involved in such activities.

HINSEY: Before your departure, you wanted to say good-bye to some people in Moscow and Leningrad who were important to you—

VENCLOVA: That's correct.

HINSEY: We have not spoken much about your friendship with Nadezhda Mandelstam, but she is one of the people you called on before leaving—

VENCLOVA: As early as 1962 or 1963, I went to Voronezh, the place of Osip Mandelstam's exile in the 1930s, looking for his traces. As I previously mentioned, I managed to find Natasha Shtempel, a close friend of the Mandelstam family, a Platonic love of the poet, and one of the most engaging women I've ever met. For many years, she taught Russian literature in one of Voronezh's schools, living modestly and maintaining an inconspicuous lifestyle. She told Nadezhda Iakovlevna about my visit. In 1967, when I was attempting to publish some of my Lithuanian translations of Mandelstam, I received a letter from Nadezhda. She wrote, among other things: "I have laughed more than once at the thought that we might be walking side by side, yet have never met." After that we started to correspond and to see each other.

HINSEY: Could you take a moment to describe your last encounter?

VENCLOVA: Nadezhda lived in a one-room apartment in a suburb of Moscow, which she had managed to obtain after much difficulty. Before that, she was virtually homeless, like her friend Akhmatova. Already frail, she was looked after by several young admirers who did her shopping and picked up her medicines. Strangely enough, she received some royalties from the West, where her two volumes of memoirs had been published—although these books were as politically explosive as Akhmatova's *Requiem* or Solzhenitsyn's works. "I have thought about leaving, but I have finally decided to stay," she said, "mainly because I have too many friends in Russia." In addition to Mandelstam and his era, we talked at length about Brodsky who was just getting established in the United States.

HINSEY: You also wanted to see Brodsky's parents—

VENCLOVA: Yes, I went to Leningrad to see them. Our visit was long and a bit chaotic. Aleksandr Ivanovich, Joseph's father, was very concerned about his son's prospects abroad, but Maria Moiseevna, his mother, did not display any external signs of worry. (It was impossible not to compare her to my own mother who had also maintained a perfect, if strained, calm.) At any rate, when I saw Brodsky, I was able to tell him that they were in reasonably good shape. They did not give me any letters or presents for him—that was accomplished by other channels.

HINSEY: You then returned to Vilnius and prepared to leave for a final time. Can you describe your last days before departure?

VENCLOVA: They were a sort of anticlimax, quiet and almost pleasant. My mother helped me in a very composed manner. Luckily, my preparations for leaving were simple, as I took next to nothing with me—just two suitcases or something like that. As was the case with every Soviet tourist at that time, I was allowed to exchange five hundred rubles into six hundred dollars (an incredible rate, since one could get ten rubles for a dollar on the black market). The only precious thing I had with me (which was more of sentimental than material value) was my father's gold watch, which I unfortunately lost in Los Angeles a year or two later.

HINSEY: What else did you take into exile? Were you able to bring all your poems and other writings with you?

VENCLOVA: My suitcases were full of my favorite books, including Pasternak's poems printed in 1965, with my father's signature (I still have it). Incidentally, a customs officer in Moscow asked me: "Why are you taking this? People usually bring them in from abroad, and not vice versa." "I cannot live a day without it," I replied, which was the truth.

I did not try to take my manuscripts—Brodsky's and other people's experiences had proved this was never allowed. But on the very last day before I left, I managed to give my manuscripts to an acquaintance working at the French Embassy in Moscow, and I was later able to collect everything in Grenoble (including my diaries, which were politically risky). But I did take, for example, the Lithuanian periodical in which my translation of three chapters of *Ulysses* had been published. Later, it found its way to the museum in James Joyce's Tower, near Dublin.

HINSEY: Petkus and other friends came to see you off at the Vilnius train station on your way to Moscow, and Sheremetyevo airport—

VENCLOVA: Yes, several dozen friends came to see me off—to tell the truth, I never expected such a large crowd. Viktoras Petkus brought a group of young people whom I did not know. Presumably there were also some KGB agents on the platform, but I chose to ignore their presence, if indeed they were there.

The previous evening we had held a party in my flat. At the time, such farewell events had their own slang name, *otval'naya* (going-away party). Petkus, Finkelstein, Pranas Morkus, and others were present, much vodka was consumed and Bulat Okudzhava's songs were sung. Mother did not attend—she preferred for us to have a separate farewell.

HINSEY: To be allowed into the United States you also needed an American visa. Before leaving you had to obtain this from the American Embassy in Moscow. Could you say a little about your encounter there with Martha Peterson?

VENCLOVA: To my astonishment, there was a sort of Soviet office inside the American Embassy. I had to give my passport to some Russian women working there and to wait an hour or two. Needless to say, it was a stressful experience, which served to remind me—and my mother, who accompanied me—that I was still a Soviet citizen, with all the possible consequences that implied. Then, a very beautiful American lady appeared, as if from nowhere, and presented me with my passport, which now contained my visa. After all the waiting, I had the impression that she was like an angel who had descended from the heavens. That was Martha Peterson (her legible signature was on the visa).

HINSEY: Though you couldn't have known anything about it at the time, Martha Peterson would later write about her experiences as a CIA agent in Moscow and how she was betrayed and expelled from the Soviet Union—

VENCLOVA: I have read about her case in American periodicals. My reaction was: "Well, I was involved in a sort of James Bond adventure, without having any knowledge of it!"

HINSEY: Would you describe your last evening in Moscow?

VENCLOVA: I spent it in a room at the immense hotel Rossiya, practically next to the Kremlin (however incredible it may sound, the hotel burned down almost immediately after my departure). My mother and my wife Natasha were present. Marina, who lived in Moscow, came to see me off as well. The day before, we had visited a historical museum located next to the hotel, and had bought some silly gifts for my relatives in the United States, whom I hardly knew. (In Vilnius, Petkus gave me a gift for Natasha Gorbanevskaya who was already in Paris—it was a woven sash adorned with Lithuanian ethnic ornaments.) As much as possible, we avoided speaking about the future.

HINSEY: On January 25, 1977, your flight left from Sheremetyevo airport. Once you were in the airport, you were separated from your family and friends in the departure area—

VENCLOVA: It was customary to wave to the people accompanying the departing person (in my case, my mother, Natasha, and Marina) before being separated from them by a glass wall that bisected the airport hall from the departure area. I was a bit confused by the customs and passport checking procedures and failed to do this. It was only then that I realized that I could no longer see the three women. I asked a border guard for permission to take a step backward for one or two seconds. "Do you have a diplomatic passport?" he muttered. "No." "Then it is not permitted."

HINSEY: Later you composed a poem about this titled "Sheremetyevo 1977." In it you write, "I didn't know who was Persephone's captive: I or they"—

VENCLOVA: Yes, it was like crossing the border between the realms of the living and the dead—but it was unclear, in this case, who were the living and who were the dead.

HINSEY: Can you say how you felt during the flight? Now that it was a reality, what were your thoughts about the prospect of leaving Vilnius and the USSR in general?

VENCLOVA: The flight was uneventful apart from some severe turbulence as we approached Paris. Nevertheless, I was anxious until we reached Orly airport. Technically, during the flight I was still, in a sense, within Soviet "jurisdiction" (the plane belonged to Aeroflot). During my farewell evening, Pranas Morkus had quipped: "Are you sure that you are going to the West? Perhaps the plane will take off, circle Moscow, and land in the yard of a psychiatric hospital." Of course, all that was black humor, but . . .

Nevertheless, my case was nontrivial. It would be immodest, if not obscene, to compare my case to Solzhenitsyn or Bukovsky who were forcefully deported (Bukovsky remained handcuffed until the plane left Soviet airspace). Nevertheless, I was one of the first to leave the country just because I had demanded the right to emigrate, but not within the context of a "family reunion" or "returning to the land of their ancestors." Emigration, in the eyes of the Soviets, was equivalent to high treason. (Most Lithuanian intellectuals did not embrace the idea of emigration either, considering it harmful to national interests, although in my particular case many showed a modicum of understanding.) The whole situation was aggravated, however, by two factors. First, I was the son of a member of the *nomenklatura*: that made my behavior all the more pernicious from the authorities' point of view. Second, there were my "counterrevolutionary" activities with the Helsinki Group. In any case, I did not feel entirely safe until I left the plane.

I was never the type of person who considered emigration fatal for a writer, so that was outside the realm of my concerns. Naturally, I anticipated that I would encounter difficulties during my adaptation to the West, that is, finding the means for my financial survival, and so forth, yet I felt—even if it was groundless—strangely confident, and this contributed to my elation. I realized I was leaving my mother, a small daughter, and my city of Vilnius forever (thank God, this proved to be untrue). But it took some time for this understanding, as painful as it was, to sink in. In general, my mood was victorious.

HINSEY: Your flight finally touched down at Orly, in a stopover before going on to the United States—

VENCLOVA: As I have said, friends employed by the French Embassy in Moscow were instrumental in transporting my archive to Grenoble. The same friends, on my last day in the USSR, also provided me with a French tourist visa. Thus I simply left the plane (which proceeded on to Washington, DC), went through customs, and arrived on French soil. Symbolically, this meant cutting my last ties with the USSR (my act was clearly inadmissible from a Soviet point of view). I was met by the young daughter of my French friends. She took me to a mansard apartment in the center of Paris where she lived with her boyfriend. I made a phone call to my mother who was still in Moscow. "Well, it must be a beautiful place," she said (she had never been to France, even though my father and Aunt Maria had lived in Paris before the war). Well, it was. A sunset *sur les toits*, the cupola of Les Invalides in the distance, and so on.

The news of my arrival reached the media—I don't remember exactly how this happened; in any case, I had nothing to do with it. The main Lithuanian newspaper, *Draugas*, appeared with the comically large headline, "Tomas

Venclova is in Paris!" The next day, I drafted a statement for the press, Radio Liberty, and Radio Free Europe, explaining that I would continue to be a member of the Lithuanian Helsinki Group, and that I did not intend to request political asylum, as I was leaving open the possibility of returning to Lithuania and resuming my Helsinki duties there.

HINSEY: In Paris you were able to make contact with other former dissident friends. You have written that exile is a bit like the afterlife—you meet people there that you didn't imagine you would meet in this lifetime—

VENCLOVA: Almost immediately after arriving, I contacted Dimitri Sesemann, who had defected to Paris several months before me and was enjoying his old French milieu. We spent half a day together in a Chinese restaurant close to Boulevard Saint Michel. That gave me a taste of my "afterlife": not a disagreeable one, to tell the truth. Then, I found Natasha Gorbanevskaya, who had emigrated a year or two earlier. I remember how we sat on a Parisian bench, both reading *Le Monde*. "Would you ever have imagined that we would be openly reading this counterrevolutionary newspaper—moreover, each with their own separate copy?" she quipped. (It should be said, however, the general mood of Paris was far from anti-Communist. On one quay, I saw a poster that stated: "Communisme, c'est la verité et l'espoir de notre temps." I must confess I had the strong urge to write *merde* next to it, but restrained myself.)

Finally, I met Leonid Chertkov, an old buddy and a recent émigré as well. Together we visited some of the seedier districts of the city where he felt rather at home. I'll not dwell on the details—the "authentic Parisian experience" remains the same throughout the ages. Suffice it to say that in one day I lost almost all the money kindly exchanged for me by the Vilnius bank.

HINSEY: After acclimatization, one of the first things you did was to be interviewed on Radio Liberty by Alexander Galich—

VENCLOVA: Alexander Galich was a famous oppositionist chansonnier, who had also left Moscow around that time and had become a Radio Liberty journalist. I only knew him slightly (he was a close friend of Aleksandras Štromas). We did a short interview for which I was paid one hundred dollars—my first income in the West. This somewhat improved my financial situation, which was pitiable at that moment.

HINSEY: As you were still a Soviet citizen, your broadcast was not an act that would have been looked upon kindly by the Soviet authorities—

VENCLOVA: That's right—it was more than reproachable: all people having anything to do with the "hostile voices" of the Western radio were denounced as CIA stooges. By the way, the topic of our talk was rather innocent, even by Soviet standards: Galich asked me about my Mandelstam translations, and I read aloud Mandelstam's poem (as far as I remember, "Phaedra," written in 1915) in Lithuanian. The translation had been published in Vilnius several years earlier.

HINSEY: In Paris you also met up with Algirdas Julien Greimas—

VENCLOVA: Greimas, a friend of Roland Barthes's and a colleague of Claude Lévi-Strauss's, was a native Lithuanian, who had emigrated in 1944. He was a leftist who had visited Soviet Lithuania, therefore I had met him once in Vilnius (he was quite interested in the work of Yuri Lotman, my semiotics teacher). As I previously mentioned, he was somewhat involved in helping to get me out of the USSR. I even spent a night at Greimas's country house. He suggested that I join the ranks of his graduate students, but I declined due to my poor knowledge of French.

HINSEY: As your stopover in Paris had not been officially approved, you had to go to Aeroflot and attempt to renew your ticket to Washington—

VENCLOVA: Naturally, I was reluctant to enter any Soviet office. I was accompanied there by the girl who had lent me her mansard. In the case of any unexpected developments she, a citizen of France, was prepared to start a row. But there were no untoward developments—only a flat refusal to renew my ticket, followed by a rather boorish lecture about how I had violated a rule to which all Soviet citizens were expected to conform.

HINSEY: In this, Jurgis Baltrušaitis's son turned out to be of help—

VENCLOVA: Some explanation is in order here. As you remember, Jurgis Baltrušaitis, who died in Paris in 1944, was a Lithuanian-Russian Symbolist poet and the topic of my never-finished doctoral thesis. His son, Jurgis Baltrušaitis Jr., was a well-known French art historian (he married the daughter of an even more famous art historian, Henri Focillon, and inherited his magnificent library). The son maintained ties with French and American diplomats (an American in Moscow had suggested that I contact him in case of trouble). Given that I was stuck in Paris with an invalid ticket, I visited Baltrušaitis and asked him for help. I spent the day with him and his wife, talking mainly about his father, who in his own time had been on friendly terms with many Russian cultural figures (Nadezhda Mandelstam valued Baltrušaitis highly). My ticket to Washington, DC (on a French plane) was easily arranged.

HINSEY: You also carried out a ceremonial act connected with Baltrušaitis's father—

VENCLOVA: Jurgis Baltrušaitis Sr., who died just before the liberation of Paris, was buried in Montrouge Cemetery, near his son's flat. Viktoras Petkus had asked me to put flowers on his grave. As I mentioned earlier, when Petkus was arrested as a young boy in Stalinist times, among other anti-Soviet acts, he was accused of possessing "counterrevolutionary" poems by Baltrušaitis (as well as the "counterrevolutionary" book by Selma Lagerlöf). I bought and laid flowers not just in Viktoras's name but also in my own.

HINSEY: In mid-February you flew to Washington, and began traveling and meeting Lithuanian émigrés, engaging in public speaking events, and giving poetry readings—

VENCLOVA: I read my poetry and spoke in New York, Philadelphia, Baltimore, and other East Coast cities where there were large Lithuanian communities. I also visited Yale and Harvard, giving short lectures to students on the situation in Lithuania. By the way, I appreciated Yale's courtyards, unaware that I would spend the better part of my professional life there. The income I received from readings and lectures seemed substantial to a Soviet citizen. It enabled me to survive and to buy a train ticket to Berkeley, California, to begin my semester teaching there.

HINSEY: As part of your responsibilities to the Lithuanian Helsinki Group, you testified before the Commission on Security and Cooperation in Europe in Washington. You appeared before the commission on February 24, 1977, accompanied by the translator Kęstutis Čižiūnas—

VENCLOVA: Yes, that occurred soon after my arrival in DC. The Congressional Commission had been established to monitor compliance with the Helsinki Accords. Vladimir Bukovsky had spoken the day before me. His testimony created a real stir—there were literally hundreds of newspaper and TV journalists. My appearance was more modestly attended—mainly by American Lithuanians and other Balts. (As you know, all three Baltic states maintained their prewar embassies in Washington and, in general, attempted to draw attention to their presence there.) Still, it was a watershed event for the Soviet era, so I tried to do my best. The Lithuanian seaman Simas Kudirka, whom I mentioned earlier (who had spent time in Soviet prisons after his unsuccessful defection, and was later permitted to emigrate to the United States), was present in the hall. We met and made friends. (Much later, he returned to independent Lithuania).

HINSEY: During these proceedings you informed the commission about the human rights situation in Lithuania—

VENCLOVA: My testimony was short, but I tried to make it as substantial as possible. Throughout my stay in the United States, I tried to follow two rules I had set for myself: first, to never overstate one's case, and to always use a neutral, even dispassionate tone. People in the West were fed up with émigrés' stories about the crimes of brutal Communist hangmen (actually, the Communists were perceptibly less harsh under Brezhnev than during the Stalinist era, even if émigrés did not distinguish between the two). Second, to not speak solely about the hardships of ethnic Lithuanians and Catholics (information about this was already readily available), but also about the problems of minorities. I adopted this stance during my testimony as well. I'm not sure it satisfied all the Lithuanians present, although no one criticized it publicly or reproached me privately.

HINSEY: In your formal statement to the commission, you also informed those present that on January 11, Ona Lukauskaitė had been called into the Prosecutor's Office for a lengthy interrogation—

VENCLOVA: That happened before my departure, therefore I had plenty of information about it. Still, in the end, Ona was left alone, perhaps because of her advanced age. She died relatively peacefully at home in 1983 (we managed to exchange several letters delivered by clandestine means—now, her correspondence is housed in Yale's Beinecke Library).

HINSEY: Later in the hearing, when addressing Commissioner Millicent Fenwick, you also warned the commission that Petkus was in imminent danger of arrest—

VENCLOVA: Alexander Ginzburg was arrested on February 3. He was approached by plainclothes police while in a phone booth next to his flat. A photo of the booth appeared in the American press (I recognized it easily since I myself had used it more than once). The arrest of Yuri Orlov, head of the Moscow Helsinki Group, followed on February 10. It was clear that Viktoras Petkus was next in line. International publicity sometimes helped in such cases, though unfortunately this was not the case with Petkus. He was arrested and released only during the Gorbachev era, after serving eleven years of his fifteen-year sentence.

HINSEY: During the hearing there was discussion of the upcoming Belgrade Conference, which would open on October 4, 1977. The conference was the first international meeting to review compliance with the Helsinki Accords since their signing in 1975—

VENCLOVA: I attempted to go to Belgrade as a representative of the Lithuanian Helsinki Group, but did not succeed (Belgrade, after all, was the capital of a Communist country). Still, some documents from Lithuania were presented there. In toto, the group managed to prepare and send to the West twelve such documents before Viktoras's arrest. I was not involved in drafting them, yet attempted to publicize them during the various dissident meetings in Rome, Madrid, and elsewhere.

HINSEY: At the Belgrade Conference, some human rights activists were disappointed with what appeared to be a lack of international pressure toward the USSR on the part of the West—

VENCLOVA: Lyudmila Alexeyeva and I did not belong to this group of disappointed dissidents. We worked together closely in the West. I used to call her, jokingly, "Vladimir Ilyich," that is, Lenin, and she repaid the compliment by calling me "Nikolai Ivanovich," that is, Bukharin. (We use these nicknames between ourselves to this day.) We understood that pressure might be being applied, though not necessarily publicly.

HINSEY: Declassified US government documents actually show that the Soviets were very concerned about the Helsinki Groups' activities—

VENCLOVA: The Soviets fully understood the potential of the Helsinki movement, and were quite unhappy with President Carter's open support of it.

HINSEY: At the time, it must have been difficult to assess the impact of the Helsinki groups. A few years earlier, in an elegant letter from 1968, Anatolii Yakobson had written that such dissident actions "cannot be measured by the yardstick of ordinary politics where every action must produce an immediate result" but rather "one must begin by postulating that truth is needed for its own sake and for no other reason."[24] In a similar vein, Lyudmila Alexeyeva points to the fact that, in Belgrade, human rights abuses in the Soviet Union were actually brought to world attention—

VENCLOVA: I fully agreed with both of them. First of all, dissident activities had a moral impact, but in this case, morality was deeply interwoven with politics (which is not often the case).

HINSEY: But at this stage, however, the costs in terms of human sacrifice, including prison sentences, intimidation, and exile were quite high, and would only increase during 1977—

VENCLOVA: Yes, they were. The cost of every human sacrifice is quite high—perhaps always too high. But that was never imposed on the dissidents—it remained a strictly personal choice, as it was for anti-Nazi activists or the Righteous among the Nations in occupied Europe. While a small minority of oppositionists may have dreamed of taking power, as Lenin and his accomplices did in 1917, this never happened in Russia or Lithuania. It did however occur in Georgia, with deplorable results. Power corrupts, as everybody knows—or should know. But perestroika and the collapse of the USSR were considerably hastened by the dissidents.

Part Three

19

Czesław Miłosz and Berkeley

HINSEY: In March 1977, after your testimony in Washington and speaking engagements across the East Coast, you arrived in Chicago—

VENCLOVA: I reached Chicago in the first half of March and stayed in my uncle's house. Uncle Pijus was my father's eldest brother. The fate of my father's family was quite typical for Lithuania. Five brothers and three sisters survived into adulthood; several other siblings died early, as often happened in peasant families—I don't even know how many, nor their names. Pijus, the eldest, was a high school teacher; he emigrated in 1944. Juozas, the second oldest, perished in a Siberian (actually, a Kazakhstani) mine as a Soviet prisoner—we have talked about him before. My father was the third in line. The two youngest brothers, Pranas and Kazys, remained in Lithuania. Pranas, a veterinarian, died of a badly treated appendicitis immediately following the war, and Kazys, an engineer, was still living in Kaunas in 1977. All the sisters, Konstancija, Izabelė, and Agota, had married and remained in their native countryside, and Izabelė escaped deportation by a hairbreadth.

In the United States, both Pijus and his wife spent the second part of their lives working in a packing plant. This exhausting and unrewarding work—which was completely at odds with their education and ambitions—nevertheless enabled them to buy a comfortable house, which would have been out of their reach in Lithuania. This was a typical Lithuanian émigré story. Pijus contributed to the Lithuanian Social-Democrat (i.e., strictly anti-Communist) press in Chicago. He was not in contact with my father, but I was surprised to find Father's works in his personal library: Soviet Lithuanian books were easily available in Chicago, in striking contrast with the reverse situation in the old country.

Chicago unquestionably possessed the largest concentration of Lithuanian diaspora anywhere. It started to develop in the nineteenth and early twentieth centuries, when Lithuanian émigrés, many of them illiterate or semiilliterate, found employment in the city's notorious stockyards. Upton Sinclair rather vividly described their experiences in *The Jungle*. The book was translated into Lithuanian more than once, and I was well-acquainted with the work. These émigrés established Lithuanian businesses, newspapers, and publishing houses, many of which survived until the 1950s, to which were added new ventures created by the next wave of émigrés. People used to say that there were more Lithuanian-speakers in Chicago than in either Vilnius or Kaunas. Actually, there were around one hundred thousand of them, living mainly in the Marquette Park neighborhood, where one could spend one's entire life with only a rudimentary knowledge of English. There were Lithuanian shops and speakeasies on every corner. There was even an opera house that staged tolerable productions in Lithuanian: opera had been the favorite pastime of prewar Lithuanian high society; they refused to abandon it despite their new lot as Chicago's unskilled workers. Uncle Pijus lived in the very middle of Marquette Park (which was later surpassed by the suburb of Cicero).

HINSEY: And then you were invited to do a public event there—

VENCLOVA: The editors of the liberal monthly *Akiračiai* organized a poetry reading for me in the neighborhood's largest hall. If my previous readings on the East Coast were attended by forty to fifty people at best, here I found an audience of five hundred. The discussion was chaotic. Many of the Chicago Lithuanians knew my father—or mother, or both—from prewar times, or even remembered me as a small child: the appearance of the son of a leading Communist writer, and an anti-Communist to boot, caused a sensation.

I was already on friendly terms with one of *Akiračiai*'s main contributors, Liūtas Mockūnas, who had visited Vilnius several years earlier. Mockūnas was one of the most enlightened, liberal, and witty personalities of the diaspora. He transformed *Akiračiai* into the first truly international Lithuanian-language venue, publishing extensive interviews with Eastern European public figures (who were also invited to Tabor Farm, where the *Akiračiai* group held discussions with them). Another person close to the monthly was Valdas Adamkus, a future president of independent Lithuania (an absolutely unimaginable fate at the time). All the *Akiračiai* people were rather far from the Lithuanian émigré mainstream: as graduates of leading American universities, they did not hesitate to visit their home country, and evaluated the situation there more soberly than anyone else, maintaining ties with the oppositionist intellectuals in Lithuania. "Well, this is my own milieu—we reason along the same lines," was my first thought as I began to make their acquaintance. *Akiračiai* and its sister quarterly, *Metmenys*, provided a venue for my poetry and essays. As you recall, my letter to Vincas Trumpa had even appeared there prior to my emigration.

HINSEY: In late March, you reached California. A Lithuanian professor at UCLA had lent you a flat in Berkeley—

VENCLOVA: I bought a train ticket from Chicago to San Francisco (strictly speaking, to Oakland), since I was eager to see at least some of the United States close up. It was a long and boring journey in a sleeping coach across the prairies and through the Rocky Mountains. That part of the United States, which fed the romantic imaginations of many Eastern European boys, thanks to Mayne Reid and O'Henry, seemed empty and abandoned to me. The only city of any size along the way was Denver, and its train station's location was a disappointment, to say the least. For the first time in the United States, I felt lonely, and thought about the unbridgeable space that separated me from Vilnius, where my family was, and from Moscow, where I had learned so much. It was somewhat comparable to the bout of despair that had occurred during my early childhood in 1941, when I had played near the railway tracks in my grandmother's friend's garden. Perhaps the landscape of the tracks was partly responsible for this. As before, it did not last long—I did my best to pass it off as mere sentimentality. Moreover, the Sierra Nevada and the valleys of California lifted my spirits. They reminded me of Georgia, the most carefree part of the Soviet Union, which I had frequently visited during my summer escapades—and had loved. At the Oakland train station, I was met by a young, attractive Russian woman, a friend of Brodsky's, who drove me to Berkeley in her car. She belonged to my Leningrad milieu, knew everyone there, and had left the country only a year or two before me.

At Ridge Road in Berkeley, a small flat was waiting. It was the summer pied-à-terre of Algirdas Avižienis, a computer science professor of Lithuanian descent at UCLA. He was close to *Akiračiai*—I had met him and his wife in Vilnius once or twice. By an unexpected twist of fate, he made a career in independent Lithuania after 1990, becoming the first rector of the reestablished Kaunas University. At the time, however, this was as unimaginable as Valdas Adamkus's presidency.

HINSEY: Your first encounter with Miłosz took place two days later. But before we talk about this meeting, I'd like to start with the remarkable story of how you first read Miłosz's *Native Realm* in Soviet Lithuania—

VENCLOVA: I have written about this several times, and I told the story to Miłosz himself, who was visibly entertained—and flattered—by it. He believed (wrongly), that his work was largely unknown to the younger generation in Poland, and totally unavailable in Vilnius, his "city without a name." But *Native Realm* had made its way to Vilnius by a rather unusual channel. There was a remarkable Lithuanian lady, Ona Šimaitė, who was a close friend of Kazys Boruta's. During the Nazi occupation, she used to visit the Vilnius ghetto, allegedly collecting university library books that Jewish students had borrowed before the war. Instead of books, however, she brought out Jewish children hidden in sacks. For her actions, she was later named a Righteous Among the Nations. Arrested and tortured by the Gestapo, she survived but deemed it prudent to stay in Paris (where she had settled after being liberated from a prison camp by Western troops) instead of returning to Lithuania. Still, she maintained some contact with her old friends in Vilnius and Kaunas, sending them letters and parcels (a veritable exception at the time). She managed to send the entire text of *Native Realm*, page by page, which took a year and a half. Some of the pages served as chocolate wrappers: that was as clever a stratagem as her wartime exploits. The excerpts were sent to several people, who knew each other well. The pages were then collected (two of which were missing), placed between innocuous covers and circulated among trusted readers.

I was lent the book by Juozas Tumelis and read it in one day. For a large part of that time, I sat on a bench next to the Neris River, where one could easily detect unwanted observers. Soon enough, I came to Miłosz's famous lines about Soviet tanks entering Vilnius in 1940:

> I went down to the river, sat on a bench, and watched the suntanned boys in their kayaks, the revolving rod of a tiny steamboat's engine, the colored boats, which you rowed standing at the back, using one long oar. I was sorry for my city because I knew every stone of it; I knew the roads, forests, lakes, and villages of this country whose people and whose landscapes had been thrown like grist into a mill. . . . The sandbars in front of the electric-power station where children were standing with fishing poles, the river current, the sky, all spoke to me of an irrevocable sentence.[25]

It was an unbelievable coincidence, but the bench was evidently the same one on which Miłosz had sat some twenty years earlier. I could see the same electric power station, similar kayaks, children with fishing poles, even the sandbar at the confluence of the Neris and the Vilnia. One could dismiss my story as a purely literary invention, but it happened to be true, and somewhat emblematic. The country had an incredible potential for survival. It could endure until the book reached its city, to be read—in the very place described in it—by a budding poet of a different generation. And that filled one with hope.

HINSEY: The ban on Miłosz's poetry was particularly strict in Lithuania, though you had managed to read some prewar poems in your father's library, published by Juozas Keliuotis—

VENCLOVA: Juozas Keliuotis, about whom we have previously spoken, was one of the most visible cultural figures in prewar Lithuania. He studied in Paris and became acquainted with some of France's avant-garde authors, painters, and theater people: he enthusiastically followed their work, in the same way as hundreds if not thousands of young East European provincials at the time. Upon returning to Kaunas, he started the monthly journal, *Naujoji Romuva*, which became a very significant intellectual publication during the 1930s. (Romuva was the name of a pagan Lithuanian sanctuary, most likely invented by medieval chroniclers: therefore, the title of the monthly meant "New Sanctuary"—a bit pretentious, if the truth be told.) Keliuotis was a liberal Catholic (more or less in the manner of Jacques Maritain) who discreetly opposed the authoritarian rule of Antanas Smetona.

In 1939, when Poland was crushed by Hitler and Stalin, Czesław Miłosz arrived in Kaunas after an adventurous journey; he found a kindred soul in Keliuotis, who befriended him and published his work (which helped Czesław earn a meager living). Both had spent time in Paris, and both shared a love for the French poet Oscar Miłosz, a Lithuanian diplomat and, as we discussed earlier, Czesław's elder relative. Several poems by Czesław appeared in *Naujoji Romuva* (he was presented as a "Lithuanian poet writing in Polish," to which he had no objections).

In Soviet times, Keliuotis landed in a prison camp, and yearly bound sets of his monthly were strictly forbidden, yet my father kept them in his private library. I found and read Czesław Miłosz's poems there at the age of ten or twelve. I can't say that I understood them. The translations were fairly poor, though one could feel a certain poetic power hidden in the text.

HINSEY: Your father and Miłosz had a friend in common, Pranas Ancevičius—

VENCLOVA: Pranas Ancevičius differed greatly from Keliuotis—he was a leftist who participated in an uprising against Smetona's regime and had to flee to Poland—to Vilnius to be precise. He maintained friendly relations with my father and especially with Kazys Boruta. Ancevičius joined the ranks of Vilnius's students and became very close to Miłosz, whom he introduced to Marxism (contributing much to his nonprovincial education, according to

Miłosz). Czesław nicknamed him "Draugas" ("Comrade" in Lithuanian). Together, they translated Boruta's poems into Polish: these were Miłosz's very first published translations. Although a Marxist (or, perhaps, because of this fact), Ancevičius was an ardent anti-Communist. He died in Canada in 1964, a manual laborer who owned a large private library consisting mainly of books on politics. My father did not hesitate to speak about him; he was one more link to the enigmatic Polish poet.

HINSEY: Later, during your trip to Poland in 1970, you had the chance to read the entirety of Miłosz's poetry, thanks to Jan Błoński and Wiktor Worosyzlski. You were particularly taken by a poem titled "Mittelbergheim"—

VENCLOVA: By then, I knew quite a bit more about Miłosz. I already possessed a good command of Polish, and as I mentioned, I had already read *Native Realm*. Jan Błoński provided me with *The Issa Valley*, and Woroszylski with *The Captive Mind*. I was literally astonished by the abundance of Lithuanian references in *The Issa Valley*: in my opinion, it belonged to Lithuanian rather than Polish literature, notwithstanding what language it was written in (there were quite a few similar cases in Lithuanian letters). I do not remember who—Błoński or Woroszylski—gave me the large collection of Miłosz's poetry, *Światło dzienne* (The Light of Day), printed in Paris. It included his prewar and wartime poetry, as well as lots of postwar work, which had been banned by the Polish censors. For me, it was a *coup de foudre*. I read it from early morning into the night, forgetting everything else around me—even if Poland was full of tempting books, exhibitions, and movies. "Mittelbergheim" was the coda to the entire collection: its topic was the poet waking up in an Alsatian village and his sudden awareness of a great approaching change that would coincide with maturity and emigration. Toward the end of the poem there is a series of incantatory lines that begin: "Fire, power, might, you who hold me / In the palm of your hand."[26] I have repeated the poem's lines to myself many times throughout my life, initially with only a semiconscious premonition of my own fate, and later when I was abroad, when my situation began to echo Miłosz's fate to a degree. Seeking a sort of release from "Mittelbergheim," I translated it into Lithuanian. One of the first poems I wrote in America, "Thanksgiving Day," was an attempt to answer Miłosz. Nothing helped: "Mittelbergheim" is still with me—a perfect work of art and a challenge.

HINSEY: You have mentioned how, under Communism, citations from certain poets became a kind of "special code." In Russia, it was Mandelstam; in Lithuania it might be Brazdžionis or Radauskas. In Poland it was Miłosz—

VENCLOVA: There was a Russian underground poem that said, "people sharing the same faith" in totalitarian countries recognized each other rather easily; one of them would start a quotation from a banned poet, and the other would finish it. There were literally dozens of such shared citations from Miłosz's works, in particular from his long *Treatise on Poetry*, which many knew by heart almost in its entirety. The remembered lines might be, for instance, a gnomic formula: "We are both the snake and the wheel. There are two dimensions."[27] Or they could be the lines addressed to an unnamed dictator in the poem "You who wronged," which were inscribed, much later, on the Gdańsk monument dedicated to the murdered Polish workers: "Do not feel safe. The poet remembers. / You can kill one, but another is born."[28]

They might also be a humorous passage about the Polish avant-garde, which Miłosz considered to be of virtually no value: *Awangardzistów było bardzo wielu* (There were a damned lot of these avant-garde poets).

HINSEY: On your first day together, Miłosz took you to dinner in San Francisco—

VENCLOVA: Well, it was lunch. Miłosz came to Ridge Road around noon. I recognized him at once as he crossed the garden that separated my rather decrepit wooden flat from the street. On the sunny brick-paved path, he looked young and slender, yet with brushy eyebrows befitting an elderly Polish nobleman. The eyebrows became shaggier each year (he was sixty-five when we met, and our acquaintance—I would not say "friendship," since I never considered myself his equal—lasted almost three decades). He reminded one somewhat of Boris Pasternak, who also looked youthful in his late sixties: this was due not so much to his outward appearance as to his brisk, sporty movements and to the wry humor of his conversation.

Miłosz suggested that we call each other by our first names, which I did with apprehension—I was a good quarter of a century younger than him. We drove in his car across the immense bridge to San Francisco. There, we boarded a tram that rolled up and down the hills, at times seemingly vertically. It was my first visit to San Francisco, which looked more Latin American than North American to me (much later, I traveled to South America and found that this was more or less correct). We reached Fisherman's Wharf, dined on shrimp and drank a good quantity of wine, which helped to dispel my timidity. (Miłosz was a good drinker—he was a wine connoisseur and, more important, a specialist in East European vodkas. Although, as an inhabitant of the USSR, I had had extensive experience with alcohol, he surpassed me—and virtually everyone—in the amount consumed, as well as in his sobriety after a drinking bout. Still, he insisted that he had learned something from me about the craft: namely, alternating glasses of vodka with glasses of water.)

We talked a bit about my recent adventures and my chances of finding work in the United States. Miłosz was more than a bit worried about my prospects as an émigré, but did not betray his anxiety during that first meeting. Our main topics of discussion were Lithuania, Vilnius, and our university. Thanks to friends who had recently visited the country, Miłosz was well-informed about our situation, even if he tended to view everything quite pessimistically, as many long-term émigrés did. I did my best to dispel some of his worries. In my opinion, Communism was in the process of falling into decay, and Lithuania's freedom was not unimaginable, although this might still take several generations. (Both of us believed we'd never see it ourselves—thank heavens, we were wrong.) Much of our discussion that day later seeped into our dialogue published by *Kultura*.

On our way back to the car, Miłosz boyishly leaped onto a tram: as it rolled through the seedy parts of San Francisco, he allowed himself a remark, which was hardly politically correct: "Here, and only here, do I agree with the Communists: one should force all these people to be engaged in some decent labor."

HINSEY: Despite the respect that existed for Miłosz's work in underground circles in Poland, when you first met him, he was still in his "desert years": he had yet to win either the Neustadt Prize—which he received in 1978—or the Nobel Prize, awarded to him in 1980. How did you find his morale at this time?

VENCLOVA: He was not really aware of his fame in the Polish underground, and only too aware of his relative obscurity in the United States. Several days after our first meeting, he brought me along to a poetry reading he was giving for an English-speaking audience. It took place in downtown San Francisco, and was attended by precisely twelve people (true, they were enthusiastic about Miłosz's work). Later, in the attic of a hut next to his Berkeley house, Miłosz read me his poem "A Magic Mountain," which begins with the names of his deceased and half-forgotten colleagues Budberg and Chen. He emphasized these lines about himself: "Wrong Honorable Professor Miłosz / Who wrote poems in some unheard-of tongue."[29]

He obviously reckoned with the possibility that he could be erased from human memory, in the same way as Chen (who was, incidentally, a Chinese poet) and Budberg. "I am just placing my manuscripts into the hollows of trees, as an old Lithuanian custom requires," he used to say jokingly. (There was a Romantic legend that ancient pagan Lithuania possessed a literature comparable to Latin and Greek, but it did not survive because the manuscripts decayed in tree hollows.)

And Miłosz was definitely not without ambitions. Once, he asked me who among the Poles, in my opinion, had a chance of being awarded the Nobel Prize. (At the time, his friends from *Kultura* were already making a stir about him to the Nobel Committee.) I mentioned, among others, the excellent—and quite famous in the West—author of science fiction, Stanisław Lem. That candidate had never crossed Miłosz's mind. "You know, I'm not that eager to receive the Nobel," he confessed, "yet I wouldn't necessarily be pleased if it were awarded to another Pole instead of me."

HINSEY: As you had both spent your university years in Vilnius, you had quite a lot of common ground for discussion. You both knew, however, that there was a need to start out on the right foot, above all concerning your "city without a name"—

VENCLOVA: In Lithuanian, the city is called Vilnius, in Polish, Wilno. To use one or the other name is, to a certain degree, a political choice (one might compare this to Dublin, which is *Duibhlinn* in Gaelic—or even *Baile Átha Cliath* in official Irish parlance). I believe Miłosz called Vilnius the "city without a name" partly because of this controversy. During our first meeting, he used the Lithuanian, not the Polish name for it, although a bit reluctantly, as if he were playing up to Lithuanian patriotism. I immediately responded with "Wilno," as if playing up to Polish patriotism. That proved to be an elegant, "diplomatic" solution, which we continued to practice for over thirty years—somewhat ironically, since both of us considered excessive patriotism a rather silly attitude.

HINSEY: But to back up a little, the Lithuania where Miłosz was born in 1911—in Szetejnie, near Kaunas—was deeply multiethnic. You have written about what the overlapping of cultures can teach an individual—

VENCLOVA: Lithuania was and remains multiethnic, even if today it is more homogeneous than before. Moreover, Szetejnie (Šeteniai) is located in a specific part of the country where Polish influence was quite strong. Only peasants (and not all of them) used Lithuanian in their daily life: the nobility, to which Miłosz's parents belonged, might have communicated with them in rudimentary Lithuanian and considered themselves Lithuanians, but they were Poles for all intents and purposes—that is, Polish patriots, totally immersed in Polish language and culture. The picture was even more multilayered due to the presence of Russians (Stolypin, the prime minister of Russia, had his manor close by), Jews, and, sometimes, Tatars. I have written once that this spatial juxtaposition of cultures gave one the feeling of their relative existence in time; their overlapping but mutual untranslatability taught one the sense of distance necessary for a writer. This situation was rather similar to Joyce's Ireland and especially the Austro-Hungarian Empire of Kafka, Musil, and Joseph Roth. More often than not, great authors are brought up in borderland regions.

HINSEY: Late in life, Miłosz took up learning Lithuanian again. When asked why he said, "In case it is the language of heaven." At the time, however, you spoke Polish together. In 1977, what did you sense was his relationship to the Lithuanian language?

VENCLOVA: Lithuanian for Miłosz was somewhat comparable to Gaelic for Yeats. It was the epitome of an ancient, almost sacred language with a specific mythological stature. Calling Lithuanian "the language of heaven" has a long tradition. Some Lithuanian Romantics insisted that it was the language of Eden, which Adam and Eve spoke before the fall.

During his early childhood, Miłosz spoke Lithuanian when playing with local peasant children. Veronika, his mother, arranged a school for these children, and she spoke Lithuanian rather fluently. In the 1970s, Czesław's interest in Lithuanian was rekindled. He was too shy to speak it and never wrote a poem or an essay in it (although his works are sprinkled with Lithuanian quotations), but he could easily read, for example, a Lithuanian newspaper. He also told me that his way of relearning the language primarily consisted of reading the New Testament in Lithuanian. (He knew the text of the Gospels by heart.)

HINSEY: This multiethnicity underwent a radical change during and after the war, particularly after Vilnius was given by the Soviets to Lithuania. One tries to imagine the infinite complexity of your overlapping experiences in the same location: Miłosz was born near Kaunas, studied in Vilnius, wrote in Polish, but cherished his early roots in the Lithuanian countryside; your family was resettled in Kaunas in 1939, you studied in Vilnius, and write in Lithuanian—

VENCLOVA: Yes, and all that was far from an exception. Virtually everyone in Lithuania has mixed roots. My father, as you know, came from a peasant, that is, Lithuanian-speaking family, but my mother's genealogy was comparable to Miłosz's (they were born the same year—1911). As we discussed at the beginning of our conversation, her parents belonged to nobility for whom the principal language was Polish. They switched to Lithuanian only after 1918–20. Oscar Miłosz, whom we have mentioned, was an even more complicated case:

his father was a Polish nobleman, his mother Jewish, he himself was born and brought up in Belarus, opted for Lithuanian citizenship, served as a Lithuanian diplomat of anti-Polish persuasion, never learned the language of his adopted country, and wrote exclusively in French.

Today, one notices a tendency to simplify the picture: a Lithuanian is a Lithuanian, a Pole is a Pole, and our nationalists dream about monoethnic countries. Vilnius is now a Lithuanian-speaking city where traces of Polishness are not necessarily encouraged. I continue to hope that this primitive attitude, fraught with conflicts, will not ultimately prevail. In this, Miłosz and I were in full agreement.

HINSEY: If one adds to this the Soviet Union's totalitarian drive to create "a new reality" in Lithuania, these overlapping historical factors present a nearly phenomenological quandary of perception—

VENCLOVA: That's right. The streets of Vilnius were the same, but their names were now Lithuanian and frequently Sovietized (Russian signboards next to Lithuanian ones were mandatory). The university's halls were the same, but the language of instruction had been changed to Lithuanian (sometimes to Russian). The old professors were gone, and references to the prewar period were erased. Yes, living in such a city was somewhat problematic. This happened, however, in many East European places: formerly German-speaking Danzig became Polish-speaking Gdańsk, Polish-speaking Lwów became Ukrainian-speaking Lviv, and the formerly echt-German Königsberg became Kaliningrad and was radically Russified (it was nearly destroyed in the process). And so on. It was as if an immense steamroller had run over a large part of Europe, changing its character forever. Yet some aspects of old Vilnius had luckily survived: the river Neris with its sandbars, the smaller Vilnia (Wilenka) with its rapids and almost vertical banks, the trees, and, first and foremost, the Gothic, Baroque, and Classicist architecture. It was not possible for Vilnius to be transformed into a standard Soviet metropolis, as the new authorities wished. For that, one would have had to raze it completely, leaving neither stone nor hillside untouched, and erect something entirely new in the leveled space. And that was even beyond Stalin's means, to say nothing of his successors. The city still evoked a "longing for world culture," in Mandelstam's words. Indeed, it was a part of that culture.

HINSEY: As one of the "last citizens of the Grand Duchy," was Miłosz able to straddle these changes better than some?

VENCLOVA: Miłosz was an "Old Lithuanian"; this type of individual existed from the fifteenth to the early twentieth centuries. These Old Lithuanians were joined, and then ousted by "New Lithuanians," who appeared in the 1880s. "Old Lithuanians" might speak various languages, but they were patriots of the Grand Duchy. For "New Lithuanians," Lithuanian was the principal, even the sole language—they opted for a small republic, exclusively consisting of Lithuanian-speaking regions. Miłosz refused to renounce either his Lithuanianness or his Polishness: his sense of nationality was somewhat fluid, and that made him uniquely situated to encourage tolerance. Vilnius, for him, was not a Polish provincial city—which it had turned into during the interwar years (and, of course, not a Soviet regional center), but one of the great Eastern European capitals. He believed it was right that it should belong to new Lithuania, as that country was the historical and legal successor to the Grand Duchy, even if it differed vastly from its medieval predecessor. To put it otherwise, Miłosz was an "Old Lithuanian" who empathized with "New Lithuanians" and possessed an intuitive feeling for their ideas. His stance looked problematic to many hardline Polish and Lithuanian patriots, yet in my opinion it was the only sensible attitude concerning Vilnius and the vagaries of its fate. I, in turn, am a "New Lithuanian," who in the course of time has learned to long for an "Old Lithuanian" identity—or, at least, empathize with it. This was, and is, also problematic for many, yet it provided a good starting point for Miłosz's and my mutual understanding.

HINSEY: This perhaps explains his openness, a bit later, to travel to Tabor Farm, near Chicago—

VENCLOVA: He always insisted that it was easier for him to find common ground with the Lithuanian diaspora than with its Polish counterpart. In Berkeley, he knew many people from the local Lithuanian community and was somewhat involved in their affairs. (Curiously, the head of the community at that time was a certain Adomas Mickevičius—which is to say, his namesake was the greatest Polish poet Adam Mickiewicz, but in its Lithuanian variant.)

Tabor Farm was a sort of manor near Lake Michigan, where Antanas Smetona, the exiled interwar president of Lithuania, had spent his last summers. Now it belonged to Valdas Adamkus, who transformed it into a center for the liberal Lithuanian diaspora. As we've discussed, once a year, people close to *Akiračiai* and *Metmenys* would gather there for an informal conference and discussion. Non-Lithuanians, including Brodsky, were invited as well. Miłosz visited Tabor Farm twice—the first time before my arrival in the United States; the second time we traveled there together (I believe it was September 1978). On that second occasion, we talked publicly about Vilnius, gave poetry readings—"Mittelbergheim" was presented in the original and in my translation—and shared a cabin. In the evenings, Valdas Adamkus manned the beer cask and collected a dollar for each glass. That was presumably the first contact Miłosz had with our future president.

HINSEY: During your first three months in California you spent quite a bit of time together. The university lectureship Miłosz had arranged for you was to teach a seminar on Yuri Lotman's semiotics. Miłosz attended these lectures—

VENCLOVA: He was fascinated by Lotman's ideas, since poetic symbols and symbolism in general had been central to his interests starting in early youth. Moreover, both he and Lotman were interested in Freemasonry. In Tartu, there was perhaps the largest collection of Masonic documents in the entire USSR, which Lotman studied zealously. And Vilnius was also an old center of Freemasonry. In his younger years, Miłosz had belonged to some para-Masonic groups.

HINSEY: Can you speak a little about the content of your lectures?

VENCLOVA: My lectures dealt with poetry from a semiotic perspective: I gave close readings of poems by Pasternak, Akhmatova, and other Russian poets, investigating in detail their rhythmic and sound symbolism, configurations of meaning, intertextual references, and so on. The lectures were attended by a dozen or so persons, including a few professors from the Slavic Department. Miłosz, who was one of these professors, was usually present. After the very first lecture, he said: "Well, I believe you can teach at an American university—don't worry too much about it."

HINSEY: Miłosz was involved in his lectures on Dostoevsky, which you also discussed—

VENCLOVA: I did not attend his class on Dostoevsky (as far as I remember, it was not given that semester), but his fascination with the great Russian writer was evident. In his course, Miłosz dwelled mainly on the problem of evil (both writers shared the conviction that the main enigma of our universe could perhaps be encapsulated in the words *unde malum*), and on Dostoevsky's political views, which were both prophetic and highly controversial. He told me a sort of a tragicomic anecdote: after a class on Dostoevsky's *The Devils*—a novel as anti-Communist as, say, Orwell's *1984*—he was approached by a student who told him: "Thank you, Professor. You have persuaded me to join the Communist Party."

HINSEY: In Berkeley there were a number of other exiles and specialists with whom you had the chance to talk and exchange ideas—

VENCLOVA: There were some figures whose names were legendary to me: for example, Gleb Struve, the first publisher of Mandelstam's collected works and a friend of Nabokov's; Simon Karlinsky, the Tsvetaeva biographer; and Alfred Tarski, a logician whose books, semiforbidden in the USSR, I had studied while learning semiotics. Berkeley offered a rich and unusual intellectual landscape, to say the least.

HINSEY: Outside of the university, you were a frequent visitor at Miłosz's house on Grizzly Peak Boulevard. He was eager to hear about the fates of people such as Juozas Keliuotis and Boruta—

VENCLOVA: Miłosz had a house on a mountain slope, with a view of San Francisco Bay. There was a large library, and sometimes we had dinner together—Miłosz preferred old Lithuanian cuisine, reminiscent of what the village nobility would eat, such as *barszcz* or *barščiai* (beetroot and cabbage soup). Sometimes, I spent the night in the attic of the garden hut—also a Lithuanian experience, the view notwithstanding. (Well, the hills of Berkeley are not so very different from the hills of Vilnius, albeit higher and drier.) But usually we met in one of Berkeley's pubs, namely, The Cheshire Cat, which was practically at the corner of Ridge Road, and drank wine together.

My time in the San Francisco area coincided with a difficult period in Miłosz's life. His wife Janina, or Pani Janka, as many used to call her, was very ill, and Miłosz was often called upon to nurse her. Moreover, in 1977, his youngest son Piotr suffered a nervous breakdown from which he never recovered. This was never discussed, and I became aware of it only much later.

I had much to tell him about our city, the university ("an older and more venerable enterprise than Harvard," he used to say), the general mood in the country and news about his friends. Lithuania's intellectual milieu was tight-knit, everybody knew everybody, and therefore I was well-acquainted with Boruta and Keliuotis. Boruta had died twelve years before my emigration, but Keliuotis was still alive: alas, he later succumbed to psychosis and, as I mentioned earlier, started to write pro-Soviet stuff after his prison-camp trials—a fate that Boruta had thankfully escaped.

HINSEY: You also discussed Pasternak and Norwid—

VENCLOVA: Miłosz highly esteemed Pasternak, though he was wary of Pasternak's "reconciliation with Soviet reality" in the early 1930s. He used to quote one of our common acquaintances, the émigré poet Naum Korzhavin, who once said that he became a Stalinist in his youth due to Pasternak's volume of poems *Second Birth*. Cyprian Norwid, a strange and complicated nineteenth-century Polish poet, whom Brodsky worshipped, was not exactly

Miłosz's cup of tea. He jokingly used the Lithuanian variant of Norwid's name, Ciprijonas Norvydas, and even invented a kolkhoz chairman in Lithuania with that name (Norwid, like Mickiewicz and Miłosz himself, was actually of Lithuanian origin, although he never knew it). Once, we discovered that one of Pasternak's poems derived from Norwid's "Chopin's Fortepiano," and became enthusiastic about this discovery. (We were not the first: Krystyna Pomorska, a Slavic scholar and the wife of the famous linguist Roman Jakobson, had also uncovered this, although we learned about that fact only a year or two later.)

HINSEY: Miłosz was very keen about any news you might have of his family's house in Szetejnie—

VENCLOVA: None of his friends who visited Lithuania had been able to go to Szetejnie, which was off-limits to foreigners. I had been there, not exactly in Szetejnie (Šeteniai) itself, but very close by, in the village of Paberžė, where a famous Catholic priest, Stanislovas Dobrovolskis, lived (he was a supporter of our Helsinki Group). I was pretty sure nothing of the Szetejnie manor had survived, and related this to Miłosz. A day or two later, he told me he had seen the manor park in a dream ("Perhaps under your influence, since you were also in the dream," he added), and a bit later wrote a beautiful poem titled "The Wormwood Star"—about trees that continued to grow though they were no more. (Luckily, I was wrong. The park and one building survived. Miłosz was able to see the trees when he visited Szetejnie after Lithuanian independence, and the building has now been transformed into a conference center.)

HINSEY: As the weeks passed, what was your own state of mind regarding exile? Were you writing poetry during your stay in Berkeley?

VENCLOVA: I was rather euphoric. I loved San Francisco Bay and Berkeley's Telegraph Avenue with its unusual cast of characters, and the university park seemed like a veritable paradise to me. Added to all this was the feeling that I had narrowly escaped a prison called the USSR. When, a year or two later, I started to experience bouts of depression, Miłosz told me: "Well, that's natural. What was *not* natural was your previous euphoria. I envy you. These days, the world pays attention to dissidents, but in my time I had to exist in a sheer vacuum, at the very bottom." He knew much better than I that my situation in America could become very difficult. But that never happened—thanks to him, to a large degree.

I did not write poetry in Berkeley: I was too busy with my lectures and getting accustomed to the new environment. Besides, my poetic bouts are infrequent and always alternate with scholarly work, essays, and so forth. My first poem written abroad, "Museum in Hobart," was composed the following year, after a trip to Australia. Incidentally, Miłosz liked it: the fate of Tasmanian aborigines reminded him of the Baltic situation.

HINSEY: Miłosz often wrote about how conflicted he was in his beliefs—about faith, God, and other important matters. Did you find him, in person, at odds with himself?

VENCLOVA: One of Miłosz's favorite ideas was the reconciliation of Christianity with Manicheism, a heretical doctrine that believed evil was a self-sufficient and mighty force, not just an absence of good, as Saint Augustine maintained. He was very interested in Bogomils, the medieval Slavic Manicheans, and even taught about them in his classes. This also coincided with his interests in Swedenborg, William Blake, and Oscar Miłosz (who was their twentieth-century heir). All that led him to antinomies and inner conflicts. Once, in my presence, he asked Leszek Kołakowski, a philosopher and authority on early Christianity: "Am I a heretic?" "Of course," Kołakowski answered half-jokingly. As far as I know, he asked the same question of Pope John Paul II, who reassured him.

HINSEY: Together you had a chance to discuss the different metrical traditions of Polish, Russian, and Lithuanian poetry. Miłosz had rather strong views about the danger of Russian classical meter applied to Polish verse—

VENCLOVA: Yes, and he also considered Russian meters a danger to Lithuanian verse. My appreciation for them looked dubious to him. Russian and Polish systems of accentuation are opposite, but Lithuanian accentuation is closer to Russian than to Polish. Therefore, classical iambs, trochees, anapests, and so on sound natural in Lithuanian, while in Polish this is not the case. Russian meters are perfectly at home in the Lithuanian tradition; to my ear, they are even more natural than the Lithuanian version of Polish syllabic verse, which I also practice from time to time.

While at Tabor Farm with Miłosz I read my translation of Norwid's "A Funeral Rhapsody in Memory of General Bem": it was more metrical than syllabic. I was timid about this and did so with some reluctance, but Miłosz remarked: "The hexameter works well in Lithuanian."

HINSEY: Concerning his work, you once observed that in it, "an irregular rhythm, elliptical images, a peculiar visionary stance were a means for conversing with the age"—

VENCLOVA: Miłosz differed considerably from the Russian tradition of Pasternak, Mandelstam, or Akhmatova, to which Brodsky and his milieu (including myself) subscribed. Once, after listening to a reading by Brodsky's friend and follower Evgeny Rein, Miłosz said: "Either Rein's work does not belong to poetry, or my work does not belong to poetry." But he liked Russian Silver Age classics and was delighted by most of Brodsky's work. I would say his visions were more "post-Rimbaldian," though he was wary of Surrealism.

HINSEY: In Miłosz's writings one finds numerous references to his philosophical influences, but less about his poetic influences, from a formal point of view. Now with hindsight, who do you think were his most critical influences, particularly among his contemporaries, or near-contemporaries?

VENCLOVA: In the very first letter Miłosz wrote to me, he said: "My attitude toward poetry written in America (and there are thousands of poets here) is mainly negative, to say nothing about France, which is in much worse shape in this respect. Thus, my attitude toward Western literatures is disdainful, and my self-dependence is considerable." In other words, his Western contemporaries did not mean too much to him. Still, he was influenced by Whitman, T. S. Eliot (whom he translated in the Warsaw underground during the Nazi occupation), perhaps also by Sandburg and Auden, but much more by an author such as William Blake. Generally, he was an "English-language-oriented" poet, while most Polish poetry of his time was "French-oriented." In Polish poetry, Miłosz valued Mickiewicz more than anyone else—for his objectivity and his feeling for material life.

HINSEY: Once Miłosz established his poetic strategy, however, it allowed him to attempt to find a way, as you have noted, to "write poetry adequate both for the disasters that are destroying cultures and for that striking strength of cultures to survive"[30]—

VENCLOVA: Miłosz was a poet of culture, first and foremost. In this, Lithuanian peasant culture meant a lot him. His poetry emphasized persistence and inner discipline, human compassion, sobriety of attitude and expression, a specific respect for the rhythms of nature, but also language as something sacred and the guarantor of one's identity. Old Lithuania, for him, was a semimythical country of tolerance, which took into account the ineluctable variety of colors of the human universe and thus resisted any *Gleichschaltung*.

HINSEY: As we have discussed in relationship to Akhmatova's poetry, for writers of Miłosz's generation, questions of form and philosophy were not merely "aesthetic choices"—

VENCLOVA: Miłosz was not a formalist—he was a metaphysical poet, for whom moral problems were of primary importance. The idea of being afraid of "lagging behind the Zeitgeist" was, for him, a source of profound error, be it in poetry or in politics. One had to be aware of one's era with all of its burdens and controversies, but one ought to be an actor in it and not risk becoming its tool (as was, in his opinion, the case of Mayakovsky and Pablo Neruda).

In this light, formal experiments might be a sort of time-serving. In certain cases, totalitarianism allowed and even encouraged avant-garde eccentricities so that poets would be caught up in such aesthetic questions and consequently not attempt to influence reality. This did not happen in Stalinist times, when pedestrian quasi-Realism was the only permitted art form, but it started to be a threat a bit later—as well as before Stalin's time. Miłosz did his best to avoid such temptations. Influencing reality was, for him, one of a poet's duties, however difficult and uncertain that might be. (Another duty, inseparable from this one, was writing well.)

HINSEY: In your essays you give, to my mind, one of the most concise and insightful analyses of the central role of memory, "persistence of matter" and the philosophical importance of history in Miłosz's work—

VENCLOVA: Like Akhmatova and Brodsky (whose poetics strongly differed from his), Miłosz was a sort of "conservative antitotalitarianist," that is, a poet of memory and history. He was aware that totalitarianism threatened the temporal dimension of humanity: the past was censored and distorted, and the future consisted of a senseless repetition of rituals forced upon the people by "leaders who know better." While history cannot stop, poets may still help to guide its intricate course, sometimes just by reminding their readers of primary values, such as "thou shalt not kill," "thou shalt not lie," "thou shalt not talk in vain."

HINSEY: These dangers still seem relevant for poets writing today. It appears that the temptation that Miłosz warned against—about poets losing themselves in cynicism, or apocalyptic nihilism—is stronger than ever—

VENCLOVA: Yes, the temptations we are discussing are stronger than ever—or, at the very least, as strong as ever. The "third choice" that Miłosz proposed requires as much courage as it did in his time, but it is never impossible.

HINSEY: To return to 1977, would you speak a bit about the impact of Miłosz's attempt to sustain a "scale of values" on the Polish dissident movement?

VENCLOVA: Miłosz's chance to actually influence history with his poetry and his stance was quite unusual, and he took full advantage of it. For many years, he was not fully aware of the position he held for Polish dissidents: he considered emigration a form of suicide, that is, severing links with his native audience and the literary developments of his native country. Then gradually, he began to feel the extent of his impact: Adam Michnik, who met with him in Paris before Poland regained its independence, told him: "Well, you have won." Still, he was surprised to learn, in the course of his first return to his country, that certain of his poems were widely read by nearly everyone there, from schoolchildren to Lech Wałęsa. Miłosz's stubborn affirmation of human values was salutary for many, and not just in Poland, during the times of ethical degradation during the Communist period. Such things are rare but not unthinkable for poets: I believe Seamus Heaney had a comparable impact on Ireland during the Troubles, and Bei Dao on China.

HINSEY: You have mentioned that, in looking back over Miłosz's work, one might categorize him, in addition to being a poet, as a "historian of ideas." Heaney writes that he believed Miłosz's mind was like a Renaissance theater of memory: "Schoolboy Latin, Thomist theology, Russian philosophy, world poetry, twentieth-century history . . ."[31] This is not, however, unique to Miłosz, in the sense that he drew upon the traditions of nineteenth- and twentieth-century education in Eastern Europe—

VENCLOVA: Miłosz was fortunate to obtain a good old-style education at Vilnius/Wilno University, and he supplemented it with extensive and judicious reading. His two-volume book on Russian thought, which appeared after his death, is on a par with Isaiah Berlin. The person who introduced him to that subject area was Marian Zdziechowski, the interwar rector of Wilno University, who died just before Hitler's attack on Poland (Miłosz wrote a poem about him, noting that he chose a perfect moment to pass away). I also believe that Miłosz was a veritable authority on the history and theology of early Christianity.

HINSEY: In addition to all his other writings, the genre of epistolary dialogue was important to Miłosz. For example, there is his correspondence during the war with Jerzy Andrzejewski, and during his exile in California with Thomas Merton—

VENCLOVA: Large volumes of his correspondence are still in the process of being published: of special importance was his exchange of letters with Jerzy Giedroyc, the editor of *Kultura*. One of his correspondents was Juozas Urbšys, Lithuania's last independent minister of foreign affairs. Urbšys had a very unusual fate: he was born fifteen years before Miłosz into a Lithuanian-speaking family in Szetejnie, he survived Stalin's prison camps, made his living in Soviet Lithuania by translating Molière and Abbé Prévost, and died at the age of ninety-five, after having time to contribute to Lithuania's new independence movement.

HINSEY: In 1978, a year after your meetings in Berkeley, you undertook a famous exchange of letters with Miłosz, "A Dialogue about a City," on the subject of Vilnius. This document is one of the most elegant texts of cultural reconciliation of our epoch. Wiktor Woroszylski first commissioned it. Can you explain how this exchange came about?

VENCLOVA: Wiktor Woroszylski was one of the editors of *Zapis*, an underground magazine that was produced abroad (in London I believe) and then smuggled into Poland. It published works by Polish authors who were banned by the censors. Incidentally, three of my own poems in Woroszylski's translation appeared there. It was *Zapis* that asked us for an essayistic dialogue about Vilnius. I wrote my part (answering Miłosz's letter) in the summer of 1978, first in Venice, then in Los Angeles. Later, the dialogue appeared in many languages and is still being reprinted. I have met more than one person for whom our dialogue was their first introduction to Lithuania's problems.

HINSEY: The exchange caused a temporary conflict in Poland—

VENCLOVA: Jerzy Giedroyc, to whom Miłosz mailed the text, immediately published it in *Kultura*, thus depriving Woroszylski and *Zapis* of the right of first publication. It resulted in a short-lived tiff between Giedroyc and the Polish underground. The traces of that imbroglio are perceptible in the Giedroyc-Miłosz correspondence and in some memoirs. A Lithuanian version of the text was printed in *Metmenys*, which leaked into the USSR. Once, I telephoned Pranas Morkus (he was in Moscow at that time, and was not shy about talking with an "enemy of the people"). He told me: "You know, I just spent half a day riding the Moscow subway and reading your exchange with that *żagarysta*" (*Żagary* was the prewar Vilnius magazine where Miłosz started his career). "Well, and how did you like it?" "It's not bad, but it could be even stronger."

HINSEY: In the spirit of the dissident movements of the period, Miłosz, Brodsky, and yourself founded a sort of cultural trio of solidarity and support, a "poetic triumvirate." Twenty-five years after the fall of the Berlin Wall, this friendship between a Russian, a Pole, and a Lithuanian, may not seem so radical now, but at the time—

VENCLOVA: As we have discussed, Brodsky had left the USSR without much information about Miłosz—his knowledge essentially amounted to our 1972 talk in a Leningrad restaurant. Immediately after Brodsky's arrival in the West,

Miłosz wrote him a letter, which Brodsky used to call the most significant letter he ever received. The older poet spoke frankly about an émigré's fate, and ended with the statement that one may write good poetry in exile after all—it depended on the caliber of one's personality (Miłosz's own example was eloquent enough). They met and became close friends. It was only natural for me to join them as a third partner, representing a smaller country with a younger culture. If one keeps in mind Russia, Poland, and Lithuania's conflicts—which seemed pretty unsolvable at that time—that was, I believe, a significant step.

HINSEY: Miłosz continued to speak about you three in this manner—a triumvirate. You issued a number of public statements together, including one in 1987, and another in 1991. During the struggle for Lithuanian independence, Soviet tanks opened fire on peaceful protesters next to the television tower in Vilnius, and the three of you signed a joint protest, which was published in the *New York Times*—

VENCLOVA: That was Miłosz's idea. As a Nobel Prize winner, he had connections at the *New York Times*, which was, moreover, quite sympathetic to Lithuania's plight. Later, Miłosz continued to speak out on Lithuania's behalf, and visited the country (which he had not seen for fifty-two years) more than once. He wrote a brilliant poetic cycle about Lithuania: I had the honor to translate it, and to read one poem from it, in Lithuanian translation, at his funeral.

The Polish-Lithuanian territorial quarrel concerning Vilnius was finally solved in 1994—Vilnius was unconditionally assigned to Lithuania, to which it was, and is, as significant as Jerusalem to Israel. The solution had already been proposed by Giedroyc and his team in the 1950s, yet Miłosz greatly contributed to its implementation (more than anybody else). He became an honorary citizen of the Lithuanian capital, and considered spending his last years in Vilnius, although he finally opted for Kraków.

HINSEY: In addition to your encounters with Miłosz, when you were in residence in Berkeley, there were visits by poets and writers who came to give lectures and readings. At one point the Russian poet Bella Akhmadulina visited—

VENCLOVA: Akhmadulina belonged to the *shestidesyatniki* (for a time, she was Yevtushenko's wife): she was perhaps the most talented and honest member of that group, also valued by Brodsky. In the company of Akhmadulina and Miłosz, I spent a night at The Cheshire Cat, where we drank several bottles of California wine, without any undesirable observers. In Akhmadulina's words, she had been instructed by the Soviet Consul in San Francisco to "not follow the bad example of Tomas Venclova." Her behavior was not exemplary for a Soviet citizen: her exit visa was only valid for Paris, but she traveled from there to the United States by American invitation and without Soviet permission. When reprimanded for that, she boldly answered: "I'm a Russian poet, not a serf."

HINSEY: In June 1977 your lectureship ended. In August you received a letter from the Soviet Consul informing you that you had been stripped of your citizenship "for activities that defile the title of a Soviet citizen"—

VENCLOVA: That was a rather interesting story. After my lectureship at Berkeley, I had around ten thousand dollars, which seemed like an immense sum to someone from the USSR. I decided to spend eight hundred dollars on a trip to Hawaii in order to explore its beaches and volcanoes and so forth. Algirdas Avižienis occupied the Berkeley flat while I was away. Once, two self-invited visitors arrived at the door and addressed him in rude Russian. He explained to them that he did not know a word of the language. "Therefore, you are not Venclova?" "No, I'm not." "Where is he?" "Well, he's not in Berkeley." "Tell him when he gets back to visit the Soviet Consulate, since we need to make a mark in his passport."

After I returned, I sent my passport to the Consulate by mail and received the answer that it would not be returned, since I had been stripped of my Soviet citizenship due to my unacceptable behavior. The decree revoking my citizenship was promulgated in June, and the Consulate people informed me only in August.

These developments were not entirely unexpected, and I was actually rather proud of them. There were only a few people who had merited such a decree, including Leo Trotsky, Svetlana Alliluyeva, and Solzhenitsyn; I was ninth in line. (In the end, approximately thirty more people joined the club.) Due to this, however, I was forced to apply for political asylum, which was granted. The next problem that I faced was finding a job. Miłosz contacted one of his Lithuanian friends, the famous archaeologist and UCLA professor, Marija Gimbutas, who managed to arrange a temporary teaching position for me. So in the fall of 1977, I moved to Los Angeles and rented a small flat from a Lithuanian businessman in Santa Monica.

20

TRAVELS

Exile as Good Luck

HINSEY: In fall 1977, following the decree revoking your Soviet citizenship, you moved to Los Angeles. There you took up a short-term position at UCLA—

VENCLOVA: After losing my Soviet citizenship and receiving political asylum, I was cut off from Lithuania—and from the entire Soviet bloc, for that matter—but that was to be expected and was, in a certain sense, even welcome. I could still exchange letters and phone calls with my family, who, it seemed, were being left alone by the authorities. That said, some anonymous individuals telephoned and insulted my mother, but she reacted with perfect calm, and soon this type of intimidation ceased. "I got used to being harassed during the Nazi occupation, when the callers accused me of being the wife of a Communist traitor," she said later. "Now, they accuse me of being the mother of an anti-Communist traitor. For all I know, they might even be the same people, just a few decades older."

That said, I was rather reconciled to my American experience. I liked the cliffs and quasi-tropical streets of Santa Monica. It might sound ridiculous, but I was rather thrilled by the fact that Lillian Gish and Alfred Hitchcock lived practically next door, that Thomas Mann had spent part of his exile in Pacific Palisades, and that the nearby suburb of Tarzana had been built on the site of a ranch belonging to Edgar Rice Burroughs, the author of *Tarzan*.

My flat, very modest by local standards but comfortable enough for me, was on Eighteenth Street, several blocks from Wilshire Boulevard; I could easily walk to the seashore, where, incidentally, I used to run into Lithuanian émigrés from 1944. Los Angeles's Lithuanian community was quite large (second only to Chicago), relatively prosperous and vibrant.

Marija Gimbutas was one of its central figures. She was a friend of Miłosz and Roman Jakobson, and an authority on Slavic, Baltic, and Indo-European archaeology (her controversial theory of the matriarchal origins of European—and Lithuanian—culture brought her world fame in feminist circles). She had a beautiful house in Topanga Canyon, which I visited on a number of occasions. She was an old Vilnius hand, just like Miłosz. As a distinguished American scholar, she was permitted to lecture in Lithuania from time to time, and visit her cousin Meilė Lukšienė, one of my beloved university teachers. In Los Angeles, there were also Algirdas Avižienis and his wife Jūratė, whose kindness was invaluable to me at that time. I was perhaps the only person there who didn't own a car, and thus reached their house via infrequent buses and sometimes stayed the night. They had many Lithuanian friends, mainly UCLA professors. My relations with my colleagues in the Slavic Languages and Literatures Department, above all Dean Worth and Henrik Birnbaum, were convivial.

My teaching at UCLA was a very different affair. I proposed a class in Lotmanian semiotics, as I had at Berkeley, but the response was rather minimal. Therefore, I had to limit myself to teaching Lithuanian, which I did for three years. Professionally, these were among my worst years in the United States. My students consisted mainly of the children of Lithuanian émigrés. Some of them spoke Lithuanian as well as I did, others did not know a word, but had been promised an expensive car by their patriotic parents if they mastered at least the basics of the language. From time to time a highly knowledgeable American linguist would join the group, whose goal was to add Lithuanian to the Sanskrit, Hittite, and Old Icelandic languages that he or she already knew. Adjusting to all these proficiency levels was beyond my abilities. Nor was I liked by the students. One positive side was that my teaching did not require much preparation, but the textbook was rather primitive, and reading folklore texts or Donelaitis with my more gifted students was a bit exhausting. Gimbutas, who had taught Lithuanian at the beginning of her scholarly career, managed to combine this with activities related to semipagan Lithuanian holidays and games, but that was not my cup of tea.

HINSEY: Despite these changes of circumstances, you maintained contact with your former friends from the Lithuanian and Moscow Helsinki groups. For instance, Lyudmila Alexeyeva had been forced to leave the USSR at this time and had also settled in the United States—

VENCLOVA: Lyudmila Alexeyeva and I left the Soviet Union at almost exactly the same time. She settled in Tarrytown, next to New York City, where her husband Nikolay Williams, a known mathematician, had found employment as a teacher. (As I mentioned, Pavel Litvinov was also working there.)

Quite quickly, Lyudmila established contacts with American human rights groups and became the most active spokesperson for the Soviet dissident movement in the United States. Her lively and amiable character helped her in this considerably. Another member of a Helsinki Group, Petro Hryhorenko, the former Soviet general of Ukrainian descent, had also been expelled from the USSR; he became connected with Ukrainian émigré circles of nationalist persuasion. Notwithstanding our different circumstances—and, in part, divergent views—we formed a three-person team that attempted to represent the Moscow, Ukrainian, and Lithuanian Helsinki Groups in the West. My friendship with Alexeyeva had already been close in the USSR. It was strengthened in the United States, and we are still close. (In 1993, Alexeyeva returned to Russia. Now in her late eighties, she plays a leading role as a democratic political figure there.)

HINSEY: In November 1977, you attended, along with Alexeyeva, the Second International Sakharov Hearing in Rome. At the hearings you spoke twice—

VENCLOVA: I remember that trip to Rome quite well, principally because of my visa problems. I had a passport from independent Lithuania, issued by Stasys Lozoraitis Jr., who performed his diplomatic duties in Rome and Washington, DC. As I have mentioned before, several Lithuanian embassies had survived in the West as curious remnants of the prewar republic. That passport had great symbolic, but little practical, value. There were some countries that honored Lithuanian passports, but their numbers were constantly shrinking. To enter Italy, one needed an invitation from the Vatican. With this, one could obtain an Italian transit visa, which, to make a long story short, I was unsuccessful in getting. I did have, however, a gray booklet called a "Refugee Travel Document," in which the necessary stamp was placed at the very last moment.

The hotel where the Sakharov Hearing participants stayed was located in a Roman suburb, and was guarded by carabinieri because our chairman, Simon Wiesenthal, had received death threats. This was the only time I met him. It was good to see that the world-famous Nazi hunter also supported our cause. Despite the guards, I could freely come and go from our hotel. Needless to say, I tried to squeeze into my tight schedule as much of Rome as was possible. It was like the old joke: "Rome in two days, Pope included" (actually, I was there four days, and the pope was Paul VI, who was old and ill—I saw him blessing the crowds from the window of his bedchamber). To my eyes, the city looked somewhat dirty, full of shops selling either devotional kitsch or Communist posters; the weed-choked hills of the Palatine reminded me of provincial Lithuanian towns. Of course, there was also the Erythraean Sibyl on the vault of the Sistine chapel, and the inscription "Animula, vagula, blandula" in Castel Sant'Angelo. While on a walk with Stasys Lozoraitis in the vicinity of the Piazza Venezia, I took in a veritable visual course of the city's history, from the early emperors to Mussolini (whom Lozoraitis remembered well). But my impressions were superficial at best: I would explore Rome in depth only during my subsequent visits—and there were many of these indeed.

I spoke twice at the Sakharov Hearing. My initial and lengthier report dealt with religious persecution in Lithuania. This was a topic more fitting for a Catholic activist (to be precise, I also mentioned the grievances of other creeds, including Muslims and Karaites). But the underlying principle remained the same: if anyone's rights are violated, everyone's rights are violated. Second, I presented Viktoras Petkus's case, who had been arrested on August 23 of that year.

HINSEY: You also continued your human rights work through other types of public events, such as during your trip to Australia—

VENCLOVA: I traveled to Australia after Rome—I took advantage of my 1977/78 winter semester break to do so. The trip was to inform the local Lithuanian diaspora, as well as the mainstream Australian media, about the situation in Lithuania. I believe I was more or less successful in this. The situation was quickly becoming rather dire—the Helsinki movement and other human rights initiatives were being crushed throughout the Soviet Union (even though the Lithuanian Helsinki Group continued its work against all odds).

I visited Sydney, Melbourne, Canberra, and Adelaide. I also traveled to Hobart in Tasmania, the very epitome of the old Australian "Gulag." As I mentioned, my poem on Hobart touches on the genocide of the Aboriginal Tasmanians, reminiscent of our own European experiences.

The Lithuanian diaspora in Australia was unusual, in that it included a high percentage of artists. There were writers, but especially painters and sculptors among the Lithuanian émigrés of 1944, who were in the process of leaving their mark on Australian art. I met and established friendships with many of them, including Lidija Šimkutė-Pocius, a poet and traveler whom I still encounter in various parts of the world. Interestingly enough, the Australian government recognized Lithuania's incorporation (as well as that of Latvia and Estonia) into the Soviet Union in 1974, but was forced to revoke that decision due to protests by the diaspora. That was one of the recurring motifs of my talks with local Lithuanians and the Australian media. People used to grimly joke that the 1974 devastation of the city of Darwin by Cyclone Tracy was God's punishment for the Australian government's pro-Soviet stance.

On my way back to Los Angeles I managed to see New Zealand (where there was also a Lithuanian community) and Tahiti. For the latter, I had no visa, but brazenly said to the Polynesian border guard, "I was told in Sydney that this document is all that I need" and was let in for a couple of days. One of them was, in a sense, a gift of fate, since crossing the International Date Line had given me an extra day.

HINSEY: You were now witnessing the situation in Lithuania and the Eastern Bloc from the outside—what was that like, after so many years on the other side?

VENCLOVA: That is a complicated question. The differences between the colorful, easygoing, and generally friendly Western world and the constrained, fearful Soviet universe were immense. A new émigré usually felt lost due to the extraordinary variety of choices. Starting in early youth, I had grasped that my country, historically and by natural inclination, was part of Europe, and yet it was cut off from its roots and condemned by brute force to stagnate. My understanding of this now became almost unbearably poignant.

This was the mood of most Soviet dissidents who found themselves in the West. On the other hand, it quickly became clear to me that we were not necessarily the Western powers' only—or even their main—concern. There were Third World problems, for instance, which were more immediate and pressing than that of Soviet totalitarianism (which was already in the process of decay). Most dissidents, however, considered their case to be the absolute priority. Among them, I sometimes met people who praised Pinochet and similar political figures as "the only ones who dared to fight back." I had reservations about this, to say the least.

HINSEY: But the fate of exile was not necessarily easy for everyone, and also sometimes revealed hidden tendencies—

VENCLOVA: Not every courageous person from the Soviet Union was able make a success of his or her newfound freedom. In the West, there was enough space for almost any public or private initiative, but at the same time there were no guarantees. In some cases, this led to despair, and there was also the question of survival—physical survival, but also social and political survival. Under such circumstances, weaknesses that had not been obvious in the USSR surfaced, including tendencies toward radical right-wing politics and conspiracy theories. I believe Soviet dissidents (in contrast to, say, Polish ones) never reached the critical point where they could present a real alternative to the regime. That may, in part, explain the failure of post-Communist Russia.

As for Lithuania's oppositional movements, I had always been allergic to right-wing and strictly nationalist viewpoints. Among the Lithuanian diaspora, such views tended to predominate. With the notable exception of those in the *Akiračiai* milieu, almost everyone longed for the prewar republic, which was, as we have discussed, authoritarian and rather backward (though of course preferable to Soviet rule). I developed a maxim: the difference between a new Lithuanian republic and the prewar one would be as great as the difference between the prewar republic and the Grand Duchy. The world had changed unimaginably, and we had to adjust to this fact. I still maintain this position, which now carries the day in Lithuania, though not without its detractors.

HINSEY: Early in this book, you recounted the story of your discovery of a large globe at your godfather Antanas Bendorius's house. Despite the pain of being separated from loved ones, how did you now feel, given that your geographic possibilities had expanded exponentially?

VENCLOVA: In 1953 Max Frisch wrote a play titled *Don Juan, or the Love of Geometry*. Jokingly, I used to call myself *Don Juan, or the Love of Geography* (or perhaps the nickname was invented by my friends). Almost immediately after my arrival in the West, I started to travel, partly because of my duties as a Helsinki Group member, and partly on my own. The allure of previously "unreachable" countries and continents was overpowering. I spent nearly all my spare funds not on the usual amenities of American life, but on journeys (in my early youth, I became accustomed to very Spartan conditions while traveling, and was good at logistics). As time passed, it became a sort of obsession. Today, the number of countries I have visited is close to a hundred, and I've seen quite a number of them more than once. Of course, I have my favorites, above all Italy, but I have been to Bolivia, Zimbabwe, and Laos as well, immersing myself in their landscapes and daily life as much as possible. While I have never succumbed to Orientalism or Buddhism, I've spent time in Nepal and Tibet, and found it very interesting. Therefore, I have almost covered my godfather's entire globe, with the exception of Antarctica. (Regretfully, I never saw Antanas Bendorius again—he passed away in America before I emigrated. His fate is material for a short story: he worked hard throughout his life, saving up money for exotic trips that were beyond his means, and died suddenly on the third day of his retirement, preparing for the first of such trips—to Greenland, I believe.)

HINSEY: In 1980, after three years in California, you received an invitation to teach at Yale University—

VENCLOVA: My contract at UCLA expired, but to tell the truth, it saved me from a routine that I wasn't particularly fond of. That said, I was facing joblessness for the first time in America, and I was truly frightened by the prospect. Brodsky reassured me by asking: "Tell me how you felt when you parted from your first girl." "I was on the verge of suicide," I answered. "And what about when you separated from your next girl?" "Well, it was bearable." "You see, it's the same with American jobs." A month or so later, I received an offer from the chairman of the Department of Slavic Languages and Literatures at Yale, Victor Erlich. He was a grand old man of Slavic studies (I knew his seminal study of Russian Formalism—one of my friends, a student in Tartu, had copied it out by hand, since it was unavailable in Soviet libraries). Moreover, he was on friendly terms with both Brodsky and Miłosz. He proposed that I teach a class in nineteenth-century Russian poetry. "Without Pushkin," he specified, "for Pushkin, we have another specialist." I was hardly a specialist on the Russian poets of Pushkin's era, but I agreed and moved to the East Coast, which proved to be a permanent arrangement.

HINSEY: During this period, you undertook a study of eight Russian poets, which was subsequently published under the title *Unstable Equilibrium*—

VENCLOVA: I launched myself into teaching Baratynsky and Tyutchev in the vein of the old Russian joke: "I've never played the violin, but if you hand me one—perhaps I'll manage." Fortunately, I did manage—in this my training with Lotman turned out to be helpful. After a year, Victor Erlich told me: "I recommend that you join the ranks of our graduate students—you may have certain prospects if you complete a PhD." Well, I applied, was accepted and went through all the required classes and exams, surviving financially due to a university loan, in part by teaching other graduate students who were a generation younger than me. *Unstable Equilibrium* was my doctoral thesis; it was composed of extensive analyses of eight separate poems, from Pushkin and Nekrasov to Akhmatova and Brodsky. Actually, it was the last thesis written under Victor Erlich's supervision, as he retired soon thereafter. After receiving my PhD, I was offered a job as assistant professor and gradually made my way up to a tenured position, teaching classes on my beloved Russian poets, less frequently on Polish literature, and sometimes in Lithuanian language as well. The Slavic team at Yale consisted of world-class scholars, such as Alexander Schenker and Robert Louis Jackson (with whom I am still on very friendly terms). My relations with students were considerably better than at UCLA. An auspicious fate, one might say.

HINSEY: Could you say a bit more about the impact of Lotmanian semiotics on these essays—

VENCLOVA: The first chapter was a summary of Lotman's method (not particularly well-known in the United States at the time). I then applied this method to poetic texts that belonged to different eras and aesthetic schools. I tried to cover all of the texts' various levels: I started with their rhythmic and phonetic configurations, then examined the rhymes and grammatical and syntactical patterns, and finally I explored semantics and intertextuality. My work's main purpose was to demonstrate how all these elements contribute to the overall sense and artistic effect of the poem. In English-language criticism, the method corresponds roughly to "New Criticism," though with considerable differences. It is also informed by Russian Formalism (Lotman subscribed to many of its tenets), the work of Roman Jakobson and the Prague Structuralist school, and so on. I introduced my own terms "microreading" (paying attention to the smallest particles of the text and their interaction) and "macroreading" (reading the text against the background of other texts, including mythological ones).

HINSEY: How did your method in *Unstable Equilibrium* differ from the semiotic approach of your colleagues in the West?

VENCLOVA: I was not very well-acquainted with French semiotics (although I had read Claude Lévi-Strauss, Roland Barthes, Julia Kristeva, and, of course, Greimas); neither did I become a fan after prolonged study. Much of it was too abstract for my taste; I found it arbitrary and somewhat sterile (for instance, I did not see much use in Greimas's "semiotic square," even if some of my students did). Lotman provided me with much more "pleasure of the text." Of course, there were areas of overlap, especially regarding intertextuality. Deconstructionism came into vogue later, but our group of Yale Slavists never embraced it.

HINSEY: In 2013, an expanded volume of these essays appeared under the title *Participants at a Feast*—

VENCLOVA: It was printed in Russian, by the Moscow publishing house NLO. This is more or less the final account of my work as a philologist: it is composed of the studies originally included in *Unstable Equilibrium* as well as many others on individual Russian (and Polish) writers and texts. Tolstoy, Chekhov, and Mickiewicz figure in it, inter alia. The title is a quotation from Tyutchev (I had in mind authors as participants in literary and nonliterary history).

HINSEY: During this period, you also published a study of the Polish poet Aleksander Wat—

VENCLOVA: I had already read Wat's poetry in Lithuania, but I had almost no idea of his fate. More than once, Miłosz, and later Stanisław Barańczak, brought him to my attention. In his youth, Wat was a radical leftist with nihilistic tendencies. Then, he became the editor of a Communist monthly, predictably landed in a Soviet prison, came back to Poland after his release and managed to escape to the West, where he wrote (with Miłosz's help) a brilliant book of memoirs, translated into English as *My Century*. His late metaphysical verses are magnificent: if there is a Polish counterpart to T. S. Eliot, it is Wat. He merited a monograph, which I wrote during the early years of my professorship at Yale. As I used to say, to do so I fought three enemies: first, my topic (which was sufficiently complicated), second, the English language (which was a challenge for me to master), and third, the computer (then a novelty). By the way, Wat's artistic and political trajectory struck a familiar note: he strongly reminded me of my father and his leftist friends (even if in the end my father's life took a completely different path).

HINSEY: To return to the political situation, at the start of your second year at Yale, martial law was declared in Poland—

VENCLOVA: For a year or so, very promising developments had been taking place on Poland's Baltic coast. In September 1980, striking workers at the Gdańsk shipyard managed to establish Solidarity, the first trade union in a Communist country that was not controlled by the ruling party. Lech Wałęsa, the shipyard electrician who led it, immediately became an emblematic figure and was supported by most of my Polish friends, including Wiktor Woroszylski and Adam Michnik. We observed all that with the keenest of interest. I even devised a rule of thumb: significant events in the East Bloc took place at twelve-year intervals. Thus, 1944 (liberation from the Nazis and the start of Communist rule), 1956 (the Hungarian uprising), 1968 (the Prague Spring), and 1980 (Solidarity). Incidentally, each interval brought the revolution closer to Lithuania. Therefore, I predicted a profound change there in 1992 (actually, it happened a year earlier). One more dictum gained currency in my milieu: if 1956 and 1968 were rehearsals, we were now perhaps awaiting the premiere. An extremely significant role in all this was played by the Polish pope John Paul II, who enjoyed incomparably more authority among the Polish people than the government. (I was lucky to meet him once at the Vatican when he granted an audience to a group of Slavists. We exchanged several words: I addressed him in Polish and he answered in Lithuanian, one of the twenty-odd languages he was familiar with.)

In late 1981, Solidarity was on the verge of taking power. It had nearly ten million members and had proclaimed a republican program, the "Self-Governing Republic." Then, almost out of the blue, there came a blow: in the early hours of December 13, 1981, Wojciech Jaruzelski, a Polish general loyal to the Soviets, declared martial law, drastically restricting public life and jailing opposition activists. There is a theory that he chose a lesser evil: had he not intervened, the Soviet army might have invaded Poland, resulting in terrible bloodshed. Martial law also meant the end of party rule, which was replaced by a military dictatorship. In any case, Michnik, Woroszylski, and thousands of other oppositionists, without any due process, found themselves in internment camps, and as many as a hundred people were killed.

In the end, martial law, which was revoked two years later, could not stifle resistance: Solidarity survived in the underground, and the 1989 Round Table Talks finally led to the liberation of Poland. Yet in December 1981, we were almost as shocked as in August 1968, when the Soviets crushed the Prague Spring.

HINSEY: Among other Polish émigrés, you discussed the situation with Barbara Toruńczyk—

VENCLOVA: As I mentioned earlier, I had met and befriended Barbara Toruńczyk in Warsaw in the fall of 1971, when we talked through the night in Michnik's apartment. Technically, she was not an émigré, but at the time was associated with Radcliffe College and had rented a flat in New Haven near to where I lived. We saw each other quite frequently—for instance, we both went to the 1980 Madrid Conference on Security and Cooperation in Europe, where she lobbied for the Polish, and I for the Lithuanian, opposition. We even attended a corrida together. "After fighting the totalitarian beast, it is very relaxing to see a regular bullfight," she said. On the morning of December 13, I immediately went to her flat and found her in very poor spirits: she was packing her suitcases to return to Poland, where she intended to join Michnik and the others in the internment camps (that was nothing new for her: she had spent three years in jail after a 1968 student demonstration). "Wait a bit," I said. "Let's go to New York, there is a wise Jewish man whom you should consult before making this decision." I had in mind Brodsky (Barbara had not yet met him, but knew his poetry).

Brodsky was as upset as we were. At that time, I believe, he was just starting his poem "A Martial Law Carol," dedicated to Woroszylski and another Polish activist Andrzej Drawicz, which evokes "the sleep of death / in the Wujek mine."[32] (The poem was smuggled into the camp where they were held and was read by its addressees; Joseph used to state that this fact gave him more pleasure than the Nobel Prize.) "No, going to jail does not make sense under the present circumstances," he said. "What makes sense is writing. You should establish a good periodical, giving voice to your generation—something like Giedroyc's *Kultura*. Such ventures are the most helpful ones."

He managed to persuade Barbara, who soon found sponsors and started *Zeszyty Literackie*, one of the best Polish cultural magazines of all time; it was first printed in Paris, then in post-Communist Warsaw where it still appears. It became the voice of all of Eastern Europe. Brodsky, Gorbanevskaya, and others contributed to it from the very beginning. I joined the editorial board "in the capacity of a Lithuanian," as we used to joke. Of course, Polish writers and intellectuals were at the helm, including (in addition to Barbara) Stanisław Barańczak, Adam Zagajewski, and Wojciech Karpiński. (The last, a brilliant essayist, was one of the principal activists of Solidarity. On December 13, we found his name on the official list of jailed oppositionists published by the Jaruzelski junta. That was a curious mistake because at the moment of the coup he was in New Haven with Barbara and me.)

HINSEY: During this time you continued your human rights activities—

VENCLOVA: I carried on my regular work, publicizing Lithuania's situation—in both the mainstream and diaspora media—and also attempted to become a link between the Polish, Russian, and Lithuanian movements. Of course I provided Alexeyeva and other Russian dissidents with information that I had received from my Polish friends. (I was one of the few recent Soviet émigrés who knew Polish well—another, and more important one, was Gorbanevskaya.)

HINSEY: Do you recall your exchanges with Czesław Miłosz regarding martial law?

VENCLOVA: These were not numerous. At the very peak of the Solidarity movement, in the summer of 1981, he visited Poland after thirty years' absence, and was given a royal welcome (he had won the Nobel Prize the year before: that had been a big boost for his country's morale, second only to the election of John Paul II to the papal throne). After the coup, he was perhaps even more despondent than we were (although we had our moments of dejection as well). He called Wojciech Karpiński and told him: "My congratulations. Now it's your turn to experience thirty years of exile." More than once, I heard him say: "I have never been, and will never be, an optimist." Still, he believed in the abilities of the Polish underground, which he witnessed—and was himself a part of—during the Nazi occupation ("Poles take to the underground like a fish to water"). He took part in the *Zeszyty Literackie* enterprise rather enthusiastically, and was pleased when new texts by Michnik (which were as nonchalant and impertinent as before, perhaps even more so) were leaked from the internment camp where he was held to the West.

HINSEY: From the beginning, your own essays have been political as well as literary. Earlier in this book we discussed your epistolary exchange with Czesław Miłosz on Vilnius and your essay "Jews and Lithuanians." Both of these texts took on controversial subjects and opened up dialogue. Another example of this is your essay "Russians and Lithuanians"—

VENCLOVA: I delivered that essay as a speech at Tabor Farm. Its main thesis was that the real interests of Russians and Lithuanians were shared—both were equally troubled by the Soviet system, and both would benefit from its dismantling. It was not a mainstream idea at the time. The consensus of the émigrés, as well as most people in Lithuania, boiled down to the idea that it was not totalitarianism, but "eternal Russian imperialism" that was our principal enemy. For my part, I believed in peoples' will to live freely more than in their incurable geopolitical (or civilizational) strivings, and was pretty sure that the system would collapse and our independence would be assured only by the effort—or, at least, with the active consent of—the Russians themselves. Since the audience at Tabor Farm was liberal, my speech was well-received; to my astonishment, it also garnered some support in Lithuania—a fact that was conveyed to me by tourists whom I met in New Haven and elsewhere. The comparatively peaceful collapse of the USSR proved, in my opinion, that my estimation was not entirely incorrect. Vladimir Putin's saber-rattling notwithstanding, I am still skeptical regarding the "innate depravity" of Russia.

HINSEY: We have just touched on your essays, but right from the start, your prose work has included a spectrum of forms—your biographical study of Wat, works related to Vilnius, collected interviews, and travel diaries. Do you feel that these different forms correspond to different aspects of your inner creativity and life, or "humors" in the medieval sense?

VENCLOVA: Every person is an amalgam of contradictory drives: in my case, opposite impulses correlate somewhat with different genres. First of all, I think there is a perceptible difference of outlook between my poetry and essays. As a poet, I tend to toward pessimism: my world is dark, enigmatic, and quite possibly absurd. As an essayist, I'm rather optimistic, even if I attempt to be as sober and cautious as possible. In the latter, I tend to believe that the world— at least the sociopolitical world directly available to us—is intelligible, if only in part, and may be improved, if only to a degree. In my poetry, I opt for individuality, for language and all the peculiarities that stem from that, including, of course, ethnic identity. In my essays, I opt for a global approach, for cosmopolitanism, that is, a certain loosening and even erasing of ethnic and national boundaries. One critic has defined my travelogues as "brutally sharp-eyed and a bit cynical." In these, I strive to describe the world as it is, taking on its grim and brutal aspects without surprise or facile indignation, though not with approbation (In this, Ryszard Kapuściński and Bruce Chatwin are my mentors.) For my philological studies—as in any scholarly work—full objectivity, neutrality, and lack of initial preconceptions are prerequisites. Do these different attitudes correspond to medieval "humors," temperaments, or personality types? Perhaps to three of the four: melancholic (poetry), sanguine (essays, including travel diaries), phlegmatic (philology). But here, I am being a bit playful.

HINSEY: In 1985 you visited South Africa. You recorded your impressions of apartheid in your "South African Diary"—

VENCLOVA: I went to South Africa on my own, amid a personal crisis—and at the very peak of the apartheid system. Nelson Mandela was in his twenty-third year of imprisonment, the "necklace" executions, terrorist attacks, and explosions were daily affairs, and the country's rulers had been condemned by most Western governments. There was a consensus that decent people should boycott the country, and refrain from traveling there. I broke that unspoken rule, consoling myself with the thought that I would describe my experience as fully and honestly as I could, which might help contribute to a better public understanding of the situation. My travel diary was first published in Lithuanian (in *Akiračiai*), then in Russian, and finally in English.

My impressions were, of course, extremely superficial. A number of the Western tourists I met along my way proved to be hopeless racists. (This was the first time I had met this type of Westerner and frequently rubbed my eyes in disbelief that they existed.) Actually, there were very few of them: the general atmosphere was that of oppressive fear. Many local white Africans (as well as many Hindus) wanted to leave as soon as they could, but were dejected by the fact that no country was eager to take them. It was difficult to make contact with black South Africans. I remember my talk with a Xhosa, who was reading a white supremacist newspaper in my presence, and asked me what "insurrection" meant. "Uprising," I replied, but he did not understand the term. "Revolution," I specified. Well, that word was fully clear to him.

HINSEY: As we mentioned earlier, your great uncle Karolis Račkauskas had been the Lithuanian consul during the interwar period in Cape Town—

VENCLOVA: Yes, I located his house, or at least the place where it had stood, with the help of a 1932 phone book, which I consulted in the city's library. It was on the slopes of Table Mountain, in a beautiful neighborhood. The white villa with my great uncle's house number had perhaps been erected on the foundations of the previous building, but the garden and the view remained. During the interwar period, there were around fifty thousand mainly Jewish Lithuanians in South Africa: their descendants still live there. Incidentally, Joe Slovo, a well-known South African antiapartheid politician, was one of them. Karolis Račkauskas witnessed the early years of the African National Congress, and was rather sympathetic to its cause.

HINSEY: You were particularly pessimistic about change in South Africa—

VENCLOVA: The feeling of mutual alienation and hate was so all-pervasive, that I simply could not imagine any way out of it, either by evolutionary or revolutionary means. Thankfully, I was wrong. The views of black radicals led by Winnie Mandela looked extremist and therefore unacceptable, and, at the time, the government was not showing the slightest inclination to release Nelson Mandela. However, he was finally freed in 1990, then dismantled the apartheid system peacefully and fostered reconciliation. These developments coincided with the dismantling of the Soviet Union. There were many parallels, but also contrasts, and not necessarily in the Soviet Union's favor. On my very first day in Johannesburg I read in a newspaper that white liberals, in a gesture of solidarity with black Africans, had rented a plane and strewn flowers over Soweto. I tried to imagine Sakharov and Alexeyeva renting a plane and scattering flowers over Vilnius in a gesture of solidarity with Lithuanian Catholics and independence fighters, but that was beyond the scope of my imagination.

HINSEY: The situation in Lithuania remained an ever-present concern for you. In the summer of 1985, a group of émigrés from the Baltics and other dissidents arranged a boat trip on the *Baltic Star* from Stockholm to Helsinki. How did this idea come about?

VENCLOVA: In March 1985, Gorbachev took over as general secretary of the Communist Party of the USSR. There were some vague stirrings in the country, even if one could not yet predict perestroika (to say nothing of its impact). I wrote in my diary: "A change analogous to the years 1953–56 is now imaginable. In reality, history after 1956 was characterized by stagnation: we are all children of 1956 and only of 1956. Now there is the possibility of some sort of concrete progress." That said, I was pretty sure that the advances would be slow and uneven.

Leading organizers among the Baltic émigrés decided to take advantage of the new political configuration to remind the Western and world powers (including Gorbachev, for that matter) about the fate of their compatriots in Lithuania, Latvia, and Estonia. The idea was simple: to rent a very modest Swedish cruise ship (the *Baltic Star*) and sail it as close as possible to the Baltics' shores. Curiously enough, this brilliant public relations coup had never occurred to anyone before (I believe Aleksandras Štromas was one of its main catalysts). Vladimir Bukovsky, as a representative of the Russian dissent movement, was invited to take part in the trip, as well as many people from the Western media. A hundred or so Lithuanian, Latvian, and Estonian activists were invited to fill the boat: I was among them.

HINSEY: Due to the political intentions of the cruise, it did not prove to be a particularly restful affair—

VENCLOVA: The Soviets reacted more nervously to the project than to most of the émigrés' other enterprises (which, to our eyes, underscored its value). Several vaguely threatening articles appeared in the official press. Finally TASS (the Soviet state news agency) published an undisguised warning. It said that the trip was obviously organized and paid for by the CIA (which was untrue), and that the CIA, known for its underhandedness, might intentionally sink the boat, along with its passengers, in an attempt to create an international incident and place the blame on the USSR. TASS declared that in such a case, responsibility would rest solely with the United States. After that, the number of potential passengers somewhat thinned. Bukovsky, Štromas, and other former Soviet citizens, as well as most people from the media, believed it was a bluff and boarded the ship in Stockholm.

That was one of the more memorable trips of my life. We sailed very close to Palanga (where my mother was in our old house at the time), along the Latvian coastline and we even caught a glimpse of the Estonian island of Saaremaa. (For years I had dreamed about visiting Saaremaa, but this was impossible as it was part of a restricted border area; one had to emigrate to get even a glimpse of its shores.) The *Baltic Star* was constantly subjected to flyovers by Soviet airplanes, and was perhaps even followed by a submarine or two, yet nothing problematic happened. Still, we felt a bit like the war correspondents under fire in Hemingway's *For Whom the Bell Tolls* (not to mention the considerable amount of alcohol consumed).

We managed to arrange several broadcasts and ceremonies in memory of Baltic citizens who had unsuccessfully tried to escape the Soviets by sea in 1944 and afterward. In Helsinki, a large demonstration was held upon our arrival.

At that time, Gorbachev's minister of foreign affairs, Eduard Shevardnadze, was visiting Finland. For some reason, Bukovsky stayed on in Helsinki, and this created a stir: we joked that he had been invited by Shevarnadze to engage in discussions. A couple of years after our trip, such an idea no longer seemed so absurd. (As I've mentioned, I had met Bukovsky previously, but we only struck up a close acquaintance on the *Baltic Star*.)

HINSEY: In November 1986, thirty years after the Hungarian Revolution, you were able to visit Budapest. There, you had a personal mission to carry out—

VENCLOVA: I had never been to Budapest. As we've discussed, in 1973 I had been invited there by my philologist friend Bojtár Endre (who wanted to publish a book of my poetry in Hungarian), but was never allowed to go. In 1986 I was attending a dissident meeting in Vienna and discovered that visas for Hungary were automatically given to American citizens upon arrival. After much grueling deliberation and a couple of drinks, I went to the airport, bought a ticket, and an hour or so later landed in the Hungarian capital. The city with its hills and bridges over the Danube was more impressive than Vienna, even though it was shabby and dark. My main goal was to visit a monument to General Bem—a hero of the Polish-Lithuanian 1830–31 uprising, and later, the 1848 Hungarian uprising. As you recall, Cyprian Norwid's poem "A Funeral Rhapsody in Memory of General Bem," which I translated into Lithuanian, is dedicated to him. I considered, and still consider, it to be one of the best in world literature (Both Brodsky and Miłosz shared my opinion.) The Hungarian Revolution of 1956 started with a demonstration at Bem's monument, where people placed carnations at its base.

As an "enemy of the people," I felt rather uneasy being in a Communist city, although there were no hitches, either at the airport or at my hotel. After an hour or two, I decided to visit Bojtár and his wife, who were, to put it mildly, astonished to see me. (Later, Bojtár recounted a practical joke he played on the Hungarian censors immediately following my emigration. As part of a grammar exercise in a Lithuanian textbook for Hungarians, he included the following Lithuanian sentence to be translated: "Could you tell me Tomas Venclova's address?" Lithuanian censors confiscated the textbook, but the Hungarian censors did not notice the inadmissible phrase.)

HINSEY: Your 1986 poem "Instruction" addresses this Hungarian experience—

Not one passerby. Put a carnation at his feet,
so that that the world may implode like a star, defeated by its own gravity.

The continent collapses into the valley, the valley into the city mist,
the city mist into the square, the square into the monument.
The carnation is the center of it all.[33]

VENCLOVA: The next morning I bought a carnation, went to the Bem monument, and placed it at the statue's base. It was a small act of solidarity with the insurrectionists of 1956—and of earlier insurrections in which Bem himself took part. Just a gesture, but for me it was significant. That day was the thirtieth anniversary of the Hungarian Revolution. I was told that the secret police were usually on duty next to the monument, confiscating flowers and checking the documents of those who brought them. This particular anniversary, however, coincided with the October Revolution holiday; therefore, they were perhaps on leave—something that might also have explained why my entire visit to Budapest was uneventful. Two hours later, the carnation was still there.

I left for Vienna by train and, to tell the truth, breathed a sigh of relief when we crossed the border. One can almost imagine "Instruction"—with a bit of irony—issuing a set of directives for an undercover agent in a totalitarian country. Thanks to Bojtár, it obtained some popularity in Hungary and was translated by several Budapest poets, at first in the underground press.

HINSEY: Two years later, in June 1988, you were finally able to return to Moscow and Leningrad with a tourist group, though you were not yet able to visit Lithuania—

VENCLOVA: In 1988, perestroika was gathering speed, although exiled dissidents were not yet allowed to visit Lithuania. Instead, I bought an eight-day package tour to Moscow and Leningrad from a travel agency—it cost around three thousand dollars—and joined a group of American businessmen. This was their first trip to the USSR and it was mainly for pleasure. It was not inconceivable to add Lithuania to the itinerary; I was reluctant to do so, however, as there were too many people who might recognize me on Vilnius's streets. (Brodsky once said that he had considered booking such a tour to Leningrad, but with his luck the facade of the Hermitage would detach itself from the building and run to the KGB to denounce him.) For me, there was also an ethical problem—Viktoras Petkus was still languishing in Siberian exile, and it would have been unacceptable to see Vilnius without meeting him (he was released in the fall of that year). Even for Moscow and Leningrad, I doubted my visa would be approved, but it was duly processed in a week or two. This was most likely due to a clerical error. My last name was transliterated into Russian as "Venklova," and there were no people with that name on the Soviet authorities' blacklists.

HINSEY: We have a tendency to read the last years before the dissolution of the Soviet Union backward, and therefore forget that it was only in early 1987 that Gorbachev had begun releasing political prisoners. While the conditions for travel in 1988 were less fraught than before, such a trip was nevertheless risky—

VENCLOVA: Perhaps I exaggerated the risks. I took a precaution that may seem comical in retrospect: namely, I wrote and notarized a document in two copies, which I left with Lyudmila Alexeyeva and with another friend. It stated, among other things: "If I publish a declaration in the Soviet media in which I express regret for my dissident activities and declare my wish to stay in the country, this could only be the result of strong physical coercion and consequently it must be ignored." Of course things never went that far (nor could they during the Gorbachev period). The KGB did not pay the slightest attention to my humble person, if only because—due to the clerical error—they were not expecting me.

HINSEY: The first person you saw when you arrived in Moscow was Natasha Trauberg—

VENCLOVA: Prior to my arrival we'd been in touch, and she came to meet me at the airport. My first question to her was whether perestroika was indeed as good as it looked from an émigré's perspective. "Yes," she answered, "it's comparable to the abolition of serfdom." From that moment on, I felt perfectly in my element, as if the gap of eleven years had never occurred. I informed our tour guide that I had seen the Kremlin and the Winter Palace on innumerable occasions and therefore I would split off from the group to pursue my own activities, returning to the hotel only at night (or not at all). The guide, a young girl, accepted this without much hesitation.

HINSEY: After a decade, you were finally able to see your mother and friends again in Moscow and Leningrad—

VENCLOVA: My arrival had been communicated to them by word of mouth. My mother traveled from Vilnius to Moscow by train and stayed unnoticed in a friend's apartment. She was seventy-six, and that was her last major trip, though she lived—in relatively good health—for another twenty years. Two of my Vilnius friends came to Leningrad to see me, namely, Zenonas Butkevičius and Pranas Morkus. Both had much to tell about developments in Lithuania. There had been a demonstration for Lithuanian independence next to the Adam Mickiewicz monument, organized by a group of former political prisoners and other dissidents who had nothing to lose. Some people I knew had taken part in the protest. The authorities did not disperse the crowd by force, but attacked it in the media. The general public, mindful of Soviet mores, had been reluctant to join in and most had observed it from a safe distance (even from Gediminas Tower, something that was impossible without strong field glasses). Well, that demonstration was akin to sounding the depths to evaluate what risky step might be taken next. Soon, a group of intellectuals was permitted to form a public movement called Sąjūdis (the name literally means "Movement"); its ostensible goal was to promote perestroika. In a rather short time, however, it became the spearhead for Lithuanian secession and political liberation. Sąjūdis was established on June 3—incidentally, I had left Leningrad and the USSR only a day or two later.

Of course, there were dozens of old friends living in Moscow and Leningrad (including Romas Katilius, employed by a scientific institute in Leningrad at the time), with whom I met as well.

HINSEY: You also tried to locate Tatyana Milovidova—

VENCLOVA: Tanya Milovidova, or Nikitina (her maiden name), had been my girlfriend many years before (I mentioned earlier how we became acquainted in Vilnius thanks to Natasha Gorbanevskaya). We parted in 1968 but exchanged letters, including after my emigration. I remembered her old Leningrad address and went there, but she had moved. In Soviet times, there was a special service that provided anyone with the whereabouts of a person, if you knew his or her patronymic, place of birth, and exact date of birth. It cost fifteen kopecks and took five minutes, as far as I remember. Some people concealed their addresses to escape government control, but this was strictly illegal and difficult to engineer. (The service was discontinued in the nineties and later replaced by the Internet, which is less reliable; a lost benefit of totalitarianism, one might say.) Well, the address booth was in its old place, next to the main railway station. In five minutes, I received Tanya's new whereabouts in a different neighborhood. She was not at home, as she had left for Moscow for a week. But I could now easily contact her. We met up in Rotterdam, where she had been invited by a friendly Dutch family (that was her first trip to the West, made possible only by perestroika). Now, in 2015, we are in our twenty-sixth year of marriage.

HINSEY: During this trip you were able to evaluate the changes at work in the country. Upon return to the West you went to see a friend at the BBC in London—

VENCLOVA: The changes were extraordinary. Political prisoners, just released from the camps, organized big rallies in the central squares of Moscow and

Leningrad, demanding liberties that were simply unimaginable even a few months earlier. More often than not, people at these rallies expressed their solidarity with separatist strivings in the Baltics. Samizdat became a public affair. Grigory Pomerants, whom I visited in Moscow, was scared by the prospect of pogroms, but these did not materialize, notwithstanding the anti-Semitic tone of some semiofficial rightist magazines. There were literally hundreds of uncensored, frequently satirical art shows and performances. While I was there, I was asked to give interviews and conduct seminars on artistic and political matters, especially about émigré activities. After one such interview, which was as frank as any interview in the West, I asked the two young journalists: "Don't you think that you might land in a camp, and I will be forcibly deported, in the best of cases?" Their answer was: "Well, let the scoundrels try: if they attempt anything of the kind, a bloody revolution will follow."

After eight very intense days, I left for London, carrying out some manuscripts by Pomerants and others (my luggage went unchecked at the airport). London was not a city I was really familiar with, even if I'd been there several times. Still, when I emerged from the underground at Piccadilly Circus, I breathed a sigh of relief and said to myself: "Thank heavens, I'm home." That was the moment when I understood that I had become an émigré in the full sense of the word. I went to a friend at the BBC, the journalist Masha Slonim, and offered her an interview about my impressions of the USSR. "Oh, that's a scoop," she said. "No one among the dissidents has been there yet." The general tenor of my long interview was that we were witnessing something akin to the Russian Revolution of 1905, luckily without any bloodshed, at least for the time being.

HINSEY: This broadcast, unfortunately, also caught the attention of the Soviet authorities—

VENCLOVA: After the collapse of the USSR, the new authorities of independent Lithuania provided me with my KGB file. After the BBC broadcast, the secret police were alerted to the fact that an "enemy of the people" had managed to visit the country unobserved. There was an entire stack of correspondence between the KGB offices in Moscow and Lithuania, attempting to establish who had been responsible for this scandalous oversight (someone was probably punished for this, although I found no traces of it in the dossier). Their final decision was to "prohibit the aforesaid enemy of the people, the bourgeois nationalist Tomas Venclova, from entering the USSR for five years, that is, until 1993" (the term could be extended).

HINSEY: What was Brodsky's reaction to your trip?

VENCLOVA: I told him about it only after my return. He was rather envious and asked me to recount my experiences in Leningrad dozens of times. But he himself never decided to travel there, even later, when it was easy to do so. There were many reasons for this, including both philosophical and purely personal ones. Still, I believe the main reason was the poor state of his health. He toyed with the idea of visiting Vilnius, either incognito or not, but this also did not come to pass. Well, it's a pity.

HINSEY: All this brings us to the annus mirabilis of 1989—the opening of Hungary's borders, the June elections in Poland. Elsewhere we have discussed how the Berlin Wall did not hold the same meaning or symbolism for people in the East. Nevertheless, where were you when you heard the news of the fall of the Berlin Wall? What were your thoughts?

VENCLOVA: I was in New Haven at that time, teaching. It was perfectly clear that the Communist system was collapsing everywhere in Eastern Europe, but the fall of the Wall still seemed to come out of the blue. As far as I know, the very decision to open the border between East and West Berlin—which seemed as unshakable as the Pyramids—was spontaneous and, at least in part, due to a misunderstanding. Until that very moment, most people, including myself, did not believe that changes in the East were irrevocable. Viktor Nekrasov, a dissident writer whom I knew well, said before his death: "What an awful disappointment the end of all this will be." Now I knew: there would be no disappointments, a new era had begun.

HINSEY: You wrote the poem "Train Schedules on the 9th of November" about this day in Berlin, based on a friend's experiences—

VENCLOVA: Marija Čepaitytė, the daughter of my old friend Virgilijus Čepaitis and Natasha Trauberg, was one of the very last people to cross the Berlin Wall before unrestricted travel was announced. It was her first trip to the West. At the Zoologischer Garten station in West Berlin, she had to wait for a morning train to Cologne. However, due to the unexpected developments, the train schedules were somewhat confused. She noticed that the square in front of the station was filling with people dancing, singing, and weeping. Having no knowledge of German, she did not understand what was going on, and thought rather naively that this was part of the West Berlin way of life. It was an emblematic moment: all East Europeans suddenly found themselves in a new era without being fully cognizant of the changes that had taken place. My poem about her experience has an epigraph from Guillaume Apollinaire: *Je partis de Deauville un peu avant minuit.* Apollinaire spoke about the start of World War I—that is, the actual start of the century—which caught people as unawares as the fall of the Berlin Wall did. My poem deals with the closure of the same century.

HINSEY: Lithuania declared its independence in March 1990, adopting the Act of the Re-Establishment of the State of Lithuania—

VENCLOVA: That happened on March 11. The declaration was symbolic, just as the country's declaration of prewar independence on February 16, 1918, had been. At that time, German troops were still present, and de facto independence came only several months later. In March 1990, the Soviets were still in power: one had to wait eighteen months for the final collapse of the empire. Still, March 11 was as historically significant as, say, the Greek Revolution of 1821 or the Easter Rising in Dublin. Lithuania became the first country to formally separate from the USSR, and the Lithuanian Parliament's act marked the empire's coming end.

HINSEY: A tragic confrontation with Soviet troops, however, still awaited Lithuania in January 1991. You had hoped to join a group of American journalists covering these events—

VENCLOVA: On January 13, 1991, Soviet tanks stormed the Vilnius TV station to halt the transmission of uncensored broadcasts. Fourteen young people died defending the station, including Ignas Šimulionis, the son of one of my former classmates. At that moment, I feared that many of my friends might perish or land in prison. I contacted Lyudmila Alexeyeva in an attempt to get a visa and reach Vilnius as a Western correspondent, but I was unsuccessful (Adam Michnik managed to enter Lithuania from Poland and express his solidarity with those defending independence). There were people, Pranas Morkus among them, who helped to reestablish free television in Kaunas. Vilnius's Parliament building was surrounded with barricades manned by an unarmed but determined crowd, and Gorbachev's troops pulled back. After that, the USSR was more or less finished, even if it took several more months for it to be formally dissolved.

HINSEY: You reflect on these January events in your poem, "A projector flickers in the somewhat cramped hall"—

VENCLOVA: A well-known Slavist, Professor Maurice Friedberg, invited me to the University of Illinois at Urbana-Champaign to present a class on Lithuanian culture. As part of that class, I showed a film on the Lithuanian events that had been leaked out of Lithuania after the January confrontation. The film stirred only moderate interest among the American students, to put it mildly. The contrast between the Vilnius TV tower and the peaceful Illinois campus with its jasmines and water sprinklers was shattering. The poem's lines expressed my mood at that time (I am "the newcomer," and Maurice Friedberg is "his neighbour"):

> He who grew up
> in a feastless state cannot bring himself
> to look at the screen. He already knows
> what's in store: dark warm bloodstains
> and mud. . . .
> Distances grow. The newcomer tells his neighbour,
> "But everything turned out well in the end—"
> and tries hard to believe what he is saying.[34]

HINSEY: In May of the same year, a Sakharov Congress was held in Moscow, in honor of the seventieth anniversary of the scientist's birth. You were finally able to attend the Congress after the intervention of Sakharov's widow, Yelena Bonner—

VENCLOVA: Andrei Sakharov was arrested in 1980 and sent into internal exile in the city of Gorky (Nizhny Novgorod), far to the east of Moscow and off-limits to foreigners. Gorbachev released him at the end of 1986, and from that time on, he played an active role in political life. But that was only for three years. He died suddenly on December 14, 1989, and his funeral was attended by several hundred thousand people.

The organizers of the memorial Sakharov Congress, led by Yelena Bonner, invited all exiled dissidents from the West to Moscow—Alexander Ginzburg, Natasha Gorbanevskaya, Lyudmila Alexeyeva, et al.—and all the invitees received visas with the exception of two people. One was Kronid Lyubarsky, the editor of a significant émigré magazine *Strana i mir* (The Country and the World); I was the other. I do not know what special animosity the authorities bore against Lyubarsky. In my case, it was most likely related to the KGB ban that had been imposed after my 1988 trip. Yelena Bonner approached Gorbachev personally, and I obtained a visa at the very last moment, virtually before boarding the plane for Moscow (Lyubarsky, I believe, received one as well). The Congress was an unusual affair indeed: at it, Gorbachev and Yeltsin rubbed shoulders with the fiercest opponents of Soviet rule. "It looks like a ceremonial assembly of Robespierre, Danton, and the royalists," Aleksandras Štromas quipped (he was also among the participants).

After the Congress, I went to Vilnius by train. The spirit of independence there was quite determined, though the January events were still very much on everyone's mind. I left for New York and then returned to Lithuania with a new visa in less than a month. This time, I also visited Latvia and Estonia, and met Yuri Lotman in Tartu.

HINSEY: After this your travel to Russia and Lithuania was no longer barred—

VENCLOVA: In August 1991, a putsch was attempted in Moscow by adherents of the ancien régime. I received the bad news in New Haven. "Gorbachev is under arrest," my wife Tanya communicated anxiously. "And what about Yeltsin?" I asked. "Seemingly he is still at large." "Then, the putschists have lost," I said. Still, I had to soothe her by reading aloud poems by Gumilev, Akhmatova, and Pasternak long into the night. The next day, we found that I had been correct in my assessment.

On August 21, Lithuania became a fully independent state, soon also recognized by Russia. From that time on, I visited and still visit it several times a year. (As for Russia, I need a visa, which is a rather troublesome affair, but I visit it frequently as well.) Even if New Haven is still my principal place of residence, my situation can hardly be called exile, and it would be ridiculous to aspire to the title of a dissident under these new conditions. Further, the very concept of emigration has dissolved in our era of jet planes and the Internet.

HINSEY: There are those in Lithuania who still criticize your "outsider" position due to your years in the West—

VENCLOVA: The idea that an "outsider" loses a feeling for his or her country—and, consequently, the right to discuss its present and future—is a typical East European myth, which was supported by the tyrannical governments once numerous in this region. It has been refuted many, many times. Interestingly, the myth never gained currency in the United States, England, or France, where expatriates always played an important cultural role. In many ways exile, and a sense of distance, may instill subtle layers of knowledge regarding one's homeland, not necessarily available to people who live there. That was the case of Alexander Herzen in the nineteenth century, and of Thomas Mann in the twentieth. As a rule, one sees the general contours of the country's development more clearly if one is not embroiled in local squabbles. For an "outsider," these contours are projected on the larger screen of history.

It would be absurd to maintain that a writer needs permanent contact with his or her native soil and withers when deprived of it. That may sometimes happen, but the work of Russians such as Tsvetaeva, Nabokov, and Brodsky, Poles such as Mickiewicz, Norwid, Miłosz, and Gombrowicz, to say nothing of numerous Germans, Czechs, and Spaniards, proves exactly the opposite. A Lithuanian example may also be instructive. Our literature began in the sixteenth century among Protestant émigrés in Königsberg. The founding father of our national revival, Jonas Basanavičius, was active in Bulgarian Varna and then Austro-Hungarian Prague. Kazys Boruta wrote his best poems in Riga and Vienna, and Henrikas Radauskas in Baltimore. I cannot equate myself with these great names, be they Lithuanian or foreign, but their experiences are significant to me.

As I wrote in my essay on Thomas Mann, "Exile as Good Luck": "If it is possible, at least in some cases, to gain a better understanding and deeper love for your own language through emigration, this means . . . that you can also better understand your own country, its uniqueness, its value in relation to Europe and the rest of the world, its faults and its merits, its particular—often tortuous and painful—destiny. . . . There are several myths that an emigrant can choose in order to endow his fate with meaning. According to literary scholars, these are the myths of Odysseus, Aeneas, and, I would add, Joseph. All three archetypal wanderers are connected to a location in space and time that is of supreme importance to them. For Odysseus, this site is Ithaca, where he will in the end find his family and his kingdom; for Aeneas, it is the razed city of Troy, the memory of which he will carry over to the shores of Latium; for Joseph, it is the Promised Land, which he carries in him no matter where he is, whether in Egyptian slavery or in the court of the Pharaoh."[35]

21

THE JUNCTION

Poems

HINSEY: In Marina Tsvetaeva's essay "The Poet and Time," she writes: "contemporality is not the whole of my time." Let's step back in this final chapter from chronological events and speak about your creative life as a poet. In our chapter on *Sign of Speech*, we discussed the impact of writing in Soviet Lithuania. But in exile the restraints of those conditions were lifted—

VENCLOVA: I'm far from a prolific poet. During my life—which is already long—I have composed around 220 poems I consider worthy of publication. In order to write a poem I usually need at least a week of undisturbed calm. Just prior to emigrating—in 1975–76—I wrote quite a lot. The poems from that period would have constituted a samizdat book—or booklet, to be precise—which I call, in retrospect, *The Shield of Achilles*. My first year in the West was simply too overwhelming to write poetry. I was often traveling and I was involved in extensive dissident and journalist activities, to say nothing of my teaching, job-hunting, and concerns related to citizenship status. My first émigré poem, "Museum in Hobart," appeared in early 1978. The following year, in Paris, I jotted down three or four poems in a very short period of time. This was a sort of a breakthrough: from that time on, I generally produced several—sometimes up to ten—poems a year on a more or less regular basis. Frequently, however, just contemplating Florence, Rome, or Greece was enough for me: these impressions found their way into diaries, though not necessarily into stanzas.

In America, there was also the problem of audience. For me, poetry is an intimate affair, which means I do not need many readers. Nevertheless, I'm still concerned with publication and consequently with critical response.

Luckily, there were some serious periodicals edited by the Lithuanian diaspora, and some good critics—one of them, Rimvydas Šilbajoris, a professor of Slavic literatures in Ohio, was on par with any American critic of that time. Now, all that is gone. Since independence, however, I have both readers and critics in Lithuania itself (I had attempted to reach my audience there earlier, of course, but with varying degrees of success). As time passed, I began working with translators among the Russian diaspora poets, including Natasha Gorbanevskaya (Brodsky translated one of my poems and printed it in the well-known émigré periodical *Kontinent* while I was still in Lithuania—presumably this expedited my departure). Stanisław Barańczak prepared an entire book of my work in Polish translation under the aegis of *Zeszyty Literackie*. This was a great honor as he is widely considered one of the best Polish translators of all time; he is responsible for masterful versions of Shakespeare, Donne, Hopkins, and many others. Editions of my work in English, Swedish, Italian, and other languages followed. The translators usually knew little or no Lithuanian, but I worked closely with them, preparing word-for-word translations with commentary and editing their versions.

HINSEY: Did you find that in your first years of exile your method of composing and your experience of inspiration remained the same?

VENCLOVA: As you remember, in Lithuania I often composed poems while walking. After I emigrated, I started to work mainly, if not exclusively, on paper, producing many pages of rough drafts decipherable only by me. For inspiration, I still needed a strong emotional experience that sometimes took months to settle into shape. Just before my departure from the USSR, I moved away from the heightened imagery and experimental technical structures of my earlier period toward a more neoclassical and narrative style, almost in an eighteenth-century vein. I also continued to pursue my interest in fixed verse forms that had never been used before in Lithuanian poetry—not only the villanelle, which we spoke about previously, but, for instance, the sestina. In fact, "Sestina" was the title of a rather nihilistic poem from *The Shield of Achilles*—it describes a winter car trip through the frigid landscape of northern Lithuania and ends in the stylized theomachic lines:

Perhaps the road

Itself is chains. I am denied the road
Into Thy forest. The earth is numbed by snow.
We're enemies reflecting. Thou art an echo.[36]

My early émigré poems, such as "Before the middle of July, Paris / Is empty," were classical in manner. Yet "In the Fire," which followed a fixed (if original) form, was practically an exercise in *écriture automatique*. It was written in California, at a moment when I had received bad news concerning my mother's health (luckily this proved to be unfounded, but it resulted, for a time, in anxiety and insomnia). It was only after I had finished composing it that I discovered it was an invocation to the four classical elements—fire, water, earth, and air.

HINSEY: In 1977 you published in Chicago a new book of poems, titled *98 Poems*—

VENCLOVA: There was a Lithuanian publishing house in Chicago (Algimanto Mackaus knygų leidimo fondas), established by the *Metmenys* and *Akiračiai* milieus. The venture was named after Algimantas Mackus, a bold and innovative émigré poet of the younger generation who died in a car accident (a figure reminiscent of Rimbaud or Kerouac, I would say). The house maintained high literary standards, and I therefore felt honored when my Chicago friends proposed that I publish a book there. This volume consisted exclusively of poems written before my emigration, including *Sign of Speech* and the abovementioned booklet *The Shield of Achilles*. Verses from my samizdat booklet *Moscow Poems* were also included in it—a series of strange, mainly experimental texts produced during my love affair in that city. Brodsky and I discussed ideas for the title of this new collection. In the end, E. E. Cummings and Dylan Thomas, who favored numerical titles (*Twenty-Six Poems* by Thomas and *95 Poems* by Cummings) served as a source of inspiration.

HINSEY: Among the poems included in this volume and written before your emigration was "Ode to a City" [1975]—

VENCLOVA: This poem, which is a cross between a song and a Horatian ode, was my last text published in Lithuania. It was printed in the almanac *Poezijos pavasaris* (Poetic Spring) that traditionally—and up to the present—appears in May. On May 9 of that same year I mailed my letter to the Central Committee of the Lithuanian Communist Party requesting my right to emigrate, an act that immediately and concretely turned me into an "unperson." "Ode to a City" was my farewell to Vilnius in anticipation of a possible departure. Incidentally, Vilnius is never named in the poem, though some of its attributes can be easily detected. Moreover, the city has been transposed to the seashore and is buffeted by winds with ancient names—Aquilon, Notos, Eurus, Boreas; this was a reference to the old Latin topos of Rome and the Roman republic as a wretched ship tossed by the storms of history. After the almanac appeared in bookshops, I was approached on a Vilnius street by a young man I knew only slightly. He said that he understood the meaning of the poem: it alluded to my decision to emigrate (a fact not yet known to the general public). "You are right to do so, even if it is a pity," he continued. My friend Judita Vaičiūnaitė read the poem as well and reached the same conclusion.

HINSEY: In *98 Poems* there is also the dark elegy "Nel mezzo del cammin di nostra vita"—

VENCLOVA: This poem is dedicated to Konstantin Bogatyrev, a Moscow friend of my first wife Marina Kedrova and mine. We spoke about his fate earlier, though only briefly: he was a talented translator of German into Russian (Pasternak believed that Bogatyrev's Rilke translations surpassed his own). In his early youth, Konstantin had been sentenced to death for an alleged plot to murder Comrade Stalin, but the sentence had been commuted to twenty-five years' imprisonment; after Stalin's death he was released. He was on friendly terms with Heinrich Böll and many others, which enabled him to transfer various samizdat materials to the West. Although this was done with the utmost discretion, the KGB apparently took note of it, and Konstantin received a blow to the head with a heavy object when returning to his flat one night. He had just enough time to tell his wife: "Well, they carried out the death sentence," before falling into a coma; he passed away two months later. While this assault could have been the work of a common criminal, few believed it. This is reflected in the elegy's ironic coda: "To tell the truth, death / Could even be fortuitous in this state."[37] The poem mentions a number of types of deaths that were typical for that period ("gasoline" refers to the self-immolation of Romas Kalanta). Generally, the text attempts to convey my mood in 1976—and the mood of numerous friends—which was far from lighthearted.

HINSEY: While the work of Pasternak and Mandelstam continued to accompany you, who were the poets who became critical to you as you began your exile?

VENCLOVA: I did not need to reread Pasternak and Mandelstam as I knew much of their work by heart. I even felt some desire to overcome my fascination with them. In Voronezh, Natasha Shtempel shared with me two words that had been coined by young Russian poets in the thirties: *pasternakip'* and *mandel'shtamp* ("nakip'" means "spume" or "froth" and "shtamp" could be translated as "cliché"). Both neologisms conveyed the "anxiety of influence" common to that generation. I have said that anxiety of influence is less acute when one crosses the language border; still, I was looking for something new.

As for the Lithuanian émigré poets, I had already become reasonably well-acquainted with their work before I left the country, although Alfonsas Nyka-Niliūnas proved to be more innovative and thrilling than I had expected. Most of the others had developed along the same lines as my Vilnius contemporaries, pursuing a search for native roots, something I did not consider a fruitful direction. The Mediterranean tradition, to which Nyka-Niliūnas (and Radauskas) subscribed, was closer to my taste. Of course there was Miłosz, whose newest work impressed me indeed. I also attempted to fill in the gaps in my knowledge of Russian diaspora poetry. Alas, most of Nabokov's verses looked weak to me: only the poems in his prewar novel *The Gift*, attributed to the protagonist Godunov-Cherdyntsev, struck me as elegant. But there was Khodasevich, a friend of Nabokov's, who died in Paris in 1939. Both Gorky and Nabokov, writers of totally opposite views and tastes, considered him to be the best Russian poet of the twentieth century; this might be an overstatement, but not much of one. I read one of his collections in Brodsky's flat in 1968, and I remembered how, in total solitude, I raised a sword that Joseph owned as a form of salute to Khodasevich's best lines. Now, I became better acquainted with his work. His poignant, sharp, stoic, modern and at the same time impeccably Classical poetry became as important to me as Pasternak, Mandelstam, or Akhmatova. On the other hand, I did not like many of Tsvetaeva's later verses (I shared this distaste with Khodasevich himself). It took time for me to get used to Brodsky's new manner, but in several years I learned to appreciate it.

Of course there was also the entire continent of English-language poetry, which I knew superficially but now probed very slowly. I read Donne, Andrew Marvell, George Herbert—that was difficult enough: my passive English was rather good, yet even today I do not feel totally at home in the language. It took a decade or two before I really got a feeling for, say, Hopkins and Wallace Stevens. At Brodsky's urging, I became acquainted with much of Auden's work. Among the poets whom I immediately admired were Elizabeth Bishop and Richard Wilbur.

HINSEY: In your next volume, published in 1990, *The Condensing Light*, one witnessed, among other themes, a coming to terms with your new environment, and a probing of the limits of familiarity and foreignness. This is particularly evident in a poem such as "Thanksgiving Day" [1980]—

VENCLOVA: I was invited to spend Thanksgiving in Ohio at the home of one of my students. During the night, I thought about my situation: it was more or less clear that I'd spend the rest of my life in my new country, never returning to Lithuania. I wrestled with the possibility of death (I did not feel particularly well at that time, and suspected that I had inherited my father's heart disease, which later proved untrue). The country was foreign, yet one had to come to terms with it: I did not want to succumb to the type of nostalgia characteristic of so many émigrés. Well, the United States had a long tradition of accepting Odyssei of all kinds—perhaps more than Ithaca itself (as you may remember, in *Pontos Axenos* I had written about an Odysseus who never returned). The American holiday was a good occasion to offer thanks for all that, including the improbability of return. Incidentally, the room where I was spending the night reminded me of my childhood room in Freda. The past surrounded me, yet at the same time, it had to be left behind. "Thanksgiving Day" was ironic yet, I hope, stoic:

> For the future foreign grave,
> For the benign weight of the stone upon it,
> For non-existence. And for Thee, Who can
> Draw something from it. If Thou dost will it.

> For the black music of the spheres . . .[38]

HINSEY: You have also written that there are moments when the process of changing cultures can result in disorientation, as in your poem "Before the middle of July, Paris" [1979]—

VENCLOVA: The narrator in this poem is lost in a maze of Paris streets somewhere in the vicinity of the Île Saint-Louis: he thinks he is going toward Notre-Dame, but he actually heads against the current of the Seine and finds himself at the Place de la Bastille. "The Bastille" is a keyword here: the poem takes place on July 14, the anniversary of the famous storming of the French prison. These days, the memory of this event means next to nothing—except the possibility to leave the hot summer city on holiday. In July 1978, Alexander Ginzburg and Natan Sharansky were tried in Russia, and Viktoras Petkus in Lithuania. We attempted to alert Western public opinion to their cases, but without much success: the latter-day Bastilles of the Gulag did not make much of an impression ("the acoustics here are different"). This was an old theme that had been addressed by Miłosz and many Eastern European exiles, who were shocked by Western indifference to the plight of their respective countries. At the time the poem was written there was in fact greater responsiveness, though this did not bring about any immediate results: our friends were given lengthy prison sentences anyway. On top of it, in "Before the middle of July, Paris," the narrator is disoriented because he is no longer sure which of the two opposing worlds he belongs to: to the world of Black Marias and barbed wire, or to his peaceful Parisian surroundings ("You live inside the rupture of the map / Outside the calendar," "You're clearly lacking in reality"). The connection between these two universes is only provided by "the print of the damp newspaper" from the poem's epigraph (taken from Pasternak) and by some sense of duty—deprived of hope—toward those who remain "in a hundred-mile morass."[39]

HINSEY: In the poem "East Rock" one finds a similar stoic assessment of place coupled with an affirmation of choice: "So then, take the shadow along with you / The black mirror, the barren land of speech / Choosing freedom every second"[40]—

VENCLOVA: This was my first poem about New Haven. The city is bounded by two symmetrical cliffs—East Rock and West Rock. For a period of time, I lived in a neighborhood at the bottom of West Rock, traveling to Yale by bus or, more often than not, by foot, which took about an hour. The neighborhood was rather rundown, but its landscape of red stone, and the leaves of the New England autumn—along with the bluejays' call mixed with motorcycles' roaring was magnificent. I also frequently climbed East Rock: it had a monument at its top, from which one could look out at the city and the adjoining bay. Nature in America, as has been noted by many others before me, substitutes for European history: my poem is intended as a sort of ecstatic anthem to this, but the theme of death is also present, and "the permafrost" of the epoch is never too far away. The narrator accepts his new universe of choice and anticipation, in full awareness of its price.

HINSEY: Another important poem from this collection, with regard to both technique and content, is "Autumn in Copenhagen." In the poem, among other themes, you address how in exile language itself can become endangered—

VENCLOVA: I often say that "Autumn in Copenhagen" is a poem about three not-too-successful love affairs. It deals with a long walk in the Danish capital: the narrator waits for his female friend who finally arrives by train for a short reunion (the friend's Scandinavian last name is anagrammatized in one stanza, that is, all of its sounds are present in various permutations—although this came as a surprise to me when I noticed it). The second love story relates to one's motherland. Lithuania is very close to Denmark—Klaipėda and Copenhagen are only separated by the Baltic Sea, which is relatively narrow at that point, yet "as wide as the Styx," since the narrator cannot cross it by

any means. Thus, the native country is represented only by a Soviet submarine, "a leaking uranium whale," which at that very moment happened to run
aground on the south coast of Sweden (as reported in the headlines). The third
love story deals with language: the narrator feels his grammar and vocabulary
are starting to escape him ("Moods, adjectives humming, / negations, / the
blindness / of infinite particles, crowded sentences, and, only now and then, /
the dry, as if unfamiliar, but breath-stopping pain / and silence").[41] This is a
danger for any exiled writer, even if it does not come to pass. Perhaps the fear
in itself has a salutary effect.

HINSEY: The central shape of this poem, and its depiction of fountains, is
reminiscent of the metaphysical poet George Herbert's sculpted poems, such
as "Easter Wings." But sculpted verse forms were also present in Russian
poetry—

VENCLOVA: The device of a sculpted or visual poem (in which the arrangement
of lines imitates the form of the object the poet is speaking about) goes back
to antiquity and was particularly popular in the Baroque era. A seventeenth-
century Russian poet, Simeon Polotsky—who had studied, incidentally, at
Wilno (Vilnius) University—used it extensively. It was later resurrected by the
Modernists, including Guillaume Apollinaire, some Russian Symbolists and
Andrei Voznesensky (in Voznesensky's case, in a rather trivial form). Brodsky
was quite fond of it and employed it in several of his texts. In "Autumn in
Copenhagen," it is applied with some reserve: it's hard to tell which object is
imitated by the shape of the stanza (the fountain's stream? the human body?).

HINSEY: Following independence, your books began to appear again in
Lithuania. One can only imagine that to publish there was its own form of
homecoming—

VENCLOVA: My homecoming started as early as 1988. At the beginning of
that year, I was still being attacked in the Soviet Lithuanian press. Probing
the limits of perestroika, I mailed a letter to a popular magazine protesting the
untruths that were being spread about me: the letter was printed in August
without any cuts or comments, which was quite unimaginable and reflected
the extent of the political sea change. In December 1988, several of my old
poems were reprinted in literary periodicals (no one asked my permission, but
that did not overly concern me), and a liberal critic, Kęstutis Nastopka, published an article about my work under the title "Rebellious Classicism." There
was also a semi-samizdat venture (the border between the regular press and
samizdat became progressively blurry at the time), which reprinted my rather
pointed essay "The Game of the Soviet Censor," which had first appeared in

the *New York Review of Books*. Soon, I received an offer to publish two large books, a volume of poetry and a collection of essays: both appeared almost simultaneously in 1991—as far as I remember, just prior to international recognition of Lithuania's independence. In 1998, *A View from an Alley* appeared. It is a book of sixty-four pages made up of new poems dealing with the new times, and therefore confirmed my return as a regular participant in the country's culture.

HINSEY: We have previously talked about the partisans during the Cold War who attempted to reach Lithuania by boat. In *A View from an Alley* you addressed this topic in the poem "The Member of the Landing Crew"—

VENCLOVA: The topic of the postwar partisan war was, and still is, emblematic for Lithuanian literature, film, and even painting. In Soviet times, the partisans were predictably maligned. However, a film called *Nobody Wanted to Die* appeared in 1966: a Socialist Realist production that received the USSR State Prize. It was slightly nuanced in its treatment of the theme, and was professionally well done (the principal roles were performed by Juozas Miltinis's Western-oriented actors). In 1947 Petras Cvirka attempted to address this topic in a novel he was planning during the last year of his life: the surviving notes show that he also favored a nuanced approach. After Lithuanian independence, many works treated the subject in a uniformly sympathetic manner, which did not necessarily contribute to their artistic value.

I tried to address the subject from an unusual perspective, describing the case of the very young émigré Justinas Dočkus, who attempted to join the partisans with the help of the Swedish and British secret services, and perished in Western Lithuania after crossing the Baltic Sea. It was a true story unearthed from the archives by my journalist friend, Liūtas Mockūnas. Other members of Dočkus's crew were arrested by the Soviets, and some of them were recruited over to the Soviet side: later, they took part in "the dark games of the Great / Powers,"[42] providing misinformation to the British intelligence service and the CIA by means of quasi-clandestine transmitters. Against that background, Dočkus's fate perhaps even looked enviable, if also sad and absurd. My poem, written in free verse though in somewhat regular stanzas, borders on a short story: it touched on subjects usually overlooked in descriptions of the partisan war, such as its international aspect, and the extent of defection among the ranks of the partisans. In the text, I was perhaps a bit influenced by Seamus Heaney's poems about Northern Ireland's Troubles.

HINSEY: Another long poem from this collection is "Henkus Hapenčkus, In Memoriam," an unlikely elegy—

VENCLOVA: This is one of my favorite poems: it deals with a person who never existed—and never could—and therefore with the topic of nonbeing as such. In Soviet times, Pranas Morkus and I saw a plaque in the window of a funeral parlor inscribed with the name "Henkus Hapenčkus" along with nonsensical birth and death dates, something like "2019–1911." Henkus, in Lithuanian, could be an unusual short form for Henrikas, but Hapenčkus is a clearly impossible last name either in Lithuanian or, I believe, any language. The shopkeepers were undoubtedly eager to avoid any coincidences with a living person. Pranas Morkus remarked that it would be a good subject for a poem. I invented a fate for a nonentity who existed only as an inscription on a funeral plaque, and created a sort of otherworld for him, which mirrored our own universe and the city of Kaunas, but was made up of nonobjects. The poem was written in quite intricate eleven-line rhymed stanzas that attempted to reflect the convolution of the subject (nothingness, I believe, is more complicated than existence—some religious thinkers, especially Buddhists, might agree with that). Actually, the poem's theme spoke to the fate of our entire generation, of my friends and acquaintances who were, so to speak, prevented from full being by the system. Henkus might have been "a chauffeur, a journalist, a petty informer, forgotten."[43] A Postmodernist statue of Henkus Hapenčkus was erected recently in a provincial Lithuanian town—a fact I'm rather proud of.

HINSEY: A year later, your *Selected Poems* was also published in Lithuania—

VENCLOVA: This book includes one hundred poems. Exactly half of them were written before my departure from Lithuania, and the other half in emigration. By this, I tried to demonstrate that exile had not necessarily been disastrous for me (well, in any case, it did not diminish my output). I had the good luck to be photographed by Inge Morath for the book's cover.

HINSEY: In this volume we find a series of poems that attempt to evaluate the past. In "Užupis" an encounter with family friends becomes a meditation on evil—

VENCLOVA: "Užupis" is the book's closing poem. It is set in a district of Vilnius that became a haven for hippies, punks, and various counterculture figures in the early years of Lithuanian independence. A shabby, yet beautiful part of Old Town, located next to the rapid Vilnia River. Užupis has its own constitution, the first paragraph of which states: "Everyone has the right to live by the River Vilnelė, and the River Vilnelė has the right to flow by everyone." Užupis also has its own newspaper. In a café built out over the Vilnia's current, I was interviewed by two of its correspondents who happened to be sons of Romas

Katilius and Virgilijus Čepaitis, respectively. We talked about ethics, art, and similar subjects, which I also used to ponder in my youth, and I found that the new generation did not differ much from my own—or, for that matter, from the Romantics or the prewar avant-gardists. The meeting led to a formula by which I attempted to describe my attitude toward history and our ability to respond to it: "I know evil never disappears, / but one can at least strive to dispel blindness."[44]

HINSEY: In the poem "For R.K." there is a summing up of things that those, who tried to oppose the Soviet regime, sought to embrace:

> These were our choices. Yet we accepted
> truth's bitter gift—we didn't extol death,
> watched angels above rails and concrete,
> fell in love, turned lights on in the library,
> called good and evil by their names, seeing
> how hard it is to tell them apart. This we
> take into the dark. This is probably enough.[45]

VENCLOVA: "R.K." is Romas Katilius, and the poem is a meditation on the Nazi and Soviet totalitarian regimes. In Eastern Europe one observes a tendency to equate them, although there were obvious differences. To begin, the Soviets were not guilty of the Holocaust: on the contrary, the Soviet victory helped to end it, even if in his later years Stalin considered launching his own "final solution." Rather, Stalin destroyed millions of people regardless of their origins; he rarely practiced genocide in the strict sense of the word. Another difference is hardly in Communism's favor: it was much more hypocritical than Nazism, which stated its murderous goals quite openly. Both, of course, were "systems of pride," and both created "bloodlands," to use Timothy Snyder's only-too-apt term. Our memories of Nazism were vague—we were children at the time—instead, we had to resist a different inhuman order if we wanted to be respected by our own children. We experienced it mainly in its declining stage, but this did not make the task any less urgent. Did we—and many, many of our contemporaries—fulfill that duty? "Irony and patience, / very rarely, courage."[46] Still, my final answer, as you see, was a tentative "yes": perhaps not only heroism, but each small act of noncompliance matters.

HINSEY: In 2005 you published the volume *The Junction*. The book's title poem is significant in its reflection of your position as a witness to multiple cultures—

VENCLOVA: The title, which is also the title of my volume of selected poems in English (2008), is a reference to a particular point on the Earth's surface, as well as to a confluence of biographical currents that have shaped my entire life. In 2001, my wife and I spent the summer months near the small town of Sejny in northeastern Poland, some five miles from Lithuania's border. Sejny is an unusual place: for decades, it was one of the hubs of Lithuanian culture, and later, a focal point of discord between Poland and Lithuania, just like Vilnius. Finally, it was given to Poland (while Vilnius was assigned to Lithuania), but a large part of the local population is still Lithuanian-speaking, and we stayed with a family of Lithuanian peasants. A number of poems in *The Junction* were written there. Krasnogruda manor, where Miłosz lived in his youth, is very close by. Moreover, my father's native village, where I spent part of my childhood during the Nazi occupation, was also not far, just on the other side of the border.

Our friend Krzysztof Czyżewski, the head of the Borderland Foundation in Sejny, once took us from our village to the point where the borders of three countries intersect. One is Poland, another is Lithuania, and the third was East Prussia (part of Germany) before World War II—the land now belongs to the Russian Kaliningrad district. The junction was established there as early as the fifteenth century. Under Communist rule it was a forbidden zone, but now you can walk right up to the warning signs ("outdated, / but one time deadly")[47] and even take a few steps into three separate countries. All three are significant to me: Lithuania is my undeniable motherland, yet the Polish and Russian languages and cultures are near native to me as well. And, for that matter, I was born in Klaipėda, a former part of East Prussia.

HINSEY: The poem employs an unusual rhyme pattern—

VENCLOVA: I borrowed the form from the twentieth-century Dutch poet Martinus Nijhoff. He used to give a specific tonality to a stanza by ending each of its lines with a syllable that stresses a specific vowel. Similarly, in my poem all of the lines in the stanza that describe Lithuania end in syllables with the stressed vowel *a*; the stanza describing Russia—in syllables with *i*; and those on Poland—with *u*. The opening and ending stanzas emphasize *e* and *o*, respectively. It creates a particular musical effect, which may be at first imperceptible, but hopefully leaves an imprint in the listener's mind. Each country is assigned a "phonetic physiognomy," relating to its depiction—in any case, that was my intent. Lithuania's vowel is colored by the melancholic memory of my early childhood; Kaliningrad—by a feeling of wreckage and stagnation; and Poland (that is, the Sejny region)—by an intimation of rural idyll.

HINSEY: You have said that there was a period, after the changes of 1989, when you sought out places where the vestiges of totalitarianism were still visible, or where one could still keenly feel the weight of their impact—for example, in your poem "Homage to Shqiperia"—

VENCLOVA: Paradoxical as it might seem, I was a bit concerned that my imagination and poetics had been nourished by my not-too-happy era, and that I might lose my ability to write after totalitarianism's winter had passed. In the end, this proved to be untrue, but the previous system's vestiges—be they in China, Romania, or the Balkans—intrigued me for a time, and became the basis of some of my poetic themes. Accompanied by my wife Tanya, I visited Albania (Shqiperia), which we reached by boat from Italy. This was immediately following the demise of the Albanian Communist regime. The Port of Durrës, where we landed, was as poor and chaotic as any Third World country, and Tirana, the capital, was perhaps in even worse shape. The landscape was dominated by bunkers. Communist Albania had prepared itself for a war against everyone—including the United States and the USSR—therefore thousands of bunkers had been built, and the mountains had been stripped of trees in anticipation of a ground assault. An inhospitable place, to put it mildly, and a warning for posterity ("there would never again be hell or paradise, / air or water, but only, and at best, fire").[48] On the other hand, the Albanian steward on the boat told us that the first country he visited after Albania's liberation was Denmark. "Why Denmark?" we asked. "Because of Elsinore," he replied. A year or so into the post-Communist period, Albanians had already translated everything from Petrarch to Solzhenitsyn, and all that was bought by avid readers.

My poem perhaps conveys some of these early impressions of a country with a totally uncertain future. Later, we returned to Albania several times and fell in love with it. The country underwent an impossibly rapid transformation.

HINSEY: A similar environment envelopes the poem "Arrival in Atlantis," which is also an elegy to Joseph Brodsky—

VENCLOVA: In his youth, Brodsky visited the Kaliningrad district on several occasions, and wrote three good poems about it. Once, he was sent there by his friend Lev Losev as a correspondent for a children's magazine where Losev was employed, and spent some time in Baltiysk, a military harbor on the Baltic Sea. Baltiysk (or Pillau) was an old and neglected German town, inhabited only by a scant number of Soviet sailors. After Brodsky's death, some Kaliningrad-based journalists started to search for his traces there, and invited me to join them.

Baltiysk—still a restricted area—was a ghostly place. One might say that a new archaeological layer had been added to its old ruins. One country had already "capsized" there, namely, Nazi Germany; now, the remnants of the Soviet empire were piled upon it. The fleet had disappeared; the beacon mentioned in one of Brodsky's poems senselessly loomed up in the distance. We found the hotel where Joseph had stayed, and a canteen where he had dined. The town represented a point of unattainable, but still imaginable communion with him. Perhaps loyalty to language became the connection:

> Stand still, close your eyes. A traveller's steps
> press into backstreets' sand. Eyesight has failed.
> We will never meet again. Wherever one turns
> one sees the airless bay and the epoch's end.
> . . .
> But under my hands, poverty
> November, grammar and flame still flicker.[49]

HINSEY: In this collection, however, the weighing of the scales is applied not only to an era, but also to intimate relationships, which are often fraught with subterranean emotions. In one of your most well-known poems, "For an Older Poet," you wrestle with the painful poignancy of conflicts and loyalties in your relationship with your father, and with others of his generation—

VENCLOVA: I am reluctant to say that "For an Older Poet" deals exclusively with my father. True, there are some domestic details and biographical facts in the poem that hint at our relationship; yet it is above all a poem that addresses issues of generational change and generational conflict. Father was only one writer among many who opted for Communism—this was a typical choice not only for leftists in Lithuania, but also in the entire interwar world including Poland, France, the United States, China, you name it. Miłosz analyzed the complications and ambiguities of that choice in *The Captive Mind*, which was drawn from painful personal experience—he himself had been tempted by Communism in his youth. It was our lot to mature in a world where the disastrous results of such choices became patently clear. There is also a separate, strictly literary dimension to the text: as everyone knows, all poets vacillate between a certain inescapable loyalty to their predecessors (if only because one learns poetic craft from them) and the overpowering desire to present an antithesis to them, to leave a distinctive mark, to be different. And this is not necessarily restricted to writing. If the task is made even more difficult due to personal or family ties—well, one has to cope with it, that's all. I can only hope my poem is honest and empathetic enough, and somewhat exceeds the limits of a strictly individual case.

HINSEY: A similar tone of unflinching reflection is present in "The Émigré." In this poem, dedicated to a friend, you present the tragic side of exile, where individuals do not entirely find their footing in their adopted country—

VENCLOVA: This poem is dedicated to Ida Kreingold, who left Lithuania and the USSR several months ahead of me. As we spoke about earlier, she lived in the New York area in relative isolation. Her husband, a painter, was unable to establish a successful career, although they were never subjected to abject poverty. Ida's workplace was, of all places, in one of the World Trade Center towers; she did not witness their destruction as she had contracted lung cancer and died several years earlier. We were quite close friends in Vilnius—though our relationship had its ups and downs. I gradually lost track of her in the United States, and learned of her death some months after it had occurred. "The Émigré" is another elegy about the communion—or lack of communion—with those who have passed away. The voice of the narrator is weighted by embarrassment and shame when he realizes the extent of his inattentiveness. It is also a poem about the contrast between East and West, marked by a feeling of interior distance from America.

HINSEY: These two poems are written in vers libre. What informed your decision to use this technique for these subjects?

VENCLOVA: With the passage of time, I started to employ vers libre more often than I had in my youth. Poets often diversify their poetic devices to avoid creative inertia. Also, vers libre seemed more appropriate for pieces that tend toward the epic—for instance, with a short story like "The Member of the Landing Crew," or "Train Schedules on the 9th of November." The poems we have just discussed, "For an Older Poet" and "The Émigré," are long narratives dealing with biographical details; to be precise, they are not short stories, but rather meditations that verge on essays, and include snippets of dialogue. Free verse seemed to embrace all that somewhat naturally. That said, vers libre is more difficult for me than traditional forms: it can easily cross the boundary of poetic speech, becoming indistinguishable from prose (and quite frequently, bad prose). Therefore, I tend to introduce some additional rules and restrictions, usually known only to me (and perhaps discernible by an attentive critic). "For an Older Poet" consists of four stanzas that I like to call "quasi-sonnets," since each of them has fourteen lines. Of course, they do not adhere to the traditional sonnet form, but some of the rules are observed: every stanza is a closed semantic unit with a strong coda. "The Émigré" is also composed of four closed stanzas of twelve lines each.

HINSEY: Sometimes, as in "After the Lecture," the layers of time present and past collapse together. In this poem, set in a university lecture hall, the reader is transported back to your friendship with Akhmatova—

VENCLOVA: Yes, at the start of the poem, the setting is one of my lectures at Yale on Russian poetry (perhaps on one of Akhmatova's poems). The lecture itself, as well as the surrounding environment, is described, not without ironic nuances. I mention the architectural style of Yale's halls and courtyards, nicknamed "Depression Gothic," since they were erected by the unemployed during the Great Depression (and reputedly induce depression among the professors and students). During a break in the class, a woman, who is never mentioned by name, arises in the memory of the lecturer. She—actually, her shade—recites a long monologue, a sort of *ars poetica*. The woman is Akhmatova, but that is not immediately obvious (one of my reviewers did not catch this). Her words are not taken from any of her writings, nor from any talks I remember, yet similar sentiments might be found in her personal philosophy. In addition to Yale in the 1990s and Moscow in the 1960s, there is a third layer to the poem. The woman speaks about the motto *Deus conservat omnia* (God preserves everything), the Latin epigraph for "Poem without a Hero." These three words transport us to neoclassical St. Petersburg (where, as we've discussed, they were inscribed above one of the gates of the eighteenth-century house where Akhmatova had a room), and therefore refer to timelessness as well.

HINSEY: In "After the Lecture," you also posit the idea that poetry exists before we do, that "a poem rests and dreams about itself" and that it is our task "to disturb these dreams" and lead the poem out into the "streets of syntax and of sound"[50]—

VENCLOVA: These words are attributed to the woman, although I agree with them. It is a variant on the age-old idea of the Platonic existence of a work of art ("a statue is hidden in a piece of stone and has to be extracted from it").

In "After the Lecture," there is a discussion about two levels of poetry. On the first (and lower) level, the creative act is guided by the inner rules of language, which dictate the poem with little conscious participation on the part of the poet. A word suggests another word, a sound pattern another sound pattern, and so on. This is the "poetic function" posited by the structuralists: the message is directed toward itself. But there is also a higher level where the message attains what I would call the "transcendental dimension." The woman states: "this requires assistance, I suspect / of someone yet more powerful than language."[51] Here the poet almost takes on the role of the Creator, inventing not just a self-enclosed combination of sounds and words, but reality—if only a partial and noneternal one. Or at least, this way of thinking corresponds to my intuition.

HINSEY: This theme of the relationship of a poem to original sacred language—and the force that guides them (a space to which we have scant access)—also appears in your "Commentary"—

VENCLOVA: "Commentary" was intended as a sort of polemical response to Miłosz's "Ars poetica?" In the latter, Miłosz develops the well-known concept of the *daimonion*, which is stronger than a human being (and which may not necessarily be a benevolent spirit): "our house is open, there are no keys in the doors, / and invisible guests come in and out at will."[52] In my poem, the focus is more on individual effort:

> Gropingly, you'll climb Jacob's ladder
> in a dream, exceeding your strength, unprotected by a net,
> until, above, someone greets you (or perhaps doesn't).[53]

This effort (and eventual meeting) leads to a purification of language ("littered with sound / and fury")[54] that is abused by history. If the message achieves a transcendental dimension, language returns to its primordial, paradisiacal state, where things are given their true names.

HINSEY: Belief in the Word, and its divine origins, is no longer a particularly popular idea in contemporary Western intellectual circles where a far more skeptical view of language prevails. However, it seems to me that one of the gifts that Central and Eastern European émigré authors brought with them into exile was precisely skepticism regarding this strictly scientific and mechanistic view of human endeavors (which ironically turns out to be not that far from a Marxist viewpoint)—

VENCLOVA: I consider myself a born skeptic, yet I am also skeptical toward skepticism ("an iconoclast of iconoclasm," as I defined Aleksander Wat in my monograph). More often than not, today's relativist and radical intellectual fashions strike me as bordering on nonsense—part of the "sound and fury" of new and not necessarily benign times. I believe Miłosz and many Eastern European writers would agree with me. A scientific worldview has its place in human affairs—I take pains to apply it when working on strictly philological questions, for instance—but it also has its limits. As for Marxism, it has the potential to explain a considerable part of human behavior and social life—just as Freudianism can—yet both are fraught with hyperbolic ambitions and therefore always risk simplifying problems. It is no wonder that both, and Marxism in particular, have resulted in grave errors. The concept of the divine Word and its paradisiacal origins may be just a metaphor, but any poet knows that metaphors are more real than most things in this world.

HINSEY: In your poems written since 2005 you have been working in Horatian metrical patterns, such as Sapphic and Alcaic stanzas—

VENCLOVA: For the past several years, I have spent considerable time in Kotor on the Adriatic (where I am currently writing the present—and final—chapter of this book). In a sense, I experience here a return to my early fascination with the Mediterranean world. Kotor is not far from Odysseus's Ithaca and Greek shores. It is not Greece proper, yet it belongs to ancient Illyria, the land of Cadmus and Harmonia.

I used Sapphic verse forms in *Pontos Axenos* many years ago. Now, reading and rereading Horace, I have become attracted to his metrics in general. This is a very challenging technique (though not unworkable in Lithuanian, given certain variations). There seems to be a kind of natural affinity between the technique and topics such as an island in Kotor Bay where local sailors are fearful of winds they perhaps believe to be contemporary incarnations of the ancient Greek demons—or Cadmus inventing the letters of the alphabet, or at least introducing them to Europe.

HINSEY: Inspired by Elizabeth Bishop, you have also undertaken a series of biblical poems—

VENCLOVA: I was impressed by Elizabeth Bishop's poem "The Prodigal," which provided a modern angle on the well-known parable by means of sharp, frank imagery and penetrating psychological insights. But it would be an overstatement to say that it was Bishop who prompted me to try my hand at Biblical topics. Akhmatova, Pasternak, and many others have explored these themes as well. Rather, it is perhaps reflective of a certain stage in a poet's development—usually his or her maturity, though this is not always the case. My poem "On a Mountain Ridge Near Jordan" is a monologue in the voice of Moses just before his death. It is half of a diptych: the other half is "Theseus Leaving Athens," a poem about the Greek hero facing expulsion from his kingdom. Rather than their mythological subjects, both primarily address the challenges of exile; moreover, I attempt to juxtapose in them Greek and Old Testament Weltanschauung. For some of the descriptions in the poem about Moses, I incorporated elements of my first-hand travel experiences. I once crossed the border between Israel and the Kingdom of Jordan, and climbed to the top of Mount Nebo, where it is legend that Moses died on the threshold of the Promised Land and was buried. One can see nearly all of Israel from there, including Jerusalem, which did not yet exist in Moses's times. The prophet intuits that the holy city will be built there, and senses that something fateful—though still obscure even to him—will happen on a hill just beyond its walls.

Another Biblical poem, "Mother of the Living Ones," owes its existence to a Lucas Cranach exhibition Tanya and I visited in Paris. The show was organized around the theme of Adam and Eve. Fifteen or so large canvases depicted their banishment from the Garden of Eden. This is not the end of the biblical story—rather the beginning of it—but artists rarely, if ever, deal with their subsequent fates. I tried to take their banishment as the starting point, and to describe Eve's life after that: hard work, the birth of sons, the death of Adam, the swelling of the tribe that develops into humanity. All women (heroic and less heroic) are Eve's descendants. The poem ends with an apostrophe to the Virgin Mary: I am an agnostic rather than a believer, but Mary represents, for me, the aesthetic element in the universe, incarnate in medieval cathedrals and frescoes.

There are several such poems, and there will probably be more. I also attempted a Christmas poem, in Brodsky's tradition (who, in turn, was following Pasternak). The Nativity story is told from the perspective of Melchior, one of the Three Magi. But I must confess I am not sure it's successful.

HINSEY: Your recent works on Vilnius include *Vilnius City Guide*, *Vilnius: A Personal History*, and *Vilniaus vardai*, an encyclopedic compendium of its inhabitants, writers, and artists. How do these works contribute to addressing the "white spaces" as they say in Polish, left by the Soviet period?

VENCLOVA: I wrote these three books on Vilnius one after the other. The first of them is a standard Baedeker guide—incidentally, the most commercially successful book I have produced in my life: it is constantly being reprinted in many languages (including Japanese and Esperanto); when it was first published it was on Lithuania's bestseller list, and for a while even topped *Harry Potter*. Susan Sontag, to whom I gave the book as a present, was nonplussed and said she would have much preferred an essayistic work in the vein of Brodsky's *Watermark*. *Vilnius: A Personal History* cannot, of course, compete with Brodsky's masterwork, yet it presents the past and culture of the city from my own viewpoint, dwelling on its landscape, architecture, and most of all, on its incredible convolutions of fate. The third book, *Vilniaus vardai* (*Vilnius: A Guide to Its Names and People*) is a sort of personal, yet more or less exhaustive encyclopedia of famous people who lived in Vilnius or paid meaningful visits to it, starting in the Middle Ages and continuing up until the present. There are approximately six hundred names (only the deceased are included—Czesław Miłosz is the last twentieth-century figure). The ethnic composition of this compendium is mind-boggling: Lithuanians prevail at the very beginning and at the very end, but the intervening centuries abound with Poles, Jews, Belarusians, Russians, and individuals of mixed background, closely followed by Germans, Italians, French (including Napoleon and Stendhal, who stayed in Vilnius in 1812), Spaniards, Greeks, and literally dozens and dozens of other nationalities. There is also one Ethiopian (an ancestor of Alexander Pushkin) and one Brazilian of African descent. In the richness and singularity of its ethnic mosaic, Vilnius can rival or exceed Prague, Trieste, and any Eastern European city—even perhaps approaching that of New York.

In Soviet times, many of these people and most facts concerning the city's history were either unmentionable or were presented in a distorted light. Lithuanian nationalists, in turn, did their best to pass over in silence Polish—and any non-Lithuanian—contributions to Vilnius's past. On the other hand, Polish authors described the city as an exclusively Polish one: that was a weak point of even the best nineteenth-century Baedeker by Adam Kirkor, and the best twentieth-century Baedeker by Juliusz Kłos. And so on. I hope my books on Vilnius are comprehensive and evenhanded. Once, a man approached me in a Vilnius bookshop and said: "Mr. Venclova, your books on our capital were written for Poles. Please write your next book for us Lithuanians." To that, I could only answer: "I believe books should not be classified as 'written for Lithuanians' or 'written for Poles.' They should be classified as honest or dishonest."

HINSEY: Returning now to "chronological time"—as we have seen, after the collapse of the Soviet empire, freedom did not save Europe from further violence. In your poem "Dunes at Watermill," the "old era" of totalitarianism touched the new shores of the civil wars in Yugoslavia—

VENCLOVA: The collapse of the Soviet empire undoubtedly made the world more peaceful and promising, at least for a decade or two. To my surprise—and perhaps to everyone's—it did not initially result in major bloodshed, if one does not count the two Chechen wars. With some trepidation, I expected events reminiscent of 1918–20, only on a larger and far more dangerous scale. This did not happen: the system simply decomposed like a piece of completely rotten wood. The republics separated without much fighting. There were victims in Lithuania, Latvia, Georgia, Azerbaijan, and elsewhere, yet their numbers were relatively small. Of course any victim is one victim too many, but I—as well as most of the people I knew—still felt immense relief: it could have been unimaginably worse.

The Yugoslav civil wars came as a complete surprise, at least to me. Yugoslavia was the most prosperous and liberal of the Communist countries of Southeast Europe. In the Soviet Union, many considered it almost a paradise. I took the risk of visiting it (from Italy) before the system collapsed, and encountered no trouble in either Sarajevo or Belgrade. It was impossible to imagine the amount of mutual hatred that had accumulated there, which exploded in 1991 and afterward. This augured things to come. Almost concurrent with the Yugoslavian events, serious friction started up between Polish and Lithuanian communities in the vicinity of Vilnius. I was quite frightened by the prospect that my city might suffer the same fate as Sarajevo: thankfully, this did not occur, as both sides demonstrated sufficient restraint—perhaps partially due, as some people have suggested, to the more temperate Baltic character.

A few of my poems deal with the Yugoslav wars. The first one, "Tu, Felix Austria," was written in Vienna in 1992. The title refers to an old motto from the Austrian empire, *Bella gerant alii, tu, felix Austria, nubes,* which means, in a slightly modernized translation, "Let others make war, you, happy Austria, make love." The poem depicts a totally peaceful Vienna, the former city of Hitler (and also Freud) next to the war zone, about which no one really cares. The concluding lines counter Francis Fukuyama's thesis, fashionable at the time, which posited a Hegelian "end of history": "Galileo, not Hegel, was right: / *eppur si muove,*" that is, history (and, consequently, destruction) goes on. "Dunes at Watermill" (1999) recounts the stories of three Yale professors, my colleagues in the Slavic Department: one of them managed to escape the Nazis at the very last moment thanks to help of the Japanese consul Sugihara; the second, along with his mother, landed in a Soviet prison camp, but was released a year or so later, and the third was an Auschwitz survivor. The news of war in the Balkans, received in the tranquil environment of Long Island, showed that not much had changed in old Europe.

HINSEY: As Václav Havel described in his *Summer Meditations,* the changes of 1989 released with them a range of suppressed, and often dangerous, political forces. In 1990 you addressed this issue for Lithuania in your essay, "On the Choice between Democracy and Nationalism"—

VENCLOVA: Yes, the Yugoslav events were only the most glaring example of the dangers that came to the fore in Eastern Europe after 1989. I was and am especially wary of nationalism, which is, in my opinion, second only to Communism in its destructive potential. Nationalist sentiment was among the strongest forces behind the Soviet collapse; after 1989, it frequently encountered no ideological competition. In Lithuania, as in many other Eastern and Central European countries (Hungary, for instance) this tendency was aggravated by an irredentist mentality, by remnants of anti-Semitism, by a tendency to exonerate Fascist sympathizers as genuine freedom fighters, and so on. Growing economic inequality and frustrations resulting from neocapitalism have only contributed to the dangers.

I do not reject nationalism in its entirety: the struggle for ethnic identity, for the particular values of a national culture may have a noble component; it can counter a tendency toward sterile unification and *Gleichschaltung*. In the final account, it can enrich our world. That said, nationalism only too easily degenerates into a supremacist worldview, xenophobia, and condoned criminality. Democracy gives voice to nationalism, among other ideologies, but nationalism is hardly conducive to democracy. That was the sense and the main thrust of my 1990 essay.

In Sarajevo before the Yugoslav collapse, I saw the symbolic footprints of Gavrilo Princip, the young Serbian nationalist who assassinated the Austrian Archduke Franz Ferdinand in 1914 and thus triggered the century of wars. They have been carefully preserved in a sidewalk, as Princip is still a hero for many. I once said that everyone in the twentieth century was a loser: Franz Joseph, Wilhelm II, and Nicholas II, Hitler, Mussolini, and Stalin, Churchill, Roosevelt, and de Gaulle, and, alas, even Mahatma Gandhi and Sakharov. The only winner was Gavrilo Princip, since his mentality has survived—indeed, it has resolutely endured. That might sound like a rhetorical flourish, but there are moments when, I'm afraid, it regrettably seems to be the truth.

HINSEY: We are concluding this conversation in 2015. Now, a quarter century after 1989, we see that such dangers are only increasing. In 2010, you addressed questions of Lithuanian isolationism in your long essay, "I'm Suffocating"—

VENCLOVA: This essay makes reference to *The Clouds*, arguably Aristophanes's best comedy, which juxtaposes the philosopher Socrates and the gardener Strepsiades. Socrates was known to everyone (he was still alive when the play was staged, and most likely saw it). Strepsiades, a character invented by the playwright, was an honest, if limited, farmer devoted to the mores and beliefs of his forefathers. For Socrates, the freethinking individual was more valuable than these collective mores and beliefs, and the universe was more fascinating than one's own small province—in other words, he was a liberal, a globalist, and a cosmopolitan. Well, today the Lithuanian right wing is doing its best to turn these characteristics into terms of abuse.

After some comical peripeteias, Strepsiades decides that Socrates is an enemy of society, since he erodes morality and poisons minds. He sets fire to the house of Socrates, whose last words in the play are "I'm suffocating." Several years after the comedy was staged, Socrates was indeed accused of corrupting the young, was tried and condemned to death. In the final analysis, Aristophanes's play was a denunciation, even if a very talented one, and relevant reading for today.

My message was clear: Strepsiades, for me, represents our native nationalists and isolationists who glorify immutable ethnic identity, limitless independence, who fight against allegedly corrupt European values, promote suspicions about one's neighbors, and so on. In my opinion, all this can only lead in the direction of Iran or North Korea.

In fact, my essay said nothing new—this is the same line of thinking I have followed since Lithuanian independence, and during the Soviet period as well. Still, it created an unexpected stir, and that is perhaps for two reasons. First, it was published on the Internet, now more popular in Lithuania than the regular press. Second, several right-wing ideologues felt profoundly insulted by it as my opinion of them as pseudo-philosophers was clear. At least fifteen essays appeared in response to it, most, if not all, of them vehemently rejecting my ideas. Droves of anonymous commentators expressed their wish that I "suffocate as soon as possible." There had been no comparable discussion in Lithuania for two decades. As a public intellectual, I can be only proud of this, even if it highlighted the extent of anachronistic thinking in my country.

HINSEY: You have continued your human rights work through initiating such dialogues in periodicals and other media. Among numerous awards and honorary titles, in 2001 you received the Borderlander Prize, which underscored your position of residing in a multiethnic part of the world. In 2015 you received the Jan Nowak-Jeziorański Award for "creative work remaining true to values representing the cornerstone of European civilization"—

VENCLOVA: These are honorable distinctions indeed. Jan Nowak-Jeziorański was one of the most significant Polish resistance fighters of World War II, who shuttled between Warsaw and the Allied governments in the West. And the Borderlander Prize is given in Sejny, the multicultural town I spoke about earlier, which, thanks to Krzysztof Czyżewski is becoming a symbol of international cooperation in Eastern Europe. To be truthful, I do not care much about honorary titles. I am reluctant to consider my journalistic activities the central part of my work. Still, I consider it a sort of duty. We are still facing the danger of repeating patterns and attitudes that brought about disaster in our part of the world more than once. We succeeded in escaping the immense cage of the Communist empire, but there are people and social forces that imprison us in the smaller but not necessarily better cages of national egoism, self-isolation, and anachronistic views. A decent person cannot give his or her consent to this.

The word "right" has a double meaning in many languages: it can signify "correct, proper, just," but also "conservative" and "reactionary," as in the phraseological construction "right wing." Incidentally, Lithuanian avoids this precarious linguistic ambiguity (which is present in Russian, Polish, Hungarian, and so on); nevertheless our rightists, like their counterparts in other countries, claim to have a monopoly on "the correct way of thinking." They often present patriotism as their exclusive domain. One must remember that Hitler and Stalin both denounced cosmopolitanism and did their best to eradicate it.

Part of the right wing's agenda is Euro-skepticism: the belief that Europe destroys national identity and threatens a nation's survival. This idea goes against the grain of the entirety of Lithuanian history. A unique and fascinating country, isolated amid its forests in the backyard of the continent, Lithuania has striven to join Europe since the thirteen century. Interestingly enough, this quest is even somewhat reflected in our coat of arms: a knight on horseback looking westward, whose name "Vytis" literally means "to quest after." Everything that is most valuable in Lithuanian culture has come from its European aspirations. We reached the culmination of our quest in 1991, and rejecting it would be disastrous. Luckily, this seems impossible.

HINSEY: In your latest poems we witness a warning that a new era is at hand. This is explored in the final stanzas of "Limbo" and in a poem you wrote in 2014, titled "Caligula at the Gates." While the latter addresses the new autocratic rule in Russia, it is also a reflection on our inability to grasp the fragility (and gift) of the post-1989 period, about which we have not been sufficiently vigilant or appreciative—

VENCLOVA: As I have said before, I do not believe in the concept of eternal and irremediable Russian imperialism. That was the common mantra of Lithuanian, Polish, and certain Russian émigrés, and dates from at least as far back as Mickiewicz and Dostoevsky. Many of my friends were not immune to this idea. My opinion was different: if, say, British and German imperialism has become a thing of the past, there is no reason to think that Russia would be an exception. And it seemed that I was right, since the Russian people accepted the collapse of their empire without much opposition. Yet gradually nationalist and revanchist attitudes started to seep back into the Russian mentality, where they had not been particularly visible in the nineties. This was a complicated process, probably the result, in part, of certain Western errors, as well as the rise of nationalism in Eastern Europe. It suffices to say that it has ended in a new incarnation of Russian autocracy under Vladimir Putin, which is perhaps more perilous than Eastern European nationalist tendencies.

A concern for the fragility of the new world order appeared in my poems perhaps as early as 2004. "Limbo" is a poem about the city of Kraków—more specifically about its Market Square, as beautiful and civilized a square as any in Florence or Vicenza, with its arcades, flagstones, cafés, and the towers of Saint Mary's Basilica where Miłosz's funeral service was held. In the poem there are slight intimations of menace: the "towers, stations, official buildings" indicated on city maps (on the café's walls) might be possible terrorist targets, the newspapers hanging inside from their wooden poles announce a "desert ambush, hostage crisis" and similar events, stones tumble "like dice" in a dangerous game. The mood intensifies, and an orchestra in the middle of the square becomes, in the last line, the orchestra on the deck of the *Titanic*—an image from Catastrophist poetry; "the most peaceful of the circles set aside for us"[55] is still a circle of the Inferno. At that time, like everyone else, I was mainly concerned about events in the Middle East, but a decade later the peril has come closer. My poem "Caligula at the Gates" refers, of course, to the Ukrainian crisis; it is written in the tradition of Miłosz or Cavafy, transposed onto an indeterminate—partly ancient, partly Renaissance—environment.

I once defined the poetry of my generation as post-Catastrophist: today, interwar Catastrophism, with its belief that history inevitably repeats itself, and that old values have been compromised by the course of events, has regained at least part of its appeal. But it is my hope that history will not repeat itself, yet that will also depend on our efforts.

HINSEY: To end, I'd like to return to the question of exile. Soviet propaganda presented two interpretations of exile—the first was an "abandonment" or "forgetting" of one's homeland (hence, a form of betrayal, or treason), the second was conversely, an eternal lament for it. Instead, in reflecting on your life and your relationship to Lithuania, the image of John Donne's compass in "A Valediction: Forbidding Mourning" comes to mind, which is to say, however far one travels, one remains rooted in that which one loves. The other compass that comes to mind is the one in your poem "We've been seized by the pull of the universe"—

VENCLOVA: The poem you have just mentioned was written just before my emigration, when I took the threat of bad luck seriously ("I attract misfortune, just as the north pulls a magnet, / As magnet pulls magnet, misfortune attracts me in turn").[56] But the poem has, I believe, also a broader meaning.

Poetry often tackles difficult and adverse subjects: it is our answer to unsolvable problems. This does not mean merely lament or surrender, but an attempt to transcend these things—to find a higher level where the contradictions are overcome. In life, the magnetic pull toward those things that most concern us is twofold: one gravitates toward one's goal—at the same time, the goal somehow attracts one's efforts. As with poetry, when one enters this magnetic field one may find a way to solve a personal or supra-personal problem.

Poetry implies escaping the mainstream, affirming your individuality, saying something that belongs only to you. If you succeed in doing this, it means finding your place in language and history, which existed before you and will continue after your death. And in this way the problem of exile may also be transcended. To live outside one's country is rarely easy: yet it provides a magnetic point to which one is attracted, as the compass's needle is attracted toward the Pole. And, in the final account, the magnetic point may become your own.

NOTES

1. Czesław Miłosz, *The Witness of Poetry* (Cambridge, MA: Harvard University Press, 1983), 3–4.

2. Resolution of the Secretariat of the CC CPSU, "On Measures for the Curtailment of the Criminal Activities of Orlov, Ginsburg, Rudenko and Ventslov," January 20, 1977, Bukovsky Archive, Soviet Archives at INFO-RUSS, folder 3.2.

3. Tomas Venclova, *Winter Dialogue*, trans. Diana Senechal (Evanston, IL: Northwestern University Press, 1997), 121.

4. Venclova, *Winter Dialogue*, 120.

5. Tomas Venclova, *Forms of Hope* (Riverdale-on-Hudson: Sheep Meadow Press, 1999), 134.

6. Giorgio Agamben, *The Signature of All Things* (New York: Zone Books, 2009), 83.

7. Osip Mandelstam, *Complete Poetry of Osip Emilevich Mandelstam*, trans. Burton Raffel (Albany: State University of New York Press, 1973), 14.

8. Anna Akhmatova, *The Complete Poems of Anna Akhmatova*, trans. Judith Hemschemeyer, vol. 2 (Somerville: Zephyr Press, 1990), 131.

9. Venclova, *Winter Dialogue*, 19.

10. Czesław Miłosz, *Emperor of the Earth: Modes of Eccentric Vision* (Berkeley: University of California Press, 1981), 67.

11. Venclova, *Winter Dialogue*, 13.

12. Venclova, *Forms of Hope*, 121.

13. Venclova, *Winter Dialogue*, 5–6.

14. Venclova, *Winter Dialogue*, 5.

15. Venclova, *Winter Dialogue*, 6.

16. Venclova, *Winter Dialogue*, 24–25.

17. Venclova, *Winter Dialogue*, 21.

18. Venclova, *Winter Dialogue*, 55.

19. Joseph Brodsky, *Part of Speech*, trans. Alan Myers (New York: Farrar, Straus and Giroux, 1973), 39.

20. Clarence Brown, *Mandelstam* (Cambridge: Cambridge University Press, 1973), 271.

21. Venclova, *Forms of Hope*, 3–4.

22. "About the Hostile Actions of the So-called Group for Assistance of Implementation of the Helsinki Agreements in the USSR," KGB Memorandum to the CC CPSU, November 15, 1976, Electronic Briefing Book no. 19, National Security Archive, George Washington University, http://nsarchive.gwu.edu/NSAEBB/NSAEBB191/KGB-Helsinki%201976-11-15.pdf

23. Resolution of the Secretariat of the CC CPSU, "On Measures for the Curtailment of the Criminal Activities of Orlov, Ginsburg, Rudenko, and Ventslov," January 20, 1977.

24. Natalia Gorbanevskaya, *Red Square at Noon* (New York: Holt, Reinhart and Winston, 1970), 284.

25. Czeslaw Milosz, *Native Realm: A Search for Self-Definition*, trans. Catherine S. Leach (Berkeley: University of California Press, 1981), 211–12.

26. Czesław Miłosz, *Selected Poems* (New York: Seabury Press, 1973), 24; excerpt trans. Richard Lourie.

27. Czesław Miłosz, *A Treatise on Poetry*, trans. Robert Hass (New York: The Ecco Press, 2001), 51.

28. Czesław Miłosz, *The Collected Poems: 1931–1987* (New York: HarperCollins, 1988), 106; excerpt trans. Richard Lourie.

29. Czesław Miłosz, *Bells in Winter*, trans. Czesław Miłosz and Lillian Valee (New York: The Ecco Press, 1974), 25.

30. Venclova, *Forms of Hope*, 119.

31. Seamus Heaney, "In Gratitude for All the Gifts," *The Guardian*, September 11, 2004.

32. Joseph Brodsky, *To Urania: Selected Poems* (London: Penguin, 1988), 62.

33. Tomas Venclova, *The Junction: Selected Poems of Tomas Venclova*, ed. Ellen Hinsey, trans. Ellen Hinsey, Constantine Rusanov, and Diana Senechal (Tarset, UK: Bloodaxe Books, 2008), 137; excerpt trans. Diana Senechal.

34. Venclova, *Winter Dialogue*, 94.

35. Tomas Venclova, "Exile as Good Luck," trans. Darius Cuplinskas, *New England Review* 29, no. 2 (2008): 132–33.

36. Venclova, *Winter Dialogue*, 38.

37. Venclova, *Winter Dialogue*, 30.

38. Venclova, *The Junction*, 117–18; excerpt trans. Diana Senechal.

39. Venclova, *The Junction*, 132; excerpt trans. Diana Senechal.

40. Venclova, *Winter Dialogue*, 77.

41. Venclova, *Winter Dialogue*, 61–62.

42. Venclova, *The Junction*, 155; excerpt trans. Diana Senechal.
43. Venclova, *The Junction*, 152; excerpt trans. Diana Senechal.
44. Venclova, *The Junction*, 41; excerpt trans. Ellen Hinsey.
45. Venclova, *The Junction*, 73; excerpt trans. Ellen Hinsey.
46. Venclova, *The Junction*, 73; excerpt trans. Ellen Hinsey.
47. Venclova, *The Junction*, 36; excerpt trans. Ellen Hinsey.
48. Venclova, *The Junction*, 57; excerpt trans. Ellen Hinsey.
49. Venclova, *The Junction*, 29; excerpt trans. Ellen Hinsey.
50. Venclova, *The Junction*, 39; excerpt trans. Constantine Rusanov.
51. Venclova, *The Junction*, 39; excerpt trans. Constantine Rusanov.
52. Miłosz, *Bells in Winter*, 31.
53. Venclova, *The Junction*, 65; excerpt trans. Ellen Hinsey.
54. Venclova, *The Junction*, 64; excerpt trans. Ellen Hinsey.
55. Venclova, *The Junction*, 67–68; excerpt trans. Ellen Hinsey.
56. Venclova, *The Junction*, 97; excerpt trans. Diana Senechal.

WORKS BY TOMAS VENCLOVA

Books Written in Lithuanian

Eumenidžių giraitė: Nauji eilėraščiai ir vertimai [The Grove of Eumenides: New Poems and Translations]. Vilnius: Versus aureus, 2016.

Optimizmo paieškos pesimizmo amžiuje: Rytų Europos nuojautos ir pranašystės [Search for Optimism in a Pessimistic Age: Eastern European Premonitions and Predictions]. With Leonidas Donskis. Vilnius: Versus aureus, 2015.

Grįžimai Lietuvon [Returns to Lithuania]. With Czesław Miłosz. Vilnius: Vaga, 2014.

Pertrūkis tikrovėje [A Break in Reality, essays]. Vilnius, 2013.

Vilnius: asmeninė istorija [Vilnius: A Personal History]. Vilnius: R. Paknio leidykla, 2011.

Visi eilėraščiai: 1956–2010 [Collected Poems]. Vilnius: Lietuvių literatūros ir tautosakos institutas, 2010.

Kitaip: poezijos vertimų rinktinė [Otherwise: Selected Translations]. Vilnius: Lietuvos rašytojų sąjungos leidykla, 2006.

Vilniaus vardai [People from Vilnius]. Vilnius: R. Paknio leidykla, 2006.

Sankirta: Eilėraščiai [The Junction: Poetry]. Vilnius: Lietuvos rašytojų sąjungos leidykla, 2005.

Ligi Lietuvos 10 000 kilometrų [10,000 Kilometers to Lithuania, journal]. Vilnius: Baltos lankos, 2003.

Vilnius: Vadovas po miestą [Vilnius City Guide]. Vilnius: R. Paknio leidykla, 2001.

Manau, kad . . . Pokalbiai su Tomu Venclova [I Think That . . . Interviews with Tomas Venclova). Vilnius: Baltos lankos, 2000.

Rinktinė [Selected Poems]. Vilnius: Baltos lankos, 1999.

Reginys iš alėjos: eilėraščiai [A View from an Alley, poetry], Vilnius: Baltos lankos, 1998.

Pašnekesys žiemą: eilėraščiai ir vertimai [Winter Dialogue, poetry]. Vilnius: Vaga, 1991.

Vilties formos: eseistika ir publicistika [Forms of Hope, essays]. Vilnius: Lietuvos rašytojų sąjungos leidykla, 1991.

Tankėjanti šviesa: eilėraščiai [The Condensing Light, poetry]. Chicago: Algimanto Mackaus knygų leidimo fondas, 1990.

Tekstai apie tekstus [Texts on Texts, essays]. Chicago: Algimanto Mackaus knygų leidimo fondas, 1985.

Lietuva pasaulyje [Lithuania in the World, essays]. Chicago: Akademinės skautijos leidykla, 1981.

98 eilėraščiai [98 Poems, poetry]. Chicago: Algimanto Mackaus knygų leidimo fondas, 1977.

Kalbos ženklas [Sign of Speech, Poetry]. Vilnius: Vaga, 1972.

Golemas, arba dirbtinis žmogus: pokalbiai apie kibernetiką [The Golem or Artificial Man, Discussions on Cybernetics]. Vilnius, 1965.

Raketos, planetos ir mes [Rockets, Planets, and Us]. Vilnius: Valstybinė grožinės literatūros leidykla, 1962.

Books Written in English

Aleksander Wat: Life and Art of an Iconoclast. New Haven, CT: Yale University Press, 1996.

Books Written in Russian

Sobesedniki na piru: Literaturnye esse [Participants in a Feast: Essays on Literature]. Moscow: ILO, 2012.

Stat'i o Brodskom [Essays on Brodsky]. Moscow: Baltrus, Novoe izdatel'stvo, 2005.

Sobesedniki na piru: Stat'i o russkoi literature [Participants in a Feast: Essays on Russian Literature]. Vilnius: Baltos lankos, 1997.

Neustoichivoe ravnovesie: vosem' russkikh poeticheskikh tekstov [Unstable Equilibrium: Eight Russian Poetic Texts]. New Haven, CT: YCIAS, 1986.

Editions in English

The Junction: Selected Poems of Tomas Venclova. Edited by Ellen Hinsey. Translated by Ellen Hinsey, Constantine Rusanov, and Diana Senechal. Tarset, UK: Bloodaxe Books, 2008.

Vilnius: City Guide. Translated by Aušra Simanavičiūtė. Vilnius: R. Paknio leidykla, 2001.

Forms of Hope. Riverdale-on-Hudson: Sheep Meadow Press, 1999.

Winter Dialogue. Translated by Diana Senechal. Evanston, IL: Northwestern University Press, 1997.

Lithuanian Literature. Translated by Algirdas Landsbergis. New York: Lithuanian National Foundation, 1979.

Index of Names

Rochester Studies in East and Central Europe

Series Editor: Timothy Snyder

Additional Titles of Interest

A complete list of titles in the Rochester Studies in East and Central Europe series may be found on our website, www.urpress.com.